MORE
THAN
WORDS

A Study of
Inspiration and
Ellen White's
Use of Sources in
The Desire of Ages

by E. Marcella Anderson King
and Kevin L. Morgan

Cover and interior design: Honor Him Publishers

Background photo: Daniel March's "thoughtful hour" quotation in *Walks and Homes of Jesus*, p. 313, adapted by Ellen White for *The Desire of Ages*, p. 83 (see comparison, Chapter 7).

Typestyles: URWTypewriterTMed, Arial, Times Roman, and TrSah Ballroom Tango

Printed by LithoTech Graphic Services

212 Harrigan Hall
Berrien Springs, Michigan 49104-0520

The authors assume full responsibility for the accuracy of all facts and quotations as cited in this book.

King, E. Marcella Anderson King, 1931 –

Morgan, Kevin L., 1957–

author of *Sabbath Rest: Is There Something Missing in Your Busy Life?* (2002)

ISBN 978-0-6152-2905-8

DEDICATION

This book is dedicated to Donald E. Mansell,
pastor, author, and friend, whose urgings were
the catalyst for the writing of this book,
and to his dear helpmeet Vesta.

ABBREVIATIONS

General

&c/etc. (Latin *et cetera*) – "and so forth"

ab. – about

Assn. – Association

Bro. – Brother

cf. (Latin *confer*) – "compare"

ed. – edition

e.g. (Latin *exempli gratia*) – *"for example"*

EGW – Ellen G. White

Eld. – Elder

ff – "and following"

fn./fns. – footnote/footnotes

GC – General Conference

i.e. (Latin *id est*) – *"that is"*

KJV – King James Version

LCRP – "Full Report of the Life of Christ Research Project"

MS/MSS – Manuscript/Manuscripts

NASB – New American Standard Bible

N.S.W. – New South Wales

OT – Old Testament

par. – paragraph

Publ. – Publishing

RSV – Revised Standard Version

R.V. – American Revised Version, 1901

sic (Latin "thus") – as in original, though incorrectly written

Sr. – Sister

Ellen G. White Writings

101 Questions – One Hundred and One Questions on the Sanctuary and on Ellen White

1*MR*, 2*MR*, 5*MR*, 7*MR*, 8*MR*, 10*MR*, 11*MR*, 12*MR*, 13*MR*, 14*MR*, 17*MR*, 18*MR*, 19*MR* – Manuscript Releases, vols. 1, 2, 5, 7, 8, 10, 11, 12, 13, 14, 17, 18, 19

1*RL* – *Redemption* Leaflets, vol. 1 (*Redemption: or the First Advent of Christ, with His Life and Ministry*)

1*SAT*, 2*SAT* – Sermons and Talks, vols. 1, 2

1*SG*, 2*SG*, 3*SG*, 4a*SG* – *Spiritual Gifts*, vols. 1, 2, 3, 4a

1*SM*, 2*SM*, 3*SM*. – Selected Messages, vols. 1, 2, 3

1*T*, 2*T*, 3*T*, 4*T*, 5*T*, 7*T*, 8*T* – Testimonies for the Church, vols. 1–5, 7, 8

2*BIO*, 3*BIO*, 4*BIO*, 5*BIO*, 6*BIO* – Ellen G. White biographies, vols. 2, 3, 4, 5, 6

2*SP*, 3*SP* – *Spirit of Prophecy*, vols. 2, 3

BEcho – *Bible Echo*

CDF – Counsels on Diet and Foods

DA – The Desire of Ages

Exhibits – "Exhibits Relating to the Writing of The Desire of Ages"

DF – White Estate Document File

EW – Early Writings

FE – Fundamentals of Christian Education

GC – The Great Controversy

LP – Sketches from the Life of Paul

MR926 – Manuscript Release, no. 926, "The Fannie Bolton Story"

PH169 – The Sufferings of Christ (1869)

PP – Patriarchs and Prophets

RH – Review and Herald

SC – Steps to Christ

ST – Signs of the Times

SW – The Southern Watchman

TSB – Testimonies on Sexual Behavior, Adultery, and Divorce

YI – The Youth's Instructor

Source Works

Barnes, 1*NG* – Notes, Explanatory and Practical, on the Gospels, vol. I

Barnes, 2*NG* – Notes, Explanatory and Practical, on the Gospels, vol. II

Beecher, *RR* – Redeemer and Redeemed

Bennett, *LHJC* – Lectures on the History of Jesus Christ

Boyd, *WH* – The World's Hope

Cumming, *LLL* – The Life and Lessons of Our Lord

Cumming, *SR-Jn* – Sabbath Evening Readings. St. John

Cumming, *SR-Lk* – Sabbath Evening Readings. St. Luke

Cumming, *SR-Mk* – Sabbath Evening Readings. St. Mark

Cumming, *SR-Mt* – Sabbath Evening Readings. St. Matthew

Deems, *WWJ* – Who Was Jesus?

Edersheim, *LTJM* – The Life and Times of Jesus the Messiah

Hanna, *LC* – The Life of Christ

Harris, *TGC* – The Great Commission

Harris, *TGT* – The Great Teacher

Ingraham, *PHD* – The Prince of the House of David

Jones, *LSFG* – Life-Scenes from the Four Gospels

Kennedy, *MP* – Messianic Prophecy

Kitto, *DBI* – Daily Bible Illustrations

Macduff, *BTS* – Brighter than the Sun

Macduff, *MO* – Memories of Olivet

March, *NS* – Night Scenes in the Bible

March, *WHJ* – Walks and Homes of Jesus

Melvill, *GL* – The Golden Lectures, Vol. 1

Melvill, *S '44* – Sermons (1844)

Melvill, *S '50* – Sermons (1850)

Miller, *W-DR* – Week-Day Religion

Neander, *LJC* – The Life of Jesus Christ

Nevin, *SBA* – A Summary of Biblical Antiquities

Nicoll, *ISLJC* – The Incarnate Saviour

Pentecost, *BS '88* – Bible Studies for 1888

Pentecost, *BS '89* – Bible Studies for 1889

Pentecost, *BBJ* – The Birth and Boyhood of Jesus

Pentecost, *IA* – Israel's Apostasy

Porter, *GCB* – The Giant Cities of Bashan

Smith, *NTH* – The New Testament History

Stanford, *ELM* – The Evening of our Lord's Ministry

Stanford, *FCA* – From Calvary to Olivet

Thayer, *SLJ* – Sketches from the Life of Jesus

Trench, *SG* – Studies in the Gospels

Wayland, *SBC* – Salvation by Christ

Winslow, *GR* – The Glory of the Redeemer

Wylie, *SB* – Scenes from the Bible

TABLE OF CONTENTS

ACKNOWLEDGEMENTS

With deep gratitude we would like to mention those who have been instrumental in bringing this book to fruition:

- *Elder Donald E. Mansell* of Nampa, Idaho, former assistant director of the Ellen G. White Estate in charge of the unpublished writings of Ellen G. White, has given invaluable editorial suggestions that have helped to shape this book.

- *Pat Mudgett* of Berkeley Springs, West Virginia, who is a wife, grandma, and gifted writer, found time in her busy schedule to proofread and edit the manuscript in the early stages of its development.

- At the White Estate, *Tim Poirier* was kind enough to review the early manuscript and offer words of encouragement. It was his suggestion to add color-coding to distinguish the degrees of literary parallelism in *The Desire of Ages*. He also helped us obtain examples of pre–*Desire of Ages* materials.

- During the development of the manuscript for this book, *Dr. Fred Veltman* lived with his wife Renie at Hendersonville, North Carolina. Dr. Veltman assisted in the composition of the book by graciously providing any and all research project materials needed for our work. We are indebted to him for many of the ideas gleaned from his excellent report for the Life of Christ Research Project and for his thoughtful input on our more recent discoveries. His gentle and supportive spirit will be greatly missed.

- In the past brief time, the Lord has wonderfully answered prayers for the completion of this project by bringing to it an editor and co-author who has been diligent and thorough in refining and polishing the original manuscript. Asking the right questions, he has been able to make the faith-building discoveries of our research shine even brighter. He and his family live at Millers Creek, North Carolina.

- There is one other who deserves acknowledgement for her painstaking efforts in editing the work upon which this book is based. *Marian Davis* sought no recognition for her labor of love, but only said, "I will be so thankful if He will use me anywhere." Expressing deep appreciation and affection for her devoted assistant and *bookmaker*,[1] Ellen White said:

> Of Sister Davis it can truly be said, "She hath done what she could." All the energies of her being were freely given to the work that she loved. Her quick appreciation of truth, and her sympathy for the seeker after truth, enabled her to work enthusiastically in preparing for the press the matter which the Lord has given me for his people. —*Review and Herald*, Feb. 16, 1905.

We can express our appreciaton for the role she played in producing *The Desire of Ages* when we see her in the resurrection.

---

[1] Ellen White's term to describe Marian Davis's role as compiler and arranger of her written materials.

PREFACE

Believe in the Lord your God, so shall ye be established; believe his prophets, so shall ye prosper. —2 Chronicles 20:20.

Not by might, nor by power, but by my spirit, saith the LORD of hosts. —Zechariah 4:6.

This researcher firmly believes that these two texts apply to the office and work of Ellen G. White. As an author she has an extraordinary record. Among other accomplishments, she is "the fourth most-translated author of all time, the most-translated *female* writer, and the most-translated *American* writer of either gender!"[1] Her book *Steps to Christ* alone has been translated into an excess of 150 languages.[2]

How is it that a woman with only a third-grade formal education was able to accomplish so much? I believe it is because she had an education that few others have been privileged to enjoy—through symbolic representations and panoramic revelations of events past, present, and future, she had Jesus and the angel of prophecy as her instructors. By the time Ellen White reached middle age, she was well read, well traveled, and had become a prolific writer and a speaker of some renown, associating with ministers and other highly educated professionals. Her writing and speaking give evidence of her grasp of deeper spiritual issues and "the truth as it is in Jesus."[3]

Through test and trial her role in the church became established.[4] As a result of her leadership, the Seventh-day Adventist Church developed worldwide missions, established numerous educational and health-related institutions, launched a massive publishing work, and took its place as a vanguard of religious liberty. Do not the development and prosperity of the ministries promoted by Ellen G. White demonstrate that the Lord was speaking through her in accordance with Zechariah 4:6? Now, a century later, there are those who would have us write Mrs. White off as a plagiarist whose literary works were the sole result of literary helpers and stolen source material! Some Adventists have, but is that a picture of the true Ellen White?

Background for the Life of Christ Research Project

In the decade or so before the inauguration of the Life of Christ Research Project, several researchers engaged in efforts to locate literary borrowing in Ellen White's writings—Walter T. Rea in *The Desire of Ages*, Donald R. McAdams in *The Great Controversy*, and Ronald L. Numbers in

---

[1] Roger W. Coon, "A 'Testimony' from the 'Other Side,'" *Perspective Digest*, Vol. 2, No. 2, p. 43. For a list of the world's top ten most translated authors (based, in part, upon 1983 research in the Library of Congress), see Roger W. Coon, *A Gift of Light* (Hagerstown, MD: Review and Herald Publ. Assn., 1983), pp. 30, 31.

[2] The Ellen G. White Estate has the latest update on the total number of translations for any given book, and also the total number of books translated per any individual language at <www.whiteestate.org>. Other helpful websites on Mrs. White are <www.ellenwhite.info>, <http://ellenwhiteanswers.org>, and <www.ellen-white.com>.

[3] "The truth as it is in Jesus" was one of Ellen White's favorite expressions for describing Biblical truth. She believed that all our understanding of Bible doctrine must be understood in relationship to Jesus.

[4] "The fact stands out to us now, that in that early time, when there was no church organization and no ecclesiastical authority among the Sabbathkeeping Adventists, the Spirit of prophecy in Ellen G. White and the faith of the believers in her divine commission constituted the sole disciplinary agent of the body, the one rallying point of the faithful, the final court of appeal. Yet how modestly, with what godly fear, in what travail of soul, did she bear her testimony!" —Arthur W. Spalding, *Origin and History of Seventh-day Adventists*, vol. 1, p. 293.

certain of her health books.[5] Seventh-day Adventist educators, scholars, and administrators recognized that the questions regarding literary borrowing and plagiarism needed to be answered.

This, however, was not the first time questions about borrowing had arisen. In 1887, *Dudley M. Canright* had publicly questioned the legitimacy of Ellen White's use of the works of other writers in producing her books. Rejecting the divine origin of Ellen White's counsels and turning his back on the Adventist Church, this one-time Seventh-day Adventist minister became Ellen White's adversary through the power of his pen.[6]

Adventist proponents of the Spirit of Prophecy,[7] like William C. White (son of E. G. White), Arthur G. Daniells (GC President, 1901–1922), Francis D. Nichol, T. Housel Jemison, and Arthur L. White (grandson of E. G. White), all acknowledged some borrowing, but, for the most part, minimized the amount of possible literary dependency in her writings. The special committee of the General Conference that examined the findings of Walter Rea and others recommended: "That we recognize that Ellen White, in her writing, used various sources more extensively than we had previously believed."[8] With such a late-coming announcement, is it any wonder that church members were wondering if there had been a cover-up somewhere along the line?

As I observed the concern of many of my fellow Seventh-day Adventists over Ellen White's "borrowing" and saw some of these give up their faith in Ellen White's inspiration and in the pillars of Adventism confirmed by the gift of prophecy, I felt the Lord leading me to get involved. At first I consented to be one of the volunteer readers for the Life of Christ Research Project, which was dedicated to the study of Ellen White's use of literary sources in the writing of *The Desire of Ages*.[9] A few months later, when the project lost its part-time

---

[5] Fred Veltman, "Full Report of the Life of Christ Research Project" [*LCRP*] (Angwin, California, Nov. 1988), Introduction. pp. 7–11. ". . . the historical portions of *The Great Controversy* that I have examined are selective abridgments and adaptations of historians. . . . In the samples I have examined I have found no historical fact in her text that is not in their text" (Donald R. McAdams, "Ellen G. White and the Protestant Historians," p. 19). This is what Ellen White told readers in the book's introduction that she was doing, making an application of "well known" facts. Arthur L. White adds that "much of the comments Ellen White had written in enlarging on Wylie's remarks had to be cut in order to fit the space"(3*BIO* 439.6). McAdams concludes: "Any honest critic must come away from a reading of *Great Controversy* impressed with the power of its message" (McAdams, p. 232). The major charge of Ron Numbers' *Prophetess of Health* has been rebutted recently by Dr. Don S. McMahon in *Acquired or Inspired?* (2005). McMahon's research shows that her health principles show a much higher degree of confirmation by modern medical science than any of the most advanced writers of her time that could have been her "sources."

[6] See article "Canright, Dudley Marvin," *Seventh-day Adventist Encyclopedia*, vol. 10, pp. 289, 290. Canright's original criticism, in the Oct. 8, 1887 *Michigan Christian Advocate*, was that she used uninspired sources. In Canright's debate with Adventist pastor William Healey in Healdsburg, California in January of 1889, the accusation of "plagiarism" was brought forward and echoed in the March 20, 1889 *Healdsburg Enterprise* in an article sponsored by the Healdsburg Pastor's Union entitled "Is Mrs. E. G. White a Plagiarist?" In the first edition of *Seventh-Day Adventism Renounced*, printed in October of 1888, Canright did accuse her of "plagiary." The reference to "plagiary" was quietly removed in the 1889 edition of the book and did not reappear until 1919 in his book *Mrs. E. G. White and Her Revelations*. (Canright seems to have forgotten in the 1914 edition of *Seventh-Day Adventism Renounced* that the 1888 edition ever existed. There he writes: "my book was not published till one year later, 1889.") A repackaging of D. M. Canright's complaints can be found in the video *Seventh-day Adventism: The Spirit Behind the Church*. The video's negative claims are evaluated by Bob Pickle in *A Response to the Video* at <www.pickle-publishing.com/papers/jeremiah-films/video-1.htm>.

[7] The term "Spirit of Prophecy," which comes from Rev. 19:10, is an inspired explanation of a phrase used in Rev. 12:17—"the testimony of Jesus." Lest we conclude that John's figure of speech refers to the testimony *about* Jesus in the New Testament, Rev. 22:9 provides one further parallel expression which shows that those with the "Spirit of prophecy" are "prophets." Thus the "spirit of prophecy" is a shorthand designation for those who possess Jesus' heavenly *gift* of prophecy (1 Cor. 12:10; John "was in the Spirit," Rev. 1:10; 4:2; cf. *DA* 55.3 regarding Simeon) and, believing that Ellen White possessed this heavenly gift, Seventh-day Adventists have applied this shorthand designation to her writings.

[8] GC Committee, quoted by Douglas Hackleman, "GC Committee Studies Ellen White's Sources," *Spectrum,* Vol. 10, No. 4 (March 1980), p. 14.

[9] Sometimes I wish I had received an education on this subject early on, as, perhaps, in a college class. However, W. C. White and D. E. Robinson's document, "Brief Statements Regarding the Writings of Ellen G. White" (1933), and Francis D. Nichol's 65-page discussion

secretary, I was asked to take her place. Shortly thereafter, I became a research assistant and then a researcher in the project, working alongside J. Paul Stauffer, a part-time research assistant, and Dr. Fred Veltman, the project director.

Before the Life of Christ Research Project, there had not been a comprehensive comparison of the works of nineteenth and pre–nineteenth-century writers on the life of Christ and *The Desire of Ages*. (Though Walter Rea had called attention to 17 possible source works for *The Desire of Ages*,[10] his principal focus had to do with the allusions from William Hanna's *Life of Christ*.[11]) Only with the completion of the Life of Christ Research Project would a more accurate sense of literary borrowing in *The Desire of Ages* come to light. The aim of our study was to be similarity in literary expression, rather than in the thoughts expressed.[12] (Though designating a sentence a "paraphrase" implies thought analysis, a thorough treatment of thought content would require a different process of analysis than we would be using, and *similarity of thought content alone does not ordinarily constitute plagiarism*.) Initially, many Adventists did not favor the Church's decision to go forward with the project. Since its completion, few Adventists have heard much about it and what they have heard is often distorted.

Many may wonder why I should now be interested in providing, from a layman's point of view, a thumbnail sketch of research that was completed 20 years ago. The answer is that I have provided this sketch in response to the encouragement of Elder Donald Mansell, former curator of the Ellen G. White unpublished writings, who knew of my experience with the Life of Christ Research Project. We were discussing a paper that summarized the Life of Christ Research Project I had presented at the Angwin Village Church, Sabbath afternoon, April 17, 1999, and it was his suggestion that a visual representation of the borrowings would be helpful if published and made available to a more general readership.[13] It is the prayer of this writer that this humble effort to acquaint others with the process and discoveries of our research—as well as more recent observations on the subject—will be truly helpful and enlightening.

E. MARCELLA ANDERSON KING

---

of literary dependency in *Ellen G. White and her Critics* (1951), pp. 403–467, have been around for decades. These are available at <www.adventistarchives.org> (*Adventist Review* for 1981, no. 23, supplement) and <www.whiteestate.org/books/egwhc/egwhctoc.html>.

[10] Review of *The White Lie* in *Forward* (San Juan Capistrano, CA: 1982), Vol. 5, No. 1, published by Christian Research Institute. The review speaks of "unequivocal copying" in Ellen White's writing, but this sweeping generalization is based on the work of Walter Rea, whose evidence and conclusions were described in his own book as "inconclusive" and "grossly exaggerated" (*The White Lie*, pp. 89, 95).

[11] We noted and compared Walter Rea's list of literary parallels to our own findings. In 17 out of 87 chapters of *The Desire of Ages*, Hanna had more than ten literary parallels with *The Desire of Ages* per chapter and ten or less in 19 others. However, this is a far cry from the early charge that Ellen White was almost wholly dependent on Hanna's *Life of Christ* for the composition of *The Desire of Ages*. Besides Hanna, there were at least 30 other possible source works involved. Regarding Rea's analysis, Jonathan Butler wrote in *Spectrum*, vol. 12, no. 4, p. 45: "Establishing ties between one author and others is a long, laborious, and tiresome process. Rea should be thanked for having undertaken this necessary and significant task. But the limited scope of his reading—and analysis—which especially qualified him as a source critic, left him decidedly unqualified to explore the significance of the parallels he found. . . . Had he produced simply an anthology of his literary exhibits, with a brief introduction which adhered modestly to the topic at hand, the importance and impact of his study might have been enhanced considerably."

[12] "We were not comparing ideas expressed but rather the actual words used to express the ideas. Individuals may express the same or very similar ideas yet never have known each other or read each other's works." —Fred Veltman, *LCRP*, Introduction, pp. 25, 26.

[13] Prior to this, Dr. Roger W. Coon (then with the White Estate) and Dr. Fred Veltman had critiqued my original paper at my request, and Dr. Robert W. Olson (former director of the White Estate) had reviewed the paper and provided helpful suggestions. Tim Poirier, now Vice Director of the Ellen G. White Estate, also made valuable suggestions.

 INVESTIGATIVE QUESTIONS

In this book you can expect to find answers (marked by the magnifying glass symbol) to the following fundamental questions regarding . . .

The writing of *The Desire of Ages*—

- Did Ellen White feel adequate to the task of putting into words what God gave her to communicate? (p. 12)
- Does the preface to *The Desire of Ages* set up any expectation that every detail in the book came from a vision? (p. 13)
- What might *The Desire of Ages* look like if it were footnoted by twenty-first century standards, marking instances of possible literary allusion? (p. 48)
- How did Ellen White use Hanna's life of Christ in *The Desire of Ages*? (p. 114)
- How should we describe Ellen White's use of sources? (p. 116)
- What conclusions can we draw from the colorized text? (p. 127)
- Why didn't Ellen White call attention to her literary sources? (p. 129)

Literary assistants—

- To what extent did Marian Davis rely on Ellen White's own words? (p. 34)
- What did Fannie Bolton testify about the work of Ellen White's assistants? (p. 37)
- How did H. C. Lacey help in the preparation of *The Desire of Ages?* (p. 41)

Plagiarism—

- What is plagiarism? (p. 133)
- In legal terms, did Ellen White make "fair use" of others' writings? (p. 136)
- Did Ellen White deny that she borrowed? (p. 139)

Inspiration—

- Can an inspired writer gather gems of truth from other writers? (p. 119)
- Whom did Ellen White consider to be the source of her messages? (p. 142)
- Does God dictate His messages to inspired writers word for word? (p. 143)
- Can an inspired writer use literary sources? (p. 147)
- How do Ellen White's writings relate to Scripture? (p. 154)
- How are Ellen White's writings "a lesser light"? (p. 155)
- Why would God need to give additional light? (p. 157)

The Life of Christ Research Project—

- How exhaustive was the scope of the investigation in the Life of Christ Research Project? (p. 173)
- How many "verbatims" were located in *The Desire of Ages*? (p. 175)

INTRODUCTION

It may be a bit of a quirk, but through the years I've always enjoyed taking pictures of people taking pictures. This book is kind of like that. It's the story behind the story of the writing of a book.

The Desire of Ages is the fullest expression of Ellen White's writing on the life of Christ. As a devotional classic, it has led thousands to a deeper appreciation of Jesus Christ, the Son of God. Unfortunately, over the past couple of decades, the beauty and insight of this inspiring book (as well as Ellen White's other writings) have been greatly neglected as a result of allegations that its author, in collaboration with her book editor, plagiarized most of the book from other writers.[1] The allegations were based on the discovery of selective phrasing in the book that was noticeably similar to that in earlier works on the life of Christ. Such allegations called for a response. Dr. Fred Veltman, Ph.D., chairman of the religion department of Pacific Union College and expert in language and source analysis, was commissioned to look into the matter.[2] After nearly eight years of careful study, he and his assistants published for the scholarly community the results of their research in a comprehensive and fair-handed report of 2,222 pages.[3] The conclusions of the report were both surprising and enlightening.

It was seen that it was not her editor Marian Davis, who had adapted wording from other writers, but Mrs. White. Marian Davis had only "compiled Mrs. White's earlier writings into scrapbook form," along with fresh material from Mrs. White, for the revitalization of Mrs. White's earlier account of the life of Christ in *Spirit of Prophecy*, Volumes 2 and 3.[4] Commenting on Mrs. White's borrowing of wording, Dr. Veltman wrote: "The issue that concerned her was the authority and truth of her messages— not their originality."[5] By this he meant that the uniqueness of her life of Christ writings was not in the particular words she used, but in the "finished product" and in the "emphasis she gave to the descriptions of the activities or viewpoints of God and His angels and of Satan and his angels."[6]

"The issue that concerned her was the authority and truth of her messages—not their originality."

Dr. Fred Veltman

From his careful examination of 15 chapters of the book, Dr. Veltman calculated that approximately 31% of the sentences of *The Desire of Ages* contain some "verbal similarity" to other previously printed volumes, the average level of dependency for these sentences being just a little higher than "loose paraphrase."[7] Was such "verbal similarity" evidence of *plagiarism*? It was Dr. Veltman's considered opinion that it was not. He wrote:

---

[1] Walter Rea, *The White Lie* (Turlock, California: M&R Publications, 1982), p. 72. Besides Walter Rea's allegations and those currently made on the Internet, the transcript of a recent presentation by an Adventist professor entitled, "The Specter of Plagiarism Haunting Adventism," has also made its rounds.

[2] At the same time, Attorney Vincent L. Ramik, expert in copyright law, was commissioned to render a legal opinion on her use of sources. His legal opinion is summarized in Chapter 8 of this book.

[3] Fred Veltman, "Full Report of the Life of Christ Research Project" [*LCRP*], available from <www.adventistarchives.org>.

[4] Fred Veltman, *Ministry*, Oct. 1990, p. 6, at <www.members.tripod.com/~Help_for_SDAs/Veltman.htm>.

[5] Veltman, Dec. 1990, p. 12.

[6] Veltman, Oct. 1990, pp. 15, 12. We will discover in this book that the uniqueness does not stop there.

[7] Veltman, p. 6. Since Veltman rated *whole sentences*, the 31% dependency rating is a bit misleading. In Chapter 3, for example, the percentage of actual words in the dependent sentences that were verbatim or near verbatim was 9.3%, or 203 out of 2,192 total

A writer can only be legitimately charged with plagiarism when that writer's literary methods contravene the established practices of the general community of writers producing works of the same literary genre within a comparable cultural context. In the process of doing our research, we discovered that Ellen White's sources had previously used each other in the same way that she later used them. At times the parallels between the sources were so strong that we had difficulty deciding which one Ellen White was using.[8]

Of course, it's not enough to plead, "Everybody's doing it!" Such a defense does not excuse immoral behavior—especially for one claiming divine inspiration. However, using that which is "community property" is not stealing, and it is not immoral. At the time that she wrote, improving one's writings with the pollen of another man's compositions was not considered unethical.

You may *steal* in the manner of bees, without wronging any one, but the *theft* of ants, who carry off a whole grain, should never be imitated.[9]

So why would Ellen White choose to use other writers' language in writing out the story of Jesus, and why would the level of literary dependency in telling that story exceed that of every other book of hers? The answer to these questions becomes apparent when we ask ourselves what *we* would have done had *we* seen what she saw and been called to write out the greatest of stories,[10] but felt limited in our command of language. "Oh that God would quicken the understanding," she would write, "for I am but a poor writer, and cannot with pen or voice express the great and deep mysteries of God."[11] Would we not have looked, after studying out what God had revealed, to the language of more gifted writers in helping us express our thoughts as she did?

Did Ellen White feel adequate for the task of putting into words what God gave her to communicate?

Notwithstanding all the power that God had given her to present scenes in the lives of Christ and His apostles and His prophets and His reformers in a stronger and more telling way than other historians, ... she always felt most keenly the results of her lack of school education. She admired the language in which other writers had presented to their readers the scenes which God had presented to her in vision, and she found it both a pleasure and a convenience and an economy of time[12] to use their language fully or in part in presenting

words. In Chapter 10, the percentage was 1.7%, or 79 out of 4,537 total words. It should also be noted that many of the sentences deemed "dependent" had no parallel *verbatim* words.

[8] Veltman, Dec. 1990, p. 14. (Similar statement found in *LCRP* 952.) When I informed Dr. Veltman that the LCRP was being used to support the charge of plagiary on the Internet, he expressed great surprise.

[9] La Mothe Le Vayer quoted by Mary Moss in "No Plagiarism," *New York Times* (Jan. 6, 1906): BR6, emphasis supplied. In his research Raymond F. Cottrell was struck by "the extent to which these nineteenth-century writers, many of them well known and respected, copied significant amounts of material from one another without once giving credit," and he "concluded that nineteenth-century literary ethics, even among the best writers, approved of, or at least did not seriously question, generous literary borrowing without giving credit"—Raymond F. Cottrell, *The Literary Relationship Between The Desire of Ages, by Ellen G. White and The Life of Christ, by William Hanna*, part I (Nov. 1, 1979), p. 6. Tilar J. Mazzeo writes of the early nineteenth century: "... writers who did not acknowledge their borrowings, even implicitly ... were not considered plagiarists, no matter how extensive the correspondences, if they had improved upon their borrowed material." —*Plagiarism and Literary Property in the Romantic Period*, p. 2.

[10] Of the two-hour March 14, 1858 vision, including the life of Christ, she wrote: "Most of the matter of the Great Controversy which I had seen ten years before, was repeated, and I was shown that I must write it out" (*2SG* 270.1).

[11] Ltr. 67, 1894, p. 10, Jan. 18, from Brighton, Victoria, Australia, to W. W. Prescott in *Exhibits* #55. ""In her early experience when she was sorely distressed over the difficulty of putting into human language the revelations of truths that had been imparted to her, she was reminded of the fact that all wisdom and knowledge comes from God and she was assured that God would bestow grace and guidance."—W. C. White, "Brief Statements Regarding the Writings of Ellen G. White," p. 5.

[12] Because of her conviction that the messages God gave her for the Church needed to come out quickly, Ellen White's *Testimonies to the Church* were released while still containing grammatical imperfections. When, in 1884, it was decided that these should be

those things which she knew through revelation, and which she wished to pass on to her readers. —Ltr. W. C. White to L. E. Froom, Jan. 8, 1928, in 3*SM* 460.3.[13]

As we learn from the preface of *The Desire of Ages*,[14] those who prepared the book were well aware of other "lives of Christ" and set up no expectation that every detail in the book came through a vision.[15]

> It is the purpose of this book to set forth Jesus Christ as the One in whom every longing may be satisfied. There is many a "Life of Christ" written, excellent books, large funds of information, elaborate essays on chronology and contemporaneous history, customs, and events, with much of the teaching and many glimpses of the many-sided life of Jesus of Nazareth. . . . It is not, however, the purpose of this work to set forth a harmony of the Gospels, or even to give in strictly chronological order the important events and wonderful lessons of the life of Christ; its purpose is to present the love of God as revealed in His Son, the divine beauty of the life of Christ, of which all may partake, and not to satisfy the desires of the merely curious nor the questionings of the critics. —Publishers, *The Desire of Ages*, preface, pp. 13, 14.

Does the preface to The Desire of Ages set up any expectation that every detail in the book came from a vision?

My own experience with *The Desire of Ages* goes back to the mid–1970s, when it was my pleasure to take a class on the life and teachings of Jesus that used *The Desire of Ages* (in addition to a Gospel harmony) as the main textbook for the class. I remember hearing someone say at that time that a student should take about two hours of study outside class for every hour spent in the classroom. I found myself reading and thinking about *The Desire of Ages* much longer than such a formula would afford. The spiritual thoughts of Ellen White captivated my heart and imagination. Just like a child receiving nutrition from a piece of whole wheat bread while unaware of all the nutrients in it, I was being fed while reading *The Desire of Ages*—even though I was unaware of all the "ingredients" used in its making! It wasn't until August of 1979 that I learned from the *Adventist Review* how the book was put together and was drawn into the excitement of author and editor as the contents of each chapter of the manuscript came into place.

Concerning my co-author, Marcella Anderson King, Dr. Fred Veltman noted in the final report of the Life of Christ Research Project: "She brought to the project a thorough knowledge of the Ellen G. White writings, a passion for hard work, and a dedication to detail" (*LCRP* ix, x). Marcella is indeed a careful researcher, and I have really been blessed in working with her on this project. I trust that you, the reader, will also be blessed as you dig beneath the surface with us and discover what went into the making of *The Desire of Ages*.

KEVIN L. MORGAN

---

corrected, she wrote: "I think that anything that shall go forth will be criticized, twisted, turned, and boggled, but we are to go forward with a clear conscience, doing what we can and leaving the result with God. We must not be long in delaying the work." 3*SM* 97.5f.

[13] W. C. White's comments about his mother's use of sources will often be cited in the footnotes of this book in corroboration of other documentary evidence in the main text.

[14] The wording of the preface was suggested by Marian Davis, who wrote: "In the preface, would it not be well to state, in some way, that this book is not a harmony of the gospels, that it does not attempt to teach chronology. Its purpose is to present the love of God, the divine beauty of the life of Christ, not to satisfy the questioning of critics."

[15] Ellen White herself referred to the impressions of the Lord that helped her to know which subjects to write upon: "This is an important time just now, the closing up of the book on life of Christ. I want quiet and restfulness, that if the Lord has anything to impress upon my mind, I can discern the subject and prepare it for the book." —Ltr. 173, 1896, written Nov. 29 from "Sunnyside," Cooranbong, N.S.W., to "Dear Son Willie."

A Glimpse of Jesus

Soon after this I had another dream. I seemed to be sitting in abject despair, with my face in my hands, reflecting like this: If Jesus were upon earth, I would go to Him, throw myself at His feet, and tell Him all my sufferings. He would not turn away from me, He would have mercy upon me, and I should love and serve Him always. Just then the door opened, and a person of beautiful form and countenance entered. He looked upon me pityingly and said: "Do you wish to see Jesus? He is here and you can see Him if you desire to do so. Take everything you possess and follow me."

I heard this with unspeakable joy, and gladly gathered up all my little possessions, every treasured trinket, and followed my guide. He led me to a steep and apparently frail stairway. As I commenced to ascend the steps, he cautioned me to keep my eyes fixed upward, lest I should grow dizzy and fall. Many others who were climbing up the steep ascent fell before gaining the top.

Finally we reached the last step and stood before the door. Here my guide directed me to leave all the things that I had brought with me. I cheerfully laid them down; he then opened the door and bade me enter. In a moment I stood before Jesus. There was no mistaking that beautiful countenance. Such a radiant expression of benevolence and majesty could belong to no other. As His gaze rested upon me, I knew at once that He was acquainted with every circumstance of my life and all my inner thoughts and feelings.

I tried to shield myself from His gaze, feeling unable to endure His searching eyes, but He drew near with a smile, and, laying His hand upon my head, said: "Fear not." The sound of His sweet voice thrilled my heart with a happiness it had never before experienced. I was too joyful to utter a word, but, overcome with ineffable happiness, sank prostrate at His feet. While I was lying helpless there, scenes of beauty and glory passed before me, and I seemed to have reached the safety and peace of heaven. At length my strength returned, and I arose. The loving eyes of Jesus were still upon me, and His smile filled my soul with gladness. His presence filled me with holy reverence and an inexpressible love. . . .

—Ellen White, *Early Writings*, pp. 79 and 80.

Pictured on this page is a profile of Jesus from the engraving, "Our Saviour," by artist John Sartain. About this engraving Abbie Kellogg Norton wrote in 1935: "I well recall seeing Brother and Sister White coming to our home many times when I was a child . . . and Sister White never failed to comment upon the picture and its likeness to the Saviour as she had seen Him in visions." Willie White wrote in 1925 that his mother "considered it the most nearly correct of any picture she had seen." Even still, there is no mention of the picture in Ellen White's writings themselves. "Neither God nor heaven nor Christ, who is the image of the Father," she wrote, "can be truly represented by the art of man" (15*MR* 105.6). She preferred to portray the Saviour through the story of His loving words and deeds while on earth. As in the words of Mary, "Be it unto me according to thy word" (Luke 1:38), so in this 1842 dream recorded in *Early Writings*, do we find evidence of the submissiveness to God that would fit young Ellen Harmon to faithfully portray the Saviour through pen and voice.

CHAPTER 1
Her Heart's Desire

The book was the fulfillment of a longing that grew up within a young woman's heart as she fell in love with Jesus and devoted her life in service to Him. Receiving inspired glimpses of His love and earthly mission, that young woman sketched out in several brief compositions what she was shown. These were later amplified to include more of Jesus' life. Describing what motivated her, she wrote:

> I was surprised and enraptured with the clear views now presented to my mind of the atonement and the work of Jesus Christ. . . . I longed to tell the story of Jesus' love. . .[1]

It was not until 1898, however, that the great longing of her heart would come to completeness. The young woman was Ellen Gould Harmon, later to become Ellen G. White. Because Ellen was forced to break off her formal education in the third grade, throughout her long writing career, she would always require the help of literary assistants of one type or another.[2]

Ellen White's first literary assistant

W. C. White, son of James and Ellen White, shared recollections about his mother's regular solicitation of help from her husband in improving the language of her compositions:

> On coming home from the *Review and Herald* Office, James White was frequently greeted by his wife with the statement, "James, I want you to hear what I have been writing." Then he would lie down on the sofa in the sitting room, and Mother would read to him what she had written during the forenoon. I can never forget the joy which they shared together as she brought out from time to time precious instruction for the church, and interesting historical articles regarding leading characters in the patriarchal and Christian age.
>
> Sometimes, she would say, "James, here is an article that ought to be printed. It is a testimony on Christian experience, and I want you to listen to it and help me prepare it for the printer." She was an unusually good reader, speaking slowly and distinctly. If her husband discovered weaknesses in the composition, such as faulty tenses of verbs, or disagreement between subjects, noun, and verb, he would suggest grammatical corrections. These she would write into her manuscript and then read on.[3]

James and Ellen White, 1864

When she wrote out the 1858 "great controversy" vision in *Spiritual Gifts*, vol. 1—a book that included her first 50 pages on the life of Christ—it was James who helped her prepare it.[4]

---

[1] Ellen G. White, *Life Sketches of James and Ellen White* (1880), p. 161.

[2] Reflecting on the stone's blow to her face that left her physically disfigured and unable to complete her formal education, Ellen White would write some nearly 50 years later: "I might never have known Jesus, had not the sorrow that clouded my early years led me to seek comfort in Him." —Ellen G. White, *RH* 11-25-1884.

[3] W. C. White, "How Ellen White's Books were Written: Addresses to Faculty and Students at the Advanced Bible School, Angwin, California," June 18, 1935, Part I, at <www.whiteestate.org/issues/HowEGWbksWCW.html>.

[4] Robert W. Olson, "How the Desire of Ages Was Written," p. 2 at <www.whiteestate.org/issues/DA-HOW/DA-How.html>.

"I am not a scholar."

During the early 1870s Ellen White began expanding her writing on the life of Christ with *The Spirit of Prophecy*, vol. 2.[5] "It was early in 1873, while James and Ellen White were in California for the first time, that she began her writing on the life of Christ. Between this date and the spring of 1875, as her travels and other work allowed, she wrote somewhat intermittently. Portions were first published in the *Review and Herald*" (Arthur L. White, 4*BIO* 376.3). Nevertheless, her book writing often had to wait for the preparation of testimonies to church leaders and other people in need. It also had to wait on Mrs. White's frailty of health—though it was not her own health, but that of her husband James, brought on by overwork, that led Ellen White to re-evaluate the logistics of her writing with James's waning assistance. We pick up hints of the struggle she was going through in excerpts from her personal diary and from letters to family:

> I spent a share of the day in writing. Walked out and sat under spruce trees. Read my manuscript to my husband and corrected it for printer. —MS 4, 1872, at Walling's Mills, Colorado, July 28.

> We rose early to prepare to go to San Francisco. My heart is inexpressibly sad. This morning I take into candid consideration my writings. My husband is too feeble to help me prepare them for the printer, therefore I shall do no more with them at present. I am not a scholar. I cannot prepare my own writings for the press. Until I can do this I shall write no more. It is not my duty to tax others with my manuscript. —MS 3, 1873, p. 5, Friday, Jan. 10, in *Exhibits #7*.[6]

> We rested well last night. This Sabbath morning opens cloudy. My mind is coming to strange conclusions. I am thinking I must lay aside my writing I have taken so much pleasure in, and see if I cannot become a scholar. I am not a grammarian. I will try, if the Lord will help me, at forty-five years old to become a scholar in the science [of writing]. God will help me. I believe He will. —MS 3, 1873, p. 5, Jan. 11 from San Francisco in *Exhibits #8*.[7]

Though she made great strides in improving her writing, she never totally mastered grammar, spelling, or syntax, and therefore continued receiving help from others in preparing her writings.

---

[5] Her earliest writings about Jesus were an 1842 dream that she first published in 2*SG* (1860) 18, 19, and revised for *EW* (1882) 79, 80 (see p. 14); five pages on the coming of the Messiah in 4*SG*, published in 1864; a 16-page pamphlet, "The Sufferings of Christ" [*PH169*], published in 1869. *PH169* was amplified during 1873–1875 and published in the *ST* articles on "The Sufferings of Christ" of November/December 1875 (85% of *PH169* makes up 44% of the *ST* articles; reprinted in August of 1879). Ellen White also wrote several articles on the birth, temptations, and sufferings of Christ for the *RH* and *YI* of 1872–1875; the 388 pages of 2*SP* (printed mid-Nov. 1876); and the 255 pages of 3*SP* (printed late Nov. 1877).

[6] At this time a "scholar" was one who applied himself/herself to some area of study, i.e., a *student*. Ellen White uses "scholar" to describe someone who makes a study of healthful cooking (2*T* 537.2).

[7] No book published before 1876 has a dependency rate higher than 1%, suggesting when Ellen White began reading in earnest to improve her writing. Aside from *DA*, the works of hers with the highest literary dependency are *GC* (1911) with 3241 lines (15.11%) for attributed material and 1084 (5.05%) for unattributed, *LP* (1883) with 1185 (12.23%), *SC* (1892) with 196 (6.23%). The lowest are 2*T* (1868–1871) with 42 lines (0.20%), 2*SM* (1958) with 20 (0.17%), and *EW* (1882) with 10 (0.14%). The documented number of lines of allusion in Ellen White's works has been carefully recorded by Tim Poirier in "Project Surprise," summarized at <www.whiteestate.org/issues/parallel.html>. The results of this tabulation agree with W. C. White and D. E. Robinson's explanation:

> ... the class of matter written by Mrs. White, in which she used the writings of others, is *comparatively small* when considering the vast field covered by her writings. It is in the delineation in prophetic and doctrinal exposition that we find that she used the words of others or had closely paraphrased them. In the vast field covering thousands of pages of messages of encouragement, reproof, and spiritual instruction, *she worked independent of all other writers*, also in her divine prediction of future experiences through which the church must pass. —"Brief Statements Regarding the Writings of Ellen White," Aug. 1933, p. 12, emphasis supplied. (Though occasionally using their words, her writing wasn't directed by their thoughts.)

I am still feeling very weak. I tried to write to San Francisco to the brethren. Wrote twenty-seven pages upon the blessings Christ pronounced upon the mount. I had some freedom in writing. —MS 4, 1873, written Feb. 4 from Santa Rosa, Calif.

It continues rainy. We walked out some distance for exercise. I again resumed my writing upon *Spirit of Prophecy*. . . .

We decided to remain at home if it continues raining. I looked over my writings with my husband. Prepared twenty pages of manuscript for a printer. —MS 4, 1873, Santa Rosa, Feb. 7, and Sabbath, Feb. 8.

As a result of the intensity of his efforts in looking after the growth and interests of the Seventh-day Adventist Church, Elder White's health took another severe blow. In April of 1873 he suffered his fourth stroke of paralysis, affecting one of his arms. In answer to prayer and anointing, the Lord restored most of the strength of the affected arm. However, it was evident that he needed more recreation. That is why the Whites found themselves, in the summer of 1873, in Colorado on the property of an old mill belonging to their relative, Mr. Walling. James had finally become "settled in regard to his duty to drop everything like burdens at Battle Creek and spend the summer in the Colorado Mountains" (MS 6, 1873, in Arthur L. White, *2BIO* 381.2). Upon arriving in Colorado, they settled comfortably into a cabin located on Mr. Walling's property.

James and Ellen White's Colorado cabin with its builder, W. H. Moore

This is a beautiful day. We walked out early and had a precious season of prayer. We wrote quite steadily upon the temptations of Christ. —MS 10, 1873, Walling's Mills, Colo., Sabbath, Aug. 2.

The Whites enjoyed their Rocky Mountain retreat until mid-November when they returned east for the twelfth annual session of the General Conference. On December 18 they headed out to Santa Rosa, California, where "Lucinda Hall had set up housekeeping for the White family in a commodious rented home. The two [little] nieces, Addie and May Walling, were with her" (*2BIO* 401.2). Both James and Ellen pursued their writing during the rainy winter months. In late April of 1874 the Whites moved to Oakland to launch a weekly publication, *The Signs of the Times*. With little more to start it than James's personal initiative, it soon became evident that they would need to raise funds for the venture. With this purpose in mind, Ellen White undertook a fundraising campaign that would take her across the country alone for the first time. From camp meeting to camp meeting she traveled, telling about the struggling but promising work out in California. Finally, she arrived in Battle Creek and took the July 3 Sabbath morning service. On August 6, James joined his wife in Battle Creek, though he would soon have to return to their home in Oakland, California where the Pacific Press publishing work would have its beginning. The dream of a press in Oakland was coming closer to reality as money was raised in pledges ($19,300) at the Yountville, California camp meeting. Soon after recovering from a serious illness in 1874, James took up the mantel of the presidency of the General Conference, shouldering heavy responsibilities. Within two years, he would again be afflicted with another paralytic stroke and its resulting debilitation (White, *2BIO* 442, 443).

In the midst of all her other activities, Ellen White continued working intermittently on the life of Christ materials that would appear in the first four of the "Life of Christ" pamphlets (also known as the *Redemption Leaflets*) and in *Spirit of Prophecy*, volume 2.[8] To her husband she wrote:

> I am trying to revise <u>Sufferings</u> of <u>Christ</u>.[9] It is called for everywhere. —Ltr. 68, 1874, written July 3 from Battle Creek, Mich.

Then a year later, she reported—

> We have just finished "<u>Sufferings</u> of <u>Christ</u>." Willie has helped me, and now we take it to the office for Uriah [Smith] to criticize it. —Ltr. 44, 1875, Battle Creek, to James White, July 17.[10]

The Whites were active in church work, and much of the time traveled together. In June of 1875, they ministered at camp meetings in the Midwest—Illinois, Wisconsin, and Minnesota (White, 2*BIO* 473.1, 2), as well as at other camp meetings in late summer. By the end of September, they were back to their "good home" in Oakland with area meetings to attend. During these busy times, they did not always travel together as the many letters that went back and forth between them testify. In her letter of April 18, 1876, Ellen White explained to her husband why she could not join him for a particular trip to Battle Creek where he had Church business as General Conference president:

> I see many subjects to write out which must be done with the greatest care. I want this summer, the whole of it, to do this work in. I must stop a day or two in the week and go somewhere or my head will break down. I begrudge every moment that I feel compelled to rest. These intensely interesting subjects weary me far more to write them out than to speak upon them. I feel that it would not be advisable for me to break off now and go East. ... I would feel pleased to meet my brethren and sisters in camp meeting. It is just such work as I enjoy. Much better than the confinement of writing. But this will break up my work and defeat the plans of getting out my books, for I cannot do both—travel and write. Now seems to be my golden opportunity. Mary [Clough—her sister's daughter] is with me, the best copyist I can ever have. Another such chance may never be mine. —Ltr. 9, 1876, pp. 1, 3, written April 18 from Oakland, California in *Exhibits* #17.

In other letters, she told James about progress on the life of Christ manuscript:

> I enjoy the presence of God and yet my soul is continually drawn out for more of His salvation. I am writing and having freedom in my writing. Precious subjects I am handling. The last I completed or about completed yesterday—Jesus healing the impotent man at the pool of Bethesda. —Ltr. 1, 1876, p. 2, March 31, in *Exhibits* #10.

> I feel that I am less than nothing, but Jesus is my all—my righteousness, and my wisdom, and my strength. —Ltr. 16a, 1876, p. 2, April 28, in *Exhibits* #23.

---

[8] 2*SP* was first released as four leaflets—nos. 1, 3, and 4 in 1877 and no. 2, from a series of 13 articles on the temptations of Christ in the *Adventist Review and Sabbath Herald*, in 1874 and 1875. 3*SP* was printed in late November 1877 (see announcement *RH* 11-22-1877), and the printed text was first advertised as the "Life of Christ" pamphlets, nos. 5–8, in *ST* 2-21-1878.

[9] In June of 1873, she had mentioned expanding her original 16-page 1869 pamphlet on Christ's suffering (3*SM* 264.4).

[10] She was always concerned that ambiguity of wording might obscure the communication of the truth. On April 8, 1876, she wrote her husband: "How will it do to read my manuscript to Elders Waggoner and Loughborough? If there is any wording of doctrinal points not so clear as might be, he might discern it. (W. I mean.)" (Ltr. 4a, 1876, pp. 1, 2, in *Exhibits* #14). Later she wrote of Marian Davis: "Tell her that she has a point about Zedekiah's having his eyes put out. That needs to be more carefully worded—also the rock, when the water flowed" (Ltr. 38, 1885 [Dec. 22] from Basel, Switzerland, in 3*SM* 121, 122). See also letter in 10*MR* 12.4.

Dear Husband: . . . Last night I again spoke to the people. This was my text—the words of Christ to the twelve, "Will ye also go away?" Peter answered, "Lord, to whom shall we go? Thou hast the words of eternal life" (See John 6:67, 68). I had perfect freedom. I never felt more sensibly the especial help from God than while speaking. The people sat as if spellbound, wide awake, although the meeting did not close till after nine o'clock. The Spirit of God was upon me. —Ltr. 18, 1876, pp. 1, 2, April, in *Exhibits #24*.

Dear Husband: . . . I have been writing more than usual, which was too much for me. I cannot and must not write more than half a day, but I continue to step over the bounds and pay for it. My mind is on my subjects day and night. I have strong confidence in prayer. The Lord hears me and I believe in His salvation. In His strength I trust. In His strength I shall complete my writings. I cling firmly to His hand with unwavering confidence. We are happy in our work and this is our world for the present. . . .

If I am blessed with health as I have been hitherto, I shall complete my first book in about four weeks. —Ltr. 21, 1876, pp. 1, 2, May 5, in *Exhibits #25*.

Dear Husband: . . . If I get my writings [for *Spirit of Prophecy*, vol. 2] all in manuscript, my part of the work is done and I shall be relieved. —Ltr. 24, 1876, p. 2, May 11, in *Exhibits #26*.

The work of writing on the life of Christ was a combination of revelation, research, which included study of Scripture and reference works such as William Hanna to help with the storyline and background information, prayer, and meditation. In her letter to James (illustrated on page 20), she mentions one other ingredient—plain "hard thinking."

There seems to be nothing to confuse and distract my mind, and with so much hard thinking my mind could not be perplexed with anything without being overtaxed. —Ltr. 13, 1876, April 24, p. 1, in *Exhibits #19*.

I cannot rush business. This work must be done carefully, slowly, and accurately. The subjects we have prepared are well gotten up. They please me. —Ltr. 14, 1876, April 25, in *Exhibits #20*.

Previously that year, when her son Willie and his wife Mary were part of her household, Mrs. White had written her husband: "Mary White has too great a pressure of work in the office reading proof and preparing matters for paper" (Ltr. 5, 1876, from Oakland, Calif., April 11). She was hoping for more help in the transcription and correction of her handwritten manuscripts. As noted earlier, her sister's daughter started working for her shortly thereafter, for she wrote to Willie and Mary: "Mary Clough will remain with me and do my work as I prepare it for her" (Ltr. 29, 1877, from Healdsburg, Calif., Oct. 26). By January of 1878, however, problems in Mary's work caused Ellen White to ask Willie, who was then at Battle Creek, Michigan, to send her some other copyists. By year's end, Mrs. White needed additional secretarial help. She suggested that Willie send Mary White, Mary Smith Abbey, or Marian Davis, and she said that James was anxious to get Marian, who had several years of experience as a proofreader at the Review and Herald publishing offices. Her "judgment on composition" would be an advantage because James made no changes to Mrs. White's writing and her copyist would "copy precisely even to wrong spelling," even though both had been schoolteachers (Ltr. 62, 1878, from Denison, Texas, Dec. 19).

Elder James White's health continued to worsen until early June of 1878, when he went to the Battle Creek Sanitarium "to rest and to receive treatments" under Dr. John Harvey Kellogg. In less than a month, he wrote Ellen: "I report myself very much improved" (White, 3*BIO* 90.3).

Pictured above are the first and last pages of a six-and-a-half-page letter that Ellen White wrote to James on the progress of the life of Christ. In the letter, she said: "Mary has just been reading to me two articles— one on the loaves and fishes, [the other on] Christ walking on the water . . . This takes fifty pages and comprises many subjects. I do think it the most precious matter I have ever written. Mary is just as enthusiastic over it. She thinks it is of the highest value. I am perfectly satisfied with it. . . . I love the Lord. I love His cause. I love His people. I feel great peace and calmness of mind" (Ltr. 13, 1876 in 3SM 106.3).

After helping with plans to build and finance the "Dime Tabernacle"[11] at Battle Creek, James was ready to leave for the mountains of Colorado for a long anticipated time of relaxation and restoration. When Ellen joined him there on August 3, she found him "every way improved" (White, 3*BIO* 93.6). Yet, she could not stay long, for she was to be called east to have a part in camp meetings in Michigan, Massachusetts, and Maine. By late winter in early 1879, the Whites were assisting with meetings in Dallas, Texas, a needy field (White, 3*BIO* 95, 96, 107).

> There was hardly a wasted hour in Ellen White's life. She learned early that serving as an effectual channel of communication for the Lord called for a total dedication. Often she had weeks and months of diligent work before her, just to convey to individuals the messages the Lord gave her for them. There was also a backlog of articles to be written for the *Review* and the *Signs*, and book preparation. While she was at home she spent almost every moment available in writing, except when she was ill ... She wrote on trains and in boats, while traveling by carriage, and sometimes during camp meetings, at a table in front of the pulpit. ... the work was ... always with her. —White, 3*BIO* 150.1.

> While still in Texas in mid-January, 1879, with Marian Davis at hand to assist, [Ellen White] began work on *Spirit of Prophecy*, volume 4 [*The Great Controversy*], work that would continue off and on for the next four years (JW to WCW, Jan. 17, 1879) —White, 3*BIO* 150.4.

From time to time James White had to be at Battle Creek "to care for the many administrative duties he willingly accepted at General Conference session, to pastor the Battle Creek church, and to push ahead with such publishing interests as the publication of *Life Sketches of James and Ellen White* and the republication of some of the earliest E. G. White pamphlets and books" (White, 3*BIO* 132.3). In *Life Sketches*, published in 1880, James White made the following claims about his wife's writing:

> In her published works there are many things set forth which cannot be found in other books, and yet they are so clear and beautiful that the unprejudiced mind grasps them at once as truth. A doctor of divinity once heard Mrs. W. speak upon her favorite theme, God in Nature. She dwelt largely upon the life and teachings of Christ. This Christian gentleman was instructed and highly edified; and at the close of the discourse, in private conversation, addressed her in these words: "Sister White, while you were speaking, I have been asking myself the question, Why is it that none of us have thought of these precious things which you have brought out this morning?" —*Life Sketches of James and Ellen White*, p. 328.

On April 6, 1880, while Ellen had to be out West, she wrote from Oakland to her husband:

> Never doubt my love for you. But I find my duty calls me from you sometimes, and I shall be obedient to the call. My influence at times will be more favorable alone than if you are with me. I shall be with you when I can, but in the future we both may have to endure the trial of separation more in our labors than in the past. —Ltr. 19, 1880 in 3*BIO* 136.2.

At about the same time he wrote to Ellen:

> I hope by your good counsel and help of the Lord to avoid any breakdown this spring. —Ltr. April 11, 1880 in 3*BIO* 136.3.

---

[11] So named because, when it was constructed to accommodate General Conference sessions, "each church member throughout the land was asked to contribute at least ten cents" (The Trustees of the Ellen G. White Publications, 4*T* 6).

On May 4 he wrote Willie:

> I undertake to do too much work. I shall not deny that I love to work, and am inclined to take too much on my hands. —3*BIO* 136.4.

The Whites took another trip together in mid-August to a camp meeting in Quebec, Canada, where they both ministered (White, 3*BIO* 143). About a year later, on July 30, 1881 at the Battle Creek Tabernacle, Elder James White stood side by side with his wife in the pulpit. Little could either have imagined that this would be the last time they would minister together. Just two days later, James suffered a severe chill that was accompanied by an attack of malaria. Though given the best of care at the sanitarium, the "tired warrior" passed to his rest on August 6, 1881 (White, 3*BIO*, Chap. 14).

> The last years of James White's life [had been] marked by notable achievements in building the church and its institutions in spite of periods impaired by illness. His rather sudden death at the age of 60 shocked both Ellen White and the church. —White, 3*BIO* 10.1.

Mrs. White was not prepared for his death. She and James had "designed to devote the coming winter to writing" (Ellen White, "A Sketch of Experience," in "In Memoriam: A Sketch of the Last Sickness and Death of Elder James White," p. 54).

> At times I felt that I could not have my husband die. But these words seemed to be impressed on my mind: "Be still, and know that I am God." Psalm 46:10. I keenly feel my loss, but dare not give myself up to useless grief. This would not bring back the dead. And I am not so selfish as to wish, if I could, to bring him from his peaceful slumber to engage again in the battles of life. Like a tired warrior, he has lain down to sleep. I will look with pleasure upon his resting place. The best way in which I and my children can honor the memory of him who has fallen, is to take the work where he left it, and in the strength of Jesus carry it forward to completion. —*Life Sketches of Ellen G. White* (1915), p. 253.

"Severely alone," but courageously continuing in ministry

"Now midway in her lifework, Mrs. White, though deprived of her husband's companionship and more than ever dependent on divine aid and support, courageously continued her ministry of writing, counseling, and public speaking across America and overseas" (White, 3*BIO* 10.2). About this period of her life, she would later write:

> I have been . . . severely alone with all the difficulties and all the trials connected with the work. God alone could help me. —MS 227, 1902 in 3*SM* 67.2.

In a few months, Ellen White moved her household from Oakland to Healdsburg. On February 24, 1882, the day after arriving at her farm, she wrote her children and gave her address as "White's Ranch," Healdsburg, California. "She drew in her family of literary and home helpers, hoping soon to settle down to a serious program of writing. But this she found hard to do" (White, 3*BIO* 194.5). Her writing during this period was rather limited. Suffering a severe chill in late August, she lapsed into a two-month long sickness (White, 3*BIO* 203.1). Failing to recover at the Health Retreat in St. Helena or at her Healdsburg home, Mrs. White hoped that, as camp meeting commenced, she would "experience a renewal of life and strength" (White, 3*BIO* 203.2). At the Healdsburg camp meeting, greatly enfeebled, Mrs. White stood up to address the congregation. As she spoke, "her voice and appearance" changed, and the people in Healdsburg witnessed an instantaneous, miraculous healing. "This event, which seemed to be a turning point in her physical condition, opened the way for a strong ministry" (White, 3*BIO* 205.1).

The events of the next decade we will now review rather quickly. At the General Conference Session of late 1884, the Committee of the Central European Mission presented their request for Mrs. White to visit Europe. After a period of deliberation, she accepted the call and spent part of three years (1885–1887) ministering in Europe, beginning with a brief stay in England, and then moving to Basel, Switzerland—a place that would become her home base.

From Basel, she, W. C. White, Sara McEnterfer, and an interpreter visited the Scandinavian countries. Returning to Basel, Ellen White received a request to go to Italy to hold meetings. However, perplexing logistical matters needed to be settled—Mrs. White was without proper literary assistance and she needed a place of retreat to continue her publishing work. Should the lack be supplied by bringing Marian Davis over from America? No, Mrs. White was content to send her writings back to Marian in America and have them published there (White, 3*BIO* 331.5). Hopefully, during the upcoming meetings in Torre Pellice, Italy, a place to relax and write could be found. Oh, how Mrs. White thrilled at being able to visit the Waldensian hideaways!

In early February 1886, Willie White, having just attended the General Conference session at Battle Creek, surprised his mother by writing that he was bringing a company of workers. This would include Marian Davis, L. R. Conradi, and Willie's wife, Mary. With these workers, Ellen White could remain in Europe for the rest of the year, prepare her books, and have them published in Europe without going back to America (White, 3*BIO* 339.3). With these matters resolved, Mrs. White visited Italy and the Scandinavian countries a second time. Then she and her helpers left for France to help in an evangelistic effort (White, 3*BIO* 355.2). On Christmas Day, 1886, Mrs. White attended the dedication of a house of worship in Tramelan, Switzerland. It was the first such dedication of a Seventh-day Adventist church in Europe (White, 3*BIO* 359.1). Before starting the long trek back toward America, Sister White and her son Willie squeezed in a visit to Zurich, stopped at a conference held at Vohwinkel, Prussia the weekend of May 27 to 29 (White, 3*BIO* 363.5), and then proceeded on to Moss, Norway, where the first European camp meeting was held, starting June 14.

W. C. White, 1880s

The sights of Europe brought remembrances from visions past to Mrs. White and motivated her to include additional material in the 1888 revision of *The Great Controversy*. W. C. White recounts an instance in Basel in which one of her "eyewitness" views of events came back to mind:

> I was reading Wylie's history of the Reformation and found a very interesting passage telling the story of a Catholic army coming against the Protestants. In this story it was represented that as soon as the Catholic army caught sight of the little Protestant band, they turned and fled as though a great army was pursuing them. After reading this, I took the book to mother's room and asked her to let me read it to her. When I had read through a page, she took up the narrative and described the experience with all the clearness and vividness of one who had seen it and she brought in a number of very interesting features not mentioned by Wylie. After she had finished her description of the scene, I said, "Mother, have you read that in Wylie's?" She said, "No, but I saw it in vision. I saw those armies come and before they reached the little company of Protestants, the heavenly hosts appeared and manifested themselves to them and the Catholic army fled in great dismay." Then I said, "Why did you not write that out and include it in your first edition of 'Great Controversy'?" And she said, "Because I did not know its relation to other parts of the history, but now that I know when and where it

occurred, I will write out what was presented to me and it can be incorporated in the next edition of the book." —Ltr. from St. Helena, Calif., July 25, 1919.[12]

Visiting the British Mission back in England, she and W. C. White finally returned home to America in mid-August (White, 3*BIO* 371, 372).

During the years 1887–1891, the servant of the Lord was kept busy with her usual activities, speaking at camp meetings and churches, sending out testimonies and various counsels, as well as preparing materials for books. To attend the General Conference session in the late fall of 1888 held at Minneapolis, Minnesota, Ellen "ventured to cross the Rocky Mountains" (White, 3*BIO* 385.1). This was a trying General Conference session for Ellen and her son Willie. Speeches were long and discussions were heated between the two camps of ministering brethren that had formed among those assembled at the conference. A number of men identified themselves with one camp or the other, influenced by the doctrinal arguments presented and by their attitude toward the Spirit of Prophecy counsels. In some cases their attitude was not wholesome.

Ellen White, the servant of the Lord, stood staunchly for the two main presenters from the West Coast, A. T. Jones and E. J. Waggoner. Well over 200 citations in her writings endorse these messengers and their message through 1896, and even longer for Elder A. T. Jones. (You can read one of her strongest endorsements in *Testimonies to Ministers and Gospel Workers*, pages 91–93, and her further evaluation of the controversy in 1*SM* 234, 235.)

For a short time after the Minneapolis General Conference, Ellen White accompanied Elder(s) Jones and/or Waggoner for a number of speaking engagements and even joined them as one of the presenters. In the General Conference sessions of 1889, 1891, 1893, 1895, 1897, and 1899, Jones and Waggoner played a prominent role in delivering several series of studies.

After the General Conference session of 1889, several in Battle Creek continued to oppose the messages of these special messengers (White, 3*BIO* 448.1). An important breakthrough in the controversy came during the General Conference session of March 1891, which Mrs. White attended. On March 8, she was awakened by the Lord at 3:00 A.M. and prompted to write out some notes from the vision God had given her a year earlier, in Salamanca, New York, but which she had to this point not related to anyone. When she arrived unexpectedly at the 5:30 early-morning ministers meeting, the brethren quickly gave her the pulpit. Upon relating her message about not removing our distinctive truths from *The American Sentinel*, the hearers were stunned. "The Holy Spirit witnessed to the testimony borne by His servant in that meeting, and instead of division, there came a spirit of unity and sweet communion" (A. T. Robinson in Arthur White, 3*BIO* 482.4).

"The 1891 General Conference session over, Ellen White hoped fervently that there would be no invitation for her to" leave home again and defeat her plans for writing (White, 3*BIO* 490.1). Despite her wishes, the call of the brethren went forward.

> The action of the Foreign Mission Board calling for Ellen White to go to Australia carried a clause that left the final decision with her. . . . As she later wrote of it, she had adopted the practice of responding to the requests of the General Conference unless she had special light to the contrary (Letter 18a, 1892). As they viewed the needs of the world field the brethren had asked her to go; in vision she had been shown conditions in Australia, which to her seemed to be an indication that she should go; and as the Lord gave her no direct word as to the course she should follow, she would go, even though she wished she might be released from going. —White, 3*BIO* 492.2, 4.

---

[12] DF #389, pp. 3, 4. Description used in *GC* 116, 117 (both the 1888 and 1911 editions). This incident explains why he wrote on Feb. 14, 1926 to L. E. Froom that, after reading D'Aubigne and Martyn "later she read a little in Wylie, but not much."

A quiet place to get out the "life of Christ"

For some time Mrs. White had been impressed that she should revise and enlarge her life of Christ chapters in *Spirit of Prophecy,* vols. 2 and 3.[13] She wrote: "I long for rest, for quietude and to get out the 'Life of Christ.'" —MS 29, 1891 in White, 3*BIO* 490.1. Now she was to have a new locale for doing this precious work—a land that was a new frontier for the Advent message, the island country of Australia. O how much Ellen White looked forward to being able to write on the life of Christ! Yet, even in going to this new and distant land, the servant of the Lord would face obstacles to the fulfillment of her great desire.

> I attended the Lansing camp meeting and malaria fastened itself upon me. But I was enabled, by the strength given me of God, to look over an accumulated mass of writing and select those things I had written in regard to the life of Christ. This book was so much needed that in counseling with my brethren it was thought advisable to take my workers with me and remain in Australia until the <u>Life of Christ</u> was ready for the press. —MS 40, 1892, diary fragment, written in Preston, Melbourne, Victoria, Feb. 13.

> Night before last I slept only two hours, but yesterday was surprised to find my head clear to write some of the life of Christ. I feel lifted up and comforted when I can write on the life of Christ. . . .

> I am thankful every day to the Lord that I have my reason and can contemplate the precious things in the life of Christ, which I try to fasten with pen and ink lest they may become *dim in my mind*,[14] and I feel refreshed in spirit as I do this. —Ltr. 163, 1892, written March 25 from Preston, Melbourne, Victoria, to "Dear Son Willie," emphasis supplied.

> This afternoon I wrote a number of pages on the life of Christ. I long for a large portion of the Spirit of God, that I may write the things which the people need. —Diary for July 12, 1892 in 4*BIO* 381.6.

> After arranging my position so as not to bring any strain on arms or shoulders, I go to work at my writing, asking the Lord to bless that which I write. I know that He helps me. . . . I am now working on the life of Christ. I know that the enemy will make every possible effort to hinder me; but I shall cling to Jesus; for He is my dependence. —Diary for July 14, 1892 in 7*MR* 143.1.

> I cannot manage to keep comfortably warm in these high rooms, with only a grate fire. I have had two severe chills, and this has greatly increased the lameness in my shoulders and hips. But notwithstanding this, I was able to spend most of yesterday writing on the life of Christ. I praise the Lord because I feel a nearness to my Saviour. My faith feeds on the rich promises of God, which are full of comfort and hope. —MS 34, 1892, diary written Friday, July 15, 1892 in Preston, Victoria, Australia in 4*BIO* 382.2.

> This is indeed a physical weakness for me, and almost absolute dependence upon others. So new is this experience to me that I have felt amazed that it should be so. But though almost helpless in body, in heart I feel no sense of age. —Ltr. 40, 1892 to O. A. Olsen, July 15, from Preston, Victoria, Australia, in *Exhibits* #42.

D. E. Robinson notes that some of her most expressive writing came during this period of eleven months in 1892–1893 in which intense suffering from rheumatism confined her to her room.

---

[13] 30% of 2*SP*/3*SP* became 20% of *DA*, calculated by WCopyfind at <www.plagiarism.phys.virginia.edu/Wsoftware.html>.

[14] In 1900 she would write: "Heavenly scenes were presented to me in the life of Christ, pleasant to contemplate, and again painful scenes which were not always pleasant for Him to bear which pained my heart" (MS 93, 1900 in 4*BIO* 383.1).

Here she had opportunity to think intensely regarding the views that the Lord had given her. She was enabled to write more feelingly than at other times. Some of the choicest passages in *The Desire of Ages* came from her pen when she was confined not only to her room, but much of the time to her bed. The secret of her power to produce this beautiful language is found in three passages . . . "Jesus was sacredly near," "I thought of Christ a great deal," and "I have written sixteen hundred pages."[15]

Ellen White's constant concern was that her words properly represent Christ.

This week I have been enabled to commence writing on the life of Christ. Oh, how inefficient, how incapable I am of expressing the things which burn in my soul in reference to the mission of Christ. I have hardly dared to enter upon the work. There is so much to it all. And what shall I say, and what shall I leave unsaid? I lie awake nights pleading with the Lord for the Holy Spirit to come upon me, to abide upon me.

I walk with trembling before God. I know not how to speak or trace with pen the large subject of the atoning sacrifice. I know not how to present subjects in the living power in which they stand before me. I tremble for fear lest I shall belittle the great plan of salvation by cheap words. I bow my soul in awe and reverence before God and say, "Who is sufficient for these things?" —Ltr. 40, 1892, p. 4, written July 15 from Preston, Victoria, Australia, to O. A. Olsen (GC president from 1888 to 1897) in *Exhibits* #42.

> "I bow my soul in awe and reverence before God and say, 'Who is sufficient for these things?'"
>
> Ellen White, 1892

My words seem inadequate. I despair of clothing the truth God has made known concerning His great redemption, which engrossed to itself His undivided attention in the only begotten Son of the Infinite One. —MS written June 6, 1896, *Exhibits* #63.

Because Sarah MacEnterfer, Mrs. White's nurse, came down with a sudden illness, Fannie Bolton had taken her place in going to Australia. It was hoped that Fannie could both accompany Sister White to report her sermons and assist in preparing her articles for publication (*4BIO* 240.3). However, the arrangement didn't work out as anticipated for Fannie also got sick.

Fannie Bolton is in very poor health. What shall I do? We think of having her go to Tasmania to rest two months; if she fails to recover there, she must go to St. Helena for treatment. Unless she does regain her health, she shall have to give up work altogether. Who shall we get to fill her place? Do you know of any one you can recommend? There is not a soul in all this country I can find. I could keep two supplied with work, but I shall be satisfied with one good brain worker who can prepare matter for the papers. Unless Fannie recovers, I must give up my articles in the papers or secure another helper. —Ltr. 21b, 1892, written Dec. 23 to "Dear Brother and Sister J. H. Kellogg" in *MR926* 10.3.

Fannie brought other problems too, but we will discuss those later.

Marian Davis, Ellen White's "bookmaker"

When Sister White went to New Zealand in early 1893, Marian Davis remained in Melbourne, the site of the newly established Australasian Bible School. There she busily gathered materials for the "life of Christ." Work on the life of Christ started slowly as a letter to W. C. White reveals:

Marian Davis

---

[15] Reprinted in *Ministry*, Feb. 1980, p. 14. The source for "Jesus was sacredly near" is Ltr. 7, 1892 in *2SM* 241.2; for "I thought of Christ a great deal" is MS 17, 1893; and for "I have written sixteen hundred pages" is MS 17, 1893 in *2SM* 241.1.

You will perhaps remember some things I said last spring about the necessity of having the matter from articles and scrapbooks, that might be available for use in the life of Christ, copied, so as to be convenient for reference. Perhaps you can imagine the difficulty of trying to bring together points relating to any subject, when these must be gleaned from thirty scrapbooks, a half-dozen bound volumes [of Mrs. White], and fifty manuscripts, all covering thousands of pages. —Ltr. from St. Kilda, Melbourne, Australia, March 29, 1893, in *Exhibits #45.*

Then we also hear from Ellen White:

Before leaving Melbourne, I again had to press Sr. Davis into the work. She prepared a large amount of testimony for certain individuals, which I could not entrust to another person. Frequently she has to be called from the work on the life of Christ to prepare these special communications, which it would not be wise to trust to any one else. Emily Campbell copies, after Sr. Davis has prepared them. I pay the latter for her time, and make no charge to the Conference. —Ltr. 3, 1894, written July 19 from Granville, New South Wales, "To whom it may concern on the General Conference Committee."

Up to this period I have done scarcely anything on the life of Christ, and have been obliged to often bring Marian to my help irrespective of the work on the life of Christ which she has to do under great difficulties, gathering from all my writings a little here and little there, to arrange as best she can. But she is in good working order, if I could only feel free to give my whole attention to the work. —Ltr. 55, 1894, p. 6, undated, from Granville, New South Wales, to Brother Olsen, in *Exhibits #56.*

Ellen White's helpers were instructed to make copies of all letters sent to workers in the field because many of these contained lessons from the Gospels, which could expand the account of *The Spirit of Prophecy.* Marian pasted these copies in scrapbooks for easier reference. W. C. White commented on the use of letters in a talk[16] he gave at College View, Nebraska, Nov. 25, 1905:

A scrapbook

Some of the most precious chapters of *Desire of Ages* are made up of matter first written in letters to men laboring under trying circumstances, for the purpose of cheering and instructing them regarding their work. Some of these beautiful lessons about Christian experience illustrated in the life of our Saviour, were first written in letters to my brother Edson, when he was struggling with many difficulties in his work in Mississippi, some were written first to Elder Corliss [in late 1894], when he was holding a discussion with a wily Campbellite in Sydney.

In a letter about the history of *The Ministry of Healing,* which he sent to Maggie Hare-Bree to review, W. C. White went into greater detail about Marian's work:

For years it was our practice to place in her [Miss Davis's] hands a copy of every article sent off for publication and of all principal letters and testimonies. These she . . . read with avidity, and . . . marked those passages that she considered especially useful for the making of chapters for books which she had in contemplation. . . .

Sister Davis had a wonderful memory, and this was of great service in her work of searching for and grouping together the choicest things that Sister White had written regarding Christ in His ministry as a Healer [and] in regard to Christ as an Example of medical missionaries and medical evangelists. . . .

---

[16] "The Integrity of the *Testimonies to the Church,*" DF #107d in <www.whiteestate.org/issues/Integrity.html>, p. 7.

Letter 64, 1897 was one of the letters from which Marian Davis took "fresh matter" for *The Desire of Ages*. Written by Ellen White to Elder Arthur Swain Hickox (Marcella Anderson King's late husband's maternal grandfather), the letter has special significance for the author. The second of two paragraphs pictured below was edited for use in *The Desire of Ages* and is *italicized* in the portion of *The Desire of Ages* quoted under the picture in which it was used.

Individual work is to be done in consecration to God. You must be prepared to receive the blessing from God, to drink of the living streams yourselves. And the rich blessings received will be within you like a well of water, springing up into everlasting life,. God hath prepared a kingdom for you; he is building for us a city. And while he is building mansions for us, we must build our character after the divine similitude. There must be no pride, no self-esteem, no self-exaltation. Everything you do in the service of God must be in no half-hearted manner, but divinely done. With you both your personal influence may be so devised and planned by the Lord that you may save souls to his glory.

As the world's Redeemer apparent failure was constantly confronting Christ. From his birth he contended with poverty. He, the Majesty of heaven, the messenger of mercy to our world, in his own estimation seemed to do so little of that work which he longed to do in uplifting and saving because of the satanic influences that were working in minds and hearts of priests and rulers to oppose his way. "Ye will

*As the world's Redeemer, Christ was constantly confront*ed with *apparent failure. He, the messenger of mercy to our world, seemed to do little of* the *work He longed to do in uplifting and saving. Satanic influences were* constantly *working to oppose His way.* But He would not be discouraged. Through the prophecy of Isaiah He declares, "I have labored in vain, I have spent My strength for nought, and in vain: yet surely My judgment is with the Lord, and My work with My God. . . . Though Israel be not gathered, yet shall I be glorious in the eyes of the Lord, and My God shall be My strength." It is to Christ that the promise is given, "Thus saith the Lord, the Redeemer of Israel, and His Holy One, to Him whom man despiseth, to Him whom the nation abhorreth; . . . thus saith the Lord: . . . I will preserve Thee, and give Thee for a covenant of the people, to establish the earth, to cause to inherit the desolate heritages; that Thou mayest say to the prisoners, Go forth; to them that are in darkness, Show yourselves. . . . They shall not hunger nor thirst; neither shall the heat nor sun smite them: for He that hath mercy on them shall lead them, even by the springs of water shall He guide them." Isa. 49:4, 5, 7–10. —*The Desire of Ages*, pp. 678–679.

When a goodly number of extracts had been gathered and grouped together as possible material for chapters, they were read to Sister White. This revived her memory of the . . . scenes presented to her, and she entered . . . into the work of rewriting many chapters, giving them a fresh touch and greater vigor, also adapting the various passages . . . more fully to the people who would read this book. . . .

Time and time again in Sister White's room, was discussed the object and the best plan for the book—(a) whom the book would serve; (b) how much room should be given to each subject; (c) what was the best relationship of the great subjects with which it should deal.

After chapters were thus formed, they were carefully read again by Sister White and then submitted to the printer. —Ltr. May 22, 1934, in *Exhibits* #89.

MS 129, 1897 is one of the manuscripts that Mrs. White wrote to give a fresh touch to an earlier *Spirit of Prophecy* chapter. The immediacy and emotion of this manuscript leave the reader with the distinct impression that Mrs. White was simply recounting what she had witnessed first hand.[17] Portions of MS 129, 1897 used in *DA*, Chapter 77, are highlighted in yellow and footnoted with references after the exhibit. That some of the wording from *Spiritual Gifts*, vol. 1 (highlighted in brown) was used in Chapter 9 of *Spirit of Prophecy*, vol. 3 (highlighted in grey) and was carried over into MS 129, shows that she likely had *Spirit of Prophecy* before her as she revisited the scene.

Condemnation of Christ.

Outside the judgment hall, the multitudes were heaving and pressing like the billows of the sea, some crying one thing, some another. Herod commanded silence. He wished to interrogate Christ himself. Herod had slain the holy prophet of God, and for a time had felt the keenest remorse.[a] But now he hoped to efface entirely from his mind the memory of that bloody head brought to him in a charger. He also desired to have his curiosity gratified, and thought that Christ would do anything he asked of him, if he was given any prospect of release.[b]

Herod ordered that the fetters of Christ should be unloosed at the same time charging his enemies with roughly treating him. He looked with compassion into the serene face of the world's Redeemer, and read in it only innocence and noble purity. He as well as Pilate knew that Christ had been brought there through malice and envy.[c]

Herod questioned Christ in many words, but throughout Christ maintained a profound silence.[d] He might have caused the heart of the king to tremble with terror; but he gave no look, no word. In reality this was the severest rebuke that Christ could have given[e] to the wicked king. Some word of rebuke would have been considered a mercy in comparison with this utter silence.[f] But not a word has the Majesty of

---

[17] "The great events occurring in the life of our Lord were presented to her in panoramic scenes . . . and . . . were *exceedingly vivid* . . ." —W. C. White, 3*SM* 459, 460, emphasis supplied. "Many times in the reading of Hanna, Farrar, or Fleetwood, she would run on to a description of a scene which had been *vividly presented* to her, but forgotten, and which she was able to describe in more detail than that which she had read." —Letter to L. E. Froom, Jan. 8, 1928 in 3*SM* 459, 460, emphasis supplied. "In the life of John the Baptist, in the life of Christ, I have tried to present that which has been presented to me." —Transcription of the handwritten diary of Ellen White (*LCRP* 61; edited version in *FE* 310.2).

heaven for him.[g] Christ stood before the king in silence, yet in calm, dignified majesty.

Then at the command of the king, the decrepit and maimed were called into the presence of Christ, and he was ordered to prove his claims by demonstrating his power before them. If thou canst work miracles for others, he said, work them now for thine own good, and it will serve thee a good purpose. But Christ was as one who heard and saw not. Still Herod continued to urge him, "Men say thou canst save the sick," he said, "I am anxious to see that thy widespread fame has not been belied.[h] Then work a miracle."

Jesus did not respond.[i] Herod felt that he was mocked, and over and over again he repeated in the ears of Christ as if to intimidate him, the exalted position he held, and how one of the prophets like himself had been treated at his hands. But no sign from Jesus gave evidence that he heard a word.[j] Herod became excited, and again commanded Christ to work a miracle. Show us a sign, he said, that thou hast the power with which rumor hath accredited thee.[k] But Jesus preserved alike his silence and his Godlike majesty. That ear that had ever been open to human woe, had no room for Herod's words. Those eyes that had ever rested upon the penitent sinner in pitying forgiving love, had no look to bestow upon Herod. Those lips that had uttered the most impressive truths, that had ever pleaded in tones of tenderest entreaty, that had been ever ready to speak pardon to the most hardened sinner, were closed to him.[l]

Herod then promised Christ if he would perform some miracle in his presence, he would release him. Christ's accusers had seen with their own eyes the mighty works wrought by his power. Their ears had heard him command the grave to give up its dead. They had beheld the grave hear his voice, the dead obey his command; and fear seized his enemies lest he should work a miracle and thus defeat their purposes. The priests and rulers, in great anxiety, came with their accusations. Raising their voices they declared, He is a traitor, a blasphemer. He works his miracles through Beelzebub, the prince of the devils. He claims to be the Son of God, the King of Israel. The hall was one scene of confusion, some crying one thing and some another.[m]

Herod interpreted the silence of Christ as an insult to himself, a contempt for his power. Turning to him he said, If you will not work a miracle, if you will give no sign of your claims, I will deliver you up to the soldiers and the people. They may succeed in making you speak. If you are an impostor, death at their hands is only what you merit; if you are the Son of God, save yourself.[n]

No sooner were these words spoken, than a rush was made for Christ. Like wild beasts they darted upon their prey, and Christ was left by the wicked king to the mercies of the mob and the soldiers, who were intoxicated with fury. He was mocked and dragged this way and that, Herod joining the mob, and making suggestions how they could best humiliate the Son of God.[o] A crown of thorns was plaited, and derisively placed upon his sacred head. At his suggestion an old kingly purple robe[p] was brought, and put upon his noble form. Then they seated the world's Redeemer upon a large block, mockingly terming it his throne. An old reed was placed in his hand, and they mockingly bowed before him. Coarse and Satanic laughter, jeering and mocking, cursing and swearing, was heard on every side.

All this mockery, —this clothing with purple and crowning with thorns, this saluting and bowing in mock worship, —was enacted in the presence of the priests and rulers, and gave them the highest pleasure. Occasionally some murderous hand struck the crown upon his brow, forcing the thorns into His temples, and sending the blood trickling down His face and beard.[q] And all this against a man who had been pronounced faultless. No accusation could be brought against him. He was the victim of the malice, the envy, and jealousy of the people who had been the chosen of God.

———

Though he had pronounced Christ entirely innocent, Pilate decided to give him over to the will of the infuriated mob, led by the priests who were inspired by Satan. Yet he was not willing that the responsibility of this act should rest upon his shoulders. In an imposing manner he took water, and washed his hands before the people, saying[,] "I am innocent of the blood of this just man." And the cry of the priests and scribes and rulers was, His blood be upon us and upon our children."

MS-129-97

E. G. White

Where text was used in *The Desire of Ages:*

a. *DA* 730.1	b. *DA* 728.3	c. *DA* 729.1	d. *DA* 729.2	e. *DA* 730.4	f. *DA* 730.2
g. *DA* 730.4	h. *DA* 729.2	i. *DA* 729.2	j. *DA* 730.1	k. *DA* 729.2	l. *DA* 730.4
m. *DA* 729.3	n. *DA* 730.5	o. *DA* 731.1	p. *DA* 739.3	q. *DA* 734.1	

Occasionally, in outlining what would be needed in the revision of *Spirit of Prophecy,* vols. 2 and 3, Mrs. White's "bookmaker" would suggest subjects for Mrs. White to write on that were extraneous to what the Lord was guiding her to write.

> I am anxious to get out the life of Christ. Marian specifies chapters and subjects for me to write upon that I do not see really need to be written upon. I may see more light in them. These I shall not enter upon without the Lord's Spirit seems to lead me. The building a tower, the war of kings, these things do not burden my mind, but the subjects of the life of Christ, His character representing the Father, the parables essential for us all to understand and practice the lessons contained in them, I shall dwell upon. —Ltr. 131, 1893, p. 3, to "Dear Son Willie" from Wellington, New Zealand, June 15, in *Exhibits* #48.

As she explains to her son Willie, she wrote on a number of subjects at one time.

> I write some every day on the life of Christ. One chapter sets my mind fresh upon other subjects so that I have several scratch books that I am writing upon. —Ltr. 132, 1893, July 2, in *Exhibits* #49.

We sense Marian Davis's excitement as the pieces of the life of Christ manuscript were gradually fitting into place. After enrolling in a class at the Melbourne training school to assist her in the arrangement of the manuscript, Marian wrote Mrs. White, who was then in New Zealand:

Now, about the book, I am so glad you are writing on the two journeys to Galilee. I was so afraid you would not bring that out. . . . I shall watch with great interest for the arrival of the promised manuscript. . . . There is such a rich field in the teachings of Christ after He left Jerusalem. —Aug. 2, 1893, in *Exhibits* #51.

I have a number of chapters prepared on life of Christ, but cannot get them copied just now. Perhaps I can on vacation. If so, I will send them to you. Am glad you are working on life of Christ and am looking eagerly for manuscript. There are chapters—or parts—that are to be prepared in what I have gone over—some things that were left incomplete, and I can be working on these till I get more manuscript. Of course I have a considerable manuscript ahead of where I am working, but it is not in regular connection, and it will be better to prepare it after I get the intervening links. —Aug. 22, 1893, in *Exhibits* #52.

Oh, when I see how we seem to be in the circles of a whirlpool, that is sweeping us faster and faster toward the great consummation, I do long to see this book go out, to reveal Christ to the people as He is, in His beauty. Let the work be done by whomever God shall choose, but Oh, I want to see it done, and I will be so thankful if He will use me anywhere. There is a very great loss in stopping, breaking off the chain of thought and beginning over again. But I am ready to do it, if necessary. But while we are studying the life of Christ and the matter is on my mind it seems like poor policy to work at something else. . . .

I sympathize with you in the constant moving. It must be very wearisome. But what a privilege the New Zealand people are having!

I shall be so glad when we can talk over the work. So many points come up that I want to ask about, and I shall appreciate the privilege of having someone to read the chapters to.

I will send you a few more chapters soon. Brother [W. F.] Caldwell copies for me Sunday forenoons[18]. . . . I am real anxious to get some chapters finished and some gaps filled before going to any other work.

These are busy days, the Bible class coming in the middle of the forenoon is rather inconvenient, but while the life of Christ is studied, I can't afford to lose it, for it is the only thing I have bearing on my work, and it wakes one's mind up, to hear the matter talked over. —Ltr. from Prahran, Melbourne, Australia, to Ellen G. White, in New Zealand, October 18, 1893, in *Exhibits* #54.

In a letter to Dr. John Harvey Kellogg, who was one of her confidants, Ellen White poured out her heart about the pressure for writing she was under, elaborating on Marian's techniques for finding thought gems from Mrs. White's writings for the life of Christ book.

Marian is working at the greatest disadvantage. I find but little time in which to write on the life of Christ. I am continually receiving letters that demand an answer, and I dare not neglect important matters that are brought to my notice. Then there are churches to visit, private testimonies to write, and many other things to be attended to that tax me and consume my time.[19] Marian greedily grasps every letter I write to others in order to find sentences that

---

[18] This likely refers to the work on the typewriter that D. E. Robinson did when he joined the staff (see p. 34).

[19] W. C. White notes: "when Sister White was busily engaged in writing she had very little time to read. Previous to her work of writing on the life of Christ and during the time of her writing, to some extent, she read from the works of Hanna, Fleetwood, Farrar, and Geikie. I never knew of her reading Edersheim. She occasionally referred to [Samuel] Andrews, particularly with reference to chronology" (3*SM* 459.1). In Ltr. 52, 1878 (Nov. 8) in 3*BIO* 103.2, Ellen White herself called attention to her use of source works. Listing several books from her library, she concludes with: "You look over my books and send all I shall really need."

she can use in the life of Christ. She has been collecting everything that has a bearing on Christ's lessons to His disciples, from all possible sources. After the camp meeting is ended, which is a very important meeting, I shall locate myself in some place where I can give myself to the work of writing on the life of Christ. . . .

There is much to be done in the churches, and I cannot act my part in keeping up the interest and do the other work that is necessary for me to do without becoming so weary that I cannot devote strength to writing on the life of Christ. I am much perplexed as to what is my duty. . . .

I have about decided to . . . devote all my time to writing for the books that ought to be prepared without further delay. . . . I will have to stop writing so much for the papers, and let the *Review and Herald*, the *Signs of the Times*, and all other periodicals go without articles from my pen for this year. All articles that appear under my signature are fresh, new writings from my pen. I am sorry that I have not more literary help. I need this kind of help very much. Fannie could help me a great deal on the book work if she had not so many articles to prepare for the papers, and so many letters and testimonies to edit to meet the demands of my correspondence and the needs of the people. It is of no use to expect anything from Marian until the life of Christ is completed. . . .

You know that my whole theme both in the pulpit and in private, by voice and pen, is the life of Christ. Hitherto nearly all that I have written on this theme has been written during the hours when others are sleeping. —Ltr. 41, 1895, pp. 1–4, written Oct. 25, 1894 from Granville, New South Wales, Australia in *Exhibits #57*.

In answer to Ellen White's pleas for more help, the Conference brethren recommended that she get her son Willie to come and assist her. Her response was that she felt the Board knew very little about the real situation. "W. C. W. has had to receive help from some of my workers in keeping up his own pressing writing," she responded (Ltr. 69, 1894, from Granville, N.S.W., "To leading brethren in the Conference and in the R&H Office"). In late August of 1895 Ellen White again appealed to Dr. Kellogg for help to obtain at least one other editor. Typists were easier to come by.

I am in need of editors to prepare manuscripts for the press. . . . Sister Bolton corrects manuscripts when she is able, but she is troubled so much with headache that often she cannot use her brain. This has become more and more marked, and is a very great hindrance to me in my work. I cannot do the things I would do. It is sufficiently taxing to do the writing, but when I have done that, there is the burden of having the matter prepared. If I had one to edit the matter, I should feel so grateful. Since completing the little book that is now in press [she likely refers to *Thoughts from the Mount of Blessing*], Sister Davis is working again on the "Life of Christ," and until that is finished cannot give much attention to anything else. We have no helpers to spare, but we want more, and those who are healthy. Two would not be too many. —Ltr. 44, 1895, written Aug. 29 from Avondale, Cooranbong, N.S.W., to J. H. Kellogg, M.D.

Earlier the same year she reiterates what she had proposed to resolve her problem:

I have considered the question, and have thought I would refrain from sending articles to the *Review and Herald*, the *Signs of the Times*, and other periodicals for the space of a year. But the first thing that needs our attention is work on "The Life of Christ." But no one seemed in favor of my plan, and therefore I furnished articles just as abundantly as I have in the past. I have had no one who could report my sermons, and have written articles to be prepared for the papers. —Ltr. 59, 1895, written April 12 from Launceston, Tasmania, to "Dear Brother and Sister Olsen" in 19*MR* 270.3.

Just the same, Marian Davis seems to bubble with enthusiasm as she writes about the "Life of Christ" in late 1895. She has one concern—that a "copy of everything" be sent to her so she can locate things Sister White has written that will bring the message of the book "close to the heart."

> We sent the letter for Sydney workers to Brother McCullagh. It was so good. I must keep all the general for my scrapbooks. Of late I have been using the matter gleaned from late letters, testimonies, etc. Have found some of the most precious things, some in those letters to Elder Corliss. They have been to me like a storehouse of treasures. There's something in these personal testimonies that are written with deep feeling, that comes close to the heart. It seems to me the things gathered in this way give a power and significance to the book that nothing else does. I hope the one who copies will not forget to send me a copy of everything. —Ltr. Nov. 25, 1895 from Granville, N.S.W. in *Exhibits* #60.

Long-time White Estate secretary, D. E. Robinson, describes how the pieces of a new manuscript were assembled. (In 1899, Robinson joined Ellen White's staff in time to assist in typing the manuscript for *Christ's Object Lessons*, the third book drawn from the life of Christ materials that Marian Davis gathered.) He describes listening as Marian Davis read from pages of various sizes.

> This I wrote on the typewriter, as it was read to me by Miss Marian Davis . . . She read mostly from typewritten copy. However, I noticed that she sometimes read from a scrap of paper, a sentence or a short paragraph that was written in her own hand. . . .[20]

Robinson later discovered where the sentences on the little scraps of paper came from.

> With a clear, comprehensive plan for the subject matter to be used in an article, or as a chapter in a book under preparation, she would sometimes read many pages of manuscript, looking for suitable or appropriate material. Usually she would mark this to be typed. However, if she ran across a brief sentence or phrase of rare beauty, she would copy it in her own handwriting from the original—she did not use the typewriter—and would file it where she could find it when the fitting place was reached in the manuscript under preparation.[21]

 To what extent did Marian Davis rely on Ellen White's own words?

Marian was indeed a conscientious worker. A few years earlier, in working on *Patriarchs and Prophets*, she had gone through an adjustment in thinking about her role as Mrs. White's editor.

> Marian will go to him [W. C. White] for some little matters that it seems she could settle for herself. . . . Her mind is on every point and the connections, and his mind has been plowing through a variety of difficult subjects until his brain reels and then his mind is in no way prepared to take up these little minutiae. She must just carry some of these things that belong to her part of the work, and not bring them before him nor worry his mind with them. Sometimes I think she will kill us both, all unnecessarily, with her little things she can just as well settle herself as to bring them before us. Every little change of a word she wants us to see. —Ltr. 64a, 1889, p. 1 in 3*SM* 92.5.

Continuing where we were in the recounting of the preparation of the "Life of Christ" manuscript—work on *Thoughts from the Mount of Blessing* had alerted Ellen White to potential problems for the life of Christ. She was obliged to wait an unrealistically long time for the woodcut illustrations.

[20] D. E. Robinson, *Ministry*, Feb. 1980, p. 12.

[21] D. E. Robinson, *Ministry*, Feb. 1980, p. 13.

It is a mystery to me that "The Sermon on the Mount" [i.e., *Thoughts from the Mount of Blessing*] has had to wait so long for the cuts. It has been ready for some time, but the cuts do not come. How long will this be delayed, and will we be obliged to wait in the same way for the cuts on the "Life of Christ"? We must know about this, because some plans must be made which will advance the work more speedily. —Ltr. 74, 1895, written to Eld. A. O. Tait from Armadale, Melbourne, Nov. 21.

I am giving the first volume of the life of Christ the last reading. I am glad it is so good, but only wish I had the power to make it a great deal better. . . . .

We will have two volumes of the life of Christ and a small book upon the parables, and may have to have one on the miracles of Christ, but the lives of the disciples and apostles is yet to be prepared. —Ltr. 140, 1896 (Jan. 23) from Avondale, Cooranbong, N.S.W., to "Dear Children."

When the "dummy" (or proof) of the book arrived, she found the illustrations unacceptable.

The dummy of "Thoughts from the Mount of Blessing," with the illustrations, I received. The illustrations I could not possibly accept under any consideration. Some of them look as if prepared for a comic almanac. That any one connected with the work in Battle Creek should think it possible for me to accept these cuts, is most astonishing. I dare not trust the book "Life of Christ" for them to illustrate; for I think their wisdom has departed from them. —Ltr. 90, 1896, written to Mr. W. O. Palmer from Avondale, Cooranbong, N.S.W., Jan. 24.

Eventually Ellen White chose the Pacific Press over Review and Herald—proper illustrations for the book being one of the deciding factors.

I have decided to negotiate with Pacific Press to publish "Life of Christ." We are now waiting for them to obtain cuts to go in the book. The first book is completed; the second is in process of completion. But every month I have to engage my workers wholly on the preparation of mail for America and different countries. This keeps us back, that we do not advance as we desire in book making. —Ltr. 150, 1896, written May 6 from "Sunnyside," Cooranbong, N.S.W., to "Dear Children Edson and Emma White."

Funding for the book was also of concern. In a letter to Sister Wessels back in July of that year, Sister White had mentioned how the preparation of the life of Christ book had cost her $3,000 for literary helpers, especially Marian Davis. (In 14*MR* 331.1 she also mentions that it was going to cost her $2,000 for her share of the book's cuts or illustrations.) Her appeal to Sister Wessels was, "Another three thousand will be needed to prepare it to be scattered broadcast through the world in two books" (Ltr. 114, 1896, p. 3, written July 16, 1896, from Cooranbong, New South Wales, Australia, in 3*SM* 119.1). From this major investment of means author and publisher were hoping for large sales.

"Fannie has been strictly forbidden to change my words for her words."

By early 1896, more problems had developed with Fannie Bolton besides her poor health. She had begun to complain that she and Marian "should be recognized as the ones [who] were putting talent" into Ellen White's works, and she claimed that Ellen White instructed her to "fill out the points" in one of Ellen White's testimonies in Fannie's own words. Working with Fannie Bolton had become so untenable by this point that Mrs. White was obliged to relieve her of her responsibilities, though not without giving Fannie "another trial." However, having only begun the task of copying and preparing a manuscript for publication, Fannie came back to Mrs. White telling her that "she could not possibly do the work" and that she felt impressed to go back to America. Mrs. White honored Fannie's decision and let her go. Wrote Mrs. White in retrospect:

> I now see why I was directed to give Fannie another trial. There were those who misunderstood me because of Fannie's misrepresentations. These were watching to see what course I would take in regard to her. They would have represented that I had abused poor Fannie Bolton. In following the directions to take her back, I took away all occasion for criticism from those who were ready to condemn me. —Letter 61, 1900 in *MR926* 96.2.

To Fannie's charges about being asked to fill in a testimony, Marian Davis responded:

> I cannot think that anyone who is acquainted with Sister White's manner of writing could possibly believe it. The burden she feels when the case of an individual is presented before her, the intense pressure under which she works, often rising at midnight to write out the warnings given her, and often for days, weeks, or even months, writing again and again concerning it, as if she could not free herself from the feeling of responsibility for that soul,—no one who has known anything of [these] experiences, could believe that she would intrust to another the writing of a testimony.

> For more than twenty years I have been connected with Sister White's work. During this time I have never been asked either to write out a testimony from oral instruction, or to fill out the points in matter already written. —Ltr. to G. A. Irwin, written April 23, 1900 from Sunnyside, Cooranbong, Australia, in *Exhibits* #80.

Marian also addressed the idea that manuscripts are more inspired or trustworthy than Mrs. White's published works.

> Many persons seem to attach far more value to an unpublished manuscript of Sister White than to the matter printed in books. But in all she has written I know of nothing better than the things to which reference has been given. In such books as *Desire of Ages*, have been carefully gathered together many of the most precious things which she has written during a score of years. —Ltr. from Cooranbong to Marius Christensen in Hayward, Minnesota in *Exhibits* #78.

In a letter written to "Miss Malcolm," an acquaintance in Australia, dated November 11, 1894, Fannie Bolton responded to the rumors that she herself had spread. In this letter she describes the work that was done by those who assisted Ellen White in her work:

> Concerning the matter of which I have written to you before, I will say that there is no reason why you or anyone else should be thrown into perplexity. Sister White is the prophet of the Lord for the remnant church, and though the Lord has seen fit to choose one for this work who is not proficient in grammar and rhetoric, and this lack is supplied by others, yet she is responsible for every thought, for every expression, in her writings. Every manuscript that is edited goes back to her for examination, and this work committed to those who have been called to labor in this branch is not done without prayer and consecration.

Fannie Bolton

> "The word of the Lord" comes to her; but if in passing through the human channel, the human imperfection in education leaves its impress, why should it be a perplexity if God should lay upon another the trifling duty of putting the subject of a sentence in harmony with its verb, or the number or gender of a thing mentioned in harmony with the fact that determines the number and gender? . . .

Now as far as changing Sister White's expressions are concerned, I can say that just as far as it is consistent with grammar and rhetoric, her expressions are left intact. —Ltr. to Miss Malcolm, Nov. 11, 1894, in 4*BIO* 248.1–3.

Though Fannie Bolton had taken substantial credit for improving Mrs. White's writing, Mrs. White could insightfully observe in 1900, after Fannie's final dismissal:

Wherein do my articles in the papers now differ from what they were when Fannie was with me? Who is it that now puts in words to supply the deficiencies of my language, my deplorable ignorance? How was this done before Fannie Bolton had anything to do with my writings? Cannot people who have reason see this? If Fannie supplied my great deficiency, how is it that I can now send articles to the papers? —Ltr. 61a, 1900, April 23, to G. A. Irwin in 4*BIO* 250.7.

Fannie confirmed Sister White's observation after she returned to the United States.

What did Fannie Bolton testify about the work of Ellen White's assistants?

The editors in no wise change Sister White's expression if it is grammatically correct, and is an evident expression of the evident thought. Sister White, as human instrumentality, has a pronounced style of her own, which is preserved all through her books and articles, that stamps the matter with her individuality. Many times her manuscript does not need any editing, often but slight editing, and again, a great deal of literary work; but article or chapter, whatever has been done upon it, is passed back into her hands by the editor, and the Spirit of Prophecy then appropriates the matter, and it becomes, when approved, the chosen expression of the Spirit of God. —"A Confession Concerning the Testimony of Jesus Christ," written in early 1901 to "Dear Brethren in the Truth," in 4*BIO* 248.4, 5.

Sister White distinguished the roles of her various workers one from another:

Dear Brother: . . . My copyists you have seen. They do not change my language. It stands as I write it.[22]

Marian's work is of a different order altogether. She is my bookmaker. Fannie never was my bookmaker. How are my books made? Marian does not put in her claim for recognition. She does her work in this way: She takes my articles which are published in the papers, and pastes them in blank books. She also has a copy of all the letters I write. In preparing a chapter for a book, Marian remembers that I have written something on that special point, which may make the matter more forcible. She begins to search for this, and if when she finds it, she sees that it will make the chapter more clear, she adds it.

The books are not Marian's productions, but my own, gathered from all my writings. Marian has a large field from which to draw, and her ability to arrange the matter is of great value to me. It saves my poring over a mass of matter, which I have no time to do.

---

[22] ". . . we find that as scenes which are similar in character and import are impressed upon her mind that she writes them out rapidly without reference to chronological order or other apparent connection." —Ltr. W. C. White to Miss Julia Malcolm, Dec. 10, 1894, in *Exhibits* #58.

"Her helpers are given the task of deciphering her hasty writing, and of putting her thoughts, using her words, into form for publication. The lengthy manuscripts are divided according to subjects. When written out with typewriter, the matter is submitted to Mother for criticism and correction, and when sent forth to the people each manuscript goes with her authority, representing her thoughts." —Ltr. W. C. White to J. J. Gorrell, May 13, 1904.

So you understand that Marian is a most valuable help to me in bringing out my books. Fannie had none of this work to do. Marian has read chapters to her, and Fannie has sometimes made suggestions as to the arrangement of the matter.

This is the difference between the workers. As I have stated, Fannie has been strictly forbidden to change my words for her words. As spoken by the heavenly agencies, the words are severe in their simplicity; and I try to put the thoughts into such simple language that a child can understand every word uttered. The words of someone else would not rightly represent me.[23]

> "The words of someone else would not rightly represent me."
> Ellen G. White

I have written thus fully in order that you may understand the matter. Fannie may claim that she has made my books, but she has not done so. This has been Marian's field, and her work is far in advance of any work Fannie has done for me. —Ltr. 61a, 1900, pp. 4, 5, April 23, to G. A. Irwin in *Exhibits* #79.[24]

Following Marian Davis's untimely death in 1904 from tuberculosis, Ellen White had this to say about her beloved editor:

We worked together, just worked together in perfect harmony all the time. . . . She takes the intensity of it as though it were a reality, and we both have entered into it with an intensity to have every paragraph that shall stand in its right place, and show its right work. . . . when she would be gathering up the precious jots and tittles that had come in papers and books and present it to me, "Now," she would say, "there is something wanted; I cannot supply it." I would look it over and in one moment I could trace the line right out. —MS 95, 1904, p. 1, Elmshaven, St. Helena, Sept. 24, 1904, in *Exhibits* #86.

By May 25, 1896, Mrs. White could write: "Fannie has now left us . . ." (Ltr. 87a, 1896, to Brother Olsen), and, by July, she could describe the return to normalcy of her family of workers.

We are all in good health with the exception of Sr. Eliza Burnham, who occasionally has nervous headaches. Sr. Burnham is a superior editor. Marian Davis also is authority on the class of books we send to the world. —Ltr. 128, 1896, written July 9 from "Sunnyside," Cooranbong, N.S.W., to Mrs. Mary Watson, "Dear Niece" in 14*MR* 332.2.

Maggie Hare takes dictation in shorthand, so she reports all my discourses and writes them out. May Israel is my bookkeeper. She is a young woman of good health. She also

---

[23] W. C. White corroborates her statement: "Mother's workers of experience, such as Sisters Davis, Burnham, Bolton, Peck and Hare, who are very familiar with her writings, are authorized to take a sentence, paragraph, or section from one manuscript and incorporate it with another manuscript where the same thought was expressed but not so clearly. But none of Mother's workers are authorized to add to the manuscripts by introducing thoughts of their own. They are instructed that it is the words and thoughts that Mother has written, or spoken, that are to be used." —Ltr. to G. A. Irwin, May 7, 1900, in *Exhibits* #81. "The secretaries and copyists who prepare Mother's writings for the printer remove repetitions so that the matter may be brought into the allotted space. They correct bad grammar and they fit the matter for publication. They sometimes carry her best expressions of thought from one paragraph to another but do not introduce their own thoughts into the matter." —Ltr. W. C. White to Miss Julia Malcolm, Dec. 10, 1894, in *Exhibits* #58.

[24] Fannie's name is supplied in "Elmshaven Leaflets," vol. 2, no. 3, "The Story of 'Steps to Christ.'" According to Edward S. Ballenger in *The Gathering Call*, Sept. 1932, pp. 20, 21, *Steps to Christ* "was her [i.e., Fannie Bolton's] product in total, but was published as Mrs. White's production." The falsity of such a claim is quickly seen by noting that *Steps to Christ* contains material that predates her employment with Mrs. White (1887)—and even predates Fannie's birth (1859). Among these are *SC* 12.1 from *RH* 12-16-1884, par. 17; *SC* 15.1 from 4*T* (1881) 563.1, 2; *SC* 35.1 from 1*T* (1857) 162.4, 163.1; *SC* 37.1–41.2 from 5*T* (1882) 635.1–641.3; *SC* 43.3 from 3*T* (1872) 106.2; *SC* 44.2, 45.1, 46.1 from 1*T* 160.1, 3, and 370.1b; *SC* 52.3 from *RH* 9-21-1886, pars. 5, 10; *SC* 83.1, 2 from 3*T* 246.2, 247.2; *SC* 85.3 from *RH* 10-27-1885, par. 6b; *SC* 92.2 from *ST* 11-18-1886, par. 15; *SC* 96.3 from 3*T* (1873) 323.2 and *ST* 8-21-1884, par. 5; and *SC* 121.2, 3, 122.1 from *RH* 2-3-1885, par. 1–4. Elder G. B. Starr credits Marian Davis with having gathered Mrs. White's statements for *Steps to Christ*.

writes shorthand. She has reported sermons at our camp meetings, but has had so much of this work placed upon her, that it was feared that she had injured her nervous system. But she has since learned better what she can bear. —Ltr. 128, 1896 in 14*MR* 328.5, 329.1.

Ellen G. White, 1899

Minnie Hawkins and Maggie Hare I now have being educated by Sister Eliza Burnham. They are girls that make me no trouble, and although my family now numbers thirteen I am getting along better than I have done for years. —Ltr. 153, 1896, written July 9 from "Sunnyside," Cooranbong, N.S.W., to "Dear Children."

Maggie does all my editing now, and copying on typewriter. She takes discourses in shorthand and writes them out. . . . Fannie failed me and she has been a great tax to me since she came to Australia. She left me for America in April, and she told me she wished to come back again. I told her I had no light to say one word of encouragement in this line. She urged me to say she might come back if she would pay her own fare. I could not do this. And, Edson, I never want her connected with me again. She would talk to my workers, especially Marian . . . was like another person. . . . Now Fannie is gone, she is herself, just as peaceable as she used to be. The workers now are wholesome, healthy, and kind, and of value to me. I am so pleased. —Ltr. 154, 1896, Aug. 2, to "Dear Children."

"I feel in such a hurry for the book to come out."

Passing on from the difficulties with Fannie Bolton, we turn again to the progress in completing the life of Christ book. We see the responsibilities that Ellen White and Marian Davis each carried in the preparation of the manuscript as it neared completion. Wrote Ellen White:

I am writing upon subjects which stir every fiber of my being. The pre-existence of Christ—how invaluable is this truth to the believer! How full of mightiness and power! What solid rock foundation we stand upon if our faith is centered in Him who was from the beginning and yet humbled Himself to humanity and gave his precious life to save a perishing world. —MS 65, 1896, diary for June 19.

> "I am writing upon subjects which stir every fiber of my being."
>
> Ellen G. White, 1896

As editor of the manuscript, it was Marian's responsibility to put in proper sequence the events described by Sister White. In the absence of direct instruction from Ellen White or clues in the materials themselves (each Gospel writer seems to follow a slightly different order), Miss Davis consulted Samuel J. Andrews' amplified harmony of the Gospels.

This morning Brother White handed me your letter of October 6, with list of cuts etc., asking me to write to you in regard to it. Had I seen them before leaving Cooranbong, where my lists and MS are, I could have written more intelligently. As it is, I can mention but few points.

1. Transposition of chapters. In the order of chapters we followed Andrews' Harmony, as given in his Life of Christ. He is generally regarded as the very best authority, and is quoted by leading writers. We know of no better arrangement than his. (The year between the first and second Passover seems to have been a period of comparative quiet and seclusion; that between the second and third, of activity and

publicity.) Those who read the MS, Professor Prescott and Sister Burnham, agreed with our arrangement. We would not like to see this chapter transposed.

"Imprisonment and Death of John." The place of this chapter is optional, of course. But no one has heretofore objected to its present position. As to the reference to John in Chapter 28, coming after the account of his death, this is not unusual in other books. See Geikie and many others. If the chapter were transposed, it would probably be best to omit the first paragraph. But not having the MS to refer to, I cannot speak with much positiveness. —Marian Davis, Ltr. Nov. 23, 1896 from Ashfield, New South Wales, Australia, to C. H. Jones in Oakland, California, in *Exhibits* #65.

When I think of the many thousands who will read the book, I want just as little human imperfection as possible to mar its divine beauty. —Ltr. April 11, 1897 to W. C. White.

Ellen White's responsibility in the book's production, was in listening to hear what God would have her write:

This is an important time just now, the closing up of the book on life of Christ. I want quiet and restfulness, that if the Lord has anything to impress upon my mind, I can discern the subject and prepare it for the book. —Ltr. 173, 1896, written Nov. 29 from "Sunnyside," Cooranbong, N.S.W., to "Dear Son Willie."

I have so much precious matter. Light came to me, you remember, before you left for America, "Gather up the fragments. Let nothing be lost."[25] Much matter should be before our people that they do not have, and I can use up my vitality in breasting difficulties that are not after all cured, but have to be met again and again. —Ltr. 200, 1897, written Nov. 26 from "Sunnyside," Cooranbong, N.S.W., to "Dear Son Willie" in 11*MR* 271.1.

I expected that the sale of Thoughts from the Mount of Blessing would help me to help in advancing the work in Australia. But the way the book was kept back in America, after being in the hands of the publishers for two years, and then coming out in a style that I could in no wise accept, had disappointed me greatly. The delay also on the "Life of Christ," preparing suitable cuts, is another drawback. The means I hoped to obtain have not answered my expectations, and now I must do all I possibly can to help in various ways the cause in this missionary field. . . .

Some felt very much dissatisfaction that Steps to Christ was given to Revell. I have received quite a sum of money,[26] more than has come to me from some books; and I think more would come to me if he had more of my books to handle. . . . There is an advantage in doing this, because they get the truth before a class that we will not reach. —MS 80, 1897, written July 4 from "Sunnyside," Cooranbong, N.S.W., no addressee.

In 1896, as the "Life of Christ" was thought to be nearing completion (4*BIO* 385), Marian worked vigorously on the first of three introductory chapters for the book—"God With Us," or, as it was originally entitled, "The Word Made Flesh." Because this chapter was so important in setting the background for Christ's earthly mission and because it was not a revision of a *Spirit of Prophecy* chapter, Marian Davis sought the counsel of Herbert Camden Lacey[27] about the arrangement of paragraphs. In response to questions

H. C. Lacey

---

[25] Ellen White also frequently used these words of Jesus from John 6:12 to call for carefulness in church finance.

[26] Some forget that she used such proceeds for needy families and students and for extending the work in Australia.

[27] He later became *Professor* Lacey at the Avondale School, and his sister married the widowed W. C. White.

about whether he had indicated that Marian Davis or he himself had written *The Desire of Ages*, Elder Lacey made several statements flatly denying these rumors.

> In 1895, upon my return to Australia from Battle Creek, Michigan Miss Marian Davis urged me repeatedly to help her in editing the MSS for *The Desire of Ages* then under preparation. I put her off as long as I could, as I did not feel capable of rendering any special assistance, but finally I yielded to her importunities and, after receiving the MSS of certain chapters, I made some suggestions which she seemed glad to accept. Now I cannot remember any details relative to those suggestions, other than that I have a vivid recollection that she seemed anxious to have certain sentences logically connected. We therefore rearranged some of them, and I have an impression that there was some necessary rewording done. But I am certain that there was no altering of the thought anywhere.

How did H. C. Lacey help in the preparation of *The Desire of Ages?*

> With reference to the first chapter,[28] I have a more vivid recollection. I remember that Sr. Davis was greatly worried about it. She did not seem to have sufficient material to fill it out sufficiently well.[29] It was repeatedly revised, and I think that Elder W. W. Prescott and Br. E. R. Palmer were frequently consulted as to its composition. Finally it assumed the form in which it now appears in the *Desire of Ages*.

> At the Bible Conference in Washington, D.C., in 1919, during a discussion on this point of the editing of Sr. White's writings, I said, that in my opinion it would be well for the clarifying of the whole question before the people if the fact that was clearly stated somewhere (I meant, on the title page or in the preface) that *The Desire of Ages* was written by Mrs. E. G. White, and edited by Miss Marian Davis.

> I did not use the words quoted "for she wrote it" [concerning the rumor about Marian Davis]. I did say that she came to me to get help to prepare the first chapter especially, as she seemed to be much concerned over its final form. Hoping these simple statements will be of service in rebutting those who seem to be persisting in misrepresenting what was really said at the Bible Conference referred to. —Ltr. to D. E. Robinson, in New York City, Aug. 17, 1931, in *Exhibits* #88.

And, in another letter he wrote:

> Miss Marian Davis, who was entrusted with the preparation of "Desire of Ages," frequently came to me in 1895 and 1896 asking help in the arrangement of the material which she gathered from Sister White's various manuscripts. Sister Davis was a warm personal friend of mine, and I did the best I knew how to aid her, especially in the first chapter. As I recall it, this help was only in the arrangement of the sentences and paragraphs, or the choice of a more suitable word. *Never at any time, was there any alteration of the thought, or the insertion of an idea that was not*

---

[28] Marian Davis describes this "new introductory chapter" in her April 11, 1897 letter to C. H. Jones: "I think that all will be pleased with it. It is fresh, containing a considerable new matter that will not be published elsewhere until after the book is issued. I hope this MS will be read by Eld. Wilcox and others. I have sent a copy to Bro. White. Whatever criticisms may be offered, will, I suppose, have to be considered by Sr. Burnham. They can be referred to Bro. White if necessary." —quoted by Fred Veltman in *LCRP*, Introduction, p. 198.

[29] With Lacey's statement about Marian's concern over having sufficient material to fill out the first chapter of *The Desire of Ages*, one might surmise that she might have been responsible for borrowing near verbatim statements from the sources to fill in the first chapter. However, each of the near verbatim statements we find in that chapter was used by Sister White in an earlier manuscript or periodical article. (See footnotes in Chapter 3.)

already expressed in the original text. The resultant "copy" was always submitted to Sister White herself for final approval.

The entire *Desire of Ages* as it is now printed is, therefore, I hold, the product of Sister White's mind and heart, guided by the good Spirit of God. And the "editing" was merely technical. —Ltr. to Samuel Kaplan, July 24, 1936, in *Exhibits* #90, emphasis supplied.

Finding a suitable name for the book was one of the final matters that Marian discussed in a letter to C. H. Jones of the Pacific Press as Sister White continued writing up to the last:

Your letter of February 2 received by last mail. I am very glad to know of the decisions in regard to the size and style of the book. I believe the plan is right, and I am thankful that no plates have been made to be thrown aside.

We noted the titles mentioned—"Desire of Ages" and "Desire of All Nations." Sister White prefers the former, as I do, with all others who have expressed an opinion.

You ask me if I cannot, by this mail, send to the press the manuscript of the parables. You also ask when the balance of the manuscript for the last book will be ready. And you request Sister White to write on the parable of the rich man and Lazarus. I fully agree with you that the "Life of Christ" should be closed up as soon as possible. But let me state the situation: Considerably more than a year ago, Sister White began writing on the trial and crucifixion of Christ. She has a number of manuscripts unfinished. It is her intention to gather these together as soon as possible and complete them for the book. Of late she has had a very heavy burden for the General Conference, as well as for individuals, and the work in South Africa and in Cooranbong. But now that the Conference is over, and she has written quite fully in regard to these other cases, she fully intends to devote her time to the manuscript. I have been almost consumed with anxiety to complete the book. I prepared some chapters with what material I had, thinking that she would not write more on these subjects. She did write on them, however, and I had my work to do over. —Ltr. to C. H. Jones, March 11, 1897, from "Sunnyside," Cooranbong, Australia, in *Exhibits* #66 (MSS from 1897 used in *DA* Chaps. 77 and 78).

Marian manifested a wholesome sense of humor under the pressure of "closing up the book" as she affirmed her role of editor—and not author—of *The Desire of Ages*.

Sister White is constantly harassed with the thought that the manuscript should be sent to the printers at once. I wish it were possible to relieve her mind, for the anxiety makes it hard for her to write and for me to work. . . . Sister White seems inclined to write, and I have no doubt she will bring out many precious things. I hope it will be possible to get them into the book. There is one thing, however, that not even the most competent editor could do—that is prepare the manuscript before it is written. —Ltr. to W. C. White, Aug. 9, 1897, from "Sunnyside," Cooranbong, Australia, in *Exhibits* #69.

> "There is one thing, however, that not even the most competent editor could do—that is prepare the manuscript before it is written."
>
> Marian Davis, 1897

As W. C. White, Ellen White, and Marian Davis looked over proofs in November of 1897, we catch a glimpse, in a letter of her son's, of what Mrs. White had seen in vision of the holy land:

On returning from Sydney I showed Mother and Sister Davis the proofs which I had brought of chapter headings, vignettes, etc., for the new book. Some of them we like very well. About others we feel much disappointed. . . .

In looking at some photographs of the Mount of Olives, Mother told us how much more beautiful the country was in the time of Christ; that the places which are now bare and dreary were then beautified by magnificent trees and groves. O, I wish we could get some pictures that would represent these places as she has seen them. But I know not how to do this. —W. C. White, from Cooranbong, Australia, to C. H. Jones in New York City, in *Exhibits #72*.

Mrs. White expresses relief as the last chapters were being finalized:

I am seeking to close up the book. I think I have about done this. It is a tax on me but I have courage and faith in God. Marian is about done now, is on the last chapter, I think. —Ltr. 201, 1897, written Dec. 1 from "Sunnyside," Cooranbong, N.S.W., to "Dear Son Willie."

Marian seems cheerful. The last chapters are done. "Oh," she says, "I could never, never have completed the book had you not been right here where you could supply the live links necessary. Now the life of the book is fully kept up to the close."

And I feel very much relieved and do not feel as if I am stealing if I take up other subjects before the book is closed. But nearly everything I could write has been on the matter which concerned the book, that she could select some things for the book and Maggie could make articles of the subjects for papers. I shall now breathe more freely. —Ltr. 209, 1897, written Dec. 12 from "Sunnyside," Cooranbong, N.S.W., to "Dear Son Willie" in 4*BIO* 391.3, 4.

I have had some most precious things for the book, the last chapter. My part is done now. Oh, thank the Lord. Praise His holy Name that He has spared my life to see the closing up of the book. —Ltr. 211, 1897, written Dec. 31 from "Sunnyside," Cooranbong, New South Wales, Australia, to "Dear Son Willie."

Early in 1898 Marian Davis went over a number of final details regarding *The Desire of Ages* and *Christ's Object Lessons* with the servant of the Lord:

This morning we mail "The Man of Sorrows," copied from the new matter you left; and the parable of the talents, for the parable book. The matter on the sower which was given to Minnie, she has copied. But that which was given to Miss Peck has not been done. If Miss Peck does not have time to do it soon, I think we will let Minnie take it, as I am anxious to get it into your hands, and you will want it all together, so as to know what you have. We will not send any on the sower till we can send all.

I have been gathering out the precious things from these new manuscripts on the early life of Jesus. Sent a number of new pages to California [to Pacific Press] by the Vancouver mail, and shall send more for later chapters by the next mail. Two of those new articles on Christ's missionary work I let Brother James have to read in church. Last Sabbath he read the one which speaks of the Saviour's denying Himself of food to give to the poor.[30] These things are unspeakably precious. I hope it is not too late to get them into the book. It has been a feast to work on this matter. . . .

I will send a copy of a little I gathered out for the chapter, "In Joseph's Tomb." It supplies a link that was missing, and I think will be a real help to the book. . . .

I learn that the work of setting the book is underway, so we want to finish up the last chapters as soon as possible. Hope you will be able to send us, soon, the rest of the matter on Christ's ministry of healing, and, as soon as convenient, the rich man and Lazarus. I do hope the book on the parables can come out at the same time with the life of Christ. —Ltr. to E. G. White, from "Sunnyside," Cooranbong, Australia, March 1, 1898, in *Exhibits #73*.

---

[30] This passage, dated Feb. 20, 1898, is found in MS 22, 1898 and was printed in *The Desire of Ages*, p. 87, which says: "He had little money to give, but He often denied Himself of food in order to relieve those who appeared more needy than He."

Minnie is sending you this morning the matter she has been copying. That on the sower is all we have—the article given to Miss Peck, and the manuscript left with me. Now, if you do not wish to add anything more, I can go on and finish the chapter, but shall wait to hear from you. The article I send, "No Reward but of Grace," the parable of the laborers, is the last of the matter that was prepared for the book. I had planned to let this close the book. The last paragraphs seem to me very precious. The parable of the talents, which comes just before this, has set forth the importance of working, using every power for God, and this shows the spirit in which the work should be done. A few sentences you will recognize as from a letter lately written—"The golden gate is not opened to the proud in spirit. But the everlasting portals will open wide to the trembling touch of a little child."[31]

You left me a manuscript on the unjust steward, and I have been collecting material to complete this, and have found some precious things to add to the closing chapters of the life of Christ. Of course I cannot compile the chapters (the last two) until I receive what you write on the ministry of healing. —Ltr. to E. G. White, from "Sunnyside," Cooranbong, Australia, March 10, 1898, in *Exhibits* #74.

The matter you sent on the ministry of healing was just what was wanted. I have used as much as I could get into the chapter, "Go Teach All Nations." When Minnie comes home I will have it copied, and send you a copy. I am so glad we could get these things into the book, for they add greatly to its value and helpfulness. Brother [W. C.] White thinks it best to send the last two chapters, "Go Teach All Nations," and "To My Father and Your Father," by the boat that goes on Sabbath. I have no idea they are ready for them yet, but he thinks it will encourage them to push forward the work, and I shall send them. I feel in such a hurry for the book to come out. I hardly know how to wait, but the waiting gives time to work up the parables, and it will be so good to have both come out at the same time.

I have used some of the new matter on the parables, and shall go right on with the work. I want to get into the book [i.e., *Christ's Object Lessons*] just as much as possible of the fresh matter on nature teaching.

These things have been a feast to me. I want my heart enlarged and my mind enlarged to take in these grand, great principles. —Ltr. from "Sunnyside," Cooranbong, N.S.W., to Ellen White, in Melbourne, March 21, 1898, in *Exhibits* #75.

Then she writes Miss E. J. Burnham at the Pacific Press:

By this mail we send index. It is not properly finished. Has been verified only to page 32. The girls worked almost all night to do that, and the revising. We must ask you to verify, as you will have to substitute the type numbering for MS numbering of pages. . . . I worked all night last night. . . .

Sister White has read all the chapters, and expresses herself much pleased with them. —Ltr. June 6, 1898, from Cooranbong, Australia, to Miss Burnham at the Pacific Press in Oakland, California, in *Exhibits* #76.

Your letter of May 16, with proofs, received. I have hastily read the pages. Except one or two trifling errors, the text is all right. I can't tell you how great relief I feel on seeing so much of the matter in type, and straight. Have been almost consumed with anxiety in thinking of the possibilities for so many insertions sent so far away. I am unspeakably thankful to God, whose good hand is over the work, that He has made it possible for you to have it in charge, and I hope that no word of mine may bring on you any needless burden. . . .

---

[31] This passage was used in *Christ's Object Lessons*, p. 404, which was published in 1900.

In the preface, would it not be well to state, in some way, that this book is not a harmony of the gospels, that it does not attempt to teach chronology. Its purpose is to present the love of God, the divine beauty of the life of Christ, not to satisfy the questioning of critics. The above may not be the best way to put it. It is intended only as a suggestion. —Ltr. from Cooranbong, Australia, to Miss E. J. Burnham at the Pacific Press in Oakland, California in *Exhibits* #77 (compare to the wording of the *DA* preface, cited on p. 13 of this book).

The reading of the proofs at times called to mind some things Ellen White wanted to add. In a letter written in mid-February, 1898, she stated:

Matters must be prepared on the "Life of Christ," and after I thought it was done. In writing the manuscript, I saw that some other things must be written. —Ltr. 8, 1898 in 4*BIO* 392.1.

Making changes to manuscripts that had been sent to the publisher and that were already set in type was frustrating and expensive, as noted by W. C. White in a letter to C. H. Jones at the Pacific Press on July 14, 1898.

The getting out of this book is a great enterprise, and though it costs us much in money and in labor and in patient forbearance, we are confident that when issued, it will be worth, to the cause, all that it has cost and many times more. And while we may truly say that it is a trying thing to work along with author and publisher so far apart, yet it may be that the book is enough better to pay for all this.

As I now have opportunity to see the volume, and the value of what Mother is now writing, I daily feel to thank the Lord that she is here in Australia, where she is comparatively free to write what the Lord presents to her mind.[32]

The only draft manuscript for *The Desire of Ages* still in existence, comprising Chapters 2 through 37, was used in Ellen White's office in Cooranbong, Australia in 1897 and 1898. Here opened to Chapter 18, these working papers were discovered by James Nix on May 16, 1979 in a box kept in an off site storage building when space for the White Estate office vault was limited (*Exhibits* #70).

---

[32] W. C. White Letter Book, 12, p. 96, in Arthur L. White, 4*BIO* 392, emphasis supplied.

The fruition of her heart's desire

Finally, by the end of July, God's servant was quite satisfied as she wrote to family:

> Sabbath I devoted to reading the pages, proof sheets, of *Desire of Ages*. I am much pleased with the book. May the Lord bless and prosper the book, that its circulation shall be extensive, is my prayer. Our people need it very much. It has scarcely an error in it. I mean typographical errors. —Ltr. 181, 1898 to Edson and Emma, written July 31 from "Sunnyside," Cooranbong, N.S.W.

Though originally planned to be two volumes, it was decided between editor, author, and publisher that the first edition of the book should come out as a single volume.[33]

> Pacific Press first published *The Desire of Ages* in a large, well-illustrated volume of 866 pages in 1898. In 1900, *The Desire of Ages* was published in two large, beautifully illustrated volumes with an aggregate of 835 pages of text for distribution to the general public.[34]

> Very near the close of the year, December 10, 1898, copies arrived at Cooranbong and were eagerly examined by Ellen White, W. C. White, and her staff of workers . . . The monumental task was completed. Now the book would bless millions in the years to come. —Arthur L. White, 4*BIO* 392.

On May 21, 1900, Ellen White wrote to G. A. Irwin from her "Sunnyside" home:

> God would be pleased to see *The Desire of Ages* in every home. In this book is contained the light He has given upon His Word. To our canvassers I would say, Go forth with your hearts softened and subdued by reading of the life of Christ. Drink deeply of the water of salvation, that it may be in your heart as a living spring, flowing forth to refresh souls ready to perish. —Ltr. 75, 1900 in *Colporteur Ministry*, pp. 126, 127.

. . . .

Unfortunately, the specter of "plagiarism," which has cast its vilifying shadow over Ellen White's originality in *The Desire of Ages*, forces us to take up a task of investigation that will not be so enjoyable as reliving Ellen White and Marian Davis's excitement over the developing life of Christ manuscript. If you, the reader, have ever done dissection in a biology or anatomy class, you will certainly remember the experience, and you will thereby have some basis for understanding the task before us. Despite your initial feelings of squeamishness in having to cut open something that was once a living organism, you likely came away from the experience with a greater respect for the Creator and a greater appreciation for the amazing complexity of God's creation. As we "dissect" the text of *The Desire of Ages*, in the next four chapters, to answer questions about the book's composition, we trust that our investigation—though distasteful for many—will bring a greater appreciation for the thought and effort that went into the composition of this inspiring book.

---

[33] "Now that the book is to be one volume . . ." —Ltr. Marian Davis to C. H. Jones, April 11, 1897, from Sunnyside in *Exhibits* #67.

[34] Arthur L. White, *Adventist Review*, Aug. 23, 1979, pp. 6, 7 at <www.whiteestate.org/vault/Inspiration.html>.

CHAPTER 2

The Charges Require an Examination

Was it an accident or was it child abuse? That was the question that needed an answer the day co-author Kevin Morgan attended the autopsy of a small child. He was present that day because of an anatomy class, but you can imagine the conflicting emotions that filled his heart and mind. Though awed by the amazing design of the human structure, he couldn't help but think about the ones who were under suspicion for the death of this little one, and he couldn't help but wonder whether the coroner's examination would clear their name.

When it comes to charges against Ellen White in the composition of *The Desire of Ages*, we must ask, how are we to account for the similarity of language between her works and earlier sources? Was her borrowing plagiarism or did she borrow language appropriately and in good faith? These are the questions we will address in the next several chapters. Though answering such questions is not the usual reason for reading *The Desire of Ages*, the charge of plagiarism has made such an investigation necessary. By comparing four chapters of *The Desire of Ages*[1] with literary works listed as possible sources of content in the Life of Christ Research Project, we will have a basis for evaluating Mrs. White's use of sources.

An explanation of marking conventions

To make the levels of literary similarity and difference between *The Desire of Ages* and the source works stand out in the exhibits of the following chapters, we will use certain markings. (A convenient color-coding key will be found at the bottom of right-handed pages.)

- Verbatim words or phrases that correspond to the source works will be colored red with solid underscoring. Breaks in underscoring will designate non-consecutive words. Verbatim strings of five or more consecutive words will be marked according to twenty-first century academic standards (see definition of Professor Irving Hexham in Chapter 8), using *guillemets* or angle quotes (« ») to distinguish from quotation marks in the original text.
- Apparent paraphrasing from a source will be colored blue with dotted underscoring.
- If there is more than one possible source of verbatim or more than one possible source of paraphrase the underscoring will be darker.
- Words from Scripture will be colored green. When not anticipated by the Gospel story line or the topic under discussion and, thus, used in the same "unique" way as a source (even if phrased differently than that source), Scripture will be underscored with breaks in underscoring for non-consecutive words. Scripture references that fall within range of the "This chapter is based on . . ." statement for the chapter will be footnoted in green.
- Sources in the footnotes that were not listed in Ellen White's libraries will be designated by the ± sign. This will help to rule out questionable source works.
- Highlighting will be used to set off wording carried over from 1*SG*, *PH169*, and 2*SP*/3*SP* or incorporated from other Ellen White "bound volumes," "articles," or "fresh matter" from her "scratch books." (Correlation of these earlier EGW materials has not been exhaustive.)

---

[1] These particular chapters were assigned to Marcella Anderson in the "Life of Christ Research Project," but the results of her study were not included in the project's analysis and conclusions.

A note on footnoting

In evaluating parallels between *The Desire of Ages* and the various sources, we have recorded in the footnotes the particular sources that most closely correspond to the words, sentences, or structure of paragraphs in *The Desire of Ages*. Keep in mind that, in an effort to exhaust as many literary parallels as possible, many words and phrases have been footnoted for nothing more than a hint of literary allusion. Though sentences are described as "paraphrase" and words as "verbatim," such designations do not *certify* that Ellen White actually derived her words directly from a particular source as she wrote rather than drawing them from her own acquired vocabulary. Other parallels are described as a "similar thought." Certain *independent thoughts* and *points unique to the DA text* will also be pointed out.

What might *The Desire of Ages* look like if it were footnoted by 21st century standards, marking every instance of possible literary allusion?

The notation of sources in the exhibits of the next four chapters may give the reader some idea of what *The Desire of Ages* could look like if it were marked and footnoted for possible sources according to twenty-first century academic standards. Of course, Ellen White, whose knowledge of literary practice was based on what she saw in the works of contemporary authors and not from a literary education, did not write *The Desire of Ages* for an academic audience (much less a twenty-first century one). Verbatim phrases from sources containing five or more consecutive words are actually quite rare,[2] and footnoting of scattered parallel verbatim words would be rather awkward.

"Reverse engineering" this devotional classic has been tricky business at best. We do not claim to have identified all the pieces. However, we trust that the inclusion of the cumbersome notation of the exhibits that follow will illustrate why Ellen White chose not to clutter the pages or compromise the spiritual impact of *The Desire of Ages* with such academic superfluity. You don't have to read every reference in the following chapters to benefit from the exhibits. Simply noting the quantity and arrangement of each color—including **black**—will tell you something about Ellen White's literary dependency. (Conclusions from the colorized text will be summarized in Chapter 7.) When you have satisfied your curiosity about possible sources and the use of Ellen White's earlier materials in *The Desire of Ages*, why not go back and read the same chapters again from an unmarked copy of *The Desire of Ages* and see what message of inspiration you receive? As Leonard Brand noted, "Study of her source books can help us understand her editorial methods—how she achieved the wording in her books" (*The Prophets and Her Critics*, p. 27). It is only when we look beyond the similarity between her writings and those of others, however, that we recognize the uniqueness of her message.

· · · · · · · · · ·

Our first exhibit is a marked and annotated version of "God With Us," the first chapter of *The Desire of Ages*. It is a Bible study on the Incarnation of Christ and how His coming to earth answered Satan's impugning of God's character of love, justice, and mercy.

---

[2] *LCRP* 879. There were two classes of verbatim sentences designated in the *Life of Christ Research Project:* **V1**, *strict verbatim*—which requires exact duplication of an entire sentence (*none* were identified for the 15 chapters), and **V2**, *not so strict verbatim*—which allows for slight modification of words or punctuation (*29* of these were identified for the 15 chapters; these are marked for consecutive verbatim in EXHIBIT A of Appendix B). In addition to verbatim, there were five other classes of dependent sentences: **P1**, *strict paraphrase*—same general structure and meaning as the identified source, though as little as a phrase or two from a source sentence; **P2**, *simple paraphrase*—the same basic meaning as the source, though not following its structure, and often containing an additional thought; **P3**, *loose paraphrase*—a very similar thought as the source, though not in the same order nor always containing significant verbatim words and frequently identified by sentences in the context that more clearly parallel the source; **B1**, *unique use of Scripture as in source*—a parallel Scripture not directly associated with the story; and **I2**, *partial independent*—strong parallelism for part of the sentence (what one might call "an allusion"), though at least half of the sentence is made up of independent wording.

CHAPTER 3

A Scriptural Tapestry—

"God With Us"

"His name shall be called Immanuel, . . . God with us."[1] {*DA* 19.1}

"The light of the knowledge of the glory of God" is seen "in the face of Jesus Christ."[2] From the days of eternity the Lord Jesus Christ was one with the Father; He was "the image of God,"[3] the image of His greatness and majesty, "the outshining of His glory." It was to manifest this glory that He came to our world.[4] To this sin-darkened earth He came to reveal the light of God's love,[5]—to be "God with us." Therefore it was prophesied of Him, "His name shall be called Immanuel." {*DA* 19.2}

By coming to dwell with us, Jesus was to reveal God both to men and to angels. He was the Word of God,—God's thought made audible.[6] In His prayer for His disciples He says, "I have declared unto them Thy name,"—"merciful and gracious, long-suffering, and abundant in goodness and truth,"—"that the love wherewith Thou hast loved Me may be in them, and I in them." But not alone for His earthborn children was this revelation given. Our little world is the lesson book of the universe. God's wonderful purpose of grace, the mystery of redeeming love, is the theme into which "angels desire to look," and it will be their study throughout endless ages. Both the redeemed and the unfallen beings will find in the cross of Christ their science and their song.[7] It will be seen that the glory shining in the face of Jesus is the glory of self-sacrificing love. In the light from Calvary it will be seen that the law of self-renouncing love is the law of life for earth and heaven; that the love which "seeketh not her own" has its source in the heart of God; and that in the meek and lowly One is manifested the character of Him who dwelleth in the light which no man can approach unto.[8] {*DA* 19.3}

---

[1] A blending of *Isa. 9:6*, *Isa. 7:14* and *Matt. 1:23*—". . . his name shall be called Wonderful, Counsellor, The mighty God, The everlasting Father, The Prince of Peace," "and shall call his name Immanuel" and "God with us."

[2] Same *unique* use of *2 Cor. 4:6* as in Winslow, *GR* 34, 38, and Harris, *TGT* 121, though *DA* and Harris paraphrase differently.

[3] A simple paraphrase, Harris, *TGT* 135, "The office of revealing and representing the character of the Deity was reserved for him who had been from eternity in the bosom of the Father [*John 1:18*]; the image of the invisible God [*Col. 1:15*]." "From the days of eternity" derives from the marginal reading of *Micah 5:2*; "image of God" is from *2 Cor. 4:4*. "One with the Father" is a conflation of *John 1:1* ("the Word was with God") and *John 10:30* ("I and my Father are one"); it is used by Winslow, p. 15; Hanna (1863), pp. 12, 31; and Andrews (1891), p. 516. Though Andrews was first published in 1862, it is the 1892 edition that is listed in the Ellen G. White office library, and Andrews is only mentioned as being used for ordering chapters (see *Exhibits* #65). Ellen White used "one with the Father" in a sermon on 11-9-1885 (MS 4, 1885) and the phrase "Christ was one with the Father" in *ST* 7-4-1895. She had earlier written in *RH* 12-17-1872, "He was in the express image of his Father, not in features alone, but in perfection of character."

[4] A very loose paraphrase, Winslow, p. 18, "But the manifestation of Christ's pre-existent glory would not be confined to the spirits in heaven. *On earth* there would be such a visible unfolding of it, as would confirm all his previous claims to infinite dignity and power."

[5] A simple paraphrase, Harris, *TGT* 114, "He had rolled away the thick darkness from before the throne of God, and had revealed him to the world as light and love . . ."

[6] A simple paraphrase, Harris, *TGT* 81, "He came forth from the bosom of the Father, as the Word, the Revealer of the infinite mind . . ." See *John 1:14, 18; Rev. 19:13*. Phrase "thought made audible" used in *YI* 6-28-1894.

[7] Highlighted is from *PP* 154.3 and from *5T* 317.2—two of the "bound volumes" used by Marian Davis (see *Exhibits* #45).

[8] Through the Scriptures, Ellen White, as a "lesser light," directs the reader's attention to Jesus, the "greater light." Note the string of Scriptural allusions—"I have declared unto them Thy name" (*John 17:26*); "merciful and gracious . . . truth" (*Ex. 34:6*);

In the beginning, God was revealed in all the works of creation. It was Christ that spread the heavens, and laid the foundations of the earth. It was His hand that hung the worlds in space, and fashioned the flowers of the field.[9] "His strength setteth fast the mountains." "The sea is His, and He made it." Ps. 65:6; 95:5. It was He that filled the earth with beauty, and the air with song. And upon all things in earth, and air, and sky, He wrote the message of the Father's love. {DA 20.1}

Now sin has marred God's perfect work, yet that handwriting remains. Even now all created things declare the glory of His excellence.[10] There is nothing save the selfish heart of man, that lives unto itself.[11] No bird that cleaves the air, no animal that moves upon the ground, but ministers to some other life. There is no leaf of the forest, or lowly blade of grass, but has its ministry. Every tree and shrub and leaf pours forth that element of life without which neither man nor animal could live; and man and animal, in turn, minister to the life of tree and shrub and leaf. The flowers breathe fragrance and unfold their beauty in blessing to the world. The sun sheds its light to gladden a thousand worlds. The ocean, itself the source of all our springs and fountains, receives the streams from every land, but takes to give. The mists ascending from its bosom fall in showers to water the earth, that it may bring forth and bud. {DA 20.2}

The angels of glory find their joy in giving,—giving love and tireless watchcare to souls that are fallen and unholy. Heavenly beings woo the hearts of men; they bring to this dark world light from the courts above; by gentle and patient ministry they move upon the human spirit, to bring the lost into a fellowship with Christ which is even closer than they themselves can know. {DA 21.1}

But turning from all lesser representations, we behold God in Jesus.[12] Looking unto Jesus we see that it is the glory of our God to give. "I do nothing of Myself," said Christ; "the living Father hath sent Me, and I live by the Father." "I seek not Mine own glory," but the glory of Him that sent Me. John 8:28; 6:57; 8:50; 7:18. In these words is set forth the great principle which is the law of life for the universe.[13] All things Christ received from God, but He took to give.[14] So in the heavenly courts, in His ministry for all created beings: through the beloved Son, the Father's life flows out to all;[15] through the Son it returns, in praise and joyous service, a tide of love, to the great

---

"that the love . . . and I in them" (*John 17:26*); "angels desire to look" (*1 Peter 1:12*); "face of Jesus" (*2 Cor. 4:6*); "seeketh not her own" (*1 Cor. 13:5*); "meek and lowly" (*Matt. 11:29*); and "in the light which no man can approach unto" (*1 Tim. 6:16*).

[9] A very loose paraphrase, Winslow, p. 8, ". . . 'All things,' all worlds, all creatures, 'created by him, and for him . . .' [*Col. 1:16*]," including the near verbatim of *Isa. 48:13*, though "laid the foundations of the earth" of *Isa. 51:13* is in 2*SP* 162.2 and in a sermon in *RH* 8-19-1884. Same thought in *PP* (1890) 574.2 and in *BEcho* 6-18-1894, including the clause "hand that hung the worlds in space."

[10] A very loose paraphrase paralleling two non-consecutive sentences, Winslow, p. 46. "In the person and work of Christ, the HOLINESS of God is revealed with equal power and lustre. It is only through this medium that we possess the most clear and perfect demonstration of this Divine and awful perfection. From nature and from providence the evidence of its existence, and the illustration of its nature, come to us more in the form of inference than of positive declaration. Sin has obliterated all traces of holiness which once existed; not a foot of this vast domain, not a shrub, nor flower, nor creature remains, to tell what the 'beauties of holiness' [*Psalm 110:3*] once were. Not a link binds the present with the world's primeval history. Sin has severed the chain, has created a vast and fearful chasm, ingulfing [*sic*] all that was ever holy and beautiful in this now fallen and defaced creation. And yet, even from its present condition, we form some faint idea of what it once was."

[11] A related thought with verbatim words, Harris, *TGC* (1854) 41, "Yet now it was that man first made the monstrous essay of living to himself. As if he had only to withdraw his allegiance from God in order to dissolve relations with the universe, selfishness now became the law of his sinful being. But such separation was impossible. Live to himself, in the sense of selfish appropriation, he might; but detach himself from the relations of dependence and influence he could not."

[12] A very loose paraphrase, Winslow, p. 52, "Of the glory of this Divine perfection, the Lord Jesus is the grand revelation."

[13] A loose paraphrase, Harris, *TGC* 37, "MUTUAL dependence and influence is the law of the universe."

[14] A strict paraphrase, ±Joseph Parker, *Ecce Deus* (1867), p. 211, "He only received that he might give; he only asked that he might distribute." However, the "±" symbol indicates that Parker was not listed in any of Ellen White's libraries.

[15] A related thought with a common verbatim word that is used differently from *DA*, Winslow, p. 24, "This covenant must be *rich* in its promises of mercy, seeing that it is made by Jehovah himself, the Fountain of all holiness, goodness, mercy, and truth, whose very essence is 'Love.' It must be *glorious*, because the second Person in the blessed Trinity became its surety."

Source of all.[16] And thus through Christ the circuit of beneficence is complete, «representing the character of the» great Giver,[17] the law of life. {*DA* 21.2}

In heaven itself this law was broken. Sin originated in self-seeking. Lucifer, the covering cherub, desired to be first in heaven. He sought to gain control of heavenly beings, to draw them away from their Creator, and to win their homage to himself. Therefore he misrepresented God, attributing to Him the desire for self-exaltation. With his own evil characteristics he sought to invest the loving Creator. Thus he deceived angels. Thus he deceived men. He led them to doubt the word of God, and to distrust His goodness. Because God is a God of justice and terrible majesty, Satan caused them to look upon Him as severe and unforgiving.[18] Thus he drew men to join him in rebellion against God, and the night of woe settled down upon the world.[19] {*DA* 21.3}

The earth was dark through misapprehension of God. That the gloomy shadows might be lightened, that the world might be brought back to God, Satan's deceptive power was to be broken.[20] This could not be done by force. The exercise of force is contrary to the principles of God's government; He desires only the service of love, and love cannot be commanded; it cannot be won by force or authority. Only by love is love awakened. To know God is to love Him; His character must be manifested in contrast to the character of Satan. This work only one Being in all the universe could do. Only He who knew the height and depth of the love of God could make it known.[21] Upon the world's dark night the Sun of righteousness must rise, "with healing in His wings." Mal. 4:2.[22] {*DA* 22.1}

The plan for our redemption was not an afterthought, a plan formulated after the fall of Adam. It was a revelation of "the mystery which hath been kept in silence through times eternal." Rom. 16:25, R.V.[23] It was an unfolding of the principles that from eternal ages have been the foundation of God's throne. From the beginning, God and Christ knew of the apostasy of Satan, and of the fall of man through the deceptive power of the apostate. God did not ordain that sin should exist, but He foresaw its existence, and made provision to meet the terrible emergency. So great was His love for the world, that He covenanted to give His only-begotten Son,[24] "that whosoever believeth in Him should not perish, but have everlasting life." John 3:16. {*DA* 22.2}

---

[16] A related thought, Harris, *TGC* 38, ". . . while the well-being of each is an ingredient in the happiness of the whole; and all, according to their respective natures, ascribe glory to Him, their centre and their source, by whom they are alike pervaded, and in whom they are all one."

[17] Verbatim for part of a phrase in the previously cited Harris, *TGT* 135, "The office of revealing and representing the character of the Deity was reserved for him who had been from eternity in the bosom of the Father; the image of the invisible God." Same thought is in *RH* 12-17-1872, "He was in the express image of his Father, not in features alone, but in perfection of character."

[18] Highlighted is from *5T* 56.1, MS 43, 1897 (*2MR* 59.5), *ST* 6-27-92, and *SC* 10.3f; verbatim phrase from *Isaiah 30:18* and *Job 37:22*. About her use of *SC*, Marian Davis wrote in 1892: "I shall want to use rather more than a page from 'Steps'" (see *Exhibits* #41). *1SG* 17f, 19 says: "Satan was insinuating against the government of GOD, ambitious to exalt himself, and unwilling to submit to the authority of Jesus . . . He must insinuate against GOD's truthfulness, create doubt whether GOD did mean as he said . . ."

[19] A similar thought for last clause (though not describing Satan), Harris, *TGT* 50, "The darkness was universal and complete. It had settled down, like a pall, over the face of the whole earth."

[20] An echo of *John 1:5*, "And the light shineth in darkness; and the darkness comprehended it not," and *John 1:18*, "No man hath seen God at any time; the only begotten Son, which is in the bosom of the Father, he hath declared him."

[21] Phrase "the exercise of force" in *RH* 9-7-1897; sentence from *SC* (1892) 14.2, in a chapter added to *SC* in 1893.

[22] Same *unique* use of *Malachi 4:2* as in Harris, *TGT* 52, and in Winslow, p. 71, though *DA* paraphrases slightly.

[23] Thought carried over from *ST* 8-24-1891, "The plan of redemption was not conceived after the fall of man to cure the dreadful evil; the apostle Paul speaks of the gospel, the preaching of Jesus Christ, as 'the revelation of the mystery, which hath been kept in silence through times eternal, but now is manifested . . .'" and *ST* 4-25-1892, "Therefore redemption was not an afterthought—a plan formulated after the fall of Adam—but an eternal purpose to be wrought out for the blessing not only of this atom of a world but for the good of all the worlds which God has created."

[24] While Ellen White paraphrases *John 3:16*, Winslow, p. 37, paraphrases *John 3:17*.

Lucifer had said, "I will exalt my throne above the stars of God; . . . I will be like the Most High." Isa. 14:13, 14. But Christ, "being in the form of God, counted it not a thing to be grasped to be on an equality with God, but emptied Himself, taking the form of a servant, being made in the likeness of men." Phil. 2:6, 7, R.V., margin. {DA 22.3}

This was a voluntary sacrifice. Jesus might have remained at the Father's side. He might have retained the glory of heaven, and the homage of the angels. But He chose to give back the scepter into the Father's hands, and to step down from the throne of the universe, that He might bring light to the benighted, and life to the perishing.[25] {DA 22.4}

«Nearly two thousand years ago, a voice of» «mysterious import was heard in heaven», «from the throne» of God,[26] "Lo, I come." "Sacrifice and offering Thou wouldest not, but a body hast Thou prepared Me. . . . Lo, I come (in the volume of the Book it is written of Me,) to do Thy will, O God." Heb. 10:5–7.[27] In these words is announced the fulfillment of the purpose that had been hidden from eternal ages. Christ was about to visit our world, and to become incarnate.[28] He says, "A body hast Thou prepared Me." Had He appeared with the glory that was His «with the Father before the world was»,[29] we could not have endured the light of His presence. That we might behold it and not be destroyed, the manifestation of His glory was shrouded. His divinity was veiled with humanity,—the invisible glory in the visible human form. {DA 23.1}

This great purpose had been shadowed forth in types and symbols. The burning bush, in which Christ appeared to Moses, revealed God.[30] The symbol chosen for the representation of

---

[25] First sentence builds on 1SG 22.2f, "He then made known to the angelic host that a way of escape had been made for lost man. He told them that he had been pleading with his FATHER, and had offered to give his life a ransom, and take the sentence of death upon himself, that through him man might find pardon. That through the merits of his blood, and obedience to the law of GOD, they could have the favor of GOD, and be brought into the beautiful garden, and eat of the fruit of the tree of life." (See *Rev. 2:7; 22:2, 14* on restoration of the tree of life.) Highlighted is from *RH* 1-9-1893 and MS 101, 1897 (12*MR* 397.2).

[26] A near verbatim, gleaned from Heman Humphrey, D.D., in his introductory essay to John Harris's *The Great Teacher*, p. xiii, "Nearly two thousand years ago, a voice of strange and mysterious import was heard in heaven; and the more mysterious, because it issued from the throne itself," an expansion of the phrase introducing *Heb. 10:5–7*, "Wherefore, when he cometh into the world, he saith . . ." The thought gem was first used in *YI* 11-21-1895 and *ST* 7-30-1896, though *ST*, which used the word "mysterious" and "wouldest not, but a body has Thou prepared Me," is a little closer to Harris's wording. The phrase "from the throne" is very common in Ellen White's earlier writings (e.g. *YI* 3-1-1874 and *RH* 8-4-1874).

[27] Same *unique* use of Scripture as in Humphrey, *TGT* xiii, though *DA* does not follow Humphrey's mixing of *Ps. 40:6–8* with *Heb. 10:5–7*. The text from Hebrews, regarding Jesus' coming in flesh, was first used in *ST* 7-22-1886.

[28] A strict paraphrase, Humphrey, *TGT* xiii, "And who is it, that thus announces his purpose to visit a guilty world, and become incarnate?" A related thought in Winslow, p. 51, "Then did this perfection appear in its most fearful form—Jesus bearing sin—Jesus enduring the curse of the law—Jesus sustaining the wrath of his Father—Jesus surrendering his holy soul a sacrifice for man's transgression."

[29] A paraphrase of *John 17:5*—"And now, O Father, glorify thou me with thine own self with the glory which I had with thee before the world was"—using a verbatim phrase used in at least four sources. Winslow, p. 14, "[skipping 26 words] the human nature of Christ never existed in any form in a pre-eternal state, consequently it could possess no glory with the Father before the world was." Hanna, p. 748, "If the saying which went before, 'It is finished,' be taken, as it well may be, as Christ's last word of farewell to the world he leaves behind, this may be taken as his first word of greeting to the new world that he is about to enter. *New* world, we say, for though, as the Eternal Son, he was but returning to the glory that he had with the Father before the world was, let us not forget that death was to the humanity of the Lord—as it will be to each and all of us—an entrance upon a new and untried state." Harris, *TGT* 68, "Astonishment is only for those to whom knowledge is novelty; but 'the glory which is to be revealed' to us, is 'the glory which he had with the Father before the world was:' the unapproachable splendors of the celestial state, he speaks of as ever present to his mind, as the natural and familiar scenes of his Father's house." Melvill, *Sermons by Henry Melvill, B. D.* (1853), vol. 1, p. 343, "Whatever the glory that was about to descend on the manhood, it could not be described as a glory which he had had with the Father before the world was . . ." Such a commonly used phrase would doubtless not require footnoting.

[30] Verbatim phrase in a related thought in Winslow, p. 73, "We have, therefore, selected from the many a single one,— *the burning bush*,—as embodying a mass of truth relating to our adorable Immanuel." Same thought as *DA* is in 4a*SG* 61.5, "The burning bush seen by Moses was also a token of the divine presence . . ."

the Deity was a lowly shrub, that seemingly had no attractions. This enshrined the Infinite.[31] The all-merciful God shrouded His glory in a most humble type, that Moses could look upon it and live.[32] So in the pillar of cloud by day and the pillar of fire by night,[33] God communicated with Israel, revealing to men His will, and imparting to them His grace. God's glory was subdued, and His majesty veiled, that the weak vision of finite men might behold it.[34] So Christ was to come in "the body of our humiliation" (Phil. 3:21, R.V.), "in the likeness of men." In the eyes of the world He possessed no beauty that they should desire Him;[35] yet He was the incarnate God, the light of heaven and earth. His glory was veiled, His greatness and majesty were hidden,[36] that He might draw near to sorrowful, tempted men. {*DA* 23.2}

God commanded Moses for Israel, "Let them make Me a sanctuary, that I may dwell among them" (Ex. 25:8), and He abode in the sanctuary, in the midst of His people. Through all their weary wandering in the desert, the symbol of His presence was with them. So Christ «set up His tabernacle in the midst of» our human encampment. He pitched His tent by the side of the tents of men, that He might dwell among us, and «make us familiar with His» divine character and life.[37] "The Word became flesh, and tabernacled among us (and we beheld His glory, glory as of the Only Begotten from the Father), full of grace and truth." John 1:14, R.V., margin. {*DA* 23.3}

Since Jesus came to dwell with us, we know that God is acquainted with our trials, and sympathizes with our griefs.[38] Every son and daughter of Adam may understand that our Creator is the friend of sinners. For in every doctrine of grace, every promise of joy, every deed of love, every divine attraction presented in the Saviour's life on earth, we see "God with us."[39] {*DA* 24.1}

---

[31] A simple paraphrase, Winslow, p. 76, "Nay; but a *bush*—the most mean and insignificant, the most lowly and unsightly of all trees—was to enshrine the Godhead of Him whom the heaven of heavens cannot contain."

[32] A similar thought to that in two sentences in Winslow, p. 74, "'. . . And Moses hid his face; for he was afraid to look upon God.' Now this type—a type it doubtless is—is radiant with the glory of Christ."

[33] "Pillar of cloud by day and the pillar of fire by night" taken from *Ex. 13:22*.

[34] A likely allusion to *Ex. 33:22* and a very loose paraphrase, Melvill, *Sermons* (1853), vol. 1, p. 43, "But he did not appear as God. He put from him, or he veiled, those effulgent demonstrations of Deity, which had commanded the homage, and called forth the admiration of the celestial hierarchy."

[35] A paraphrase of *Isa. 53:2*—"no beauty that we should desire him," adapting verbatim wording in Winslow, p. 77, "Behold, too, the *meanness* of Christ in the world's eye. In him it sees no glory and traces no beauty; his outward form of humiliation veils it from their view." Ellen White used the expression "in the eyes of the world" in 1*SG* 127.1 and in a sermon in *RH* 8-25-1885.

[36] A simple paraphrase, Melvill, p. 43, "He was still God, and could not, for a lonely instant, cease to be God. But he did not appear as God. He put from him, or he veiled, those effulgent demonstrations of Deity which had commanded the homage, and called forth the admiration of the celestial hierarchy," building on the "veil" of *Heb. 10:20*. *RH* 12-31-1872 has a closer thought, "The Son was the brightness of the Father's glory, and the express image of his person [*Heb. 1:3*]. He possessed divine excellence and greatness. He was equal with God [*Phil. 2:6*]. It pleased the Father that in him all fullness should dwell [*Col. 1:19*]."

[37] Near verbatim, gleaned from Harris, *TGT* 137, "Like the moveable sanctuary which accompanied the Israelites in the wilderness, he was the *tabernacle of witness;* having been made flesh, he came and set up his tabernacle in the midst of the human encampment, pitched his tent side by side with our tents, to attest the presence of God, to make us familiar with his character and sensible of his love." Thought gem was first adapted for *ST* 1-20-1890. It is a beautiful metaphor for describing what Ellen White had written in 1*SG* 23.1f, quoted in next footnote.

[38] Independent thought built on *Isa. 53:3*, *Heb. 12:1*, and *Heb. 2:17*, previously expressed in 1*SG* 23.1f, "He would leave all his glory in heaven, appear upon earth as a man, humble himself as a man, become acquainted by his own experience with the various temptations with which man would be beset, that he might know how to succor those who should be tempted . . ."

[39] Phrase "friend of . . . sinners" from *Matt. 11:19*. A very loose paraphrase and same use of *Matt. 1:23* as in Harris, *TGT* 137, "The great inscription of Immanuel, *God with us*, was so legible on every part, that the thoughtful and reverent could not raise their eye to Christ, without being conscious of feelings of reverence and awe, like those awakened by the sight of a temple."

Satan represents God's law of love as a law of selfishness. He declares that it is impossible for us to obey its precepts. «The fall of our first parents»,[40] with all the woe that has resulted, he charges upon the Creator, leading men to look upon God as the author of sin, and suffering, and death. Jesus was to unveil this deception. As one of us He was to give an example of obedience. For this He took upon Himself our nature, and passed through our experiences. "In all things it behooved Him to be made like unto His brethren." Heb. 2:17. If we had to bear anything which Jesus did not endure, then upon this point Satan would represent the power of God as insufficient for us. Therefore Jesus was "in all points tempted like as we are." Heb. 4:15. He endured every trial to which we are subject. And He exercised in His own behalf no power that is not freely offered to us. As man, He met temptation, and overcame in the strength given Him from God. He says, "I delight to do Thy will, O My God: yea, Thy law is within My heart." Ps. 40:8. As He went about doing good, and healing all who were afflicted by Satan, He made plain to men the character of God's law and the nature of His service. His life testifies that it is possible for us also to obey the law of God.[41] {DA 24.2}

By His humanity, Christ touched humanity; by His divinity, He lays hold upon the throne of God. As the Son of man, He gave us an example of obedience; as the Son of God, He gives us power to obey. It was Christ who from the bush on Mount Horeb spoke to Moses saying, "I AM THAT I AM. . . ."[42] Thus shalt thou say unto the children of Israel, I AM hath sent me unto you." Ex. 3:14. This was the pledge of Israel's deliverance. So when He came "in the likeness of men," He declared Himself the I AM. The Child of Bethlehem, the meek and lowly Saviour, is God "manifest in the flesh." 1 Tim. 3:16. And to us He says: "I AM the Good Shepherd." "I AM the living Bread." "I AM the Way, the Truth, and the Life."[43] "All power is given unto Me in heaven and in earth." John 10:11; 6:51; 14:6; Matt. 28:18. I AM the assurance of every promise. I AM; be not afraid. "God with us" is the surety[44] of our deliverance from sin, the assurance of our power to obey the law of heaven. {DA 24.3}

In stooping to take upon Himself humanity, Christ revealed a character[45] the opposite of the character of Satan. But He stepped still lower in the path of humiliation.[46] "Being found in fashion as a man, He humbled Himself, and became obedient unto death, even the death of the cross." Phil. 2:8. «As the high priest laid aside his gorgeous pontifical robes, and officiated in the white linen

---

[40] A common verbatim phrase in a different context, Edersheim, *LTJM* (1886), vol. 2, p. 573, "The instant before and after sin represents the difference of feeling as portrayed in the history of the Fall of our first parents." Used in *ST* 8-7-1879 (first printed in 1875), "The fall of our first parents was caused by the indulgence of appetite." Such a phrase would not require footnoting.

[41] Other highlighted in this paragraph is from *ST* 5-30-1895 and Testimony No. 58, 1890 in MS 141, 1901 (17*MR* 337.4f); "went about doing good . . ." from *Acts 10:38*.

[42] A loose paraphrase built on *Ex. 3:1*, "mountain of God" at "Horeb"; *3:4*, "out of the midst of the bush"; and *3:14*, "I AM THAT I AM"; as in Harris, *TGT* 61, "When from the midst of the burning bush Jehovah proclaimed himself, *I am that I am*, he announced his independent existence and self-sufficient perfections; in other words, he declared *what he is in himself.*"

[43] Same *unique* use of *John 10:11, 14* and *14:6* as in Harris, *TGT* 61, for two expressions; though Harris has "I am the bread of life" (*John 6:35, 48*). *ST* 10-11-1899 uses the same Biblical phrases as Harris: "What fulness is expressed in the words: 'I am the Light of the world.' 'I am the Bread of life.' 'I am the Way, the Truth, and the Life.' 'I am the good Shepherd.' 'I am come that they might have life, and that they might have it more abundantly.'" (There could have been a pre-*DA* manuscript that formed the basis for both EGW texts.) Walter Rea asserted that Ellen White used Scriptures from other authors as "fillers" (*The White Lie*, p. 24), however, the discriminating reader will recognize that she used Scripture thoughtfully and purposefully, independent of the other authors' "free handling," or paraphrasing, of the Biblical text.

[44] A loose paraphrase, Winslow, p. 12, "What a stable truth for faith in its weakest form to deal with,—to have a glorious incarnate I AM for an atoning sacrifice—the I AM for a Redeemer—the I AM for a Surety . . . the I AM as the centre in whom all the promises are 'yea and amen' . . ." The word "surety" is from *Heb. 7:22*. "Be not afraid" is used throughout Scripture.

[45] A loose paraphrase, Winslow, p. 39, "But God has revealed himself. He has stooped to our nature . . ."

[46] Highlighted is from a testimony marked "Basle, Switzerland, March 10, 1887" in MS 141, 1901 (17*MR* 339.3) and from *ST* 2-20-1893.

dress of» the «common priest, so Christ» «took the form of a servant, and offered sacrifice, Himself the priest, Himself the victim.»[47] "He was wounded for our transgressions, He was bruised for our iniquities: the chastisement of our peace was upon Him." Isa. 53:5. {*DA* 25.1}

Christ «was treated as we deserve», «that we might be treated as He» deserves. «He was condemned for our sins, in which He had no share, that we might be justified by His righteousness, in which we had no share.»[48] He suffered the death which was ours, that we might receive the life which was His. "With His stripes we are healed." {*DA* 25.2}

By His life and His death, Christ has achieved even more than recovery from the ruin wrought through sin. It was Satan's purpose to bring about an eternal separation between God and man; but in Christ we become more closely united to God than if we had never fallen.[49] In taking our nature, the Saviour has bound Himself to humanity by a tie that is never to be broken. Through the eternal ages He is linked with us. "God so loved the world, that He gave His only-begotten Son." John 3:16. He gave Him not only to bear our sins, and to die as our sacrifice; He gave Him to the fallen race.[50] To assure us of His immutable counsel of peace, God gave His only-begotten Son to become one of the human family, forever to retain His human nature. This is the pledge that God will fulfill His word. "Unto *us* a child is born, unto *us* a son is given: and the government shall be upon His shoulder."[51] God has adopted human nature in the person of His Son, and has carried the same into the highest heaven.[52] It is the "Son of man" who shares the throne of the universe. It is the "Son of man" whose name shall be called, "Wonderful, Counselor, The mighty God, The everlasting Father, The Prince of Peace." Isa. 9:6. The I AM is the Daysman between God and

---

[47] The only near verbatim sentence gleaned from Charles Beecher's chapter on "Azazel" in *Redeemer and Redeemed, An Investigation of the Atonement and of Eternal Judgment* (1864), p. 65, "As the high-priest laid aside his gorgeous pontifical robes, and officiated in the white linen dress of a common priest, so Christ emptied himself, and took the form of a servant [*Phil. 2:7*], and offered sacrifice, himself the priest, himself the victim." Thought gem first appeared in MS 57, 1896 (18*MR* 362.2), which was used in *RH* 9-7-1897. A similar thought is found in a manuscript used in *DA*, Chapters 77 and 78—MS 101, 1897 (12*MR* 398.1), "Priest and victim combined . . ."

[48] This longest verbatim for *DA*—an expanded paraphrase of *2 Cor. 5:21*—was gleaned and condensed from a chapter on the paschal lamb in Robert Boyd's *The World's Hope; or The Rock of Ages* (1873), pp. 381, 382, "He was treated as we deserved, in order that we might be treated as he deserved. He came to earth and took our sins, that we might take his righteousness and go to heaven. He was condemned for our sins, in which he had no share, that we might be justified by his righteousness, in which we had no share." Ellen White first abridged this thought gem in MS 24, 1888 (12*MR* 193.4, marked for parallels to Boyd): "Jesus becoming our sin-bearer that He might become our sin-pardoning Saviour. He was treated as we deserve to be treated. He came to our world and took our sins that we might take His righteousness." She used more of it in Ltr. 16, 1892 and in *RH* 3-21-1893: "The world's Redeemer was treated as we deserve to be treated, in order that we might be treated as he deserved to be treated. He came to our world and took our sins upon his own divine soul, that we might receive his imputed righteousness. He was condemned for our sins, in which he had no share, that we might be justified by his righteousness, in which we had no share." Boyd's source may have been John Cumming, *Prophetic Studies; or, Lectures on the Book of Daniel* (1853), p. 379: "Jesus was condemned for our sins, in which he had no share; we shall be justified by his righteousness, in which we have had no personal part whatever." 1*SG* 23.1f gives the underlying concept of His being our sin-bearer when it says that Jesus was "hung up between the heavens and the earth as a guilty sinner . . ."

[49] First two sentences of the paragraph, a very loose paraphrase, Harris, *TGT* 113, "That he should have raised our world from the gloomy suburbs of hell, and have lifted it into the radiance of an orbit next his throne; . . . and have educed from our evil a greater good than would have otherwise existed . . ." For "death" and "life," see *Rom. 5:10*.

[50] Highlighted is a mix of *RH* 12-17-1889 and *SC* 14.3, 72.1; *Heb. 9:28* has "bear the sins of many."

[51] Highlighted is from *RH* 4-3-1894; phrase "counsel of peace" is from *Zech. 6:13*; same use of *Isa. 9:6* as in Hanna, p. 30, and in Humphrey, *TGT* xiii, though they quote the entire verse.

[52] Harris, *TGT* 113, ". . . that he should have adopted our nature into the person of his Son, and have carried it to the highest throne of the highest heavens . . ." and Melvill, p. 342, "If so, that nature must ascend in the person of our representative; we are still chained to earth, if Christ, as our forerunner, have not passed into the heavens." Both are paraphrases of *Heb. 4:14*. Highlighted is from *YI* 7-29-97.

humanity,[53] laying His hand upon both. He who is "holy, harmless, undefiled, separate from sinners," is not ashamed to call us brethren. Heb. 7:26; 2:11. In Christ the family of earth and the family of heaven are bound together. Christ glorified is our brother. Heaven is enshrined in humanity and humanity is enfolded in the bosom of Infinite Love. {*DA* 25.3}[54]

Of His people God says, "They shall be as the stones of a crown, lifted up as an ensign upon His land. For how great is His goodness and how great is His beauty!" Zech. 9:16, 17. The exaltation of the redeemed will be an eternal testimony to God's mercy. "In the ages to come," He will "show the exceeding riches of His grace in His kindness toward us through Christ Jesus." "To the intent that . . . unto the principalities and the powers in the heavenly places might be made known . . . the manifold wisdom of God, according to the eternal purpose which He purposed in Christ Jesus our Lord." Eph. 2:7, 3:10, 11, R.V. {*DA* 26.1}

Through Christ's redeeming work the government of God stands justified. The Omnipotent One is made known as the God of love. Satan's charges are refuted, and his character unveiled. Rebellion can never again arise. Sin can never again enter the universe. Through eternal ages all are secure from apostasy. By love's self-sacrifice, the inhabitants of earth and heaven are bound to their Creator in bonds of indissoluble union.[55] {*DA* 26.2}

The work of redemption will be complete. In the place where sin abounded, God's grace much more abounds. The earth itself, the very field that Satan claims as his, is to be not only ransomed but exalted. Our little world, under the curse of sin the one dark blot[56] in His glorious creation, will be honored above all other worlds in the universe of God.[57] Here, where the Son of God tabernacled in humanity; where the King of glory lived and suffered and died,—here, when He shall make all things new, the tabernacle of God shall be with men, "and He will dwell with them, and they shall be His people, and God Himself shall be with them, and be their God." And through endless ages as the redeemed walk in the light of the Lord, they will praise Him for His unspeakable Gift,— *Immanuel, "God with us."*[58] {*DA* 26.3}

Brief analysis and conclusions

In the 24 paragraphs of this chapter, we have footnoted nine different possible source works— those of John Harris, Charles Beecher, Robert Boyd, Octavius Winslow, John Cumming, Alfred Edersheim, Joseph Parker, and Henry Melvill. Harris authored two different source works, *The Great Teacher* and *The Great Commission*. As part of the first of these, Humphrey's introductory essay, which had several literary parallels, was not counted as a separate source work. Seven of these source works were in Ellen White's library at the time of her death. Five were in her private library— Harris's *The Great Commission* and the works by Melvill, Winslow, and Boyd. Three were in her

---

[53] A strict paraphrase, Winslow, p. 12, ". . . —the I AM as a Day's-man between God and the soul—the I AM as an Advocate, and unceasing intercessor at the court of heaven, pleading each moment his own atoning merits . . ." "Daysman" comes from *Job 9:33*.

[54] Highlighted is from *4T* 396.1.

[55] Highlighted is from Testimony, no. 58, 1890 in MS 141, 1901 (17*MR* 338.2), and *BEcho* 7-15-1893.

[56] 1*SM* 394.1 from *Bible Students' Library Series*, April 1893, based on *Rom. 5:20*. "One dark blot" is a phrase used in Charlotte Elliott's hymn "Just As I Am" (1834)—"to rid my soul of *one dark blot*," a hymn Ellen White quoted in *ST* 7-22-1875.

[57] A loose paraphrase from a part of a 205-word sentence, Harris, *TGT* 113, "That he should have raised our world from the gloomy suburbs of hell, and have lifted it into the radiance of an orbit next his throne: . . . and have educed from our evil a greater good than would have otherwise existed . . ."

[58] Last part of the sentence, a verbatim word and a paraphrase of *2 Cor. 9:15*—"Thanks be unto God for his unspeakable gift," a Scripture quoted in Winslow, p. 28; also quoted in ⊥Flavel (1716), vol. 1, pp. 110, 156; same use of *Matt. 1:23* as in Harris, *TGT* 137.

COLOR CODING: Scripture verbatim «5 consecutive» paraphrase 1*SG* 2*SP* book article fresh

office library, bearing her handwritten signature—*The Great Teacher*[59] by Harris and the works by Beecher and Cumming. Considering the content of Winslow's book, one can see where Ellen White could have absorbed some thought content for this chapter from his book, however, there is very little verbal similarity to link the two. We do know that Mrs. White read his book, for verbatim words and phrases from pages 128–135 of Winslow's book were incorporated into a diary entry of Ellen White's on Christ's temptations in 1890 and in 1897, though the entries were not used in *DA*, Chapters 12 and 13 (see *LCRP* 149–151, 153–157, 169). The parallels to Winslow's work for *DA* Chapter 1 were often so vague that, in verifying Marcella's notation for this chapter, we had a hard time locating which sentences it was that she had originally considered to be parallels. By contrast, the majority of the parallels from Harris's two books were considerably more definite, though most were loose paraphrase and only two were a near verbatim (and one of those was from Heman Humphrey). Based on the number of times they are referenced in the footnotes, Harris and Winslow's works are rated as major sources for the chapter (i.e., having more than ten parallels).

Even though the parallel from Cumming predates Boyd (indicating that Boyd likely borrowed from Cumming), the closer similarity to Boyd would indicate that it was the source for the thought gem. It is very possible that the common parallel phrase from Edersheim that parallels *DA* 24.2 and the short sentence from Parker that parallels *DA* 21.2 are actually Ellen White's own expressions, for she could easily have written them without reference to the sources. (Edersheim was in her library listings, though without her signature; Parker's *Ecce Deus* was not.[60]) Though we have noted three possible parallels in Melvill, these are made less certain by the first being derived from Scripture, the second being paralleled by the *Review and Herald* of December 31, 1872, and the third being less exact than the quotation in Hanna. We note that several fresh manuscripts were used in the chapter.

You can likely see why this has always been one of Marcella Anderson King's favorite chapters in *The Desire of Ages*. Its simple elegance and its careful Biblical exposition on the incarnation of Christ have helped confirm her belief that God's Spirit was at work, directing the selection and adaptation of the source works used in this chapter. The chapter's emphasis on Satan's behind-the-scenes controversy over God's law and character makes a unique statement for any life of Christ work.[61] Walter Rea refers to Ellen White's adapted use of thought gems from other writers as the "abuse and misuse of others' materials" (*The White Lie*, p. 24). However, one would hardly say that Ellen White's simplified adaptations of the five select sentences gleaned from Humphrey (used only in this chapter), Harris, Beecher (used once in *DA*, Chap. 79), and Boyd (used minimally in *DA*, Chaps. 18, 72, and 77) are an abuse of their expressions. Rather, they provide a distinctive accent to a beautiful tapestry of Scriptural truth, made up largely of sentences and paragraphs without discernable borrowing. That these verbatims appeared in earlier Ellen White manuscripts and articles point to Ellen White as the one who gleaned from the four authors and not Marian Davis. Even by today's more rigid standards of attribution, these four recognizable gleanings would be the only

---

[59] There could be no copyright infringement in Ellen White's use of Harris's phrasing—especially as it was adapted and minimally used in this chapter. *The Great Teacher* was published in 1836 in Amherst, Massachusetts and protected by U.S. copyright law for 28 years plus a possible extension of 14 years. Harris died in 1856. If his heirs renewed the copyright in 1864, then it would not have gone into the public domain until 1878. By the time *DA* was published in 1898, Harris's book had been in the public domain for at least 20 years. See <www.ellengwhite.info/desire_of_ages_ch_5_rea_m.htm>.

[60] By the time of her death, Ellen White's private and office libraries contained 1200 volumes, an estimate based on *A Bibliography of Ellen G. White's Private and Office Libraries*, Ellen G. White Estate, Third Revised Edition, April 1993, Warren H. Johns, Tim Poirier, and Ron Graybill, compilers. Some of her books have "X"s or tiny marks in their margins. *The Great Teacher* does have marks, but most of the parallels to *DA* are not marked. There were no markings in Beecher or in Jones.

[61] E. W. Thayer, who was ruled out as a source author for these first two chapters, gives a hint of awareness of the cosmic aspect of Christ's coming to earth (though without Ellen White's emphasis on the controversy over God's law), "Other worlds than ours were also in the posture of keen expectation." —*Sketches from the Life of Jesus, Historical and Doctrinal* (1891), p. 23. Hanna's *Life of Christ* begins with Luke 1:26–56 and does not deal with the issues of the cosmic controversy.

strings of verbatim wording of sufficient length and significance to require any kind of marking in the chapter (and the "verbatims" from the *LCRP* in Appendix B could only be marked with difficulty). One might assume that, this being the first chapter in the book, there would be a similar amount of near verbatim borrowing throughout the rest of the book. However, in all our comparison of *The Desire of Ages* and the "sources," we never encountered this much verbatim borrowing—the two sentences from Boyd are the absolute maximum for any chapter of the book.[62]

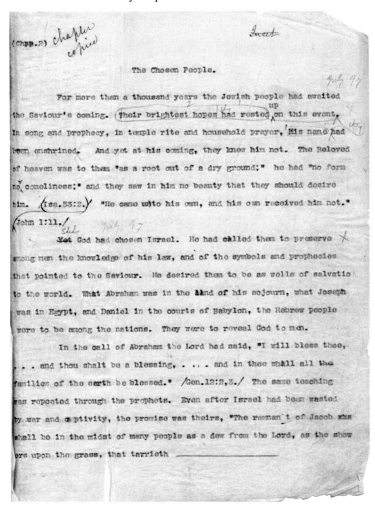

No working manuscripts for "God With Us" are known to be in existence. The facsimile to the left is the first page of the working manuscript for "The Chosen People," together with Ellen White's final handwritten corrections (pictured to the right, © 2008 EGW Estate). These corroborate Ellen White's statement in Ltr. 133, 1902 (3*SM* 90.6), "I read over all that is copied, to see that everything is as it should be. I read all the book manuscript before it is sent to the printer." Even though eager to quickly get *Christ's Object Lessons* into print, Marian Davis wrote C. H. Jones at Pacific Press on March 11, 1897: "About the parables: Before we send the book for press, Sr. White must read it" (*LCRP*, "Introduction," p. 130).

. . . .

In our next exhibit, we will "savor the flavor" of Ellen White's writing when it has only a trace of possible "seasoning" from other writings. Together with Chapters 1 and 3 of *The Desire of Ages*, Chapter 2, "The Chosen People," provides background for the story of Jesus' mission to planet Earth.

---

[62] The only other to come close was a verbatim-paraphrase found outside the *LCRP* in Harris, *TGT* 265, 266: "He became one flesh with us, in order that we might become one spirit with him. Here is a two-fold bond subsisting between Christ and his people: but the former of these they possess only in common with all mankind, it allies him to the species, and by virtue of it, all the ungodly shall be raised. The *spiritual* bond, however, is peculiar to themselves; it has been tied by his own hand, and nothing shall be able to separate it. By virtue of this union it is that believers shall arise; not merely by an act of his power, for thus the wicked shall arise, but by an extension of his life as their life." The sentences in *DA* 388.1 read: "Christ «became one flesh with us, in order that we might become one spirit with Him.» [cf. *John 1:14; 1 Cor. 6:17*] It is by virtue of this union that we are to come forth from the grave,—not merely as a manifestation of the power of Christ, but because, through faith, His life has become ours."

CHAPTER 4
A Sampling of Her Literary Style—

The Chosen People

FOR more than a thousand years the Jewish people had awaited the Saviour's coming.[1] Upon this event they had rested their brightest hopes. In song and prophecy, in temple rite and household prayer, they had enshrined His name. And yet at His coming they knew Him not.[2] The Beloved of heaven was to them "as a root out of a dry ground;" He had "no form nor comeliness;" and they saw in Him no beauty that they should desire Him. "He came unto His own, and His own received Him not." Isa. 53:2; John 1:11. {*DA* 27.1}

Yet God had chosen Israel. He had called them to preserve among men the knowledge of His law, and of the symbols and prophecies that pointed to the Saviour. He desired them to be as wells of salvation to the world.[3] What Abraham was in the land of his sojourn, what Joseph was in Egypt, and Daniel in the courts of Babylon, the Hebrew people were to be among the nations. They were to reveal God to men. {*DA* 27.2}

In the call of Abraham the Lord had said, "I will bless thee; . . . and thou shalt be a blessing: . . . and in thee shall all families of the earth be blessed." Gen. 12:2, 3. The same teaching was repeated through the prophets. Even after Israel had been wasted by war and captivity, the promise was theirs, "The remnant of Jacob shall be in the midst of many people as a dew from the Lord, as the showers upon the grass, that tarrieth not for man, nor waiteth for the sons of men." Micah 5:7. Concerning the temple at Jerusalem, the Lord declared through Isaiah, "Mine house shall be called an house of prayer for all peoples." Isa. 56:7, R.V. {*DA* 27.3}

But the Israelites fixed their hopes upon worldly greatness. From the time of their entrance to the land of Canaan, they departed from the commandments of God, and followed the ways of the heathen. It was in vain that God sent them warning by His prophets. In vain they suffered the chastisement of heathen oppression. Every reformation was followed by deeper apostasy. {*DA* 28.1}

Had Israel been true to God, He could have accomplished His purpose through their honor and exaltation. If they had walked in the ways of obedience, He would have made them "high above all nations which He hath made, in praise, and in name, and in honor." "All people of the earth," said Moses, "shall see that thou art called by the name of the Lord; and they shall be afraid of thee." "The nations which shall hear all these statutes" shall say, "Surely this great nation is a wise and understanding people." Deut. 26:19; 28:10; 4:6. But because of their unfaithfulness, God's purpose could be wrought out only through continued adversity and humiliation. {*DA* 28.2}

They were brought into subjection to Babylon, and scattered through the lands of the heathen. In affliction many renewed their faithfulness to His covenant. While they hung their

---

[1] Verbatim wording found in *YI* 2-1-1873, "From the lofty mountains of Nazareth he looked forth upon a land that had waited a thousand years for his coming." *2SP* (1877) 395.1 uses the phrase "more than a thousand years" in describing God's "favored people." The last seven paragraphs of this chapter (*DA* 28.5–30.2) were adapted for *SW* 3-28-1905.

[2] An adaptation of ***John 1:10, 11*** as in Nevin, *SBA* 253, "In the fulness of time, the long-expected Christ, the Son of the living God, came. But the nation knew Him not; 'he came to his own, and his own received him not.'"

[3] Highlighted is from *PP* 314.2. "Wells of salvation" is from ***Isa. 12:3***.

harps upon the willows, and mourned for the holy temple that was laid waste,[4] the light of truth shone out through them, and a knowledge of God was spread among the nations. The heathen systems of sacrifice were a perversion of the system that God had appointed; and many a sincere observer of heathen rites learned from the Hebrews the meaning of the service divinely ordained, and in faith grasped the promise of a Redeemer. {DA 28.3}

Many of the exiles suffered persecution. Not a few lost their lives because of their refusal to disregard the Sabbath and to observe the heathen festivals. As idolaters were roused to crush out the truth, the Lord brought His servants face to face with kings and rulers, that they and their people might receive the light. Time after time the greatest monarchs were led to proclaim the supremacy of the God whom their Hebrew captives worshiped. {DA 28.4}

By the Babylonish captivity the Israelites were effectually cured of the worship of graven images. During the centuries that followed, they suffered from the oppression of heathen foes, until the conviction became fixed that their prosperity depended upon their obedience to the law of God. But with too many of the people obedience was not prompted by love. The motive was selfish. They rendered outward service to God as the means of attaining to national greatness. They did not become the light of the world,[5] but shut themselves away from the world[6] in order to escape temptation to idolatry. In the instruction given through Moses, God had placed restrictions upon their association with idolaters; but this teaching had been misinterpreted. It was intended to prevent them from conforming to the practices of the heathen. But it was used to build up a wall of separation between Israel and all other nations. The Jews looked upon Jerusalem as their heaven, and they were actually jealous lest the Lord should show mercy to the Gentiles.[7] {DA 28.5}

After the return from Babylon, much attention was given to religious instruction. All over the country, synagogues were erected, where the law was expounded by the priests and scribes. And schools were established, which, together with the arts and sciences, professed to teach the principles of righteousness. But these agencies became corrupted. During the captivity, many of the people had received heathen ideas and customs, and these were brought into their religious service. In many things they conformed to the practices of idolaters. {DA 29.1}

As they departed from God, the Jews in a great degree lost sight of the teaching of the ritual service. That service had been instituted by Christ Himself. In every part it was a symbol of Him; and it had been full of vitality and spiritual beauty. But the Jews lost the spiritual life from their ceremonies, and clung to the dead forms.[8] They trusted to the sacrifices and ordinances themselves, instead of resting upon Him to whom they pointed. In order to supply the place of that which they had lost, the priests and rabbis multiplied requirements of their own; and the more rigid they grew,

---

[4] Phrases are from *Ps. 137:2* and *79:7*.

[5] From *Matt. 5:14*, based on *Isa. 42:6*, "a light of the Gentiles," and *Isa. 60:3*, "the Gentiles shall come to thy light."

[6] A description used of the Pharisees in *2SP 216.1*.

[7] A simple paraphrase, Harris, *TGT* (1836) 97, with a more direct explanation of the Jews' heaven, "And, when in addition to this, it is remembered,—that the whole of their law had become rabbinized and overlaid with traditions; that notwithstanding their sacrificial types, the doctrine of pardon procured by a vicarious expiation, was 'to the Jews a stumbling block;' that all that was supernatural in their temple worship had been long since recalled to heaven, and all that was spiritual suffered to depart; that any of their moral duties were compounded for a pecuniary consideration; that the only heaven they knew, was suspended, in their imagination, over the land of Judea; and that they were actually jealous of the Divine Being, lest he should take within the pale of salvation, any part of the gentile world . . ." Highlighted sentences were adapted from *YI* 7-29-1897, pars. 2, "In the instruction of Christ to Moses, to be given to his people, restrictions were placed upon their association with idolatrous nations"; and 4, "Jerusalem was their heaven, and they were actually jealous lest the Lord should show mercy to the Gentile world" and *ST* 1-1-1894, "The scribes and Pharisees had built up a wall of separation between their nation and every other people."

[8] A very loose paraphrase, Harris, *TGT* 314, "Devotion, which to be pure and vital must derive its supplies like the living stream, by hidden communication with the parent ocean, he found cut off from the great Fountain of life, and made to consist in artificial jet-works and devices for proud and public display." Highlighted is from *RH* 3-20-1894.

the less of the love of God was manifested. They measured their holiness by the multitude of their ceremonies, while their hearts were filled with pride and hypocrisy.[9] {*DA* 29.2}

With all their minute and burdensome injunctions, it was an impossibility to keep the law. Those who desired to serve God, and who tried to observe the rabbinical precepts, toiled under a heavy burden. They could find no rest from the accusings of a troubled conscience. Thus Satan worked to discourage the people, to lower their conception of the character of God, and to bring the faith of Israel into contempt. He hoped to establish the claim put forth when he rebelled in heaven—that the requirements of God were unjust, and could not be obeyed. Even Israel, he declared, did not keep the law. {*DA* 29.3}

While the Jews desired the advent of the Messiah, they had no true conception of His mission. They did not seek redemption from sin, but deliverance from the Romans. They looked for the Messiah to come as a conqueror, to break the oppressor's power, and exalt Israel to universal dominion.[10] Thus the way was prepared for them to reject the Saviour. {*DA* 29.4}

At the time of the birth of Christ the nation was chafing under the rule of her foreign masters, and racked with internal strife. The Jews had been permitted to maintain the form of a separate government; but nothing could disguise the fact that they were under the Roman yoke, or reconcile them to the restriction of their power. The Romans claimed the right of appointing and removing the high priest, and the office was often secured by fraud, bribery, and even murder.[11] Thus the priesthood became more and more corrupt. Yet the priests still possessed great power, and they employed it for selfish and mercenary ends. The people were subjected to their merciless demands, and were also heavily taxed by the Romans. This state of affairs caused widespread discontent. Popular outbreaks were frequent. Greed and violence, distrust and spiritual apathy, were eating out the very heart of the nation. {*DA* 30.1}

Hatred of the Romans, and national and spiritual pride, led the Jews still to adhere rigorously to their forms of worship. The priests tried to maintain a reputation for sanctity by scrupulous attention to the ceremonies of religion. The people, in their darkness and oppression, and the rulers, thirsting for power, longed for the coming of One who would vanquish their enemies and restore the kingdom to Israel. They had studied the prophecies, but without spiritual insight.[12] Thus they overlooked those scriptures that point to the humiliation of Christ's first advent, and misapplied those that speak of the glory of His second coming. Pride obscured their vision. They interpreted prophecy in accordance with their selfish desires.[13] {*DA* 30.2}

---

[9] A very loose paraphrase, Harris, *TGT* 315, "Reprobating this shameless ostentation as hypocrisy, he assigned to it its only legitimate reward, the notice of man, the barren applause of congenial hypocrisy—and left it withering under the frown of God." Highlighted is from *RH* 3-20-1894 and 2*SP* 108.2.

[10] A loose paraphrase, Harris, *TGT* 315, 316, "Having secularized their religion, and thus prepared themselves for the delusion, their early conquests, their miraculous history, and the glowing descriptions of prophecy combined to foster the expectation of their coming greatness and universal empire; while the galling pressure of the Roman yoke rendered the vision doubly precious, and heightened its splendors, and filled them with a frenzy of impatience to behold it realized." This is consistent with earlier Ellen White statements—4a*SG* (1864) 115, "By many he was looked for to come as a mighty monarch. The Jews had boasted to the Gentiles of his coming, and had dwelt largely upon the great deliverance which he would bring them, that he would reign as king, and put down all authority. Every kingdom and nation would bow to him, and the Jewish nation would reign over them"; *RH* 12-24-1872, "They declared that the power and authority they were then compelled to respect and obey, would soon come to an end; for Messiah would take the throne of David, and, by force of arms, restore the Jews to their liberty, and their exalted privileges"; and *RH* 12-17-1872, "Their ambitious desire was the establishment of a temporal kingdom, which they supposed would reduce the Romans to subjection, and exalt themselves with authority and power to reign over them." Highlighted from *ST* 4-29-1897.

[11] Verbatim words in a similar thought, Harris, *TGT* 315 (see above); highlighted from 2*SP* 41.1.

[12] A similar thought, Harris, *TGT* 315, 316 (see above), building on *Isa. 9:2* and *Matt. 4:16*.

[13] For the last two sentences of the paragraph, a very loose paraphrase, Harris, *TGT* 315 (see above); however, the concept is found in *RH* 12-17-1872, "Had they, with humble minds and spiritual discernment, studied the prophecies, they would not have

Brief analysis and conclusions

No pre-*DA* manuscript for this chapter survives, but we do have the typewritten manuscript for the entire chapter with Ellen White's final handwritten corrections (see p. 58). Chapter 2 of *The Desire of Ages* is less than one half the length of Chapter 1. In it we were able to locate only ten possible borrowings, with only a single source work represented—*The Great Teacher* (1836) by John Harris. Note, however, that the concepts behind these paraphrased statements are found in articles in the *Review and Herald* and in *Spiritual Gifts*, vol. 4a. There might also have been Old Testament source works that would have fed into a composition on this subject, however, in carefully reviewing the possible works from Ellen White's library in this category, we found no literary parallels.

The borrowings for this chapter are mostly loose paraphrases. Out of the seven or eight sentences attributed to Harris, only four have very recognizable literary parallels. One of these is paralleled by a similar thought in the *Review and Herald* that predates Ellen White's access to Harris's book. Though *The Great Teacher* was published in 1836, the flyleaf of her well-worn personal copy of Harris's *The Great Teacher* (pictured to the right) is marked "Purchased in Oakland California." For this reason, though she could possibly have read the book elsewhere, her earliest conceivable opportunity for purchasing the book was the evening of September 25,  1872, when she and James quickly passed through Oakland for the first time on their way to San Francisco.[14] Since Ellen White's sentences in the *Review* articles are not paraphrases of Harris, this would mean that she either quickly and thoroughly digested the content of his book before writing the articles—which would be quite a feat with her busy schedule during these three short months—or she had an understanding of the subject from another source previous to her purchase of the book.

Of the 82 sentences in this chapter, only about 1% is close paraphrase, and another 6% is loose paraphrase. With so little apparent borrowing, one can reasonably say that Chapter 2 of *The Desire of Ages* gives a sampling of Ellen White's writing style—enhanced by Marian Davis's editing—with only traces of "flavoring" from the sources.[15] As Fannie Bolton wrote in 1901, "Sister White as human instrumentality has a pronounced style of her own." That style comes through in this brief chapter.

· · · · · · · · · ·

In our next exhibit, we will examine the literary parallels in *The Desire of Ages*, Chapter 77— "In Pilate's Judgment Hall"—a chapter built on Ellen White's earlier narrative of events that led up to Jesus' crucifixion. This earlier account is found in *Spirit of Prophecy*, vol. 3.

---

been found in so great error as to overlook the prophecies which pointed to his <u>first advent in humility</u>, and misapply those which spoke of his <u>second coming</u> with power and great <u>glory</u>" and 4a*SG* 115.2, 116.3, "They had the events of the <u>first</u> and <u>second</u> comings of Christ <u>confounded together</u>. . . . The self-righteous, <u>proud</u>, unbelieving Jews expected their Saviour and King would come into the world clothed with majesty and power, compelling all Gentiles to yield obedience to him. They did not expect any <u>humiliation</u> and suffering would be manifested in him" (last two sentences carried over into *RH* 12-31-1872).

[14] Arthur L. White, 2*BIO* 356.1. The fall of 1872 is likely when she purchased Daniel March's *Night Scenes in the Bible* (1872), for it was in December of that year that she first used the quotation about "<u>every shadow of uncertainty</u>" (*NS* 201, 202) in her writing (Ltr. 22, 1872 in 2*BIO* 369.5, 370.1), a thought gem she adapted again in 5*T* 69 (written June 20, 1882, see Chapter 7 for full quotation). She mentions that she also bought Melvill's *Sermons* in Oakland [Ltr. 52, 1878].) Interestingly, there were no recognizable parallels found between *TGT* and the *Spirit of Prophecy*, vols. 2 and 3.

[15] Dr. Fred Veltman assessed Chapter 56 to be 99% strictly independent, and the readers of the *LCRP* found 19 other chapters to be virtually parallel free—*DA*, Chapters 6, 9, 20, 22, 30, 34, 38, 42, 43, 44, 48, 50, 59, 60, 61, 68, 70, and 81.

CHAPTER 5
Her Earlier Narrative Refined—
*In Pilate's Judgment Hall**

Chapter 77 of *The Desire of Ages*, like most chapters in the book, is a refinement of a narrative found in *Spirit of Prophecy*. In this chapter, Ellen White enhances her account of the "CONDEMNATION OF JESUS" before Pilate from Chapter 9 of *Spirit of Prophecy*, vol. 3. In this chapter, they are presented side by side, with *Spirit of Prophecy*, vol. 3, on the left and *The Desire of Ages*, Chapter 77, on the right. Paragraphs follow the order of the earlier account, with carry over from 3*SP* into *DA* marked in grey. Such a comparison serves to illustrate how Marian Davis revised Mrs. White's earlier account, using descriptions drawn from her letters, articles, and fresh manuscripts. Marking conventions are those outlined in Chapter 2 of this book. We encourage the reader to take note of explanations in the footnotes regarding possible sources, Scriptural references, and references to her earlier works. Special notice should also be taken of the highlighted material that was carried over from Mrs. White's earlier works. The comparison begins with the first two paragraphs of *The Spirit of Prophecy* that were not carried over into *The Desire of Ages*.

WHEN Jesus was asked the question, Art thou the Son of God? he knew that to answer in the affirmative would make his death certain; a denial would leave a stain upon his humanity.[1] There was a time to be silent, and a time to speak. He had not spoken until plainly interrogated. In his lessons to his disciples he had declared, "Whosoever, therefore, shall confess me before men, him will I confess also before my Father who is in Heaven." When challenged, Jesus did not deny his relationship with God. In that solemn moment his character was at stake and must be vindicated. He left on that occasion an example for man to follow under similar circumstances. He would teach him not to apostatize from his faith to escape suffering or even death. {3*SP* 127.1}

Had the Jews possessed the authority to do so, they would have executed Jesus at once upon the hasty condemnation of their judges; but such power had passed from them into the hands of the Romans, and it was necessary that the case be referred to the proper authorities of that government for final decision. The Jews were anxious to hasten the trial and execution of Jesus, because if it were not brought about at once there would be a delay of a week on account of the immediate celebration of the passover. In that case Jesus would be kept in bonds, and the intense excitement of the mob that was clamoring for his life, would have been allayed, and a natural reaction would have set in. The better part of the people would have become aroused in his behalf, and in all probability his release would be accomplished. The priests and rulers felt that there was no time to lose.[2] {3*SP* 127.2}

---

* This chapter is based on *Matt. 27:2, 11–31; Mark 15:1–20; Luke 23:1–24; John 18:28–40; 19:1–16.*

[1] A loose paraphrase, Hanna (1863), p. 672, "The only way to free his character as a man from the stain of such egregious vanity and presumption, is to recognise him as the Son of the Highest. If the divinity that was in him be denied, the humanity no longer stands stainless." Scripture is verbatim of *Luke 22:70* minus "then."

[2] A loose paraphrase, Hanna, 672, "CHRIST'S trial before the Jewish Sanhedrim closed in his conviction and condemnation. The strange commotion on the bench, in the midst of which the sentence was pronounced, and the outbreak of brutal violence on the part of the menials in the hall, being over, there was an eager and hurried consultation as to how that sentence could most speedily be executed."

The whole Sanhedrim, followed by the multitude, escorted Jesus to the judgment hall of Pilate, the Roman governor, to secure a confirmation of the sentence they had just pronounced. The Jewish priests and rulers could not themselves enter Pilate's hall for fear of ceremonial defilement, which would disqualify them for taking part in the paschal feast.[3] In order to condemn the spotless Son of God, they were compelled to appeal for judgment to one whose threshold they dared not cross for fear of defilement. Blinded by prejudice and cruelty, they could not discern that their passover festival was of no value, since they had defiled their souls by the rejection of Christ.[4] The great salvation that he brought was typified by the deliverance of the children of Israel, which event was commemorated by the feast of the Passover. The innocent lamb slain in Egypt, the blood of which sprinkled upon the door-posts caused the destroying angel to pass over the homes of Israel, prefigured the sinless Lamb of God, whose merits can alone avert the judgment and condemnation of fallen man. The Saviour had been obedient to the Jewish law, and observed all its divinely appointed ordinances. He had just identified himself with the paschal lamb as its great antitype, by connecting the Lord's supper with the Passover. What a bitter mockery then was the ceremony about to be observed by the priestly persecutors of Jesus! {3SP 128.1}

IN the judgment hall of Pilate, the Roman governor, Christ stands bound as a prisoner. About Him are the guard of soldiers, and the hall is fast filling with spectators. Just outside the entrance[5] are the judges of the Sanhedrin, priests, rulers, elders, and the mob.[6] {DA 723.1}

After condemning Jesus, the council of the Sanhedrin had come to Pilate[7] «to have the sentence confirmed» and executed.[8] But these Jewish officials would not enter the Roman judgment hall. According to their ceremonial law they would be defiled thereby, and thus prevented from taking part in the feast of the Passover.[9] In their blindness they did not see that murderous hatred had defiled their hearts. They did not see that Christ was the real Passover lamb, and that, since they had rejected Him, the great feast had for them lost its significance. {DA 723.2}

When the Saviour was brought into the judgment hall, Pilate looked upon Him with no friendly eyes. Assuming his severest expression, he turned to see what kind of man he had to examine, that he had been called from his repose at so early an hour. He knew that it must be someone whom the Jewish authorities were anxious to have tried and punished with haste.[10] {DA 723.3}

---

[3] Fleetwood (1860), p. 338; Jones, p. 372; Farrar (1874), p. 623, and ±Bennett, LHJC (1828), vol. 2, p. 388, are all expanded paraphrases of John 18:28, "and they themselves went not into the judgment hall, lest they should be defiled; but that they might eat the passover." Fleetwood has "priests," "themselves," and "hall"; Farrar has "Jewish" and "ceremonial"; Bennett has "defiled."

[4] Sentences in this paragraph up to this point, a loose paraphrase, Hanna, p. 673, with key verbatim words, "a house to cross whose threshold at such a time as this—on the very eve of the passover—was to disqualify the entrant from all participation in the holy rite."

[5] Based on John 18:28. Highlighted is from MS 112, 1897.

[6] Based on Luke 23:1, "And the whole multitude of them arose . . ."

[7] A very loose paraphrase, Kitto, DBI (1853), vol. 7, p. 409, "THE Sanhedrim had pronounced sentence of death against Jesus; but the power of life and death having been taken from them, the sentence they had given could not be executed without the sanction of the Roman governor."

[8] A very loose paraphrase, Hanna, p. 675, ". . . Pilate meant to open up or re-try the case, or, at least, to get at and go over, upon his own account, the ground of their condemnation ere he ratified it." The unexceptional verbatim phrase "to have the sentence confirmed" is found in Jones (1868), p. 371.

[9] Fleetwood, p. 338; Robinson, Scripture Characters, vol. 2 (1849), p. 437; Kitto (1859), p. 410; and Anderson (1864), p. 674 are all paraphrases of John 18:28. "Prevented" in ±Rufus Clark (1860), p. 269, Edersheim, LTJM (1886), vol. 2, p. 565.

[10] For the last two sentences, a very loose paraphrase of several sentences, Hanna, p. 674. Exact phrase "at so early an hour" (a paraphrase of John 18:28, "it was early") is found in Andrews (1891), p. 536, fn. 4. What is the likelihood that Ellen White got her wording from a footnote in a work—either here or in the other parallels?

Pilate beheld, in the accused, a man bearing the marks of violence, but with a serene and noble countenance and dignified bearing.[11] Many cases had been tried before the Roman governor, but never before had there stood in his presence a man like this. He discovered no trace of crime in his face;[12] and something in the prisoner's appearance excited his sympathy and respect. He turned to the priests, who stood just without the door, and asked, "What accusation bring ye against this man?"[13] {3*SP* 129.1}

The Roman governor had been called from his bedchamber in haste,[14] and he determined to do his work as quickly as possible. He was prepared to deal with the prisoner with magisterial severity. Pilate looked at the men who had Jesus in charge, and then his gaze rested searchingly on Jesus. He had had to deal with all kinds of criminals; but never before had a man bearing marks of such goodness and nobility been brought before him. On His face he saw no sign of guilt, no expression of fear, no boldness or defiance. He saw a man of calm and dignified bearing, whose countenance bore not the marks of a criminal, but the signature of heaven.[15] {*DA* 724.1}

Christ's appearance made a favorable impression upon Pilate.[16] His better nature was roused.[17] He had heard of Jesus and His works.[18] His wife had told him something of the wonderful deeds performed by the Galilean prophet, who cured the sick and raised the dead. Now this revived as a dream in Pilate's mind. He recalled rumors that he had heard from several sources. He resolved to demand of the Jews their charges against the prisoner.[19] {*DA* 724.2}

Who is this Man, and wherefore have ye brought Him? he said. What accusation bring ye against Him? The Jews were disconcerted. Knowing that they could not substantiate their charges against Christ,[20] they did not desire a public examination. They answered that He was a deceiver called Jesus of Nazareth. {*DA* 724.3}

Again Pilate asked, "What accusation bring ye against this Man?"[21] The priests did not answer his question, but in words that showed their

---

[11] Verbatim words in a very loose paraphrase, Jones, p. 373; "dignified" is used in connection with Jesus' appearance in Hanna, pp. 674, 698; and, in connection with His "face" in Jones, though 3*SP* is closer to 1*SG* 53.1f. "He bore no marks of being a criminal.... Even Herod and Pilate were greatly troubled at his noble, GOD-like bearing."

[12] A very loose paraphrase, Hanna, p. 674.

[13] As with many quotations from Christ's trials, Pilate's question, found only in *John 18:29*, is used by multiple source works—Hanna, p. 675; J. S. C. Abbott (1872), p. 128; and Farrar, p. 624.

[14] A very loose paraphrase, Hanna, p. 674.

[15] The whole paragraph, a loose paraphrase, Hanna, p. 674; however, the last two sentences in the paragraph appear to be more like Jones, p. 373, "He saw their purpose: and saw the calm and dignified face before him, the noble expression of features, the grandeur even yet marked upon that brow." However "dignified" is used in connection with Jesus' appearance in Kitto (1853), p. 413, and "dignified" and "criminal" are used in Hanna, pp. 674. 1*SG* 53.1f predates Jones and Hanna with "criminal" and "bearing." Several use "calm" to describe Jesus' demeanor. Highlighted is from MS 40, 1897.

[16] A loose paraphrase, with verbatim words from sentences on separate pages, Hanna, pp. 674 and 675; Ellen White used the expression "favorable impression" in a sermon in *RH* 9-20-1892.

[17] A simple paraphrase, Hanna, p. 675, "there was something in the very first impression that our Lord's appearance made upon Pilate which touched the better part of his nature, and not only stirred within his heart the wish to know what it was of which they accused such a man ..." "Roused" is from previous paragraph.

[18] A simple paraphrase, Andrews, p. 531, "We can scarce doubt, however, that he had some knowledge of Jesus, of His teaching, works, and character." A loose paraphrase, Kitto, p. 411, "It cannot be doubted that Pilate had already heard some things concerning Jesus ..." Hanna, p. 674, a much more tentative paraphrase, "He must have heard something, perhaps much, of Jesus of Nazareth before."

[19] A loose paraphrase, Jones, p. 373.

[20] A paraphrase, Hanna, p. 675, inferred from their insistence in *John 18:30*—"If he were not a malefactor, we would not have delivered him up unto thee."

[21] Verbatim use of Pilate's question of *John 18:29* as in Hanna, p. 675; J. S. C. Abbott, p. 128; and Farrar, p. 624.

They were not prepared for this question. They had not designed to state the particulars of the alleged crime of Jesus. They had expected that Pilate would, without delay, confirm their decision against the Saviour. However they answered him that they had tried the prisoner according to their law and found him deserving of death. **Said they,** "If he were not a malefactor we would not have delivered him up unto thee."[22] But Pilate was not satisfied with the explanation of the Jews, and reminded them of their inability to execute the law. He intimated that if their judgment only was necessary to procure his condemnation, it was useless to bring the prisoner to him.[23] Said he, "Take ye him, and judge him according to your law."[24] {3SP 129.2}

irritation, **they said,** "If He were not a malefactor, we would not have delivered Him up unto thee."[25] When those composing the Sanhedrin, the first men of the nation, bring to you a man they deem worthy of death, is there need to ask for an accusation against him?[26] They hoped to impress Pilate with a sense of their importance, and thus lead him to accede to their request without going through many preliminaries. They were eager to have their sentence ratified;[27] for they knew that the people who had witnessed Christ's marvelous works could tell a story very different from the fabrication[28] they themselves were now rehearsing. {DA 724.4}

The priests thought that «with the weak and vacillating» Pilate they could carry through their plans without trouble.[29] Before this he had signed the death warrant hastily,[30] condemning to death men they knew were not worthy of death.[31] In his estimation the life of a prisoner was of little account; whether he were innocent or guilty was of no special consequence. The priests hoped that Pilate would now inflict the death penalty on Jesus without giving Him a hearing. This they besought as a favor on the occasion of their great national festival.[32] {DA 724.5}

But there was something in the prisoner[33] that held Pilate back from this. He dared not do it. He read the purposes of the priests.[34] He remembered how, not long before, Jesus had raised Lazarus, a man that had been dead four days; and he determined to know, before signing the sentence of condemnation, what were the charges against Him,[35] and whether they could be proved. {DA 725.1}

If your judgment is sufficient, he said, why bring the prisoner to me? "Take ye Him, and judge Him according to your law." Thus

[22] The priests' response of *John 18:30*, used in Hanna, p. 675; Abbott, p. 128; ⊥Clark (1860), p. 269; Farrar, p. 624; and Jones, p. 373.

[23] A loose paraphrase from *John 18:31*, Hanna, p. 676.

[24] Pilate's retort of *John 18:31* in Hanna, p. 676 (slightly paraphrased); Abbott, p. 128; Farrar, p. 624; and Jones, p. 373.

[25] The priests' response of *John 18:30* in Hanna, p. 675, and at least four other source works, though Hanna is not specific about who was speaking.

[26] A paraphrase, Hanna, p. 675, using "worthy of death" from *Luke 23:15*.

[27] A very loose paraphrase, Hanna, p. 675, using verbatim word "ratified" but from the Jewish leaders' point of view rather than from Pilate's.

[28] A word possibly derived from the phrase "fabricate such a crime" of Hanna, p. 677.

[29] A loose paraphrase with a verbatim partial phrase, Hanna, p. 676; "weak" and "vacillating" are used by many authors to describe Pilate. See ±Cumming, *Luke SR-Lk* (1854) 498, and Robert Boyd, *WH* (1873) 380.

[30] A paraphrase, ±Deems, *WWJ* (1880) 646, and ⊥Thayer (1891), p. 321. "Death warrant" is used in Hanna, p. 675. (Deems seems to parallel many expressions in Hanna. Because it was not in Ellen White's libraries, it is less likely as a source.)

[31] To this point in the paragraph, a loose paraphrase, Hanna, p. 675, using "worthy of death" from *Luke 23:15*, a very common expression in the sources (see Hanna, p. 692).

[32] A loose paraphrase, Hanna, p. 675, "doom him to death. They had hoped that to save himself the trouble of investigation, and in compliment to them at this passover season ..."

[33] Near verbatim "there was something in this prisoner which strangely influenced him;" ±Deems, p. 655, and Hanna, p. 675, "there was something in the very first impression that our Lord's appearance made upon Pilate ..." Ellen White used the assimilated expression in a sermon in *RH* 8-27-1895, "There was something in his countenance that awed and terrified them."

[34] To this point, a loose paraphrase, Jones, p. 373.

[35] A paraphrase, Pentecost, *BS '88*, p. 177, inferred from *John 18:29*.

The treacherous priests felt that they were outwitted; they saw that it would not do to specify the grounds for their condemnation of Jesus. The charge of blasphemy would be regarded by Pilate as the expression of religious bigotry and priestly jealousy; and the case would be at once dismissed. But if they could excite the apprehensions of the Roman governor that Jesus was a leader of sedition, their purpose would be accomplished. Tumults and insurrections were constantly arising among the Jews against the Roman government, for many affirmed that it was against the Jewish law to pay tribute to a foreign power. The authorities had found it necessary to deal very rigorously with these revolts among the people, and were constantly on the watch for developments of that character, in order to suppress them at once. But Jesus had always been obedient to the reigning power. When the scheming priests sought to entrap him by sending spies to him with the question, "Is it lawful to render tribute to Cæsar?"[36] he had directed their attention to the image and superscription of Caesar upon the tribute money, and answered, "Render unto Cæsar the things which are Cæsar's."[37] Jesus himself had paid tribute and had taught his disciples to do so. {3SP 129.3}

pressed, the priests said that they had already passed sentence upon Him, but that they must have Pilate's sentence to render their condemnation valid. What is your sentence? Pilate asked. The death sentence, they answered; but it is not lawful for us to put any man to death. They asked Pilate to take their word as to Christ's guilt, and enforce their sentence.[38] They would take the responsibility of the result. {DA 725.2}

Pilate was not a just or a conscientious judge; but weak though he was in moral power,[39] he refused[40] to grant this request. He would not condemn Jesus until a charge had been brought against Him. {DA 725.3}

The priests were in a dilemma. They saw that they must cloak their hypocrisy under the thickest concealment. They must not allow it to appear that Christ had been arrested on religious grounds.[41] Were this put forward as a reason, their proceedings would have no weight with Pilate. They must make it appear that Jesus was working against the common law; then He could be punished as a political offender.[42] Tumults and insurrection against the Roman government were constantly arising among the Jews. With these revolts the Romans had dealt very rigorously, and they were constantly on the watch to repress everything that could lead to an outbreak. {DA 725.4}

Only a few days before this the Pharisees had tried to entrap Christ with the question, "Is it lawful for us to give tribute unto Caesar?"[43] but Christ had unveiled their hypocrisy. The Romans who were present had seen the utter failure of the plotters, and their discomfiture at His answer, "Render therefore unto Caesar the things which be Caesar's."[44] Luke 20:22–25. {DA 725.5}

---

[36] Same *unique* use of the question of **Mark 12:14**, "Is it lawful to give tribute to Caesar, or not?" as in Hanna, p. 677, suggested by **Luke 23:2**, though Hanna turns Jesus' question into a statement— "These very men . . . had tried to get him to pass his judgment upon the abstract question as to whether it was lawful to pay tribute to Cæsar or not . . ."

[37] Same use of **Matt. 22:21** as in +Cumming, *SR-Lk* 493.

[38] A few verbatim words and use of *John 18:31* as by Hanna, pp. 675, 676, and at least three other source works. Highlighted is from MS 51, 1897.

[39] Words used in Abbott, p. 129.

[40] Hanna, p. 676, has "weak" and "refusal" (separated by four sentences), though the refusal itself is found in *John 18:31*.

[41] A loose paraphrase, Hanna, p. 676, inferred from their political accusation in *Luke 23:2*. Only later did they reveal the religious nature of their condemnation (see *John 19:7*).

[42] The thought that Jesus was being tried as a "political offender" and not as a "religious" one is a possible loose paraphrase, Kitto, p. 410, "The Sanhedrim, therefore, concluded most dishonestly to shift their ground, and to present to Pilate, as a political offender dangerous to Rome . . ." Same thought with verbatim "common law" is in Hanna, p. 677.

[43] Same *unique* use of the question of **Mark 12:14** as in Hanna, p. 677, though Hanna converts Jesus' question into a statement.

[44] Verbatim use of **Luke 20:25** unlike any source.

In their extremity the priests called the false witnesses to their aid. "And they began to accuse him, saying, We found this fellow perverting the nation, and forbidding to give tribute to Cæsar, saying that he himself is Christ, a king."[45] {3SP 130.1}

Pilate was not deceived by this testimony. He now became confident that a deep plot had been laid to destroy an innocent man, who stood in the way of the Jewish dignitaries.[46] He turned to the prisoner and "asked him, saying, Art thou the King of the Jews? And he answered him and said, Thou sayest it."[47] Jesus stood before Pilate, pale, bruised, and faint from loss of sleep and food. He had been hurried from place to place, and subjected to insult and violence; yet his bearing was noble, and his countenance was lighted as though a sunbeam were shining upon it. {3SP 130.2}

Now the priests thought to make it appear that on this occasion Christ had taught what they hoped He would teach.[48] In their extremity they called false witnesses to their aid, "and they began to accuse Him, saying, We found this fellow perverting the nation, and forbidding to give tribute to Caesar, saying that He Himself is Christ a King."[49] Three charges, each without foundation. The priests knew this,[50] but they were willing to commit perjury could they but secure their end. {DA 725.6}

Pilate saw through their purpose. He did not believe that the prisoner had plotted against the government.[51] His meek and humble appearance was altogether out of harmony with the charge. Pilate was convinced that a deep plot had been laid to destroy an innocent man[52] who stood in the way of the Jewish dignitaries. Turning to Jesus he asked, "Art Thou the King of the Jews?" The Saviour answered, "Thou sayest it"[53] And as He spoke, His countenance lighted up as if a sunbeam were shining upon it. {DA 726.1}

---

[45] Verbatim use of **Luke 23:2** as in Hanna, p. 677; ±Clark, p. 270; ±Cumming, SR-Lk 493; and Jones, p. 373, though no source work quotes "and they began to accuse Him, saying . . ." 3SP varies from one time to another as to which author it matches in Scripture use.

[46] A loose paraphrase, Hanna, p. 678, "He did not entertain, because he did not believe the charge of his being a seditious and rebellious subject." However, this can be inferred from **Matt. 27:18**, "For he knew that for envy they had delivered him," and 1SG 54.1 has the same thought: "Pilate from the first was convicted that he was no common man, but an excellent character. He believed him to be entirely innocent." The word "plot" is used by many authors. Phrase "innocent man" was used in Hanna (1863), p. 716; Neander (1848), p. 417; ±Richard C. Trench, SG (1867) 294; and ±Ingraham, PHD (1855) 384, 386, 387. "Innocent" is from **Matt. 27:4**.

[47] The verbatim statements of Pilate and Jesus of **Luke 23:3** (or **Mark 15:2**), Hanna, p. 678 (though Hanna adds "—I am the king of the Jews"); ±Cumming, SR-Lk 493, 494; and Jones, p. 374. That of Pilate alone is used by ±Clark, p. 270; Farrar, p. 625; Kitto, p. 412; and Neander, (1848) p. 414. Only ±Clark has "asked him, saying."

[48] A very loose paraphrase, ±Cumming, SR-Lk 493, "First of all, when the multitude came to Pilate, 'they began to accuse him,' that is, Jesus, alleging against him falsehoods which his whole life contradicted." Ellen White is more specific than Cumming—it is the priests who make the allegations.

[49] Verbatim use of Luke 23:2 as in Hanna, p. 677, and in at least three source works, though none quotes the introductory phrase as does Ellen White.

[50] A very loose paraphrase, Hanna, p. 677, "They here bring three different accusations against him, not one of which—in that sense in which alone they desire that Pilate should understand them—they know is true; and one of which, the second, they know is absolutely, and in every sense of it, false." Verbatim phrase "three charges" is from Farrar, p. 625.

[51] To this point, a paraphrase, Hanna, pp. 677, 678, "Pilate had no faith in their sincerity. He saw through their designs. Perhaps it was now that, for the first time, he recognized that it was with Jesus of Nazareth, of whom he had heard so much, that he had to do. He did not entertain, because he did not believe, the charge of his being a seditious and rebellious subject." His statement can be inferred from Matt. 27:18, "For he knew that for envy they had delivered him."

[52] A loose paraphrase with verbatim phrase, Hanna, p. 683, verbatim word "plot" is from a separate paragraph; highlighted is from MS 112, 1897 and 3SP 130.2; a similar thought is in Farrar, p. 626, and in 1SG 54.1. Phrase "innocent man" used by many sources. "Innocent" is from Matt. 27:4.

[53] Verbatim statements from Luke 23:3 (or Mark 15:2) are used in Hanna, p. 678, and in at least three other source works.

When his answer was heard by Caiaphas, who stood at the threshold of the judgment hall, the high priest joined with others in calling Pilate to witness that Jesus had admitted his crime by this answer, which was a virtual acknowledgment that he was seeking to establish a throne in Judah in opposition to the power of Cæsar. Priests, scribes, and rulers, all united in noisy denunciations of Jesus, and in importuning Pilate to pronounce sentence of death upon him. The lawless uproar of the infuriated priests and dignitaries of the temple confused the senses of the Roman governor. Finally, when some measure of quiet was secured, he again addressed Jesus, saying, "Answerest thou nothing? behold how many things they witness against thee. But Jesus yet answered nothing; so that Pilate marveled."[54] The silence of the Saviour perplexed him. He saw in the prisoner no marks of a seditious character, and he had no confidence in the accusations of the priests.[55] Hoping to gain the truth from him, and to escape from the clamor of the excited crowd, he requested Jesus to step with him into his house. When he had done so, and the two were alone, Pilate turned to Jesus, and in a respectful voice asked him, "Art thou the King of the Jews?"[56] {3SP 131.1}

When they heard His answer, Caiaphas and those that were with him called Pilate to witness that Jesus had admitted the crime with which He was charged. With noisy cries, priests, scribes, and rulers demanded that He be sentenced to death. The cries were taken up by the mob, and the uproar was deafening. Pilate was confused. Seeing that Jesus made no answer to His accusers, Pilate said to Him, "Answerest Thou nothing? Behold how many things they witness against Thee. But Jesus yet answered nothing."[57] {DA 726.2}

Standing behind Pilate, in view of all in the court, Christ heard the abuse; but to all the false charges against Him He answered not a word.[58] His whole bearing gave evidence of conscious innocence. He stood unmoved by the fury of the waves that beat about Him. It was as if the heavy surges of wrath, rising higher and higher, like the waves of the boisterous ocean, broke about him, but did not touch Him.[59] He stood silent, but His silence was eloquence.[60] It was a light shining from the inner to the outer man. {DA 726.3}

Pilate was astonished at His bearing.[61] Does this Man disregard the proceedings because He does not care to save His life? he asked himself.[62] As he looked at Jesus, bearing insult and mockery without retaliation, he felt that He could not be as unrighteous and unjust as were the clamoring priests.[63] Hoping to gain the truth from Him and to escape the tumult of the crowd, Pilate took Jesus aside with him, and again questioned, "Art Thou the King of the Jews?"[64] {DA 726.4}

[54] Use of *Mark 15:4, 5* unlike sources.

[55] Two words used in Hanna, pp. 677, 678, though "sedition" is in *Luke 23:25* and "accusation" in *John 18:29*.

[56] Hanna, p. 678, has the verbatim repetition of the question of *John 18:33*, "Art thou the King of the Jews?"

[57] Verbatim use of *Mark 15:4, 5* unlike sources.

[58] Near verbatim, ±Didon, pp. 338, "Jesus answered him not a word," a paraphrase of *Matt. 27:12*, "he answered nothing," and *Luke 23:9*, "he answered him nothing." Phrase "not a word" by itself is used in Boyd, *WH* 382; ±Deems, pp. 650, 651; and Edersheim, *LTJM* (1886), vol. 2, p. 563; and by Ellen White in various sermons, e.g. *RH* 1-4-1887.

[59] A loose paraphrase, Edersheim, p. 571, 572, "It was as if the surging of the wild waves broke far beneath against the base of the rock, which, untouched, reared its head far aloft to the heavens. But as He stood in the calm silence of Majesty, Pilate greatly wondered. Did this Man not even fear death; was He so conscious of innocence . . ." Also a possible loose paraphrase, Hanna, p. 681, which uses "whole," "bearing," and "innocence."

[60] A loose paraphrase, Pentecost, *BS '88*, p. 178, and *BS '89* 344. Hanna, p. 682, and ±Didon, p. 338, also use the word "silence," implied by *Matt. 27:14* and *Mark 15:5*, "Jesus yet answered nothing; so that Pilate marvelled."

[61] ±Didon, p. 338, "His silence astonished Pilate," implied by *Mark 15:5* and *Matt. 27:14* "And he answered him to never a word; insomuch that the governor marvelled greatly."

[62] A simple paraphrase, Edersheim, p. 572 (see above).

[63] A very loose paraphrase, Farrar, p. 626.

[64] Hanna, p. 678, has Pilate's repetition of the question of *John 18:33*.

Page 70

Jesus did not directly answer this question. He knew that conviction was awakened in the heart of Pilate, and he wished to give him an opportunity to acknowledge how far his mind had been influenced in the right direction. He therefore answered, "Sayest thou this thing of thyself, or did others tell it thee of me?"[65] The Saviour wished a statement from Pilate whether his question arose from the accusations just made by the Jews, or from his desire to receive light from Christ. Pilate longed for a more intelligent faith. The dignified bearing of Jesus, and his calm self-possession when placed in a position where there would naturally be developed a spirit of hate and revenge, astonished Pilate and won his deep respect. The direct question just asked him by Jesus was immediately understood by him, which evidenced that his soul was stirred by conviction. But pride rose in the heart of the Roman judge and overpowered the Spirit of God.[66] "Pilate answered, Am I a Jew? Thine own nation and the chief priests have delivered thee unto me; what hast thou done?"[67] {3SP 131.2}

Pilate's golden opportunity had passed.[68] Jesus, however, did not leave him without farther light. At his desire God sent an angel to Pilate's wife; and, in a dream, she was shown the pure life and holy character of the man who was about to be consigned to a cruel death. Jesus did not directly answer the question of Pilate as to what he had done; but he plainly stated to him his mission:— {3SP 132.1}

"My kingdom is not of this world; if my kingdom were of this world, then would my servants fight, that I should not be delivered to the Jews; but now is my kingdom not from hence. Pilate therefore said unto him, Art thou a king then? Jesus answered,

Jesus did not directly answer this question. He knew that the Holy Spirit was striving with Pilate, and He gave him opportunity to acknowledge his conviction. "Sayest thou this thing of thyself," He asked, "or did others tell it thee of Me?"[69] That is, was it the accusations of the priests, or a desire to receive light from Christ, that prompted Pilate's question? Pilate understood Christ's meaning; but pride arose in his heart. He would not acknowledge the conviction that pressed upon him.[70] "Am I a Jew?" he said. "Thine own nation and the chief priests have delivered Thee unto me; what hast Thou done?"[71] {DA 726.5}

Pilate's golden opportunity had passed.[72] Yet Jesus did not leave him without further light. While He did not directly answer Pilate's question, He plainly stated His own mission. He gave Pilate to understand that He was not seeking an earthly throne. {DA 727.1}

"My kingdom is not of this world," He said; "if My kingdom were of this world, then would My servants fight, that I should not be delivered to the Jews; but now is My kingdom not from hence. Pilate therefore said unto Him, Art Thou a king then? Jesus answered,

---

[65] Verbatim use of *John 18:34* as in Hanna, p. 678, and in Neander, p. 414; with slightly different wording, in Abbot, p. 128; Farrar, pp. 625, 626; and Jones, p. 374.

[66] A strict paraphrase, Hanna, p. 679, "The pride of the Roman, the judge, swells up within his breast, overbearing his eternal interests as a man, a sinner—and so he haughtily replies: 'Am I a Jew?'"

[67] Verbatim use of *John 18:35* as in Abbott, p. 128. Verbatim quoting of Pilate in Hanna, p. 679; Jones, p. 374; and, with slight paraphrasing, in Farrar, p. 626.

[68] A very loose paraphrase, Farrar, p. 629, "And now came the golden opportunity for him to vindicate the grandeur of his country's imperial justice ..."; Hanna, p. 679, "The chance of reaching ... has passed"; however, "golden opportunity" was a familiar expression for Mrs. White. In Ltr. 9, 1876, April 18, for example, she wrote: "Now seems to be my golden opportunity."

[69] Verbatim use of *John 18:34* as in Hanna, p. 678; Neander, p. 414; and, with slightly different wording, in at least three other source works.

[70] A very loose paraphrase, Hanna, p. 679.

[71] Verbatim use of *John 18:35* as in Abbott, p. 128. Verbatim words of Pilate as in Hanna, p. 679; Jones, p. 374; and, with slight paraphrasing, in Farrar, p. 626.

[72] A very loose paraphrase, Farrar, p. 629; however, the last word "passed" is used by Hanna, p. 679, in a similar thought. "Golden opportunity" was a familiar expression for Mrs. White.

Thou sayest that I am a king. To this end was I born, and for this cause came I into the world, that I should bear witness unto the truth. Every one that is of the truth heareth my voice."[73] {*3SP* 132.2}

Jesus thus sought to convince Pilate that he was innocent of aspiring to kingly honors upon earth. Pilate had been confused by the disturbed and divided elements of the religious world, and his mind grasped eagerly at the words of Jesus declaring that he had come into the world to bear witness to the truth. Pilate had heard many voices cry, Here is the truth! I have the truth![74] But this man, arraigned as a criminal, who claimed to have the truth, stirred his heart with a great longing to know what it was, and how it could be obtained. He inquired of Jesus, "What is truth?"[75] But «he did not wait for» a reply;[76] the tumult of the excited crowd was continually increasing; their impatient cries jarred upon his ears, and recalled him to his judicial position. He went out to the Jews, who stood beyond the door of the hall, and declared in an emphatic[77] voice, "I find in him no fault at all."[78] {*3SP* 132.3}

Those words, traced by the pen of inspiration, will forever stand as a proof to the world of the base perfidy[79] and falsehood of the Jews in their charges against Jesus. Even the heathen magistrate pronounced him innocent.[80]

---

[73] Verbatim use of the statements of Pilate and Jesus in *John 18:36, 37* as in Hanna, p. 680; Jones, p. 374; and, with slight paraphrasing, in Abbott, p. 128.

[74] A very loose paraphrase, Hanna, p. 680, "Truth, moral truth, religious truth, was the one proclaimed object of research, of which some were saying, Lo, here it is, and others, Lo, there it is . . ."

[75] Verbatim use of Pilate's question of *John 18:38* as in Hanna, p. 680, and in at least nine other source works.

[76] Nearly verbatim sentence from Jones, p. 374, "He did not wait for an answer to this question, but went out before the expectant crowds, who were eager for his return." Implied by his not waiting for an answer to his question before returning to the crowd in *John 18:38*.

[77] The nearly verbatim word "emphatically" is from Hanna, p. 680. Fleetwood, p. 341, also has "out to the Jews," a phrase based on *John 18:32*, "he went out again to the Jews, and saith. . ."

[78] Verbatim use of Pilate's declaration of *John 18:38* as used in Hanna, p. 680; Abbott, p. 128; and Farrar, p. 626.

[79] "Perfidy" means "treachery."

[80] A common verbatim word, Farrar, p. 626.

Thou sayest that I am a king. To this end was I born, and for this cause came I into the world, that I should bear witness unto the truth. Everyone that is of the truth heareth My voice."[81] {*DA* 727.2}

Christ affirmed that His word was in itself a key which would unlock the mystery to those who were prepared to receive it. It had a self-commending power, and this was the secret of the spread of His kingdom of truth. He desired Pilate to understand that only by receiving and appropriating truth could his ruined nature be reconstructed.[82] {*DA* 727.3}

Pilate had a desire to know the truth. His mind was confused. He eagerly grasped the words of the Saviour, and his heart was stirred with a great longing to know what it really was, and how he could obtain it. "What is truth?"[83] he inquired. But «he did not wait for an answer».[84] The tumult outside recalled him to the interests of the hour; for the priests were clamorous for immediate action. Going out to the Jews, he declared emphatically, "I find in Him no fault at all."[85] {*DA* 727.4}

These words from a heathen judge were a scathing rebuke to the perfidy and falsehood of the rulers of Israel who were accusing the Saviour.

---

[81] Verbatim use of the statements of Pilate and Jesus in *John 18:36, 37* as in Hanna, p. 680; Jones, p. 374; and, with slight paraphrasing, in Abbott, p. 128.

[82] Thought of this paragraph not found in Hanna.

[83] Verbatim use of Pilate's question of *John 18:38*, as in Hanna, p. 680, and in at least nine other source works.

[84] Verbatim sentence, a partial sentence in Jones, p. 374, "He did not wait for an answer to this question . . ." Implied by *John 18:38*, this self-evident fact would hardly require footnoting.

[85] A loosely paraphrased sentence with the verbatim use of Pilate's declaration of *John 18:38*, prefaced by the verbatim word "emphatically" of Hanna, p. 680.

As Pilate thus spoke, the rage and disappointment of the priests and elders knew no bounds.[86] They had made great efforts to accomplish the death of Jesus, and now that there appeared to be a prospect of his release they seemed ready to tear him in pieces. They lost all reason and self-control, and gave vent to curses and maledictions against him, behaving more like demons than men. They were loud in their censures of Pilate, and threatened the vengeance of the Roman law against him if he refused to condemn one who, they affirmed, had set himself up against Caesar. {3SP 133.1}

During all this uproar, Jesus stood unmoved,[87] uttering no word in answer to the abuse that was heaped upon him. He had spoken freely to Pilate when alone with him, that the light of his truth might illuminate the darkened understanding of the Roman governor; and now he could say nothing more to prevent him from committing the fearful act of condemning to death the Son of God. Pilate turned again to Jesus and inquired, "Hearest thou not how many things they witness against thee?[88] And he answered him to never a word; insomuch that the governor marveled greatly." {3SP 133.2}

Angry voices were now heard, declaring that the seditious influence of Jesus was well known throughout all the country.[89] Said they, "He stirreth up the people, teaching throughout all Jewry, beginning from Galilee to this place."[90] Pilate at this time had no thought of condemning Jesus, because he was certain that he was the victim of the envious and designing priests. As he afterward stated to Jesus, he had the power to condemn or to release him; but he dreaded the ill-will of the people; so when he heard that Jesus was a Galilean and was under the jurisdiction of Herod, he embraced the opportunity to spare himself from farther difficulty, and refused to decide

As the priests and elders heard this from Pilate, their disappointment and rage knew no bounds.[91] They had long plotted and waited for this opportunity. As they saw the prospect of the release of Jesus, they seemed ready to tear Him in pieces. They loudly denounced Pilate, and threatened him with the censure of the Roman government. They accused him of refusing to condemn Jesus, who, they affirmed, had set Himself up against Caesar. {DA 727.5}

Angry voices were now heard, declaring that the seditious influence of Jesus was well known throughout the country,[92] The priests said, "He stirreth up the people, teaching throughout all Jewry, beginning from Galilee to this place."[93] {DA 728.1}

Pilate at this time had no thought of condemning Jesus. He knew that the Jews had accused Him through hatred and prejudice. He knew what his duty was. Justice demanded that Christ should be immediately released. But Pilate dreaded the ill will of the people. Should he refuse to give Jesus into their hands, a tumult would be raised, and this he feared to meet.[94] When he heard that Christ was from Galilee, he decided to

---

[86] A very loose paraphrase, ±Clark, p. 271, "This announcement, so contrary to their expectations and wishes, filled them with the greatest rage." Farrar, p. 650, also uses "rage," inferred from "more fierce" of *Luke 23:5*.

[87] Same thought, using verbatim word "unmoved," Hanna, p. 681.

[88] "Had spoken freely to Pilate" is used in *DA* 736.4. Verbatim use of Pilate's question in *Matt. 27:13* as in Hanna, p. 682, and in ±John Flavel, *The Whole Works of* (1716), vol. 1, sermon 24, neither using *Matt. 27:14*.

[89] A very loose paraphrase of *Luke 23:5*, with verbatim words, Hanna, p. 683, "the setting forth of Christ as a ringleader of sedition. 'He stirreth up the people,' . . . preaching rebellion through the whole country . . ."

[90] Verbatim use of their reply of *Luke 23:5* as in Abbott, p. 130; ±Cumming, *SR-Lk*, p. 494; Jones, p. 375; and, with slight rewording, ±Clark, p. 271. Hanna, p. 683, has only "He stirreth up the people."

[91] A very loose paraphrase, ±Clark, p. 271, based on *Luke 23:5*.

[92] A very loose paraphrase of *Luke 23:5*, using verbatim words from Hanna, p. 683.

[93] Verbatim use of *Luke 23:5* as in Abbott, p. 130, and in at least three other source works.

[94] To this point in the paragraph, a paraphrase with verbatim words, ±Didon (1893), pp. 337, 338, though the first sentence is from *3SP* (1878) 134.1. Highlighted is from MS 51, 1897.

the case, sending him to Herod, who was then in Jerusalem.[95] {3SP 134.1}

Jesus was faint and weary from loss of sleep and food, and the ill-treatment he had received; yet his suffering condition awakened no pity in the hearts of his persecutors. He was dragged away to the judgment hall of Herod amid the hooting and insults of the merciless mob. Besides escaping responsibility in regard to the trial of Jesus, Pilate thought this would be a good opportunity to heal an old «quarrel between himself and Herod».[96] He thought that this act on his part would be regarded by Herod as an acknowledgment of his superior authority, and would thus bring about a reconciliation. In this he was not wrong, for the two magistrates made friends over the trial of the Saviour.[97] {3SP 134.2}

When Herod had first heard of Jesus and the mighty works wrought by him, he was terror-stricken, and said, "It is John whom I beheaded; he is risen from the dead;" "therefore mighty works do show forth themselves in him."[98] Herod had never before met Jesus,

send Him to Herod, the ruler of that province, who was then in Jerusalem.[99] By this course, Pilate thought to shift the responsibility of the trial from himself to Herod.[100] He also thought this a good opportunity to heal an old «quarrel between himself and Herod».[101] And so it proved. The two magistrates made friends over the trial of the Saviour.[102] {DA 728.2}

Pilate delivered Jesus again to the soldiers, and amid the jeers and insults of the mob He was hurried to the judgment hall of Herod. "When Herod saw Jesus, he was exceeding glad." He had never before met the Saviour, but "he was desirous to see Him of a long season, because he had heard many things of Him; and he hoped to have seen some miracle done by Him."[103] This Herod was he whose hands were stained with the blood of John the Baptist.[104] When Herod first heard of Jesus, he was terror-stricken, and said, "It is John, whom I beheaded; he is risen from the dead;" "therefore mighty works do show forth themselves in him."[105] Mark 6:16; Matt. 14:2. {DA 728.3}

---

[95] A paraphrase of *Luke 23:7*, "he sent him to Herod, who himself also was at Jerusalem at that time." Phrase "then in Jerusalem" is used in ±Angus (1853), p. 258, "But hearing that He had been in Galilee, under Herod's jurisdiction, and that Herod was then in Jerusalem . . ."

[96] A paraphrase of *Luke 23:12*, "And the same day Pilate and Herod were made friends together: for before they were at enmity between themselves," Hanna, p. 684, "Herod recognized and appreciated the compliment; and whatever else Pilate lost by the line of conduct he pursued that day, he at least gained this—he got the quarrel between himself and Herod healed." (See context in Appendix A.) ±Angus, p. 258, has "heal" and "old." The word "quarrel" was used in *Mark 6:19* of Herodias' attitude toward John the Baptist.

[97] A paraphrase with verbatim words, ±Angus, p. 258, "he sent Him to that king—an act of courtesy against Christ, which healed old feuds and made the two governors friends." The words "made friends," from *Luke 23:12*, were used in *1SG 55.1*.

[98] *1SG 55.1*, "His murdering John left a stain upon his conscience which he could not free himself from, and when he heard of Jesus, and the mighty works done by him, he thought it was John risen from the dead." Hanna, p. 687, quotes from *Matt. 14:2*, while 3SP 135.1 quotes from *Mark 6:16* and *Matt. 14:2*. The single word "terror" is used in Hanna, p. 689.

[99] A paraphrase of *Luke 23:7*, "he sent him to Herod, who himself also was at Jerusalem at that time." Phrase "then in Jerusalem" is found in ±Angus, p. 258.

[100] A paraphrase, Hanna, p. 684, "Pilate will send the case to him; and thus get the responsibility of deciding it shifted from his own shoulders, by laying it upon one who not only may be quite willing to assume it, but may regard as a compliment the reference of the case to his adjudication." ±Deems (1880), p. 652, apparently borrowing from Hanna, has "shifted the responsibility." The thought of *shifting the responsibility* is implied by *Luke 23:7*. Matthew, Mark, and John do not mention the trial before Herod.

[101] A paraphrase of the phrase "at enmity" of *Luke 23:12*, using "quarrel," Hanna, p. 684 (context in Appendix A).

[102] A paraphrase with verbatim words, ±Angus, p. 258. The words "made friends," from *Luke 23:12*, were used in *1SG 55.1*.

[103] Verbatim use of *Luke 23:8*.

[104] A very loose paraphrase, Hanna, p. 687, "when he looks at Jesus, it is with no disturbing remembrances of that bloody head once brought to him upon a charger . . ." Highlighted in this paragraph is from MS 112, 1897.

[105] Verbatim carried over from *1SG 55.1*. Hanna, p. 687, quotes from *Matt. 14:2*, while Ellen White quotes from *Mark 6:16* and *Matt. 14:2*. "Terror" used in Hanna, p. 689.

but he had long desired to see him,[106] and witness his marvelous power. He was pleased that he was brought to him a prisoner, for he made no doubt that he could force him to work a miracle[107] as a condition of saving his life. Herod's conscience[108] was far less sensitive than when he had trembled with horror at the request of Herodias for the head of John the Baptist. For a time he had felt the keen stings of remorse[109] for the terrible act he had committed to gratify the revenge of a cruel woman; but his moral perceptions had become more and more degraded by his licentious life,[110] till his sins appeared but trifles in his eyes. The men who are capable of the worst crimes are those who have once been convicted by the Spirit of truth, and have turned away from the light into the darkness of iniquity. Herod had very nearly become a disciple of John; but at the very point of decision, he had fallen into the snare of Satan and put to death one whom he knew to be a true prophet. {3SP 135.1}

As the Saviour was brought before Herod, the rabble surged and pressed about, crying out against the prisoner, some charging him with one crime and some with another. Herod commanded silence and directed that Jesus be unbound, for he wished to interrogate him.

Yet Herod desired to see Jesus.[111] Now there was opportunity to save the life of this prophet, and the king hoped to banish forever from his mind the memory of that bloody head brought to him in a charger.[112] He also desired to have his curiosity gratified,[113] and thought that if Christ were given any prospect of release, He would do anything that was asked of Him.[114] {DA 728.3}

Herod's conscience was now far less sensitive than when he had trembled with horror at the request of Herodias for the head of John the Baptist. For a time he had felt the keen stings of remorse for his terrible act; but his moral perceptions had become more and more degraded by his licentious life.[115] Now his heart had become so hardened that he could even boast of the punishment he had inflicted upon John for daring to reprove him. And he now threatened Jesus, declaring repeatedly that he had power to release or to condemn Him. But no sign from Jesus gave evidence that He heard a word.[116] {DA 730.1}

A large company of the priests and elders had accompanied Christ to Herod. And when the Saviour was brought in, these dignitaries, all speaking excitedly, urged their accusations against Him. But Herod paid little regard to their charges. He commanded silence, desiring an opportunity to question Christ.[117]

---

[106] Paraphrase of *Luke 9:9* and *Luke 23:8*, Hanna, p. 687, and Farrar, p. 628; but see earlier 1SG 55.1, "Herod was glad to see JESUS."

[107] Similar phrase "working of miracles" in Hanna, p. 688.

[108] Loose paraphrase and commonly used verbatim word "conscience" in Hanna, p. 687, but see 1SG 55.1, "Herod was hardened."

[109] Verbatim phrase "stings of remorse" is from Hanna, p. 686.

[110] From "Herod's conscience" to this point, a very loose paraphrase from two separate paragraphs in Hanna, pp. 686 and 687, using words "for a . . . time," "stings of remorse," and "licentiousness."

[111] Paraphrase of *Luke 9:9* and *23:8*, "He desired to see him" Hanna, p. 687, and Farrar, p. 628.

[112] A paraphrase, Hanna, p. 687, "He has come to be once more on such good terms with himself; so much at ease, that when he looks at Jesus, it is with no disturbing remembrances of that bloody head once brought to him upon a charger . . ." Verbatim words "head," "charger," and "brought" are from *Matt. 14:8, 11*.

[113] Hanna, pp. 674, 688, 689; Farrar, p. 628; Edersheim, p. 572; Kitto, p. 413; Neander (1848), p. 415; ±Didon, p. 339; and ±Deems, p. 651, all use the word "curiosity." Except for Neander, all are predated by 1SG 55.1, which has "gratify his curiosity." There is no evidence that Ellen White had Neander at this early date.

[114] From the first of the paragraph to this point, a very loose paraphrase, Hanna, p. 687.

[115] To this point, a paraphrase, Hanna, pp. 686, 687.

[116] ±Deems (1880), pp. 650, 651, uses "licentious," "life," "time," "conscience," and "hardened," though the unique words "life" and "time" are from 3SP (1878) 135.1, and 1SG 55.1 has "Herod was hardened." Highlighted is from 3SP 136.2 and MS 129, 1897.

[117] Verbatim phrase, Jones, p. 375, but highlighted in this paragraph is from MS 112, 1897 and MS 129, 1897.

He looked with curiosity,[118] mingled with an impulse of pity, upon the pale, sad face of the Saviour, which was marked with deep wisdom and purity, but showed extreme weariness and suffering. Herod, as well as Pilate, knew from his acquaintance with the character of the Jews, that malice[119] and envy had caused them to condemn this innocent man. {*3SP* 135.2}

Herod urged Jesus to save his life by working a miracle that would give evidence of his divine power. But the Saviour had no such work to do. He had taken upon himself the nature of man, and was not to perform a miracle to gratify the curiosity[120] of wicked men, nor to save himself[121] one jot of the pain and humiliation that man would suffer under similar circumstances. Herod urged him to prove that he was not an impostor by demonstrating his power before the crowd. He summoned for the purpose maimed, crippled, and deformed persons, and in an authoritative manner, commanded Jesus to heal these subjects in his presence, urging that if he had really worked such remarkable cures as were reported of him, he still had power to do like wonders, and could now turn it to his own profit by procuring his release.[122] {*3SP* 136.1}

But Jesus stood calmly before the haughty ruler as one who neither saw nor heard. Herod repeatedly urged his proposition upon Jesus, and reiterated the fact that he had the power to release or to condemn him. He even dared to boast of the punishment he had inflicted upon the prophet John for presuming to reprove him. To all this, Jesus made no answer either by word or look. Herod was irritated by the profound silence of the prisoner,[123] which indicated an utter indifference to the

He ordered that the fetters of Christ should be unloosed, at the same time charging His enemies with roughly treating Him. Looking with compassion into the serene face of the world's Redeemer, he read in it only wisdom and purity. He as well as Pilate was satisfied that Christ had been accused through malice[124] and envy. {*DA* 729.1}

Herod questioned Christ in many words, but throughout the Saviour maintained a profound silence.[125] At the command of the king, the decrepit and maimed were then called in, and Christ was ordered to prove His claims by working a miracle. Men say that Thou canst heal the sick, said Herod. I am anxious to see that Thy widespread fame has not been belied. Jesus did not respond, and Herod still continued to urge: If Thou canst work miracles for others, work them now for Thine own good, and it will serve Thee a good purpose. Again he commanded, Show us a sign that thou hast the power with which rumor hath accredited Thee. But Christ was as one who heard and saw not. The Son of God had taken upon Himself man's nature. He must do as man must do in like circumstances. Therefore He would not work a miracle to save Himself[126] the pain and humiliation that man must endure when placed in a similar position. {*DA* 729.2}

Herod was irritated by this silence.[127] It seemed to indicate utter

---

[118] Same word, Farrar, p. 628 (see Appendix A).

[119] Same word, Jones, p. 378.

[120] Two verbatim words "gratify" and "curiosity" are used in Hanna, pp. 687, 688, and "miracle" and "curiosity" are used in Farrar, p. 628 (see Appendix A). Ellen White had previously written in *1SG* 55.1, "Herod was glad to see JESUS, for he expected that he would work some mighty miracle for his satisfaction. But it was not the work of JESUS to gratify his curiosity."

[121] Two words from Hanna, p. 688, "And if he wrought them to save others, surely he will do so to save himself." Verbatim is based on *Mark 15:30*, "save thyself."

[122] Same word, Hanna, p. 687.

[123] Jones, p. 375, uses "irritated" and "silence," while Hanna, p. 688, uses only "silence." *1SG* 55.2 has "Herod was enraged because JESUS did not appear to fear his power . . ."

[124] Same word, Jones, p. 378.

[125] Farrar, p. 628, "questioned Him in many words," a paraphrase of *Luke 23:9*.

[126] A very loose paraphrase, Hanna, p. 688; based on *Mark 15:30*, "save thyself." Highlighted for these two paragraphs is from MS 129, 1897.

[127] Jones, p. 375, uses "irritated" and "silence," while Hanna, p. 688, uses only "silence."

royal personage before whom he had been summoned. Open rebuke would have been more palatable to the vain and pompous ruler than to be thus silently ignored. {3SP 136.2}

Had Jesus desired to do so, he could have spoken words which would have pierced the ears of the hardened king. He could have stricken him with fear and trembling by laying before him the full iniquity of his life, and the horror of his approaching doom. But Jesus had no light to give one who had gone directly contrary to the knowledge he had received from the greatest of prophets.[128] The ears of Christ had ever been open to the earnest plea of even the worst sinners; but he had no ear for the commands of Herod. Those eyes, that had ever rested with pity and forgiveness upon the penitent sinner, however defiled and lowly, had no look to bestow upon Herod. Those lips, that had dropped precious words of instruction, and were ever ready to answer the questions of those who sought knowledge, and to speak comfort and pardon to the sinful and desponding, had no words for proud and cruel Herod.[129] That heart, ever touched by the presence of human woe, was closed to the haughty king who felt no need of a Saviour.[130] {3SP 137.1}

indifference to his authority. To the vain and pompous king, open rebuke would have been less offensive than to be thus ignored. Again he angrily threatened Jesus, who still remained unmoved and silent.[131] {DA 730.2}

Christ might have spoken words to Herod that would have pierced the ears of the hardened king. He might have stricken him with fear and trembling by laying before him the full iniquity of his life, and the horror of his approaching doom. But Christ's silence was the severest rebuke that He could have given. Herod had rejected the truth spoken to him by the greatest of the prophets, and no other message was he to receive. Not a word had the Majesty of heaven for him.[132] That ear that had ever been open to human woe, had no room for Herod's commands. Those eyes that had ever rested upon the penitent sinner in pitying, forgiving love had no look to bestow upon Herod. Those lips that had uttered the most impressive truth, that in tones of tenderest entreaty had pleaded with the most sinful and the most degraded, were closed to the haughty king who felt no need of a Saviour.[133] {DA 730.4}

Herod promised that if Christ would perform some miracle in his presence,[134] He should be released. Christ's accusers had seen with their own eyes the mighty works wrought by His power.[135] They had heard Him command the grave to give up its dead.

---

[128] From the beginning of the paragraph to this point, Hanna, pp. 688, 689, expresses a similar thought. ±Bennett, pp. 399, 400, provides a paraphrase of the same two sentences, "Herod, who, instead of benefiting by the greatest prophet ever born of woman, had killed the faithful reprover; and, therefore, Jesus, instead of the little vanity and selfishness which makes us fond of outshining each other, displays a high regard for this faithful minister, by refusing to speak one word to his murderer." The phrase "the greatest of prophets" is adapted from *Luke 7:28*, "not a greater prophet than John the Baptist . . ."

[129] A paraphrase, ±Bennett, p. 400 (see above).

[130] Based on *Luke 23:9*, a very loose paraphrase, Hanna, p. 688, "It does not appear that, from the time when he was presented to Herod, to the time when he was sent away from him, a single word ever passed the Saviour's lips. That deep and death-like silence, the silence of those lips which opened with such pliant readiness when any word of gentle entreaty or hopeful warning was to be spoken, how shall we interpret it?"

[131] Abbott, p. 126, Boyd, p. 382, ±Cumming, *SR-Lk* 495, ±Deems, p. 651, and Kitto, p. 413, all use "silent." Highlighted in last sentence is from 3SP 137.2.

[132] From the beginning of the paragraph to this point, Hanna, pp. 688, 689, and ±Bennett, pp. 399, 400, express a similar thought. Phrase "the greatest of the prophets" is adapted from *Luke 7:28*.

[133] Based on *Luke 23:9*, these last four sentences, an apparent parallel to Hanna, p. 688. Highlighted is from MS 129, 1897.

[134] Strickland (1854), p. 159, uses the words "perform . . . miracle in his presence." Hanna, p. 688, has a looser paraphrase, "Herod tries in every way he can think of, to induce him to work some wonder in his presence." Both are paraphrases of *Luke 23:8*, "and he hoped to have seen some miracle done by him."

[135] Strickland also uses the word "power."

The silence of Jesus could no longer be borne by Herod; his face grew dark with passion, and he angrily threatened Jesus; but the captive still remained unmoved. Herod then turned to the multitude and denounced him as an impostor. His accusers well knew that he was no impostor; they had seen too many evidences of his power to be thus misled. They knew that even the grave had opened at his command, and the dead had walked forth, clothed again with life. They had been greatly terrified when Herod commanded him to work a miracle; for of all things they dreaded an exhibition of his divine power, which would prove a death-blow to their plans, and would perhaps cost them their lives. Therefore the priests and rulers began to cry out vehemently against him, accusing him of working miracles through the power given him of Beelzebub, the prince of devils. {3SP 137.2}

Some cried out that he claimed to be the Son of God, the King of Israel. Herod, hearing this, said, in derision, A king, is he? Then crown him, and put upon him a royal robe, and worship your king. Then turning to Jesus he angrily declared that if he refused to speak, he should be delivered into the hands of the soldiers, who would have little respect for his claims or his person; if he was an impostor it would be no more than he deserved; but if he was the Son of God he could save himself by working a miracle. No sooner were these words uttered than the mob, at the instigation of the priests, made a rush toward Jesus. Had not the Roman soldiers forced them back, the Saviour would have been torn in pieces. {3SP 138.1}

They had seen the dead come forth obedient to His voice. Fear seized them lest He should now work a miracle. Of all things they most dreaded an exhibition of His power. Such a manifestation would prove a deathblow to their plans, and would perhaps cost them their lives. Again the priests and rulers, in great anxiety, urged their accusations against Him. Raising their voices, they declared, He is a traitor, a blasphemer. He works His miracles through the power given Him by Beelzebub, the prince of the devils.[136] The hall became a scene of confusion, some crying one thing and some another.[137] {DA 729.3}

The mission of Christ in this world was not to gratify idle curiosity. He came to heal the brokenhearted. Could He have spoken any word to heal the bruises of sin-sick souls, He would not have kept silent.[138] But He had no words for those who would but trample the truth under their unholy feet. {DA 730.3}

Herod's face grew dark with passion. Turning to the multitude, he angrily denounced Jesus as an impostor. Then to Christ he said, If You will give no evidence of Your claim, I will deliver You up to the soldiers and the people. They may succeed in making You speak. If You are an impostor, death at their hands is only what You merit; if You are the Son of God, save Yourself by working a miracle. {DA 730.5}

No sooner were these words spoken than a rush was made for Christ. Like wild beasts, the crowd darted upon their prey. Jesus was dragged this way and that, Herod joining the mob in seeking to humiliate the Son of God.[139] Had not the Roman soldiers interposed, and forced back the maddened throng, the Saviour would have been torn in pieces. {DA 731.1}

---

[136] An argument they had used in *Matt. 12:24*.

[137] Highlighted is from MS 129, 1897.

[138] Kitto (1859), p. 413, has "But it was no part of our Lord's calling to gratify an idle curiosity ..." The expression is common to several of the life of Christ authors, such as Neander (1848), p. 415, has "But it was no part of the Saviour's calling to satisfy an idle curiosity." ±Bennett (1828), p. 399, has "in refusing to gratify the idle curiosity of a king ..." See also Hanna (1863), p. 688. *1SG* (1858) 55.1 has "But it was not the work of JESUS to gratify his curiosity." Highlighted is from MS 112, 1897.

[139] Farrar, p. 636, used phrase "wild beasts," though not in connection with the manhandling of Jesus. Herod's joining the mob is a thought based on *Luke 23:11*, "And Herod with his men of war set him at nought, and mocked [him], and arrayed him in a gorgeous robe, and sent him again to Pilate." Highlighted is from MS 129, 1897.

At the suggestion of Herod, a crown was now plaited from a vine bearing sharp thorns, and this was placed upon the sacred brow of Jesus; and an old tattered purple robe, once the garment of a king, was placed upon his noble form, while Herod and the Jewish priests encouraged the insults and cruelty of the mob. Jesus was then placed upon a large block, which was derisively called a throne, an old reed was placed in his hand as a scepter, and, amid satanic laughter, curses, and jeers, the rude throng bowed to him mockingly as to a king. Occasionally some murderous hand snatched the reed that had been placed in his hand, and struck him on the head with it, forcing the thorns into his temples, and causing the blood to flow down his face and beard.[140] {3SP 138.2}

Satan instigated the cruel abuse of the debased mob, led on by the priests and rulers, to provoke, if possible, retaliation from the world's Redeemer, or to drive him to deliver himself by a miracle from the hands of his persecutors, and thus break up the plan of salvation. One stain upon his human life, one failure of his humanity to bear the terrible test imposed upon it, would make the Lamb of God an imperfect offering, and the redemption of man would be a failure.[141]

"Herod with his men of war set Him at nought, and mocked Him, and arrayed Him in a gorgeous robe." The Roman soldiers joined in this abuse. All that these wicked, corrupt soldiers, helped on by Herod and the Jewish dignitaries, could instigate was heaped upon the Saviour. Yet His divine patience failed not. {DA 731.2}

Christ's persecutors had tried to measure His character by their own; they had represented Him as vile as themselves. But back of all the present appearance another scene intruded itself,—a scene which they will one day see in all its glory. There were some who trembled in Christ's presence. While the rude throng were bowing in mockery before Him, some who came forward for that purpose turned back, afraid and silenced. Herod was convicted. The last rays of merciful light were shining upon his sin-hardened heart. He felt that this was no common man; for divinity had flashed through humanity.[142] At the very time when Christ was encompassed by mockers, adulterers and murderers, Herod felt that he was beholding a God upon His throne.[143] {DA 731.3}

Satan led the cruel mob in its abuse of the Saviour. It was his purpose to provoke Him to retaliation if possible, or to drive Him to perform a miracle to release Himself, and thus break up the plan of salvation.[144] One stain upon His human life, one failure of His humanity to endure the terrible test, and the Lamb of God would have been an imperfect offering, and the redemption of man a failure.

---

[140] A paraphrase, Farrar, p. 634. Same key words appeared earlier in 1SG 50.1, "They then took the reed from his hand, and smote him with it upon the head, causing the thorns to penetrate his temples, sending the trickling blood down his face and beard." The words "reed" and "hand" are from *Matt. 27:29*. Unlike 3SP, DA does not mention a reed in the mockery of Herod and his soldiers, but only of Pilate and his soldiers (see DA 734.1). 1SG 51.1 adds an eyewitness detail omitted in 3SP and DA, "They spit in his face—that face which they will one day desire to be hid from, which will give light to the city of God, and shine brighter than the sun—but not an angry look did he cast upon the offenders. He meekly raised his hand, and wiped it off." This is a description found in none of the sources—including Ingraham, whose book Ellen White could have read before writing 1SG. These eyewitness details were likely left out of DA because of an editorial policy that Marian Davis described to J. E. White, which excluded "statements for which the Bible seems to furnish no proof" —Ltr. Dec. 22, 1895 (4BIO 386.6).

[141] This entire independent thought bears resemblance to 1SG 49.1, "Satan hoped that such insult and sufferings would call forth from the SON of GOD some complaint or murmur; or that he would manifest his divine power, and wrench himself from the grasp of the multitude, and thus the plan of salvation at last fail." 1SG 61.1 has "He had hoped that he could break up the plan of salvation; but it was laid too deep."

[142] Ellen White used "was no common man" in 1SG 54.1 and "this was no common man" in a sermon in ST 8-6-1885, and "divinity flashed through humanity" in a sermon in RH 4-9-1889. Similar expressions to the latter are found in DA 734.3, "flashing forth of His divine majesty," and DA 753.4, "Had His glory flashed forth from the cloud."

[143] Highlighted this page is from MS 112, 1897.

[144] This entire independent thought bears close resemblance to 1SG 49.1, using a key phrase from 1SG 61.1.

But he who could command the heavenly hosts, and in an instant call to his aid legions of holy angels, one of whom could have immediately overpowered that cruel mob,—he who could have stricken down his tormentors by the flashing forth of his divine majesty,—submitted to the coarsest insult and outrage with dignified composure. As the acts of his torturers degraded them below humanity, into the likeness of Satan, so did the meekness and patience of Jesus exalt him above the level of humanity. {3SP 139.1}

When Herod saw that Jesus submitted passively to all the indignity that was heaped upon him, preserving an unparalleled serenity through it all, he was moved by a sudden fear that after all this might not be a common man who stood before him. He was greatly perplexed when he looked upon the pure, pale face of the prisoner, and questioned if he might not be a god come down to earth. The very silence of Jesus spoke conviction to the heart of the king, such as no words could have done. Herod noticed that while some bowed before Jesus in mockery, others, who came forward for the same purpose, looked into the sufferer's face and saw expressed there a look so like a king that they turned back, ashamed of their own audacity. Herod was ill at ease, and, hardened[145] as he was, dared not ratify the condemnation of the Jews; and he therefore sent Jesus back to Pilate. {3SP 139.2}

The Saviour, tottering with weariness, pale and wounded, wearing a robe of mockery and a crown of thorns, was mercilessly hurried back to the court of the Roman governor. Pilate was very much irritated; for he had congratulated himself on being rid of a fearful responsibility when he referred the accusers of Jesus to Herod. He now impatiently inquired of the Jews what they would have him do. He reminded them that he had already examined the prisoner and found no blame in him;

But He who by a command could bring the heavenly host to His aid[146]—He who could have driven that mob in terror from His sight by the flashing forth of His divine majesty—submitted with perfect calmness[147] to the coarsest insult and outrage. {DA 734.3}

Christ's enemies had demanded a miracle as evidence of His divinity. They had evidence far greater than any they had sought. As their cruelty degraded His torturers below humanity into the likeness of Satan, so did His meekness and patience exalt Jesus above humanity,[148] and prove His kinship to God.[149] His abasement was the pledge of His exaltation. The blood drops of agony that from His wounded temples flowed down His face and beard were the pledge of His anointing with "the oil of gladness" (Heb. 1:9) as our great high priest. {DA 734.4}

Hardened[150] as he was, Herod dared not ratify the condemnation of Christ. He wished to relieve himself of the terrible responsibility, and he sent Jesus back to the Roman judgment hall. {DA 731.4}

Pilate was disappointed and much displeased.[151] When the Jews returned with their prisoner, he asked impatiently what they would have him do. He reminded them that he had already examined Jesus, and found no fault in Him; he «told them that they had brought»[152] complaints against Him,

---

[145] Same word, Hanna, p. 685, though 1SG 55.1 had previously stated, "Herod was hardened."

---

[146] See 1SG 50.1f, "He knew that if he should desire it of his FATHER, angels would instantly release him." The description of Jesus being a perfect offering in the previous sentence is unique to Ellen White.

[147] Jones, p. 379, uses the word "calmness," while Farrar, p. 635, uses the word "calm."

[148] Highlighted is from MS 112, 1897. Phrase "meekness and patience," ± Flavel, p. 109; a similar thought in Hanna, p. 697.

[149] A similar thought for this sentence, Jones, p. 379, and ±Deems, p. 677, though 1SG 55.2.f had previously stated, "Herod was astonished at the noble, God-like appearance of JESUS, when shamefully abused, and feared to condemn him, and he sent him again to Pilate."

[150] Used by many, including, Hanna, p. 685 and 1SG 55.1.

[151] A paraphrase, Hanna, p. 691, "He was disappointed in this hope." For phrase "much displeased," see *Mark 10:14, 41*.

[152] Verbatim phrase, Farrar, p. 629, "told them that they had brought . . ." Would such an unexceptional verbatim phrase require footnoting?

that his accusers had failed to sustain a single charge against him; that he had sent Jesus to Herod, a tetrarch of Galilee,[153] and one of their own nation, who also found nothing worthy of death against the prisoner. Said Pilate, "I will therefore chastise him and release him."[154] {3SP 140.1}

Here Pilate exposed his weakness. He had declared that Jesus was innocent of the crimes of which he was accused, yet he was willing to make a partial sacrifice of justice and principle in order to compromise with an unfeeling mob; he was willing to suffer an innocent man to be scourged,[155] that their inhuman wrath might be appeased. But the fact that he proposed to make terms with them placed Pilate at a disadvantage with the ungovernable crowd, who now presumed upon his indecision,[156] and clamored the more for the life of the prisoner. Pilate turned to the people, and represented to them that the priests and elders had not substantiated in any degree the charges brought against Jesus. He hoped by this means to raise their sympathy for him, so they would be willing to release him. Meanwhile Jesus had fallen through exhaustion upon the marble pavement. Just then a messenger pressed through the crowd, and placed in Pilate's hand a letter from his wife, which ran thus:[157]— {3SP 140.2}

but they had not been able to prove a single charge. He had sent Jesus to Herod, the tetrarch of Galilee,[158] and one of their own nation, but he also had found in Him nothing worthy of death. "I will therefore chastise Him," Pilate said, "and release Him."[159] {DA 731.5}

Here Pilate showed his weakness. He had declared that Jesus was innocent, yet he was willing for Him to be scourged[160] to pacify His accusers. He would sacrifice justice and principle in order to compromise with the mob. This placed him at a disadvantage. The crowd presumed upon his indecision, and clamored the more for the life of the prisoner. If at the first Pilate had stood firm, refusing to condemn a man whom he found guiltless, he would have broken the fatal chain that was to bind him in remorse and guilt as long as he lived. Had he carried out his convictions of right, the Jews would not have presumed to dictate to him. Christ would have been put to death, but the guilt would not have rested upon Pilate. But Pilate had taken step after step in the violation of his conscience.[161] He had excused himself from judging with justice and equity, and he now found himself almost helpless in the hands of the priests and rulers. His wavering and indecision proved his ruin.[162] {DA 731.6}

While Pilate was hesitating as to what he should do, a messenger pressed through the crowd, and handed him the letter from his wife, which read:[163] {DA 732.2}

---

[153] Near verbatim first phrase from *Luke 23:7*, "he sent him to Herod," and *Luke 3:1*, "tetrarch of Galilee," Hanna, p. 691, "he had sent Jesus off to Herod," and Farrar, p. 629, "that he had then sent Him to Herod."

[154] Phrase "nothing worthy of death" is from *Luke 23:15*. Verbatim use of *Luke 23:16* as in Hanna, p. 691; Abbot, p. 132; and ±Cumming, *SR-Lk* 497.

[155] Abbott, p. 128, "Then Pilate, though he had already declared Jesus to be innocent, infamously ordered him to be scourged, that he might conciliate the favor of the Jews." Hanna, pp. 691, 692, uses words "weak" and "innocent" from *Matt. 27:4*. In this same context, Farrar, p. 630, uses the word "weakness."

[156] Same word "indecision," Hanna, p. 700.

[157] The description is carried over from 1SG 54.1, "The messenger bearing the communication pressed hastily through the crowd, and handed it to Pilate."

[158] Paraphrasing *Luke 23:7*, "he sent him to Herod," Farrar, p. 629, has "he had then sent Him to Herod" and Hanna, p. 691, has "he had sent Jesus off to Herod." Expression "Tetrarch of Galilee" is from *Luke 3:1*.

[159] Verbatim use of *Luke 23:16* as in Hanna, p. 691, and in at least two other source works.

[160] Paraphrase, Abbott, p. 128. Hanna, pp. 691, 692, uses the words "weak" and "innocent" from *Matt. 27:4*. In this same context, Farrar, p. 630, uses the word "weakness."

[161] Two highlighted sentences from 3SP 147.1 and 142.2.

[162] Same word "indecision," Hanna, p. 700. ±Ingraham, p. 384, also speaks of Pilate's "indecision." Verbatim sentence carried over from 3SP 147.1.

[163] Based on *Matt. 27:19*, which says: "when he was set down on the judgment seat, his wife sent unto him, saying . . ." The description in *DA* is carried over through 3SP 140.2 from 1SG 54.1, "The messenger bearing the communication pressed hastily through the crowd, and handed it to Pilate."

"Have thou nothing to do with that just man; for I have suffered many things this day in a dream because of him."[164] «Pilate's wife was not a Jew»;[165] but the angel of God had sent this warning[166] to her, that, through her, Pilate might be prevented from committing the terrible crime of delivering up to death the divine Son of God. {3SP 141.1}

Pilate turned pale[167] when he read the message; but the priests and rulers had occupied the interval in farther inflaming the minds of the people,[168] till they were wrought up to a state of insane fury. The governor was forced to action; he turned to the crowd and spoke with great earnestness:

---

[164] Verbatim use of the statement of Pilate's wife of *Matt. 27:19* as in Hanna, p. 692; Abbott, p. 130; and ‡Clark, p. 274.

[165] Verbatim clause "Pilate's wife was not a Jew . . ." Hanna, p. 692. Robert W. Olson writes that one "reason why Ellen White at times used the works of other writers is that she relied on these authorities for historical and geographical information not revealed to her in vision." —"Ellen G. White's Use of Uninspired Sources," p. 9.

[166] Farrar, p. 629, refers to Pilate's wife's dream as "a *second* solemn warning," and Hanna, p. 693 to "sending a warning," though the same thought was previously in 1SG 54.1, "to save him from engaging in the awful act of delivering JESUS to be crucified, an angel was sent to Pilate's wife, and gave her information through a dream that it was the SON of GOD in whose trial Pilate was engaged, and that he was an innocent sufferer. She immediately sent word to Pilate that she had suffered many things in a dream on account of JESUS, and warned him to have nothing to do with that holy man." Both are extended paraphrases of *Matt. 27:19.*

[167] 1SG 54.1 has "As he read it he trembled and turned pale."

[168] A very loose paraphrase if Hanna, p. 693, using the word "inflaming."

"Have thou nothing to do with that just Man; for I have suffered many things this day in a dream because of Him."[169] {DA 732.3}

Even now Pilate was not left to act blindly. A message from God warned[170] him from the deed he was about to commit. In answer to Christ's prayer, the wife of Pilate had been visited by an angel from heaven, and in a dream she had beheld the Saviour and conversed with Him. «Pilate's wife was not a Jew»,[171] but as she looked upon Jesus in her dream, she had no doubt of His character or mission. She knew Him to be the Prince of God. She saw Him on trial in the judgment hall. She saw the hands tightly bound as the hands of a criminal. She saw Herod and his soldiers doing their dreadful work. She heard the priests and rulers, filled with envy and malice, madly accusing. She heard the words, "We have a law, and by our law He ought to die." She saw Pilate give Jesus to the scourging, after he had declared, "I find no fault in Him." She heard the condemnation pronounced by Pilate, and saw him give Christ up to His murderers. She saw the cross uplifted on Calvary. She saw the earth wrapped in darkness, and heard the mysterious cry, "It is finished." Still another scene met her gaze. She saw Christ seated upon the great white cloud,[172] while the earth reeled in space, and His murderers fled from the presence of His glory. With a cry of horror she awoke, and at once wrote to Pilate words of warning. {DA 732.1}

Pilate's face grew pale.[173] He was confused by his own conflicting emotions. But while he had been delaying to act, the priests and rulers were still further inflaming the minds of the people.[174] Pilate was forced to action.

---

[169] Verbatim use of *Matt. 27:19* as in Hanna, p. 692; Abbott, p. 130; and ‡Clark, p. 274.

[170] A very loose paraphrase, Farrar, p. 629; near verbatim wording and other highlighted this page are from MS 112, 1897, "A message from God warned Pilate from the deed he was about to commit." 1SG 54.1 has "warned him to have nothing to do with that holy man." "Warned" is used by Jones, p. 376; Edersheim, pp. 569, 577; Neander, p. 416; and ±Ingraham, p. 386. *Matt. 2:12, 22* speaks of being "warned" in a dream.

[171] Verbatim clause, Hanna, p. 692.

[172] The "great white cloud" is mentioned by Sylvester Bliss in *Memoirs of William Miller* (Boston: Published by Joshua V. Himes, 1853), p. 310, and was used by Ellen White in 1SG 206.1. The "great white cloud" of judgment is likely derived from the "great cloud" of *Eze. 1:4* and the "white cloud" of *Rev. 14:14*. What Ellen White says Pilate's wife saw in her dream is not mentioned by other writers.

[173] 1SG 54.1 has "As he read it he trembled and turned pale."

[174] A very loose paraphrase of Hanna, p. 693, using the word "inflaming."

"Whom will ye that I release unto you? Barabbas, or Jesus who is called Christ?"[175] It was customary at this feast for the governor to release one prisoner,[176] whomsoever the people desired to be set at liberty. Pilate seized this as an opportunity to save Jesus; and by giving them a choice between the innocent Saviour and the notable robber and murderer, Barabbas, he hoped to rouse them to a sense of justice. But great was his astonishment when the cry, "Away with this man, and release unto us Barabbas!"[177] was started by the priests, and taken up by the mob, resounding through the hall like the hoarse cry of demons. {3SP 141.2}

He now bethought himself of a custom which might serve to secure Christ's release. It was customary at this feast to release some «one prisoner whom the people might» choose. This custom was of pagan invention; there was not a shadow of justice in it, but it was greatly prized by the Jews.[178] The Roman authorities at this time held a prisoner «named Barabbas, who was under sentence of death».[179] This man had claimed to be the Messiah.[180] He claimed authority to establish a different order of things,[181] to set the world right. Under satanic delusion he claimed that whatever he could obtain by theft and robbery was his own. He had done wonderful things through satanic agencies, he had gained a following among the people, and had excited sedition[182] against the Roman government. Under cover of religious enthusiasm he was a hardened and desperate villain,[183] bent on rebellion and cruelty. By giving the people a choice between this man and the innocent Saviour, Pilate thought to arouse them to a sense of justice. He hoped to gain their sympathy for Jesus in opposition to the priests and rulers. So, turning to the crowd, he said with great earnestness, "Whom will ye that I release unto you? Barabbas, or Jesus which is called Christ?"[184] {DA 733.1}

Like the bellowing of wild beasts came the answer of the mob, "Release unto us Barabbas!" Louder and louder swelled the cry, Barabbas! Barabbas![185] Thinking that the people had not understood his question, Pilate asked, "Will ye that I release unto you the King of the Jews?" But they cried out again, "Away with this Man, and release unto us Barabbas"![186]

---

[175] Verbatim use of *Matt. 27:17* as in Hanna, p. 692.

[176] Hanna, p. 692, "a customary thing . . . to release whatever prisoner." "Release" and "prisoner" are from *Matt. 27:15* and *Mark 15:6*. "Custom" is from *John 18:39*.

[177] Exact use of *Luke 23:18* as in Hanna, p. 693; ±Cumming, SR-Lk, p. 497; Fleetwood, p. 347; and Jones, p. 376.

[178] The last two sentences to this point, a paraphrase, Farrar, p. 629, using verbatim word "bethought." Modified verbatim phrase "any one prisoner whom the people might name" is found in Kitto, p. 414, though "prisoner" and "whom they would" are from *Matt. 27:15*. A similar thought is in Hanna, p. 692, "a customary thing . . . to release whatever prisoner." "Release" and "prisoner" are from *Matt. 27:15* and *Mark 15:6*. "Custom" is from *John 18:39*. 1SG 54.1f says Pilate "would labor to deliver him." Only Ellen White refers to this custom being of "pagan invention."

[179] For the last two sentences, a loose paraphrase, Edersheim, p. 576. Verbatim phrase "named Barabbas, who was under sentence of death" is found in ±Talmage (1893), p. 373, though Ellen White uses the phrase "sentence of death" 73 times (e.g. see 1SG 22.2f and 3SP [1878] 131.1), and the longer phrase "under sentence of death," 14 times. Description of the history and characteristics of Barabbas is unique to Ellen White.

[180] Raised as a possibility by ±Trench, SG 300–302; ±Stanford, ELM 205; and Edersheim, p. 577.

[181] ±Trench, SG 300–302, describes Barabbas' efforts to overthrow Rome.

[182] Word used by Andrews, p. 536, and Anderson, p. 690, drawing on *Luke 23:19*.

[183] The word "villain" is used by ±Deems, p. 655, within the same context of the scene about Barabbas, though the composite history and characteristics of Barabbas are only found in Ellen White's description.

[184] *Matt. 27:17* with a minor word substitution, Hanna, p. 692.

[185] Verbatim use of the cry from *Luke 23:18* with near verbatim words, Hanna, p. 693, though the words "swelling" and "cry" come later in the narrative in connection with "Crucify him! Crucify him!" and not with "Barabbas! Barabbas!" as in 3SP; "like the bellowing of wild beasts" was used in ST 3-26-1894.

[186] Verbatim use of Pilate's question of *Luke 23:18* as in Hanna, p. 693; ±Cumming, SR-Lk 497; Fleetwood, p. 347; and Jones, p. 376. Highlighted this page is from MS 112, 1897.

Pilate was dumb with surprise and disappointment; but by appealing to the people, and yielding his own judgment, he had compromised his dignity, and lost control of the crowd. The priests saw that though he was convinced of the innocence[187] of Jesus, he could be intimidated by them, and they determined to carry their point. So when Pilate inquired, "What shall I do then with Jesus, who is called Christ?" they with one accord cried out, "Let him be crucified!" {3SP 142.1}

"And the governor said, Why, what evil hath he done? But they cried out the more, saying, Let him be crucified."[188] Here Pilate again revealed his weakness, in submitting the sentence of Jesus to a lawless and infuriated mob. How true were the words of the prophet: "Judgment is turned away backward, and justice standeth afar off; for truth is fallen in the street, and equity cannot enter." [Isa. 59:14] The governor's cheek paled as he heard the terrible cry: "Crucify him!" He had not thought it would come to that—a man whom he had repeatedly pronounced innocent, to be consigned to the most dreaded of deaths.[189] He now saw what a terrible thing he had done in placing the life of a just man in the balance against the decision of those, who, from envy and malice, had delivered him up to trial. Pilate had taken step after step in the violation of his conscience, and in excusing himself from judging with equity and fairness, as his position demanded he should do, until now he found himself almost helpless in the hands of the Jews. {3SP 142.2}

Again he asked the question, "Why, what evil hath he done?" and again they cried out, "Crucify him!"[190] Once more Pilate expostulated with them against putting to death one against whom they could prove nothing. Again, to conciliate them, he proposed to chastise him and let him go. It was not enough that the Saviour of

"What shall I do then with Jesus which is called Christ?"[191] Pilate asked. Again the surging multitude roared like demons. Demons themselves, in human form,[192] were in the crowd, and what could be expected but the answer, "Let Him be crucified"? {DA 733.2}

Pilate was troubled.[193] He had not thought it would come to that. He shrank from delivering an innocent man to the most ignominious and cruel death that could be inflicted.[194] After the roar of voices had ceased, he turned to the people, saying, "Why, what evil hath He done?" But the case had gone too far for argument.[195] It was not evidence of Christ's innocence that they wanted, but His condemnation. {DA 733.3}

Still Pilate endeavored to save Him. "He said unto them the third time, Why, what evil hath He done? I have found no cause of death in Him: I will therefore chastise Him, and let Him go."[196] But the very mention of His release stirred the people to a tenfold frenzy.[197]

---

[187] A verbatim word, in this same context, Fleetwood, p. 347, though *Matt. 27:4* has "innocent."

[188] Verbatim use of quotations from *Matt. 27:22, 23.*

[189] A strict paraphrase, Hanna, p. 693, "most ignominious of all deaths."

[190] Verbatim use of *Mark 15:14* as in Hanna, p. 694.

[191] Same use of *Matt. 27:22* as in Hanna, p. 693, though Hanna reverses "do" and "then."

[192] A unique eyewitness detail from MS 112, 1897.

[193] Abbott, p. 130, has "Pilate was seriously troubled." *1SG* 53.1f has "Herod and Pilate were greatly troubled at his noble, GOD-like bearing."

[194] Several sources—including Hanna, p. 693; Fleetwood, p. 351; Kitto, p. 418; and ±Flavel, p. 116—use the phrase "the most ignominious … death." Jones, p. 377, provides the most complete parallel for the whole, using the words "ignominious," "cruel," and "inflicted" in a 98-word sentence! "Ignominious" is commonly used, as in ±Weiss (1894), p. 356; Andrews, p. 537; ±Clark, p. 277; Jones, p. 377; Winslow, p. 9; and ±Ingraham, p. 361. Highlighted is from MS 40, 1897.

[195] Verbatim use of Pilate's question in *Matt. 27:23* (also *Mark 15:14* and *Luke 23:22*), with a very loose paraphrase, Hanna, p. 694. "Roar of voices" is from MS 51, 1897.

[196] Verbatim use of Pilate's statement of *Luke 23:22* as in Hanna, p. 694.

[197] A paraphrase, Hanna, p. 694, and Fleetwood, p. 353, based on *Luke 23:23*, "And they were instant with loud voices," and *Matt. 27:23*, "But they cried out the more."

the world, **faint with weariness and covered with wounds,** must be subjected to the shameful humiliation of such a trial; but his sacred flesh must be bruised and mangled to gratify the satanic fury of the priests and rulers. Satan, with his hellish army had gained possession of them. {*3SP* 142.3}

Pilate, in the vain hope of exciting their pity,[198] that they might **decide this was sufficient punishment,** now caused Jesus to be scourged in the presence of the multitude.

"Crucify Him, crucify Him," they cried. Louder and louder swelled the storm that Pilate's indecision had called forth.[199] {*DA* 733.4}

Jesus was taken, **faint with weariness and covered with wounds,** and scourged in the sight of the multitude. "And the soldiers led Him away into the hall, called Praetorium: and they call together the whole band. And they clothed Him with purple, and platted a crown of thorns, and put it about His head, and began to salute Him, Hail, King of the Jews! And they ... did spit upon Him, and bowing their knees worshiped Him." Occasionally some wicked hand snatched the reed that had been placed in His hand, and struck the crown upon His brow, forcing the thorns into His temples, and sending the blood trickling down His face and beard.[200] {*DA* 734.1}

When **Pilate** gave Jesus up **to be scourged** and mocked, he thought to excite the pity of the multitude.[201] He hoped they would **decide that this was sufficient punishment.**[202] Even the malice of the priests, he thought, would now be satisfied.[203] But with keen perception the Jews saw the weakness of thus punishing a man who had been declared innocent.[204] They knew that Pilate was trying to save the life of the prisoner,[205] and they were determined that Jesus should not be released. To please and satisfy us, Pilate has scourged Him, they thought, and if we press the matter to a decided issue, we shall surely gain our end. {*DA* 735.2}

---

[198] Hanna, p. 697, puts words in Pilate's mouth, "'behold and pity, behold and be satisfied—behold, and suffer me, now that I have thus chastised him, to let him go!'" "Pity" is also used by Fleetwood, p. 349.

[199] A very loose paraphrase, Hanna, p. 694, "The very mention of letting him go stirs the crowd to a tenfold frenzy, and now the voices of the chief priests themselves are heard swelling and intensifying the cry, 'Crucify him! crucify him!' Before a storm like this who can stand?" Hanna, p. 700 has "indecision." Starting with "But the very mention of " to the end of the paragraph is a loose paraphrase, ±Didon, p. 342, "The cries of the multitude were redoubled." That the cries grew "louder and louder" can be inferred from the repetition of "Let him be crucified" in *Matt. 27:22, 23* and "they were the more fierce" of *Luke 23:5.* "Crucify him, crucify him" is from *Luke 23:21.*

[200] An expanded paraphrase of *Matt. 27:29, 30,* using the same verbatim words "crown of thorns," "reed in his right hand," "spit," and "smote him on the head" as Hanna, p. 697, "But they tire even of that mock homage; the demon spirit that is in them inspires the merriment with a savage cruelty; and so, as if ashamed even of that kind of homage they had rendered, they snatch impatiently the reed out of his hand, and smite with it the crown of thorns, and drive it down upon his pierced and bleeding brow, and spit upon him, and smite him with their hands." Kitto, p. 415, has "snatch," "reed," "His hand," "crown," though other verbatim phrasing was carried over from 1*SG* 50.1 through 3*SP* 138.2 to MS 129, 1897.

[201] Neander (1848), p. 416, has "excite the sympathy of the multitude"; ±Clark (1860), p. 274, has "excite their sympathy"; Andrews (1891/1862), p. 539, has "excite popular compassion"; and Hanna, p. 697, puts words in Pilate's mouth, using the verbatim word "pity."

[202] A similar thought with no verbatim words, Jones, p. 378, inferred from "chastise him and let him go" of *Luke 23:22.*

[203] A paraphrase, Jones, p. 378. Word "malice" is commonly used. Several source works express the same general idea as the first three sentences of the paragraph (or parts of them)—Neander, p. 416; ±Clark, p. 274; Robinson, p. 415; ±Pentecost, *IA* (1890) 371–373; and Kitto, p. 415.

[204] Jones, p. 388, uses the word "innocent" from *Matt. 27:4.*

[205] A loose paraphrase, ±Nicoll (1881), p. 302, "Pilate even yet hoped to save Him." Same thought is in Neander, p. 416, and a possible very loose paraphrase in ±Clark, p. 273, and ±Deems, p. 657.

The pale sufferer, with a crown of thorns upon his head, and stripped to the waist,[206] revealing the long, cruel stripes, from which the blood flowed freely, was then placed side by side with Barabbas. Although the face of Jesus was stained with blood, and bore marks of exhaustion and pain,[207] yet his noble character could not be hidden, but stood out in marked contrast with that of the robber chief, whose every feature proclaimed him to be a debased and hardened desperado. {3SP 143.1}

Pilate was filled with sympathy and amazement as he beheld the uncomplaining patience of Jesus.[208] Gentleness and resignation were expressed in every feature;[209] there was no cowardly weakness in his manner, but the strength and dignity of long-suffering.[210] {3SP 143.2}

There stood the Son of God, wearing the robe of mockery and the crown of thorns[211]. Stripped to the waist,[212] His back showed the long, cruel stripes, from which the blood flowed freely. His face was stained with blood, and bore the marks of exhaustion and pain; but never had it appeared more beautiful than now. The Saviour's visage was not marred before His enemies. Every feature expressed gentleness[213] and resignation and the tenderest pity for His cruel foes. In His manner there was no cowardly weakness, but the strength and dignity of long-suffering.[214] In striking contrast[215] was the prisoner at His side. Every line of the countenance of Barabbas proclaimed him the hardened ruffian that he was. The contrast spoke to every beholder. Some of the spectators were weeping. As they looked upon Jesus,[216] their hearts were full of sympathy.[217] Even the priests and rulers were convicted that He was all that He claimed to be. {DA 735.4}

Pilate was filled with amazement at the uncomplaining patience of the Saviour.[218]

---

[206] Verbatim phrase "stripped to the waist," Geikie (1877), p. 547 (context in Appendix A). There is uncertainty about whether Ellen White had access to Geikie for 3SP since Geikie and 3SP were both printed in late 1877 (though 3SP carries the publication date of 1878).

[207] A very loose paraphrase, Jones, p. 389, "They looked toward the cross; and they there saw the marks of agony; the anguish apparent in his face, and in the spasms and convulsions of his body;—that face so gentle and calm, and so God-like always, but now clouded with the pain which expressed itself in every line and feature;—the eyes now bloodshot;—the brow and form wounded and bloody;—the languor of exhaustion stealing over the limbs and frame." (See in context in Appendix A.) "Agony" is used in *Luke 22:44*.

[208] A loose paraphrase, Hanna, p. 697, using verbatim phrase "uncomplaining patience" and using the word "gentle" in the next sentence.

[209] A loose paraphrase, Jones, p. 389, see above and in context in Appendix A.

[210] A simple paraphrase, Hanna, p. 697, "There is no weakness in that patience; but a strength, a power, a dignity."

[211] Commonly used verbatim expression "robe of mockery," Taylor (1856), p. 686; Geikie (1877), vol. 2, p. 542; ±Cumming, *LLL* (1880) 461; and ±Deems (1880), p. 652. While the expression "wearing a robe of mockery and a crown of thorns" was carried over from 3SP 140.1.

[212] Verbatim phrase "stripped to the waist" found in Geikie, p. 547, five pages after "robe of mockery."

[213] Starting with "His face was stained," a very loose paraphrase, Jones, p. 389 (see in context in Appendix A).

[214] Starting with "gentleness and resignation" to this point, a simple paraphrase, Hanna, p. 697, "There is no weakness in that patience; but a strength, a power, a dignity."

[215] ±Deems (1880), p. 654, uses the words "Barabbas," "striking," and "contrast" in this same context; however, Ellen White previously used "marked contrast" in 3SP 143.1.

[216] Starting with "The Saviour's visage was not marred" to this point, a very loose paraphrase by ±Mackenzie (1896), p. 264.2.

[217] Verbatim word "sympathy," Hanna, p. 697, describing what Pilate hoped to stir.

[218] A loose paraphrase, Hanna, p. 697, using verbatim phrase "uncomplaining patience"; a similar thought, Barnes, 2NG (1854) 380.

Pilate did not doubt that the sight of this man, who had borne insult and abuse in such a manner, when contrasted with the repulsive criminal by his side, would move the people to sympathy, and they would decide that Jesus had already suffered enough. But he did not understand the fanatical hatred[219] of the priests for Christ, who, as the Light of the world, had made apparent their darkness and error. {3SP 143.2}

Pilate, pointing to the Saviour, in a voice of solemn entreaty said to priests, rulers, and people, "Behold the man." "I bring him forth to you that ye may know that I find no fault in him." But the priests had moved the mob to mad fury; and, instead of pitying Jesus in his suffering and forbearance, they cried, "Crucify him, crucify him!" and their hoarse voices were like the roaring of wild beasts. Pilate, losing all patience with their unreasoning cruelty,[220] cried out despairingly, "Take ye him, and crucify him; for I find no fault in him." {3SP 144.1}

The Roman governor, familiarized with cruel scenes, educated amid the din of battle, was moved with sympathy for the suffering prisoner, who, contemned and scourged, with bleeding brow and lacerated back, still had more the bearing of a king[221] upon his throne

He did not doubt that the sight of this Man, in contrast with Barabbas, would move the Jews to sympathy. But he did not understand the fanatical hatred of the priests for Him, who, as the Light of the world, had made manifest their darkness and error.[222] They had moved the mob to a mad fury, and again priests, rulers, and people raised that awful cry, "Crucify Him, crucify Him." At last, losing all patience with their unreasoning cruelty,[223] Pilate cried out despairingly, "Take ye Him, and crucify Him; for I find no fault in Him." {DA 736.1}

Pilate now sent for Barabbas to be brought into the court. He then presented the two prisoners side by side,[224] and pointing to the Saviour he said in a voice of solemn entreaty, "Behold the Man!" "I bring Him forth to you, that ye may know that I find no fault in Him." {DA 735.3}

The Roman soldiers that surrounded Christ were not all hardened; some were looking earnestly into His face for one evidence that He was a criminal or dangerous character.[225] From time to time they would turn and cast a look of contempt upon Barabbas. It needed no deep insight to read him through and through. Again they would turn to the One upon trial. They looked at the divine sufferer[226] with feelings of deep pity. The silent submission[227] of Christ stamped upon their minds the scene, never to be effaced until they either acknowledged Him as the Christ, or by rejecting Him decided their own destiny. {DA 735.5}

The Roman governor, though familiar with cruel scenes, was moved with sympathy for the suffering prisoner, who, condemned and scourged, with bleeding brow and lacerated back, still had the bearing of a king[228] upon his throne. But the priests declared,

---

[219] Similar description, Hanna, p. 697, "Alas! he knew not the intensity of such fanatic hatred as that which those high priests and rulers cherished, and had, for the time, infused into the obedient crowd; how it quenches every impulse of kindliness in the human heart, and nerves the human hand for deeds of utmost cruelty."

[220] Words "cruelty" and "wild," Hanna, p. 697, used in a different sense.

[221] Hanna, p. 698, uses "kingly."

[222] The first two sentences, a loose paraphrase, Barnes, 2NG 380. Similar thought, Edersheim, p. 586, using "sympathy" and "fanatical hatred," though Edersheim was predated by 3SP (1878) 143.2, leaving us to wonder if Edersheim could have drawn his wording from Hanna's phrase "fanatic hatred"!

[223] A sentence using the verbatim word "cruelty," Hanna, p. 697.

[224] A common verbatim phrase, Farrar, p. 631, from MS 112, 1897.

[225] ±Weiss, p. 356, describes Barabbas as being a "dangerous character."

[226] "Sufferer," Jones, p. 388; ±Deems, p. 657; Edersheim, p. 579; and Farrar, p. 633. All are predated by 1SG 54.1, "that he was an innocent sufferer." Ellen White used the assimilated expression "divine sufferer" in a sermon in ST 11-25-1889.

[227] Hanna, p. 697, uses words "pity," "silent," and "submitting."

[228] Hanna, p. 698, uses the word "kingly."

than that of a condemned criminal. But the hearts of his own people were hardened against him. The priests declared, "We have a law, and by our law he ought to die, because he made himself the Son of God."[229] {3SP 144.2}

Pilate was startled by these words;[230] he had no correct idea of Christ and his mission; but he had an indistinct faith in God and in beings superior to humanity.[231] The thought that had once before passed through his mind now took more definite shape, and he questioned if it might not be a divine personage who stood before him, clad in the purple robe of mockery, and crowned with thorns,[232] yet with such a noble bearing that the stanch Roman trembled with awe as he gazed upon him. {3SP 144.3}

"When Pilate therefore heard that saying, he was the more afraid; and went again into the judgment hall, and saith unto Jesus, Whence art thou? But Jesus gave him no answer."[233] Jesus had already told Pilate that he was the Messiah, that his kingdom was not of this world; and he had no farther words for a man who so abused the high office of judge as to yield his principles and authority to the demands of a blood-thirsty rabble. Pilate was vexed at the silence of Jesus,[234] and haughtily addressed him:— {3SP 145.1}

"We have a law, and by our law He ought to die, because He made Himself the Son of God."[235] {DA 736.2}

Pilate was startled.[236] He had no correct idea of Christ and His mission; but he had an indistinct faith in God and in beings superior to humanity.[237] A thought that had once before passed through his mind now took more definite shape. He questioned whether it might not be a divine being that stood before him,[238] clad in the purple robe of mockery, and crowned with thorns.[239] {DA 736.3}

Again he went into the judgment hall, and said to Jesus, "Whence art Thou?" But Jesus gave him no answer.[240] The Saviour had spoken freely to Pilate, explaining His own mission as a witness to the truth. Pilate had disregarded the light. He had abused the high office of judge by yielding his principles and authority to the demands of the mob. Jesus had no further light for him.[241] Vexed at His silence,[242] Pilate said haughtily: {DA 736.4}

---

[229] Verbatim use of *John 19:7* as in Hanna, p. 698.

[230] A paraphrase, Jones, p. 379, "the governor was startled," and Farrar, p. 636, "this word, unheard before, startled Pilate," based on "he was the more afraid" of *John 19:8*.

[231] A simple paraphrase, Hanna, p. 698, "Like so many of the educated Romans of his day, he had thrown off all faith in their divinity, and yet somehow there still lingered within, a faith in something higher than humanity, some beings superior to our race."

[232] A loose paraphrase, Hanna, p. 698.

[233] Verbatim use of Pilate's question "Whence art thou?" of *John 19:9* as in Farrar, p. 636, and, with the verbatim response, as in Hanna, p. 698.

[234] For the underlined portion, a paraphrase, Hanna, p. 699, "Annoyed by this silence, this calmness, this apparent indifference of Jesus, Pilate, in all the pride of office, says, "Speakest thou not to me . . .""

[235] Verbatim use of *John 19:7* as in Hanna, p. 698.

[236] A paraphrase, Jones, p. 379 (see context in Chapter 7), and Farrar, p. 636, based on "he was the more afraid" of *John 19:8*.

[237] A simple paraphrase with verbatim words, Hanna, p. 698, "Like so many of the educated Romans of his day, he had thrown off all faith in their divinity, and yet somehow there still lingered within, a faith in something higher than humanity, some beings superior to our race."

[238] A paraphrase, Andrews, p. 540, "Was then his prisoner, whose appearance, words, and conduct had so strangely and so deeply interested him, a divine being?" "Divine being" also used by Hanna, p. 746, and ±Didon, p. 344.

[239] Beginning with "clad in" a loose paraphrase, Hanna, p. 698, "And what if this Jesus were one of these! never in all his intercourse with men had he met one the least like this, one who looked so kinglike, so Godlike: kinglike, Godlike, even there as he now stands with a robe of faded purple and a crown of plaited thorns." *3SP* (1878) 144.3 has verbatim words. ±Angus, p. 258; Abbott, p. 129; Andrews (1862), pp. 540, 552; Hanna, pp. 697, 701; Jones, p. 378; Kitto, pp. 413, 414; and Neander, p. 415, all have the "purple robe" and "crown of thorns" of *John 19:2, 5*.

[240] To this point in the paragraph, a loose paraphrase, but same use of Pilate's question "Whence art thou?" of *John 19:9* as in Farrar, p. 636. Hanna, p. 698, uses the same verbatim question and response from *John 19:9*, "But Jesus gave him no answer."

[241] Starting with "The Saviour had spoken" to this point, a very loose paraphrase, ±Pentecost, *IA* (1890) 375. Predated by *3SP* 133.2 and 145.1.

[242] A paraphrase, Hanna, p. 699.

"Speakest thou not unto me? Knowest thou not that I have power to crucify thee, and have power to release thee? Jesus answered, Thou couldest have no power at all against me, except it were given thee from above; therefore he that delivered me unto thee hath the greater sin."[243] Jesus here laid the heaviest burden of guilt upon the Jewish judges, who had received unmistakable evidence of the divinity of Him whom they had condemned to death, both from the prophecies and his own teachings and miracles. What a scene was this to hand down to the world through all time! The pitying Saviour, in the midst of his intense suffering and grief, excuses as far as possible the act of Pilate,[244] who might have released him from the power of his enemies. {3SP 145.2}

"Speakest Thou not unto me? Knowest Thou not that I have power to crucify Thee, and have power to release Thee?" {DA 736.5}

Jesus answered, "Thou couldest have no power at all against Me, except it were given thee from above: therefore he that delivered Me unto thee hath the greater sin."[245] {DA 736.6}

Thus the pitying Saviour, in the midst of His intense suffering and grief, excused as far as possible the act of the Roman governor who gave Him up to be crucified. What a scene[246] was this to hand down to the world for all time! What a light it sheds upon the character of Him who is the Judge of all the earth![247] {DA 736.7}

"He that delivered Me unto thee," said Jesus, "hath the greater sin." By this Christ meant Caiaphas, who, as high priest, represented the Jewish nation.[248] They knew the principles that controlled the Roman authorities. They had had light in the prophecies that testified of Christ, and in His own teachings and miracles. The Jewish judges had received unmistakable evidence of the divinity of Him whom they condemned to death. And according to their light would they be judged.[249] {DA 737.1}

The greatest guilt and heaviest responsibility belonged to those who stood in the highest places in the nation,[250] the depositaries of sacred trusts that they were basely betraying. Pilate, Herod, and the Roman soldiers were comparatively ignorant of Jesus.[251] They thought to please the priests and rulers by abusing Him. They had not the light which the Jewish nation had so abundantly received. Had the light been given to the soldiers, they would not have treated Christ as cruelly as they did. {DA 737.2}

---

[243] Verbatim use of *John 19:10, 11* as in Jones, p. 379, and in Abbott, p. 129, though omitting "against me." Hanna, p. 699, has minor changes in the words for Pilate's question, but not for Jesus' response.

[244] A simple paraphrase, Hanna, p. 699, "sufferings so acute . . . and excuses, as far as he is able, the actings of Pilate."

[245] Verbatim use of *John 19:10, 11* as in Jones, p. 379. Hanna, p. 699, uses the same two verses with minor changes.

[246] A simple paraphrase, Hanna, p. 699, "There is something surely very impressive here; that, sunk as Jesus was beneath the weight of his own sufferings—sufferings so acute that they well might have engrossed his thoughts and feelings, he yet so calmly weighs in the judicial balance the comparative guilt of the actors in this sad scene, and excuses, as far as he is able, the actings of Pilate."

[247] The thought of this whole paragraph, plus the word "judge," possibly from ⊥Mackenzie, p. 262.

[248] A very loose paraphrase of this sentence, Anderson, p. 689.

[249] For the last two sentences, a very loose paraphrase, +Pentecost, *IA* 376.

[250] A simple paraphrase, Edersheim, p. 580, "Nay, not absolute power, all power came from above; but the guilt in the abuse of power was far greater on the part of apostate Israel and its leaders . . ." A similar thought, with verbatim words is in the earlier work of ⊥Bonar (1874), 409, "They are a declaration of the great guilt of the Jewish nation and its rulers, in asking Pilate to exercise his God-given authority against the Son of God." Note the similar description in the earlier 3SP 145.2, "Jesus here laid the heaviest burden of guilt upon the Jewish judges, who had received unmistakable evidence of the divinity of Him whom they had condemned to death, both from the prophecies and his own teachings and miracles." Highlighted is from MS 95, 1897.

[251] A very loose paraphrase, ⊥Pentecost, *IA* (1890), p. 376, highlighted to the end of the paragraph is from MS 101, 1897 (12MR 395.1).

Pilate was now more convinced than before of the superiority of the man before him, and tried again and again to save him. "But the Jews cried out, saying, If thou let this man go, thou art not Cæsar's friend; whosoever maketh himself a king speaketh against Cæsar."[252] This was touching Pilate in a weak point. He had been looked upon with some suspicion by the government; and he knew that a report of unfaithfulness on his part would be likely to cost him his position.[253] He knew that if the Jews became his enemies he could hope for no mercy at their hands; for he had before him an example of the perseverance with which they sought to destroy one whom they hated without reason. {3SP 145.3}

The implied threat in the declaration of the priests, regarding his allegiance to Cæsar, intimidated Pilate, so that he yielded to the demands of the mob,[254] and delivered Jesus up to the crucifixion rather than risk losing his position.[255] But

Again Pilate proposed to release the Saviour.[256] "But the Jews cried out, saying, If thou let this man go, thou art not Caesar's friend."[257] Thus these hypocrites pretended to be jealous for the authority of Caesar. Of all the opponents of the Roman rule, the Jews were most bitter.[258] When it was safe for them to do so, they were most tyrannical in enforcing their own national and religious requirements; but when they desired to bring about some purpose of cruelty, they exalted the power of Caesar. To accomplish the destruction of Christ, they would profess loyalty to the foreign rule which they hated.[259] {DA 737.3}

"Whosoever maketh himself a king," they continued, "speaketh against Caesar." This was touching Pilate in a weak point.[260] He was under suspicion by the Roman government, and he knew that such a report would be ruin to him.[261] He knew that if the Jews were thwarted, their rage would be turned against him. They would leave nothing undone to accomplish their revenge. He had before him an example of the persistence with which they sought the life of One whom they hated without reason. {DA 737.4}

Pilate yielded to the demands of the mob.[262] Rather than risk losing his position, he delivered Jesus up to be crucified.[263] But

---

[252] Verbatim use the Jews' response in *John 19:12* as in Hanna, p. 699; Abbott, p. 130; ±Clark, p. 275; Fleetwood, p. 352; Jones, p. 379; Kitto, p. 416; and ±Pressensé (1866), p. 515. Farrar, pp. 637, 638, and Neander, p. 417, paraphrase their response.

[253] A strict paraphrase, Hanna, p. 699, "Pilate knew that already he stood upon uncertain ground with the imperial authorities; he knew that a fresh report of anything like unfaithfulness to Cæsar would cost him his office." Andrews, p. 541, uses "suspicion" and Farrar, p. 638, uses "suspicions."

[254] Paraphrasing *Mark 15:15*, "willing to content the people," Hanna, p. 699, has "yielding to this last pressure . . ."

[255] A paraphrase, Hanna, p. 699, "The risk of losing all that by occupying that office he had hoped to gain, he was not prepared to face, and so, yielding to this last pressure, he

gives way, and delivers up Jesus to be crucified."

[256] Based on *John 19:12*, "And from thenceforth Pilate sought to release him."

[257] Exact use of the Jews' response in *John 19:12* as in Hanna, p. 699, and in at least six other source works. Two others paraphrase it.

[258] A paraphrase, Cumming, *SR-Jn* (1856) 363, "Now they really hated the supremacy of Cæsar . . ."

[259] The last half of the sentence, a paraphrase, Cumming, *SR-Jn* 363, 364, "insisting on the supremacy of Cæsar, when it suited their purpose . . ." Highlighted is from MS 95, 1897.

[260] A similar thought, Hanna, p. 699, with verbatim use of the Jews' response from *John 19:12*.

[261] A strict paraphrase, Hanna, p. 699, using verbatim words, and a less strict paraphrase, Abbott, p. 130, using "report." ±Clark, p. 275; Pentecost, *BS '88*, p. 181; and Kitto, pp. 416, 417, use "ruin." ±Stalker (1880), p. 140 (see Appendix A), expresses a similar thought; and ±Renan (1863), p. 286, expresses a related thought, using the word "report," but there is no direct paraphrase.

[262] Paraphrasing *Mark 15:15*, "willing to content the people," Hanna, p. 699, has "yielding to this last pressure . . ."

[263] A paraphrase, Hanna, p. 699, "The risk of losing all that by occupying that office he had hoped to gain, he was not prepared to face, and so, yielding to this last pressure, he gives way, and delivers up Jesus to be crucified." Farrar, p. 639, has a loose paraphrase. Phrase "he delivered Jesus" is from *Luke 23:25*.

the very thing he dreaded came upon him afterward in spite of his precautions. His honors were stripped from him; he was cast down from his high office; and stung by remorse and wounded pride, he committed suicide not long after the crucifixion.[264] {3SP 146.1}

"When Pilate saw that he could prevail nothing, but that rather a tumult was made, he took water, and washed his hands before the multitude, saying, I am innocent of the blood of this just person; see ye to it."[265]

Caiaphas answered defiantly, "His blood be on us, and on our children;" and his words were echoed **by the priests and rulers, and** taken up by the crowd in an inhuman roar of voices. "Then answered all the people and said, His blood be on us, and on our children."[266] {3SP 146.2}

---

[264] A very loose paraphrase, Farrar, p. 639, "Stripped of his Procuratorship very shortly afterwards, on the very charges he had tried by a wicked concession to avoid, Pilate, wearied out with misfortunes, died in suicide and banishment, leaving behind him an execrated name." Lyman Abbott, p. 473, also uses "stripped."

[265] Verbatim use of *Matt. 27:24* as in Hanna, p. 694, though Hanna reverses "that" and "rather."

[266] Verbatim use of the people's cry of *Matt. 27:25* as in Farrar, p. 639, and Hanna, p. 704. Geikie, 547, describes the scene, "'Yes! yes!' cried the furious priests and rabble, 'willingly! We and our children will take the blame!'" Only Ellen White, as an "eyewitness" of what took place, specifically describes Caiaphas as the instigator of the cry.

in spite of his precautions, the very thing he dreaded afterward came upon him. His honors were stripped from him, he was cast down from his high office, and, stung by remorse and wounded pride, not long after the crucifixion he ended his own life. So all who compromise with sin will gain only sorrow and ruin.[267] "There is a way which seemeth right unto a man, but the end thereof are the ways of death." Prov. 14:12. {DA 738.3}

Pilate then «took his place on the judgment seat,»[268] and again presented Jesus to the people, saying, "Behold your King!" Again the mad cry was heard, "Away with Him, crucify Him." In a voice that was heard far and near, Pilate asked, "Shall I crucify your King?" but from profane, blasphemous lips went forth the words, "We have no king but Caesar."[269] {DA 737.5}

Thus by choosing a heathen ruler, the Jewish nation had withdrawn from the theocracy. They had rejected God as their king. Henceforth they had no deliverer. They had no king but Caesar.[270] To this the priests and teachers had led the people. For this, with the fearful results that followed, they were responsible. A nation's sin and a nation's ruin were due to the religious leaders. {DA 737.6}

"When Pilate saw that he could prevail nothing, but that rather a tumult was made, he took water, and washed his hands before the multitude, saying, I am innocent of the blood of this just Person: see ye to it."[271] {DA 738.1a}

When Pilate declared himself innocent of the blood of Christ, **Caiaphas answered defiantly, "**His blood be on us, and on our children."[272] The awful words were taken up **by the priests and rulers, and** echoed **by the crowd in an inhuman roar of voices.** The whole multitude answered and said, "His blood be on us, and on our children." {DA 738.4}

---

[267] A very loose paraphrase, Farrar, p. 639, followed by a sentence containing the verbatim "gain," Hanna, p. 699; a very loose paraphrase, ±Thayer, p. 322. "Stripped," used by Farrar, p. 640, and Lyman Abbott, p. 473.

[268] An unexceptional verbatim phrase, Kitto, p. 411, paraphrasing *Matt. 27:19*, "he was set down on the judgment seat."

[269] Fleetwood, p. 353; and Andrews, p. 541 (quoted in Appendix A); ±Deems, p. 659; ±Didon, p. 345; Geikie, p. 554; and Jones, p. 380, use all the statements in *John 19:14, 15*. Hanna, p. 712, leaves out "Shall I crucify your King?"

[270] A loose paraphrase, Andrews, p. 541, "an open renunciation of their allegiance to Jehovah and of the covenant which He had made with the house of David . . ." (See context in Appendix A.) Highlighted this page is from MS 95, 1897.

[271] Verbatim use of *Matt. 27: 24* as in Hanna, p. 694, though Hanna reverses "that" and "rather."

[272] Verbatim use of the people's cry of *Matt. 27:25* as in Hanna, p. 704, and Farrar, p. 639. However, Ellen White is original in specifically describing Caiaphas as the instigator of the cry.

At this exhibition of satanic madness,[273] the light of conviction[274] shone more clearly upon the mind of Pilate. He had never before witnessed such rash presumption and heartless cruelty. And in strong contrast with the ungovernable passion of his persecutors was the dignified repose of Jesus. In his own mind Pilate said, He is a god, and thought he could discern a soft light shining about his head. Looking thus upon Christ he turned pale with fear and self-condemnation; then, confronting the people with a troubled countenance, he said, I am clear of his blood. Take ye him and crucify him;[275] but mark ye, priests and rulers, I pronounce him a just man, and may He whom he claims as his Father judge you for this day's work, and not me. Then turning to Jesus he continued, Forgive me for this act; I am not able to save you. {3SP 146.3}

Only a short time before, the governor had declared to his prisoner that he had power to release or to condemn him; but he now thought that he could not save him, and also his own position and honor; and he preferred to sacrifice an innocent life rather than his own worldly power.[276] Had he acted promptly and firmly at the first, carrying out his convictions of right, his will would not have been overborne by the mob; they would not have presumed to dictate to him. His wavering and indecision proved his irredeemable ruin. How many, like Pilate, sacrifice principle and integrity, in order to shun disagreeable consequences. Conscience and duty point one way, and self-interest points another;[277]

In fear and self-condemnation Pilate looked upon the Saviour. In the vast sea of upturned faces, His alone was peaceful. About His head a soft light seemed to shine. Pilate said in his heart, He is a God. Turning to the multitude he declared, I am clear of His blood. Take ye Him, and crucify Him.[278] But mark ye, priests and rulers, I pronounce Him a just man. May He whom He claims as His Father judge you and not me for this day's work. Then to Jesus he said, Forgive me for this act; I cannot save You. And when he had again scourged Jesus, he delivered Him to be crucified.[279] {DA 738.1b}

Pilate longed to deliver Jesus. But he saw that he could not do this, and yet retain his own position and honor. Rather than lose his worldly power, he chose to sacrifice an innocent life.[280] How many, to escape loss or suffering, in like manner sacrifice principle. Conscience and duty point one way, and self-interest points another.[281]

---

[273] Same word, Jones, p. 380.

[274] Same word, Hanna, p. 700, though not in connection with the cry of the Jews, which he does not cite until p. 705.

[275] Verbatim use of *John 19:6* as in Hanna, p. 697.

[276] Verbatims are a composite of several sources. ±Pressensé, p. 515, has "Pilate openly sacrifices Jesus to his ambition, knowing that he is condemning an innocent man . . ." Farrar, p. 630, has "stirring up a new and apparently terrible rebellion rather than condescend to a simple concession . . ." Neander, p. 417, has "his personal security was more to him than the life of an innocent man." Hanna, p. 701, has "He allowed worldly interest to predominate over the sense of duty." The earlier 1SG 56.1 has "if he did not deliver Jesus to be crucified, he would lose his power and worldly honor, and would be denounced as a believer on the impostor, as they termed him. . . . For his own selfish interest, and love of honor from the great men of earth, he delivered an innocent man to die."

[277] More verbatim than strict paraphrase, Hanna, p. 701, "when conscience and duty pointed in the one direction, and passion and self-interest pointed in the other . . ."

[278] Verbatim use of *John 19:6* as in Hanna, p. 697.

[279] The last half of the sentence, a paraphrase in Hanna, p. 699, from *Mark 15:15*.

[280] Verbatims are a composite of several sources. The same elements are in 1SG 56.1, "They suggested to him that if he did not take any part in condemning JESUS, others would; the multitude were thirsting for his blood; and if he did not deliver Jesus to be crucified, he would lose his power and worldly honor, and would be denounced as a believer on the impostor, as they termed him. . . . For his own selfish interest, and love of honor from the great men of earth, he delivered an innocent man to die. If Pilate had followed his conviction, he would have had nothing to do with condemning JESUS." "Innocent" is from *Matt. 27:4*.

[281] More verbatim than strict paraphrase, Hanna, p. 701.

and the current, setting strongly in the wrong direction,[282] sweeps away into the thick darkness of guilt[283] him who compromises with evil. {3SP 147.1}

Satan's rage was great as he saw that all the cruelty which he had led the Jews to inflict upon Jesus had not forced the least murmur[284] from his lips. Although he had taken upon himself the nature of man, he was sustained by a Godlike[285] fortitude, and departed in no particular from the will of his Father. {3SP 147.2}

«Wonder, O Heavens! and be astonished, O earth!»[286] Behold the oppressor and the oppressed. A vast multitude inclose [sic] the Saviour of the world. Mocking and jeering are mingled with the coarse oaths of blasphemy.[287] His lowly birth and humble life are commented upon by unfeeling wretches. His claim to be the Son of God is ridiculed by the chief priests and elders,

---

[282] A simple paraphrase with key verbatim words, Hanna, p. 701, "we have acted over and over again the very part of Pilate; hesitated and wavered, and argued and debated, and opened our ears to what others told us, or allowed ourselves to be borne away by some strong tide that was running in the wrong direction."

[283] Farrar, p. 641, uses the word "guilt" in this same context.

[284] Hanna, p. 697, uses "unmurmuring," though verbatim phrasing for 3SP is carried over from 1SG 57.1, "Satan's rage was great as he saw that all the cruelty which he had led the chief priests to inflict on JESUS had not called forth from him the least murmur." Compare Jesus' use of "murmur" in John 6:43.

[285] Same word, Hanna, p. 698; Farrar, p. 635; Jones, p. 389 (see Appendix A); but earlier in 1SG 53.1f, "his noble, GOD-like bearing."

[286] Near verbatim "Wonder … religious frenzy" carried over from Ellen White's "The Sufferings of Christ" [PH169], (1869) 7.2. The phrase "wonder, O heavens, and be astonished, O earth" was adapted from Isa. 1:2, "Hear, O heavens," and Jer. 2:12, "Be astonished, O ye heavens," and is found in Melvill's Sermons, vol. 1 (1853), p. 44, although there were no other significant parallels between Melvill and PH169, and Ellen White probably did not gain access to Melvill until 1872; she did use the sermon that this phrase is in for "Christ Man's Example" (RH 7-5-1887), though not this specific phrase in that article. This apt interjection was frequently used in the 1700s and 1800s—e.g. Paul Wright, The New and Complete Life of Our Blessed Lord (1810), p. 63; and Andrew Gray, "The Cause, Symptoms, and Cure, of Indifference to Religion," The Scotch Preacher (1779), p. 221. Near verbatims of the phrase are in Harris, The Great Teacher (1836), p. 53, "Hear, O heavens; and be astonished, O earth!"; Fleetwood (1860), p. 356, "Hear, O heavens! O earth, earth, earth, hear!"; and +Flavel (1716), p. 109, "Blush, O ye Heavens, and tremble, O Earth." To whom should Ellen White give credit?

[287] For the last two sentences, a very loose paraphrase, Hanna (1863), p. 697, though the verbatim wording "Behold the oppressor" through "passed from lip to lip" is from PH169 (1869), p. 7.2.

The current sets strongly in the wrong direction,[288] and he who compromises with evil is swept away into the thick darkness of guilt.[289] {DA 738.2}

Satan's rage was great as he saw that all the abuse inflicted upon the Saviour had not forced the least murmur[290] from His lips. Although He had taken upon Him the nature of man, He was sustained by a godlike[291] fortitude, and departed in no particular from the will of His Father. {DA 735.1}

«Wonder, O heavens! And be astonished, O earth!»[292] Behold the oppressor and the oppressed. A maddened throng enclose the Saviour of the world. Mocking and jeering are mingled with the coarse oaths of blasphemy.[293] His lowly birth and humble life are commented upon by the unfeeling mob. His claim to be the Son of God is ridiculed,

---

[288] A simple paraphrase with key verbatim words, Hanna, p. 701.

[289] Farrar, p. 641, uses the word "guilt" in this same context.

[290] The word "unmurmuring" is used in the same context by Hanna, p. 697, though verbatim phrasing is carried over through 3SP 147.2 from 1SG 57.1, "Satan's rage was great as he saw that all the cruelty which he had led the chief priests to inflict on JESUS had not called forth from him the least murmur."

[291] The word "godlike," Hanna, p. 698; Farrar, p. 635; Jones, p. 389; though 1SG 53.1f has "his noble, GOD-like bearing."

[292] Near verbatim "Wonder … lip to lip" carried over from PH169 7.2. Verbatim phrase "wonder, O heavens, and be astonished, O earth" adapted from Isa. 1:2, "Hear, O heavens," and Jer. 2:12, "Be astonished, O ye heavens." Expression is used in Melvill, p. 44; etc.; near verbatims in +Flavel, p. 109; Harris, TGT 53; and Fleetwood (1860), p. 356. To whom should she give credit? Ellen White also uses this expression to call attention to the wonder of Jesus' birth in DA 49.2.

[293] For the last two sentences, a very loose paraphrase, Hanna, p. 697.

and the vulgar jest and insulting sneer are passed from lip to lip. Satan has full control of the minds of his servants. In order to do this effectually, he had commenced with the chief priests and the elders, and imbued them with a religious frenzy. This they had communicated to the rude and uncultivated mob, until there was a corrupt harmony in the feelings of all, from the hypocritical priests and elders down to the most debased. Christ, the precious Son of God, was led forth and delivered to the people to be crucified.[294] {3SP 148.1}

[294] Phrase carried over from *1SG* 57.1, "The SON of GOD was delivered to the people to be crucified. They led the dear SAVIOUR away." Description is from *Matt. 27:31; Luke 23:26;* and *John 19:16.*

and the vulgar jest and insulting sneer are passed from lip to lip.[295] {DA 734.2}

The people of Israel had made their choice. Pointing to Jesus they had said, "Not this man, but Barabbas." Barabbas, the robber and murderer, was the representative of Satan. Christ was the representative of God. Christ had been rejected; Barabbas had been chosen.[296] Barabbas they were to have. In making this choice they accepted him who from the beginning was a liar and a murderer.[297] Satan was their leader. As a nation they would act out his dictation.[298] His works they would do. His rule they must endure. That people who chose Barabbas in the place of Christ were to feel the cruelty of Barabbas as long as time should last. {DA 738.5}

Looking upon the smitten Lamb of God, the Jews had cried, "His blood be on us, and on our children." That awful cry ascended to the throne of God. That sentence, pronounced upon themselves, was written in heaven. That prayer was heard. The blood of the Son of God was upon their children and their children's children, a perpetual curse.[299] {DA 739.1}

Terribly was it realized in the destruction of Jerusalem.[300] Terribly has it been manifested in the condition of the Jewish nation for eighteen hundred years,—a branch severed from the vine, a dead, fruitless branch, to be gathered up and burned.[301] From land to land throughout the world, from century to century, dead, dead in trespasses and sins![302] {DA 739.2}

---

[295] Unique taunts are from *PH169* 7.2. Specific eyewitness details are not in Hanna, March, or Jones.

[296] A very loose paraphrase of the paragraph to this point, Andrews, p. 541. The descriptions "robber" and "murderer" are taken from *John 18:40* and *Luke 23:19*. Several of the life of Christ authors, such as Jones, p. 381; Kitto, p. 414; ±Heinrich Ewald, *The Life of Jesus Christ* (1865), p. 321; and Robinson, p. 439, use the double designation. ±William S. Plumer, *The Rock of our Salvation* (1867), p. 185, has only "murderer." The double designation was also used in *3SP* 141.2. Neither Hanna, March, or Jones describe Barabbas being the representative of Satan; only Ellen White does so.

[297] Description of Satan as liar and murder from *John 8:44*. While ±Ellicott (1863), p. 321, speaks of "the clinging desperation of the last assaults of Satan." Only Ellen White calls attention to Satan's role in inspiring the hatred of the Jews toward Jesus.

[298] Highlighted in this paragraph is from MS 112, 1897.

[299] Whole paragraph, a very loose paraphrase, Edersheim, p. 578 (see context in Chapter 7), using verbatim words from *Matt. 27:25*; see also Farrar, pp. 639, 640.

[300] A similar thought, Farrar, p. 640.

[301] Words "gathered" and "burned" are from *Matt. 13:40*. Words "fruitless branch" are an allusion to *John 15:1–5*.

[302] Two verbatim phrases from Edersheim, p. 581, which, according to 21st century academic standards of attribution, would not require quotation marks or a footnote. "With this cry Judaism was, in the person of its representatives guilty of denial of God, of blasphemy, of apostasy. It committed suicide; and, ever since, has its dead body been carried in show from land to land, and from century, to century; to be dead, and to remain dead, till He come a second time, Who is the Resurrection and the Life!" (See context in Chapter 7.) Phrase "dead in trespasses and sins" is from *Eph. 2:1*. Highlighted is from MS 95, 1897.

Terribly will that prayer be fulfilled in the great judgment day. When Christ shall come to the earth again,[303] not as a prisoner surrounded by a rabble will men see Him. They will see Him then as heaven's King. Christ will come in His own glory, in the glory of His Father, and the glory of the holy angels. Ten thousand times ten thousand, and thousands of thousands of angels, the beautiful and triumphant sons of God, possessing surpassing loveliness and glory, will escort Him on His way.[304] Then shall He sit upon the throne of His glory,[305] and before Him shall be gathered all nations. Then every eye shall see Him, and they also that pierced Him.[306] In the place of a crown of thorns, He will wear a crown of glory,—a crown within a crown. In place of that old purple kingly robe,[307] He will be clothed in raiment of whitest white, "so as no fuller on earth can white them."[308] Mark 9:3. And on His vesture and on His thigh a name will be written, "King of kings, and Lord of lords."[309] Rev. 19:16. Those who mocked and[310] smote Him will be there. The priests and rulers will behold again the scene in the judgment hall. Every circumstance will appear before them, as if written in letters of fire.[311] Then those who prayed, "His blood be on us, and on our children," will receive the answer to their prayer. Then the whole world will know and understand. They will realize who and what they, poor, feeble, finite beings, have been warring against. In awful agony and horror they will cry to the mountains and rocks, "Fall on us, and hide us from the face of Him that sitteth on the throne, and from the wrath of the Lamb: for the great day of His wrath is come; and who shall be able to stand?"[312] Rev. 6:16, 17. {*DA* 739.3}

. . . .

In our last exhibit, we turn to "Calvary," Chapter 78 of *The Desire of Ages*, and the literary parallels we find there. "Calvary" approaches the crucifixion of Christ from the vantage point of an eyewitness. It includes many details that are unique to Ellen White.[313]

Because of the interrelated nature of Chapters 77 and 78 of *The Desire of Ages*, our analysis of these chapters will be combined in Chapter 7 of this book—"*Evaluating Ellen White's Use of Sources.*"

---

[303] A related paraphrase "till He come a second time," following the two verbatim phrases of Edersheim, p. 581.

[304] "In His own glory" is from *Luke 9:26* and "in the glory of His Father with the holy angels" is from *Mat. 16:27* and *Mark 8:38*. Ellen White used the phrase "will escort him on His way" to describe these multitudes of angels in 1*SG* 61.2f, "All the heavenly host will escort him on his way with songs of victory, majesty and might, to him that was slain, yet lives again a mighty conqueror" (cf. *Rev. 5:12*). She also used it in *ST* 4-8-1889 and in a sermon in *ST* 6-17-1889.

[305] Highlighted is used in MS 39, 1898.

[306] Verbatim phrases from *Matt. 16:27*; *Rev. 5:11*; *Matt. 25:31, 32*; and *Rev. 1:7*.

[307] The expression "kingly robe" is in ±Ingraham, p. 388, though the exact expression "old purple, kingly robe" is carried over from 1*SG* 50.1. The "purple robe" of *John 19:2* and the mock obeisance of the soldiers in *Matt. 27:29* are used by most of the source works.

[308] Highlighted is from MS 112, 1897.

[309] Highlighted is from *ST* 4-8-1889, "He is coming with clouds and with great glory. A multitude of shining angels, 'ten thousand times ten thousand, and thousands of thousands,' will escort him on his way. He will not wear that simple, seamless robe, but robes of glory, white, 'so as no fuller on earth can white them;' and on his vesture and on his thigh a name will be written, 'King of kings, and Lord of lords.'"

[310] Highlighted is from MS 111, 1897.

[311] Highlighted is from MS 39, 1898.

[312] Unique use of *Rev. 6:16, 17*, with Hanna's word "cry," but not following his loose paraphrase of the text. Ellen White uses "rocks and mountains" in *RH* 4-1-1875. Highlighted is from MS 112, 1897.

[313] James White wrote that, there are many things in her writings "as truthful as they are beautiful and harmonious, which cannot be found in the writings of others" (*Life Sketches of James and Ellen White*, 1880, pp. 328, 329).

CHAPTER 6

An Eyewitness Account—

Calvary*

"AND when they were come to the place, which is called Calvary, there they crucified Him."

"That He might sanctify the people with His own blood," Christ "suffered without the gate." Heb. 13:12. For transgression of the law of God, Adam and Eve were banished from Eden. Christ, our substitute, was to suffer without the boundaries of Jerusalem. He died outside the gate,[1] where felons and murderers were executed. Full of significance are the words, "Christ hath redeemed us from the curse of the law, being made a curse for us." Gal. 3:13. {*DA* 741.2}

A vast multitude followed Jesus from the judgment hall to Calvary. The news of His condemnation had spread throughout Jerusalem, and people of all classes and all ranks flocked toward the place of crucifixion. The priests and rulers had been bound by a promise not to molest Christ's followers if He Himself were delivered to them, and the disciples and believers from the city and the surrounding region joined the throng that followed the Saviour. {*DA* 741.3}

As Jesus passed the gate of Pilate's court, the cross which had been prepared for Barabbas was laid upon His bruised and bleeding shoulders.[2] Two companions of Barabbas were to suffer death at the same time with Jesus, and upon them also crosses were placed.[3] The Saviour's burden was too heavy for Him in His weak and suffering condition.[4] Since the Passover supper with His disciples, He had taken neither food nor drink.[5] He had agonized in the garden of Gethsemane in conflict with satanic agencies.[6] He had endured the anguish of the betrayal, and had seen His disciples forsake Him and flee. He had been taken to Annas, then to Caiaphas, and then to Pilate. From Pilate He had been sent to Herod, then sent again to Pilate. From insult to renewed insult, from mockery to mockery, twice tortured by the scourge,—all that night there had been scene after scene of a character to try the soul of man to the uttermost.[7] Christ had not failed. He had spoken no word but that tended to glorify God.

---

* This chapter is based on *Matt. 27:31–53; Mark 15:20–38; Luke 23:26–46; John 19:16–30.*

[1] A paraphrase of *Heb. 13:12*, Farrar (1874), p. 647. Highlighted in this paragraph is from MS 101, 1897 in 12*MR* 396.5.

[2] Two verbatim words, Hanna (1863), p. 701. The eyewitness detail of where He was when the cross was laid upon Him is not in Hanna. Hall (1860), p. 581, has "At last, O Saviour, there thou comest out of Pilate's gate, bearing that which shall soon bear thee."

[3] Several of the life of Christ authors develop the thought of *Mark 15:7*, "bound with them that had made insurrection"—e.g. ±Macduff, *BTS* (1878) 367, "They are bound with ropes, and are walking in the same dismal procession." See also ±Simons (1877), p. 216.

[4] A loose paraphrase, ±Macduff, *BTS* 365, "the torture of mind ... the nigh-watch of agony—the sleeplessness and scourgings." Verbatim words, 1*SG* 57.2 "He was weak and feeble through pain and suffering, caused by the scourging and blows which he had received, yet they laid on him the heavy cross upon which they were soon to nail him. But JESUS fainted beneath the burden."

[5] A strict paraphrase, Edersheim, *LTJM*, vol. 2, p. 586, "Since the Paschal Supper Jesus had not tasted either food or drink."

[6] A strict paraphrase, Edersheim, p. 586, "There had he agonised in mortal conflict ..." Also treating this thought are Pentecost, *BS* '88, p. 185, and ±Lange (1872), p. 283. Ellen White's words which predate Edersheim, 3*SP* 184.1, has the fundamental thought, "With what intense interest had they followed the closing scenes of the conflict! They had beheld the Saviour enter the garden of Gethsemane, his soul bowed down by a horror of darkness that he had never before experienced."

[7] Starting with "He had endured the anguish" to this point, Edersheim, p. 586, bears the closest resemblance (without "His disciples" and "scene"); Farrar, pp. 643, 644, describes the events mentioned from the same starting point to the end of the paragraph,

All through the disgraceful farce of a trial «He had borne Himself with» firmness and dignity.[8] But when after the second scourging the cross was laid upon Him, human nature could bear no more. He fell fainting beneath the burden.[9] {DA 741.4}

The crowd that followed the Saviour saw His weak and staggering steps, but they manifested no compassion.[10] They taunted and reviled[11] Him because He could not carry the heavy cross. Again the burden was laid upon Him, and again He fell fainting to the ground.[12] His persecutors saw that it was impossible for Him to carry His burden farther.[13] They were puzzled to find anyone who would bear the humiliating load. The Jews themselves could not do this, because the defilement would prevent them from keeping the Passover. None even of the mob that followed Him would stoop to bear the cross. {DA 742.1}

At this time a stranger, Simon a Cyrenian, coming in from the country, meets the throng.[14] He hears the taunts and ribaldry of the crowd; he hears the words contemptuously repeated, Make way for the King of the Jews! He stops in astonishment at the scene; and as he expresses his compassion, they seize him and place the cross upon his shoulders.[15] {DA 742.2}

Simon had heard of Jesus. His sons were believers in the Saviour, but he himself was not a disciple. The bearing of the cross to Calvary was a blessing to Simon, and he was ever after grateful for this providence. It led him to take upon himself the cross of Christ from choice, and ever cheerfully stand beneath its burden.[16] {DA 742.3}

Not a few women are in the crowd that follow the Uncondemned to His cruel death. Their attention is fixed upon Jesus.[17] Some of them have seen Him before. Some have carried to Him their sick and suffering ones.[18] Some have themselves been healed. The story of the scenes that have taken place is related. They wonder at the hatred of the crowd toward Him for whom their own hearts are melting and ready to break.[19] And notwithstanding the action of the maddened throng, and the angry words of the priests and rulers, these women give expression to their sympathy. As Jesus falls fainting beneath the cross, they break forth into mournful wailing.[20] {DA 742.4}

---

but uses "night," "garden," "Herod," "scourging," and "scenes." Pentecost, *BS '88* 185, 186; Strickland 163.2; and Schauffler 121 also parallel. Gladys King-Taylor, *Literary Beauty of Ellen G. White's Writings*, p. 97, cites this paragraph as a good example of *iteration*.

[8] A paraphrase, Edersheim, p. 586, "All throughout He had borne Himself with a Divine Majesty . . ."

[9] For the last two sentences, a loose paraphrase, Farrar, pp. 643, 644, and ±Lange, p. 283; Kitto, *DBI* (1853), vol. 7, p. 419; Edersheim, p. 587; and ±Macduff, *BTS* 365; so also 3*SP* 150.1, though EGW uses "fainting," "beneath," and "burden." J. S. C. Abbott, p. 131, has "fainting beneath the load," and Stalker (1880), p. 144, has "fainting beneath the burden of the cross." Highlighted in this paragraph is from MS 95, 1897, a manuscript that also uses the recognizable "land to land" statement of Edersheim.

[10] Hanna, p. 702, in this same context says: "But compassion has no place in the hearts of these crucifiers . . ."

[11] Possibly derived from the "tauntings and revilings" of Jones (1868), p. 386.

[12] "Burden" and "faint" within six sentences in ±Bennett, p. 435.

[13] A loose paraphrase, Kitto, p. 419.

[14] A paraphrase of *Mark 15:2*, "who passed by," from the previous sentence, though used more figuratively, Hanna, p. 702. A paraphrase, Farrar, p. 644; Jones, p. 385; and ±Macduff, *BTS* 366. 3*SP* 150.3 has "coming from an opposite direction."

[15] A paraphrase of *Luke 23:26*, Pentecost, *BS '88*, p. 186; Kitto, pp. 419, 420; and 3*SP* 150.3. Phrase "cross upon his shoulders" is found in ±Didon (1893), vol. 2, p. 349, and ±Ingraham, *PHD* (1855) 393. Only Ellen White gives the eyewitness detail of Simon's compassion.

[16] For the last two sentences, a loose paraphrase (not including "cross"), Hanna, p. 702, and, a very loose paraphrase without verbatim, Kitto, pp. 419, 420. A similar thought is found in ±Weiss (1894), p. 363, and ±Smith, *NTH* (1876) 329.

[17] Nearly verbatim, Hanna, p. 703; phrasing assimilated by Mrs. White and used throughout her writings.

[18] Ellen White used the phrase "their sick and suffering ones" in a sermon in *RH* 4-9-1889.

[19] A very loose paraphrase of two sentences with near verbatim words, Hanna, p. 703.

[20] Words "sympathy" and "wailing" are used in this same context by Jones, p. 386.

This was the only thing that attracted Christ's attention.[21] Although full of suffering, while bearing the sins of the world,[22] He was not indifferent to the expression of grief.[23] He looked upon these women with tender compassion.[24] They were not believers in Him; He knew that they were not lamenting Him as one sent from God, but were moved by feelings of human pity.[25] He did not despise their sympathy, but it awakened in His heart a deeper sympathy for them.[26] "Daughters of Jerusalem," He said, "weep not for Me, but weep for yourselves, and for your children." From the scene before Him, Christ looked forward to the time of Jerusalem's destruction.[27] In that terrible scene, many of those who were now weeping for Him were to perish with their children.[28] {*DA* 743.1}

From the fall of Jerusalem the thoughts of Jesus passed to a wider judgment.[29] In the destruction of the impenitent city He saw a symbol of the final destruction to come upon the world.[30] He said, "Then shall they begin to say to the mountains, Fall on us; and to the hills, Cover us. For if they do these things in a green tree, what shall be done in the dry?"[31] By the green tree, Jesus represented Himself, the innocent Redeemer.[32] God suffered His wrath against transgression to fall on His beloved Son. Jesus was to be crucified for the sins of men. What suffering, then, would the sinner bear[33] who continued in sin? All the impenitent and unbelieving would know a sorrow and misery that language would fail to express. {*DA* 743.2}

Of the multitude that followed the Saviour to Calvary, many had attended Him with joyful hosannas and the waving of palm branches as He rode triumphantly into Jerusalem.[34] But not a few who had then shouted His praise, because it was popular to do so, now swelled the cry of "Crucify Him, crucify Him."[35] When Christ rode into Jerusalem, the hopes of the disciples had been raised to the highest pitch. They had pressed close about their Master, feeling that it was a high honor to be connected with Him. Now in His humiliation they followed Him at a distance. They were filled

---

[21] A paraphrase with the verbatim words "only" and "attracted," Hanna, p. 703. ±Deems (1880), p. 665, has the verbatim words "only" and "attention"; however, his work is not listed in the Ellen G. White libraries.

[22] Phrase "the sins of the world" is from *John 1:29*.

[23] A strict paraphrase, Hanna, p. 704, "Jesus does not reject, the expression of their pity"; cf. ±Deems, pp. 664, 665.

[24] A paraphrase, ±Clark (1860), p. 281, "Turning, therefore, to the mourners, he said in mild, yet empathetic tones"; but verbatim words "with tender compassion" are from 3*SP* 151.1. Phrase "these women" used in Hanna, p. 703.

[25] A very loose paraphrase from two sentences seven sentences apart, Hanna, p. 703; Jones, p. 386, also uses "lamenting."

[26] A paraphrase, Hanna, p. 704, and ±Deems, p. 664.

[27] Simple paraphrase, Hanna, p. 708, ". . . the coming destruction of Jerusalem was present to his thoughts during the last days and hours of his earthly ministry." Highlighted is from MS 96, 1894.

[28] A paraphrase from four sentences, Hanna, p. 704; ±Lange, p. 285, and 3*SP* 151.2 contain a similar thought.

[29] A loose paraphrase, Hanna, p. 705.

[30] A loose paraphrase, Hanna, p. 705.

[31] Verbatim use of *Luke 23:30* with a paraphrase of *Luke 23:31*, Hanna, pp. 704, 707.

[32] The word "innocent," from *Matt. 27:4*, is used in this context by Farrar, p. 646, but not directly connected to the "green tree." 3*SP* (1878) 151.3 has "The innocent were represented by the green tree."

[33] Starting with "Jesus was to be crucified" to this point, a possible very loose paraphrase, Kennedy, *MP* (1860) 455, "If such sufferings are executed upon me, the innocent, what shall befall those who are steeped in crime?" and ±Cumming, *SR-Lk* (1854) 499, based on "And if the righteous scarcely be saved, where shall the ungodly and the sinner appear?" of *1 Peter 4:18*.

[34] Thought in Hanna, p. 695; Kitto, pp. 414, 420; Matthew Henry (1828), vol. 5, p. 328; Hall (1860), p. 582; Wylie, *SB* (1867) 279; and ±Henry Ward Beecher, vol. 2, p. 252. However, the verbatim wording is carried over from 3*SP* 151. *John 12:13* supplies two of the verbatim terms, "Took branches of palm trees . . . and cried, Hosanna." *Matt. 21:10* supplied another—"into Jerusalem."

[35] A loose paraphrase, ±Angus (1853), p. 267; ±Trench (1860), p. 296; and Cumming *SR-Jn* (1856) 204, 205. Verbatim cry is from *Luke 23:21*, and actual phrasing is from 3*SP* 152.1.

---

with grief, and bowed down with disappointed hopes. How were the words of Jesus verified: "All ye shall be offended because of Me this night: for it is written, I will smite the shepherd, and the sheep of the flock shall be scattered abroad." Matt. 26:31. {*DA* 743.3}

Arriving at the place of execution,[36] the prisoners were bound to the instruments of torture. The two thieves wrestled in the hands of those who placed them on the cross; but Jesus made no resistance.[37] The mother of Jesus, supported by John the beloved disciple, had followed the steps of her Son to Calvary. She had seen Him fainting «under the burden of the cross»,[38] and had longed to place a supporting hand beneath His wounded head, and to bathe that brow which had once been pillowed upon her bosom. But she was not permitted this mournful privilege. With the disciples she still cherished the hope that Jesus would manifest His power, and deliver Himself from His enemies.[39] Again her heart would sink as she recalled the words in which He had foretold the very scenes that were then taking place. As the thieves were bound to the cross, she looked on with agonizing suspense. Would He who had given life to the dead suffer Himself to be crucified? Would the Son of God suffer Himself to be thus cruelly slain? Must she give up her faith that Jesus was the Messiah? Must she witness His shame and sorrow, without even the privilege of ministering to Him in His distress? She saw His hands stretched upon the cross; the hammer and the nails were brought, and as the spikes were driven through the tender flesh, the heart-stricken disciples bore away from the cruel scene the fainting form of the mother of Jesus.[40] {*DA* 744.1}

The Saviour made no murmur of complaint. His face remained calm and serene, but great drops of sweat stood upon His brow.[41] There was no pitying hand to wipe the death dew from His face, nor words of sympathy and unchanging fidelity to stay His human heart. While the soldiers were doing their fearful work, Jesus prayed for His enemies, "Father, forgive them; for they know not what they do."[42] His mind passed from His own suffering to the sin of His persecutors, and the terrible

---

[36] A strict paraphrase, Kitto, p. 420, based on *Luke 23:33*, "And when they were come to the place, which is called Calvary . . ." Also using "place of execution" are Abbott (1872), p. 131; Andrews (1891), p. 553; ±Angus, p. 259; Edersheim (1886), pp. 583, 584, 585, and 587; Farrar, p. 646; Fleetwood, p. 354; Geikie (1877), vol. 2, p. 562; Hanna, p. 701; ±Ingraham, p. 389; Jones, p. 386; ±Lange, pp. 284, 290, 299, 305, and 323; Neander (1848), pp. 417, 418; ±Smith, *NTH* (1876) 330; and ±Stalker (1880), pp. 141, 142. Verbatim carried over from 3*SP* 153.1.

[37] Verbatim phrase, ±Ingraham, p. 401, though Ingraham has the first thief resisting, but not the second one. 1*SG* 59.1, on the other hand, agrees with *DA* 744.1, "The thieves were taken by force, and after much resistance on their part, their arms were thrust back and nailed to their crosses. But JESUS meekly submitted. He needed no one to force his arms back upon the cross."

[38] Phrase "under the burden of the cross," ±Lange (1872), p. 283. ±Macduff, *BTS* (1878) 366 has "When He fell under the burden of the cross, He may first have heard their bitter sobs." 3*SP* 150.1 has "beneath the heavy burden of the cross."

[39] Description of Mary carried over from 1*SG* 58.1a, "The mother of JESUS was there. Her heart was pierced with anguish, such as none but a fond mother can feel. Her stricken heart still hoped, with the disciples, that her SON would work some mighty miracle, and deliver himself from his murderers. She could not endure the thought that he would suffer himself to be crucified." For "the mother of Jesus," see *Acts 1:14*; the word "pierced" comes from the prophecy to Mary in *Luke 2:35*.

[40] ±Ingraham, p. 401, "The piercing nails, rending his tender flesh, made it quiver, and caused Him to turn deadly pallid . . ." Verbatim carried over through 3*SP* 153.1 from 1*SG* 58.1b, "Her stricken heart still hoped, with the disciples, that her SON would work some mighty miracle, and deliver himself from his murderers. . . . But the preparations were made, and they laid JESUS upon the cross. The hammer and the nails were brought. The heart of his disciples fainted within them. The mother of JESUS was agonized, almost beyond endurance, and as they stretched JESUS upon the cross, and were about to fasten his hands with the cruel nails to the wooden arms, the disciples bore the mother of JESUS from the scene, that she might not hear the crashing of the nails, as they were driven through the bone and muscle of his tender hands and feet." The use of "the mother of Jesus," "some mighty miracle," and "not hear the crashing of the nails" in close proximity in ±Ingraham, p. 399 suggests that Ellen White may have read Ingraham prior to writing 1*SG*, though her description of the scene differs widely in critical details. For "nails," see *John 20:25*.

[41] Last half of sentence, nearly verbatim, ±Ingraham, p. 401, but closer to 1*SG* 58.1f, "JESUS murmured not; but groaned in agony. His face was pale, and large drops of sweat stood upon his brow," which borrows language from *Luke 22:44*.

[42] A paraphrase with same use of *Luke 23:34*, Hanna, p. 713, and Fleetwood, p. 355.

retribution that would be theirs.[43] No curses were called down upon the soldiers who were handling Him so roughly. No vengeance was invoked upon the priests and rulers, who were gloating over the accomplishment of their purpose.[44] Christ pitied them in their ignorance and guilt. He breathed only a plea for their forgiveness,—"for they know not what they do."[45] {*DA* 744.2}

Had they known that they were putting to torture One who had come to save the sinful race from eternal ruin, they would have been seized with remorse and horror. «But their ignorance did not» remove their guilt;[46] for it was their privilege to know and accept Jesus as their Saviour. Some of them would yet see their sin, and repent, and be converted. Some by their impenitence would make it an impossibility for the prayer of Christ to be answered for them. Yet, just the same, God's purpose was reaching its fulfillment. Jesus was earning the right to become the advocate of men in the Father's presence. {*DA* 744.3}

That prayer of Christ for His enemies embraced the world. It took in every sinner that had lived or should live, from the beginning of the world[47] to the end of time. Upon all rests «the guilt of crucifying the» Son of God. To all, forgiveness is freely offered.[48] "Whosoever will" may have peace with God, and inherit eternal life. {*DA* 745.1}

As soon as Jesus was nailed to the cross, it was lifted by strong men, and with great violence thrust into the place prepared for it.[49] This caused the most intense agony to the Son of God.[50] Pilate then wrote an inscription in Hebrew, Greek, and Latin, and placed it upon the cross, above the head of Jesus.[51] It read, "Jesus of Nazareth the King of the Jews." This inscription irritated the Jews. In Pilate's court they had cried, "Crucify Him." "We have no king but Caesar." John 19:15. They had declared that whoever should acknowledge any other king was a traitor. Pilate wrote out the sentiment they had expressed. No offense was mentioned, except that Jesus was the King of the Jews.[52] The inscription was a virtual acknowledgment of the allegiance of the Jews to the Roman power.[53] It declared that whoever might claim to be the King of Israel would be judged by them worthy of death.[54] The priests had overreached themselves. When they were plotting the death of

---

[43] A similar thought, using near verbatim "sufferings," Neander, pp. 417, 418, though Neander doesn't speak of His persecutors, but of "the blinded people, over whose heads he saw impending the judgments of GOD . . ."

[44] A very loose paraphrase, Neander, p. 419, ". . . He did not invoke the Divine judgments upon the heads of those who had, returning evil for good, inflicted such terrible tortures upon him . . ." Hanna, p. 713, uses "handling" and "no invoking of vengeance."

[45] For the last two sentences of the paragraph, including part of *Luke 23:34*, a similar thought over three paragraphs, ±Nicoll (1881), p. 312; Hanna, p. 713, and Barnes, 2*NG* (1854) 164.

[46] A paraphrase of *1 Cor. 2:8*, Hanna, p. 713, "Had they known what they did, . . . they would not have crucified the Lord of glory" and a near verbatim "But their ignorance did not take away their guilt." Similar thought, Barnes, 2*NG* 164; Pentecost, *BS* '89 354.

[47] A verbatim phrase used in *Acts 15:18* and *Eph. 3:9*.

[48] Two sentences in loose paraphrase, Farrar, p. 649. ±Angus, p. 268, and ±Bonar, p. 337, have "the guilt of crucifying the Lord."

[49] A loose paraphrase, Geikie, p. 563; and a very loose paraphrase, Farrar, p. 649; ±Ingraham, p. 401; and Melvill, *GL* (1856), vol. 1, p. 707, though Melvill does not mention it being thrust into the place prepared for it. Notice the greater similarity to 1*SG* 59.1, "They raised the cross after they had nailed JESUS to it, and with great force thrust it into the place prepared for it in the ground, tearing the flesh, and causing the most intense suffering."

[50] A paraphrase, Geikie (1877), p. 563. See 1*SG* 59.1 above and 3*SP* (1878) 154.2, "the most excruciating agony."

[51] Several sources mention the inscription of *Luke 23:38* and *John 19:20*—Hanna, p. 711; J. S. C. Abbott, p. 132; ±Clark, p. 286; Wylie, p. 278; ±Smith, *NTH* 331; Cumming, *SR-Jn* 364; and ±Thompson (1876), p. 389. Highlighted is from MS 95, 1897.

[52] A paraphrase from *Mark 15:26*, Fleetwood, p. 356. A similar thought in Barnes, 1*NG* 329.

[53] A simple paraphrase, Hanna, p. 712, "Pilate took them at their word, and put over Christ's head such a title as implied that any one claiming to be king of the Jews might, on that ground alone, whatever his rights and claims—on the ground simply of the allegiance which the Jews owed, and which the chief priests had avowed, to the Roman emperor—be justly condemned to death." Only Ellen White points out the implications of their hypocrisy (see end of paragraph).

[54] A paraphrase from the sentence cited above, Hanna, p. 712. Phrase "worthy of death" is from *Luke 23:15*.

Christ, Caiaphas had declared it expedient that one man should die[55] to save the nation. Now their hypocrisy was revealed. In order to destroy Christ, they had been ready to sacrifice even their national existence. {*DA* 745.2}

The priests saw what they had done, and asked Pilate to change the inscription.[56] They said, "Write not, The King of the Jews; but that He said, I am King of the Jews." But Pilate was angry with himself because of his former weakness, and he thoroughly despised the jealous and artful priests and rulers.[57] He replied coldly, "What I have written I have written."[58] {*DA* 745.3}

A higher power than Pilate or the Jews had directed the placing of that inscription above the head of Jesus. In the providence of God it was to awaken thought, and investigation of the Scriptures. The place where Christ was crucified was near to the city. Thousands of people from all lands were then at Jerusalem, and the inscription declaring Jesus of Nazareth the Messiah would come to their notice. It was a living truth, transcribed by a hand that God had guided.[59] {*DA* 745.4}

In the sufferings of Christ upon the cross prophecy was fulfilled.[60] Centuries before the crucifixion, the Saviour had foretold the treatment He was to receive. He said, "Dogs have compassed Me: the assembly of the wicked have enclosed Me: they pierced My hands and My feet. I may tell all My bones: they look and stare upon Me. They part My garments among them, and cast lots upon My vesture." Ps. 22:16–18.[61] The prophecy concerning His garments was carried out without counsel or interference from the friends or the enemies of the Crucified One. To the soldiers who had placed Him upon the cross, His clothing was given. Christ heard the men's contention as they parted the garments among them.[62] His tunic was woven throughout without seam,[63] and they said, "Let us not rend it, but cast lots for it, whose it shall be." {*DA* 746.1}

In another prophecy the Saviour declared, "Reproach hath broken My heart; and I am full of heaviness: and I looked for some to take pity, but there was none: and for comforters, but I found none. They gave Me also gall for My meat; and in My thirst they gave Me vinegar to drink." Ps. 69:20, 21. To those who suffered death by the cross, it was permitted to give a stupefying potion, to «deaden the sense of pain».[64] This was offered to Jesus; but when He had tasted it, He refused it.

---

[55] A verbatim phrase from *John 18:14*.

[56] A strict paraphrase, Cumming, *SR-Jn* 364, "They ran to Pilate and wished to alter this inscription . . ." is based on *John 19:21*, a verse mentioned in numerous sources.

[57] ±Clark, p. 269, mentions Pilate's despising the Jews, but says nothing about being angry with himself.

[58] Several life of Christ authors venture a tone to Pilate's reply of *John 19:22*. ±Didon, p. 352, says: "He answered contemptuously"; Geikie, p. 565, says he "dismissed them the laconic answer" (both were preceded by verbatim words in 3*SP* 155.1); and ±Ingraham, p. 404, says he answered "coldly." Here Ellen White says Pilate answered "coldly" because he "was angry with himself because of his former weakness." This is an explanation that is absent from ±Ingraham and from the other source works.

[59] Cumming, *SR-Jn* 364, has "the inscription that was literal truth." A similar thought is found in ±Blunt (1843), pp. 211, 212, and Anderson (1864), p. 703. Highlighted in this paragraph is from MS 95, 1897.

[60] Derivatives of the words "fulfill" and "prophecy" are used in this same context by Farrar, p. 652, and in 3*SP* 171.2.

[61] Unique use of *Ps. 22:16–18* as in Geikie, p. 563, and in ±Smith, *NTH* 331, though worded differently.

[62] In this same context and in two sentences back, the word "garments" is used in Edersheim, p. 592, and in Farrar, p. 652, though it is, of course, suggested by *Ps. 22:18*.

[63] Words "without seam," "woven," and "throughout" are from *John 19:23* and are used, among others, by Kitto, p. 422, and ±Smith, *NTH* 331. ±Crosby (1871), p. 494, uses only "woven."

[64] A paraphrase, Hanna, p. 711, using his verbatim words "deaden the sense of pain." Phrase "stupefying potion" used by Farrar, p. 648; Fleetwood, p. 354; Jones, p. 387; and ±Lange, p. 290. Geikie, p. 563, has "stupefying bitter drug"; Neander, p. 418, has "stupifying drug"; Edersheim (1886), p. 593, has "stupefying wine"; Kennedy (1860), p. 455, and ±Didon (1893), p. 350,

He would receive nothing that could becloud His mind.[65] His faith must keep fast hold upon God. This was His only strength. To becloud His senses[66] would give Satan an advantage. {*DA* 746.2}

The enemies of Jesus vented their rage upon Him «as He hung upon the cross.»[67] Priests, rulers, and scribes joined with the mob in mocking the dying Saviour. At the baptism and at the transfiguration the voice of God had been heard proclaiming Christ as His Son. Again, just before Christ's betrayal, the Father had spoken, witnessing to His divinity. But now the voice from heaven was silent. No testimony in Christ's favor was heard. Alone He suffered abuse and mockery from wicked men.[68] {*DA* 746.3}

"If Thou be the son of God," they said, "come down from the cross." In the wilderness of temptation Satan had declared,[69] "If Thou be the Son of God, command that these stones be made bread." "If Thou be the Son of God, cast Thyself down" from the pinnacle of the temple. Matt. 4:3, 6. And Satan with his angels, in human form, was present at the cross.[70] The archfiend and his hosts were co-operating with the priests and rulers. The teachers of the people had stimulated the ignorant mob to pronounce judgment against One upon whom many of them had never looked, until urged to bear testimony against Him. Priests, rulers, Pharisees, and the hardened rabble were confederated together in a satanic frenzy.[71] Religious rulers united with Satan and his angels. They were doing his bidding. {*DA* 746.4}

Jesus suffering and dying, heard every word as the priests declared, "He saved others; Himself He cannot save. Let Christ the King of Israel descend now from the cross, that we may see and believe."[72] Christ could have come down from the cross. But it is because He would not save Himself that the sinner has hope of pardon and favor with God.[73] {*DA* 749.1}

In their mockery of the Saviour, the men who professed to be the expounders of prophecy[74] were repeating the very words which Inspiration had foretold they would utter upon this occasion. Yet in their blindness they did not see that they were fulfilling the prophecy. Those who in derision uttered the words, "He trusted in God: let Him deliver Him now, if He will have Him: for He said, I am the Son of God," little thought that their testimony would sound down the ages. But although spoken in mockery, these words led men to search the Scriptures as they had never done before. Wise men heard, searched, pondered, and prayed. There were those who never rested until, by comparing scripture with scripture, they saw the meaning of Christ's mission. Never before was there such a

---

have "stupifying/stupefying drink." Ellen White, *LP* 277.2f (1883) has "stupefying draughts offered him in his dying agony."

[65] For the last two sentences, an expanded paraphrase of *Matt. 27:34*, giving the reason for his refusal and using "offered" and "nothing," Hanna, p. 711. Other expanded paraphrases of the verse are ±Deems, p. 667; Kitto, p. 421; Fleetwood, p. 355; Neander, p. 418; Geikie, p. 563; ±Pentecost, *IA* (1890), p. 386; Pentecost, *BS '88*, pp. 186, 187; and ±Stanford *FCA* (1893), p. 667. Renan, p. 346, has "He preferred to go out of life with his mind perfectly unclouded . . ." ±Adams (1878), p. 336, has "His mind was clear."

[66] Fleetwood, p. 355, uses the words "faith" and "strength." "Cloud His faculties" is used in Geikie, p. 563.

[67] Verbatim phrase, Hanna, p. 765, and Kitto, p. 421, though predated by 1*SG* 61.2f, "They cried to him mockingly, as he hung upon the cross . . ." Would quotation marks be needed for such an unexceptional phrase?

[68] Hanna, p. 714, uses the word "mockery" in this same context. Highlighted is from MS 101, 1897 in 12*MR* 396.4.

[69] Edersheim, p. 596, uses words "Wilderness" and "Temptation." Same thought expressed in Matthew Henry, p. 334. The phrase "wilderness of temptation" was a common expression for Ellen White.

[70] As mentioned in *DA* 733.2, this is an aspect of the crucifixion scene that only Ellen White described, having the curtain of spiritual realities pulled aside to reveal the conflict of the ages playing out at the cross. Highlighted is from MS 112, 1897.

[71] Highlighted is from MS 40, 1897.

[72] Fleetwood, p. 358; Hanna, p. 714; etc. use *Matt. 27:42*. Only Ellen White uses *Mark 15:31, 32* as in 1*SG* 59.2f and 61.2f.

[73] Exposition of *Matt. 27:42* with verbatim, ±Cumming, *SR-Mk* (1853) 220; ±Cumming, *LLL* (1880) 460; ±Mackenzie (1896), p. 271; Pentecost, *BS '88*, p. 189; and Matthew Henry, p. 334.

[74] Phrase "who profess to be the expounders of prophecy," was carried over from *RH* 12-17-1872 via 3*SP* 156.1.

COLOR CODING: Scripture verbatim «5 consecutive» paraphrase 1*SG* 3*SP PH169* article fresh

general knowledge of Jesus as when He hung upon the cross. Into the hearts of many who beheld the crucifixion scene, and who heard Christ's words, the light of truth was shining.[75] {*DA* 749.2}

To Jesus in His agony on the cross there came one gleam of comfort. It was the prayer of the penitent thief.[76] Both the men who were crucified with Jesus had at first railed upon Him;[77] and one under his suffering only became more desperate and defiant. But not so with his companion. This man was not a hardened criminal; he had been led astray by evil associations, but he was less guilty than many of those who stood beside the cross reviling the Saviour. He had seen and heard Jesus, and had been convicted by His teaching, but he had been turned away from Him by the priests and rulers. Seeking to stifle conviction, he had plunged deeper and deeper into sin, until he was arrested, tried as a criminal, and condemned to die on the cross. In the judgment hall and on the way to Calvary he had been in company with Jesus. He had heard Pilate declare, "I find no fault in Him." John 19:4. He had marked His godlike bearing, and His pitying forgiveness of His tormentors. On the cross he sees the many great religionists shoot out the tongue with scorn, and ridicule the Lord Jesus. He sees the wagging heads. He hears the upbraiding speeches taken up by his companion in guilt: "If Thou be Christ, save Thyself and us."[78] Among the passers-by he hears many defending Jesus. He hears them repeat His words, and tell of His works. The conviction comes back to him that this is the Christ.[79] Turning to his fellow criminal he says, "Dost not thou fear God, seeing thou art in the same condemnation?" The dying thieves have no longer anything to fear from man. But upon one of them presses the conviction that «there is a God to fear», a future to cause him to tremble.[80] And now, all sin-polluted as it is, his life history is about to close.[81] "And we indeed justly," he moans; "for we receive the due reward of our deeds: but this Man hath done nothing amiss." {*DA* 749.3}

There is no question now. There are no doubts, no reproaches.[82] When condemned for his crime, the thief had become hopeless and despairing;[83] but strange, tender thoughts now spring up. He calls to mind all he has heard of Jesus, how He has healed the sick and pardoned sin. He has heard the words of those who believed in Jesus and followed Him weeping. He has seen and read the title above the Saviour's head. He has heard the passers-by repeat it, some with grieved, quivering lips, others with jesting and mockery.[84] The Holy Spirit illuminates his mind, and little

---

[75] Highlighted is from *RH* 12-28-1897. Phrase "comparing scripture with scripture" was used 63 times in the EGW writings.

[76] ±Lange, p. 302, calls this request of the penitent thief a "prayer of faith."

[77] Other lives of Christ have difficulty reconciling this fact from *Matt. 27:44* with his later reproof of his fellow criminal. The description of the history of the penitent thief is unique to Ellen White.

[78] Verbatim use of *Luke 23:39* as in Jones, p. 389, though Jones lacks the phrase "wagging heads" of *Matt. 27:39* and *Mark 15:29*. 1SG 59.2, however, has "As JESUS hung upon the cross, some who passed by reviled him, wagging their heads, as though bowing to a king . . ." Hanna, p. 715, has both "wagging heads" and verbatim "upbraiding speeches," but lacks the reference to *Luke 23:39*.

[79] Hanna, p. 716, uses the words "conviction" and "Christ." In harmony with *DA*, ±Trench, SG (1867) 289, asks if acceptance of the penitent thief required his "being convinced and converted by all the wondrous evidences of a divine grace and love which shone out in the suffering Lord?"

[80] Simple paraphrase with verbatim, Hanna, p. 716, "he does not need to say, Dost thou not fear man? for man has already done all that man can do. But, 'Dost not thou fear God?' He knows then that there is a God to fear . . ."

[81] For the last two sentences, a similar thought, ±Trench, SG 306.

[82] A very loose paraphrase, with near verbatim words used by others, Hanna, p. 716. Word "reproaches" is from *Ps. 69:9*.

[83] Farrar, p. 655, has "half-despairing" for the repentant thief; ±Lange, pp. 302, 303, uses "despairing" for the unrepentant one.

[84] A very loose paraphrase for two sentences, making the same point, ±Nicoll, pp. 313, 314, "When all were mocking and deriding the Saviour, and when the other thief was calling upon Him to take Himself and them from the Cross, this robber saw a greater nobility in His continuing to hang there, read aright the words written over His head, and trusted Him through all the scorn as 'Lord.'" Though mentioned by Hanna, p. 717, Ellen White's eyewitness account distinguishes between the reactions of "the passers-by."

by little the chain of evidence is joined together.[85] In Jesus, bruised, mocked, and hanging upon the cross, he sees the Lamb of God, that taketh away the sin of the world.[86] Hope is mingled with anguish in his voice as the helpless, dying soul casts himself upon a dying Saviour. "Lord, remember me," he cries, "when Thou comest into Thy kingdom."[87] {*DA* 750.1}

Quickly the answer came. Soft and melodious the tone, full of love, compassion, and power the words: Verily I say unto thee today, Thou shalt be with Me in paradise.[88] {*DA* 750.2}

For long hours of agony, reviling and mockery have fallen upon the ears of Jesus. As He hangs upon the cross, there floats up to Him still the sound of jeers and curses. With longing heart He has listened for some expression of faith from His disciples. He has heard only the mournful words, "We trusted that it had been He which should have redeemed Israel."[89] How grateful then to the Saviour was the utterance of faith and love from the dying thief![90] While the leading Jews deny Him, and even the disciples doubt His divinity, the poor thief, upon the brink of eternity, calls Jesus Lord.[91] Many were ready to call Him Lord when He wrought miracles, and after He had risen from the grave; but none acknowledged Him as He hung dying upon the cross save the penitent thief who was saved at the eleventh hour.[92] {*DA* 750.3}

The bystanders caught the words as the thief called Jesus Lord. The tone of the repentant man arrested their attention. Those who at the foot of the cross[93] had been quarreling over Christ's garments, and casting lots upon His vesture, stopped to listen. Their angry tones were hushed. With bated breath they looked upon Christ, and waited for the response from those dying lips. {*DA* 751.1}

As He spoke the words of promise, the dark cloud that seemed to enshroud the cross was pierced by a bright and living light. To the penitent thief came the perfect peace of acceptance with God.[94] Christ in His humiliation was glorified. He who in all other eyes appeared to be conquered was a Conqueror.[95] He was acknowledged as the Sin Bearer.[96] Men may exercise power over His human body. They may pierce the holy temples with the crown of thorns. They may strip from

---

[85] A paraphrase with verbatim words, Hanna, p. 717, "He takes them up, collects, combines; the enlightening Spirit shines upon the evidence thus afforded, shines in upon his quickened soul; and there brightly dawns upon his spirit . . ."

[86] A very loose paraphrase, Neander, p. 420, "All that he could feel (and that he *did* feel) was a consciousness that his sufferings were the result of the sins of men, and a deep sympathy with the sufferings brought upon mankind by sin. Under these pangs of soul and body he sees before him the Holy One, persecuted, mocked, proved in the bitterest sufferings, yet steadfastly trusting in GOD, as described in the twenty-second Psalm . . ."

[87] Verbatim use of *Luke 23:42* in most source works.

[88] A paraphrase, Hanna, p. 720, "the prayer has scarce been offered when the answer comes . . ." Unlike Hanna, Ellen White mirrors a literal rendering of the Greek of *Luke 23:43*, "Verily unto thee I say today with Me thou shalt be in paradise."

[89] Same use of *Luke 24:21* as in Hanna, p. 717, though Hanna substitutes the word "hoped" for "trusted."

[90] A loose paraphrase, Hanna, p. 719. Nicoll, p. 259, also uses "how grateful."

[91] Same thought at expressed in the four sentences beginning with "With longing heart" in ±Nicoll (1881), p. 315, though the thought and verbatim sentence "While the leading . . . brink of eternity" is found earlier in *3SP* (1878) 158.2.

[92] A very loose paraphrase, Hanna, p. 718.

[93] "At the foot of the cross" is a phrase used by many sources, e.g. Andrews, p. 545; ±Didon, p. 352; Farrar, p. 646; ±Lange, p. 296; March, *WHJ* (1866) 313. It is a phrase used frequently by Ellen White, as seen in *2T* (1869) 285.2 and in the address of Mrs. E. G. White at the General Conference session held in Battle Creek, Nov. 19, 1883 (*RH* 7-1-1884). Only Ellen White gives the eyewitness description of those around the cross hearing Jesus' conversation with the thief.

[94] Two key words in a two-sentence description, ±Bennett, p. 457.

[95] A loose paraphrase, Edersheim, p. 588, "And, if proof were required of His Divine strength, even in the utmost depth of His Human weakness—how, conquered, He was Conqueror . . ." However, the idea was expressed earlier in *1SG* 67.1, "Satan and his angels had enjoyed a little moment of triumph . . . For as Jesus walked forth from his prison house a majestic conqueror . . ."

[96] Neander, p. 420, describes Jesus' sense "that his sufferings were the result of the sins of men."

Him His raiment, and quarrel over its division.[97] But they cannot rob Him of His power to forgive sins. In dying He bears testimony to His own divinity and to the glory of the Father. His ear is not heavy that it cannot hear, neither His arm shortened that it cannot save. It is His royal right to save unto the uttermost all who come unto God by Him.[98] {*DA* 751.2}

I say unto thee today, Thou shalt be with Me in Paradise. Christ did not promise that the thief should be with Him in Paradise that day. He Himself did not go that day to Paradise. He slept in the tomb, and on the morning of the resurrection He said, "I am not yet ascended to My Father." John 20:17. But on the day of the crucifixion, the day of apparent defeat and darkness, the promise was given. "Today" while dying upon the cross as a malefactor, Christ assures the poor sinner, Thou shalt be with Me in Paradise. {*DA* 751.3}

The thieves crucified with Jesus were placed "on either side one, and Jesus in the midst."[99] This was done by the direction of the priests and rulers. Christ's position between the thieves was to indicate that He was «the greatest criminal of the three».[100] Thus was fulfilled the scripture, "He was numbered with the transgressors."[101] Isa. 53:12. But the full meaning of their act the priests did not see. As Jesus, crucified with the thieves, was placed "in the midst,"[102] so His cross was placed in the midst of a world lying in sin. And the words of pardon spoken to the penitent thief kindled a light that will shine to the earth's remotest bounds.[103] {*DA* 751.4}

With amazement the angels beheld the infinite love of Jesus, who, suffering the most intense agony of mind and body, thought only of others,[104] and encouraged the penitent soul to believe. In His humiliation He as a prophet had addressed the daughters of Jerusalem; as priest and advocate He had pleaded with the Father to forgive His murderers; as a loving Saviour He had forgiven the sins of the penitent thief.[105] {*DA* 752.1}

As the eyes of Jesus wandered over the multitude about Him, one figure arrested His attention. At the foot of the cross stood His mother, supported by the disciple John.[106] She could not endure to

---

[97] A paraphrase, Hanna, p. 720, based on *Luke 23:34*, "They may strip his mortal body of its outward raiment, which these soldiers may divide among them as they please; his human soul they may strip of its outer garment of the flesh, and send it forth unclothed into the world of spirits." Ellen White would certainly take exception to the latter half of this statement!

[98] A loose paraphrase, Hanna, p. 720, "But his kingly right to dispense the royal gift of pardon, his power to save, can they strip him of that?" an expression of the extent of God's ability to save described in *Isa. 59:1* and *Heb. 7:25*.

[99] A paraphrase of *Matt. 27:38* with verbatim quoting of *John 19:18*, ⊥Bennett, p. 439. Compare 1SG 59.1, "With him they crucified two thieves, one on either side of JESUS."

[100] ⊥Ingraham, p. 398, "as if He himself were the greatest criminal of the three . . ." Same verbatim phrase is found in other sermons on the crucifixion. From the beginning of the paragraph to this point, same thought as in Pentecost, *BS '88*, p. 188, and in Matthew Henry, pp. 333, 643.

[101] Also using *Isa. 53:2*, Cumming, SR-Mk 220, has a similar thought, "And in order to degrade him, and show in what category they placed him, he was crucified between two thieves."

[102] A loose paraphrase of *John 19:18*, similar to Taylor, p. 601, and to Matthew Henry, p. 333.

[103] Common description "penitent thief," Edersheim (1893), p. 598; predated by 3SP (1878) 157.2.

[104] Verbatim phrase "thought only of others" carried over from 3SP (1878) 159.2, which predates its use in Edersheim, p. 570. ⊥Bennett, p. 470, uses the words "torment," "body," "mind," and "others"; Jones, p. 390, uses the word "love" in this same context; Kitto, p. 422, uses the words "thought" and "others"; the descriptions of the angels at the crucifixion are not in the sources, but are in 1SG 59.2f, "The angels who hovered over the scene of CHRIST's crucifixion . . ." and 1SG 60.1, "The angels had viewed the horrid scene of the crucifixion of their loved commander, until they could behold no longer . . ."

[105] This paragraph is a good example of a literary device used throughout Mrs. White's writings. "Balanced sentences are used most strikingly. . . . their effect is such as to give the reader the impression that Mrs. White was fond of balancing ideas." —Gladys King-Taylor, *Literary Beauty of Ellen G. White's Writings*, p. 73.

[106] A paraphrase, Geikie, p. 569, "as His eyes wandered over the crowd, He saw, through the gloom, John, standing by His mother's side." Verbatim wording, "The eyes of Jesus wandered over the multitude" carried over from 3SP 159.2.

remain away from her Son;[107] and John, knowing that the end was near, had brought her again to the cross. In His dying hour, Christ remembered His mother. Looking into her grief-stricken face and then upon John, He said to her, "Woman, behold thy son!" then to John, "Behold thy mother!"[108] John understood Christ's words, and accepted the trust. He «at once took Mary to his home», and from that hour cared for her tenderly.[109] O pitiful, loving Saviour; amid all His physical pain and mental anguish, He had a thoughtful care for His mother![110] He had no money with which to provide for her comfort; but He was enshrined in the heart of John, and He gave His mother to him as a precious legacy. Thus He provided for her that which she most needed,—the tender sympathy of one who loved her because she loved Jesus. And in receiving her as a sacred trust, John was receiving a great blessing. She was a constant reminder of his beloved Master. {*DA* 752.2}

The perfect example of Christ's filial love[111] shines forth with undimmed luster from the mist of ages. For nearly thirty years Jesus by His daily toil had helped bear the burdens of the home. And now, even in His last agony, He remembers to provide for His sorrowing, widowed mother.[112] The same spirit will be seen in every disciple of our Lord. Those who follow Christ will feel that it is a part of their religion to respect and provide for their parents. From the heart where His love is cherished, father and mother will never fail of receiving thoughtful care and tender sympathy.[113] {*DA* 752.3}

And now the Lord of glory was dying, a ransom for the race. In yielding up His precious life, Christ was not upheld by triumphant joy.[114] All was oppressive gloom. It was not the dread of death that weighed upon Him. It was not the pain and ignominy of the cross that caused His inexpressible agony. Christ was the prince of sufferers;[115] but His suffering was from a sense of the malignity of sin,[116] a knowledge that through familiarity with evil, man had become blinded to its enormity. Christ saw how deep is the hold of sin upon the human heart, how few would be willing to break from its power. He knew that without help from God, humanity must perish, and He saw multitudes perishing within reach of abundant help. {*DA* 752.4}

Upon Christ as our substitute and surety was laid the iniquity of us all. He was counted a transgressor, that He might redeem us from the condemnation of the law. The guilt of every descendant of Adam was pressing upon His heart. The wrath of God against sin,[117] the terrible

---

[107] Extra-biblical explanation is from 1*SG* 59.2f, "She could not remain away from the suffering scene" via 3*SP* 160.2. Though taken away so she wouldn't hear the "crashing of the nails," a mother's heart just couldn't leave her Son to suffer alone!

[108] Verbatim use of Jesus' words of *John 19:26, 27* in almost every source work.

[109] Starting with "John understood Christ's words" to this point, a loose paraphrase, ±Lange, p. 298, "John understood Him even in this moment. From that hour he took Mary, as his mother, unto his own home." This description is based on *John 19:27*, "And from that hour that disciple took her unto his own *home*." Similar statements are in J. S. C. Abbott, p. 132; Andrews, p. 557, "John at once took Mary to his home"; and the earlier 1*SG* 59.2f, "And from that hour John took her to his own house."

[110] Hanna, p. 730, uses the words "thoughtful care" in this same context.

[111] Verbatim within paraphrase, Hanna, p. 731, "let us hail the great and perfect example of filial affection he has left behind him." Kitto (1853), pp. 422, 423, also has "filial affection," while ±Macduff, *BTS* (1878) 374, ±Clark, p. 288, and ±Smith, *NTH* 333, have "filial love"; Jones, p. 390, has just "love." The absolute verbatim phrase is from 3*SP* (1878) 161.1.

[112] Jones, p. 390, uses the word "mother" in this same context.

[113] For the last two sentences of the paragraph, a very loose paraphrase, Hanna, p. 731.

[114] Gladys King-Taylor, *Literary Beauty*, p. 59, calls attention to Ellen White's careful word selection in these two sentences.

[115] Several of the life of Christ authors use the word "sufferer" or "sufferers" in describing Jesus—Jones, p. 388; Farrar, pp. 653 and 656; and Winslow, *GR* (1855) 141. The verbatim phrase "Christ was the prince of sufferers" comes from 3*SP* 162.1.

[116] Jones, p. 391, uses "malignity" in this same context; 3*SP* 162.1 has the verbatim phrase "a sense of the malignity of sin."

[117] ±Adams (1878), p. 334, a very loose paraphrase, without "substitute" and "of the law," is predated by 3*SP* 162.2, of which *DA* is a reordered near verbatim, "As man's substitute and surety, the iniquity of men was laid upon Christ; he was counted a transgressor

manifestation of His displeasure because of iniquity, filled the soul of His Son with consternation. All His life Christ had been publishing to a fallen world the good news of the Father's mercy and pardoning love. Salvation for the chief of sinners was His theme. But now with the terrible weight of guilt He bears, He cannot see the Father's reconciling face.[118] The «withdrawal of the divine countenance» from the Saviour in this hour of supreme anguish pierced His heart with a sorrow that can never be fully understood by man.[119] So great was this agony that His physical pain was hardly felt.[120] {DA 753.1}

Satan with his fierce temptations wrung the heart of Jesus. The Saviour could not see through the portals of the tomb. Hope did not present to Him His coming forth from the grave a conqueror, or tell Him of the Father's acceptance of the sacrifice. He feared that sin was so offensive to God that Their separation was to be eternal.[121] Christ felt the anguish which the sinner will feel when mercy shall no longer plead for the guilty race.[122] It was the sense of sin, bringing the Father's wrath upon Him as man's substitute, that made the cup He drank so bitter, and broke the heart of the Son of God.[123] {DA 753.2}

With amazement angels witnessed the Saviour's despairing agony. The hosts of heaven veiled their faces from the fearful sight.[124] Inanimate nature expressed sympathy with its insulted and dying Author.[125] The sun refused to look upon the awful scene.[126] Its full, bright rays were illuminating the earth at midday, when suddenly it seemed to be blotted out. Complete darkness, like a funeral pall, enveloped the cross. "There was darkness over all the land unto the ninth hour."

---

that he might redeem them from the curse of the law. The guilt of every descendant of Adam of every age was pressing upon his heart; and the wrath of God, and the terrible manifestation of his displeasure because of iniquity, filled the soul of his Son with consternation." The very common words "substitute" and "of the law" are in ±Williams (1853), p. 326. Ellen White used the assimilated phrase "substitute and surety" in a sermon in 2SAT 59.1. "Surety" is from *Heb. 7:22*, "the iniquity of us all" is from *Isa. 53:6*, and "that he might redeem us" is from *Titus 2:14*. The phrase "from the condemnation of the law" is found in ST 3-7-1878, "There is but one name given under heaven and among men that can save the sinner from the condemnation of the law."

[118] A loose paraphrase, ±Williams, p. 326, has "weight," and Pentecost, *BS '88*, p. 184, has word "guilt" and the same thought to the end of the paragraph. Same thought in ST 8-21-1879 (1875 reprint), "It was not bodily suffering which so quickly ended the life of Christ upon the cross. It was the crushing weight of the sins of the world, and a sense of his Father's wrath that broke his heart. The Father's glory and sustaining presence had left him . . ." and later expression "hiding of His Father's face."

[119] Similar thought with verbatim phrase "withdrawal of the divine countenance" in Macduff, *MO* (1868) 323; similar thought in ±Ellicott (1863), p. 321; Hanna, p. 739, using "withdrawn"; Foote (1862), pp. 223, 229; ±Halsey (1860), p. 114; Hall, p. 585; Matthew Henry, p. 336; and ±Balfern (1858), p. 233. The entire verbatim sentence is carried over from 3SP 162.2.

[120] A very loose paraphrase, Strickland, p. 168; but verbatim is carried over from 3SP 163.1.

[121] This unique description is carried over from *PH169* 10.1, "He could not see through the portals of the tomb. Bright hope did not present to him his coming for from the tomb a conqueror and his Father's acceptance of his sacrifice. . . . He was tempted to fear that sin was so offensive in the sight of his Father, that he could not be reconciled to his Son."

[122] Beginning with "He feared that sin," two very loose paraphrased sentences, Pentecost, *BS '88*, p. 190; but *PH169* 10.1 has near verbatim of the sentence on the "portals of the tomb" and "Hope did not present . . ."; 3SP (1878) 11.2 has "mercy . . . entreats . . . no longer"; and Ellen White used the phrase "sin . . . was so offensive to God that man could have no communion with his Maker" in a sermon in ST 7-31-1884, and the verbatim part of this phrase is from *PH169* 10.1.

[123] Ellen White used "broke the heart of the Son of God" in a sermon in RH 3-6-1888.

[124] A loose paraphrase with verbatim words, Jones, p. 393, but not about angels. Notice DA's similarity to the earlier 1SG 60.1, "The angels had viewed the horrid scene of the crucifixion of their loved commander, until they could behold no longer; and veiled their faces from the sight." The verbatims sentence "The hosts of heaven veiled their faces from the fearful sight" is found in Ellen White's sermon reported in ST 11-25-1889.

[125] A near verbatim, Harris, *TGT* 93, "all nature expressed its sympathy with its injured Maker," though the near verbatim is in 3SP 163.2, in ST 8-21-1879 (1875 reprint), "Yet inanimate nature groans in sympathy with her bleeding, dying Author," and in *PH169* (1869) 11.1, "Nature sympathized with the suffering of its Author," and no other recognizable parallels from *TGT* were in 2SP/3SP, in the 1875 ST series, or in *PH169*, and the publication of *PH169* predates Ellen White's purchase of *TGT*.

[126] *Personification* (King-Taylor, p. 97) is from 1SG 60.1, "The sun refused to look upon the dreadful scene," not Hanna, p. 734.

There was no eclipse or other natural cause for this darkness, which was as deep as midnight without moon or stars.[127] It was a miraculous testimony given by God that the faith of after generations might be confirmed.[128] {*DA* 753.3}

In that thick darkness God's presence was hidden.[129] He makes darkness His pavilion, and conceals His glory from human eyes.[130] God and His holy angels were beside the cross. The Father was with His Son. Yet His presence was not revealed. Had His glory flashed forth from the cloud, every human beholder would have been destroyed. And in that dreadful hour Christ was not to be comforted with the Father's presence.[131] He trod the wine press alone, and of the people there was none with Him.[132] {*DA* 753.4}

In the thick darkness, God veiled the last human agony of His Son.[133] All who had seen Christ in His suffering had been convicted of His divinity. That face, once beheld by humanity, was never forgotten. As the face of Cain expressed his guilt as a murderer, so the face of Christ revealed innocence, serenity, benevolence,—the image of God. But His accusers would not give heed to the signet of heaven. Through long hours of agony Christ had been gazed upon by the jeering multitude. Now He was mercifully hidden by the mantle of God.[134] {*DA* 754.1}

The silence of the grave seemed to have fallen upon Calvary. A nameless terror held the throng that was gathered about the cross. The cursing and reviling ceased in the midst of half-uttered sentences. Men, women, and children fell prostrate upon the earth. Vivid lightnings occasionally flashed forth from the cloud, and revealed the cross and the crucified Redeemer. Priests, rulers, scribes, executioners, and the mob, all thought that their time of retribution had come. After a while some whispered that Jesus would now come down from the cross.[135] Some attempted to grope their way back to the city, beating their breasts and wailing in fear.[136] {*DA* 754.2}

At the ninth hour the darkness lifted from the people, but still enveloped the Saviour. It was a symbol of the agony and horror that weighed upon His heart.[137] No eye could pierce the gloom that surrounded the cross, and none could penetrate the deeper gloom that enshrouded the suffering soul of Christ.[138] The angry lightnings seemed to be hurled at Him as He hung upon the cross. Then "Jesus

---

[127] Hanna, p. 733, "hangs a funereal pall around the cross: no darkness of an eclipse . . ." Many sources use "eclipse."

[128] A similar description, using "eclipse," ±Ellicott, p. 320, fn. 2. Other loose paraphrases are in Farrar, p. 657; Neander, p. 421, footnote; and Fleetwood, p. 363, "for it was at once a miraculous testimony given by the Almighty."

[129] Hanna, p. 733, describes "darkness"; Matthew Henry, p. 645, uses phrase "thick darkness." *Ex. 20:21; Deut. 4:11; 5:22; 1 Kings 8:12;* and *2 Chron. 6:1* associate "thick darkness" with the hiding of God's presence.

[130] Imagery adapted from *Ps. 18:11*.

[131] A very loose paraphrase, Hanna, p. 739.

[132] A close paraphrase from *Isa. 63:3*, ±Adams (1878), p. 334; predated by 3*SP* 153.2.

[133] ±Ellicott, p. 321, uses "agony in the garden," "those hours of darkness," and "the last assaults of Satan." Fleetwood, p. 365 has "veil of darkness." Similar thoughts, using some verbatim words, Wylie, pp. 277, 278; and +Williams, p. 326.

[134] Hanna, p. 734, "Men gazed rudely on the sight, but the sun refused to look on it, hiding his face for a season." Highlighted on this page is from MS 91, 1897 in 12*MR* 385.3, 4.

[135] Unique statement by Ellen White, using a verbatim phrase from *Matt. 27:42*. Following the darkness, Ingraham, p. 408, does have a believer named Rabbi Amos joyfully declaring: "And we shall behold him next descend from the cross."

[136] A very loose paraphrase, Jones, pp. 392, combined with a paraphrase of *Luke 23:48*—"smote their breasts, and returned"; a loose paraphrase, Farrar, p. 661. Phrases "grope their way" and "to the city" carried over from *PH169* 11.1.

[137] "Agony" (of Mary), "horror" (of the scene), and "darkness" are used in Farrar, p. 657; a loose paraphrase, Jones, p. 393, and Hanna, p. 734; key words also in 3*SP* 163.2. Only Ellen White, in *DA*, calls the darkness a "symbol."

[138] A paraphrase, Hanna, p. 734, "No eye perhaps may have pierced the outer darkness that shrouded his suffering body; still less may any human eye penetrate that deeper darkness which shrouded his suffering soul." A similar thought in Jones, p. 392, and +Smith, *NTH* 333; but verbatim is from 3*SP* 164.1.

cried with a loud voice, saying, Eloi, Eloi, lama sabachthani?" "My God, My God, why hast Thou forsaken Me?"[139] **As the outer** gloom **settled about** the Saviour, **many voices exclaimed:** The vengeance of heaven is upon Him. The bolts of God's wrath are hurled at Him, because He claimed **to be the Son of God. Many who believed on Him** heard His despairing cry.[140] Hope left them. If God had forsaken Jesus, in what could His followers **trust?** {*DA* 754.3}

When the darkness lifted from the oppressed spirit of Christ, He revived to a sense of physical suffering,[141] and said, "I thirst." One of the Roman soldiers, touched with pity as he looked at the parched lips, took a sponge on a stalk of hyssop, and dipping it in a vessel of vinegar, offered it to Jesus.[142] But the priests mocked at His agony. When darkness covered the earth, they had been filled with fear; as **their terror abated, the** dread **returned that Jesus** would yet escape them.[143] His words, "Eloi, Eloi, lama sabachthani?" they had misinterpreted. With bitter contempt and scorn they said, "This man calleth for Elias." [144] The last opportunity to relieve His sufferings they refused. "Let be," they said, "let us see whether Elias will come to save Him." {*DA* 754.4}

The spotless son of God hung upon the cross, His flesh lacerated with stripes; those hands so often reached out in blessing, nailed to the wooden bars; those feet so tireless on ministries of love, spiked to the tree; that royal head pierced by the crown of thorns;[145] those quivering lips shaped to the cry of woe. And all that He endured—the blood drops that flowed from His head, His hands, His feet, the agony that racked His frame, and the unutterable anguish that filled His soul at «the hiding of His Father's face»—**speaks to** each child of humanity, declaring, It is for thee that the Son of God consents to bear this burden of guilt; **for thee** He spoils the domain of death, and opens the gates of Paradise.[146] He who stilled the angry waves and walked the foam-capped billows, who made devils tremble and disease flee, who opened blind eyes and called forth the dead to life,— offers Himself upon the cross **as a sacrifice, and** this from love to thee.[147] He, the Sin Bearer, **endures** the wrath of divine justice, **and for thy sake becomes sin itself.** {*DA* 755.1}

In silence the beholders watched for the end of the fearful scene. The sun shone forth; but the cross **was still enveloped in** darkness. **Priests and rulers looked toward Jerusalem; and lo, the dense cloud had settled over the city and the plains of Judea.**[148] The Sun of righteousness, the Light of the

---

[139] Though many source works use *Matt. 27:46*, few, like Fleetwood, p. 365, quote the Aramaic of *Mark 15:34*.

[140] Use of two verbatim words, "despairing cry," Hanna, p. 735, and Geikie, p. 562.

[141] A very loose paraphrase, Hanna, p. 741; near verbatim, **3***SP* **165.1**.

[142] More tentative than Ellen White are Andrews, pp. 559, 560, who has "One of those present, perhaps a soldier, perhaps a spectator, moved by a sudden feeling of compassion, prepares the vinegar . . ."; Hanna, p. 743, who has "pity" and "perhaps a Roman soldier"; and ±Ingraham, p. 409, who has "some, pitying his sufferings, ran to give him wine and hyssop, to deaden them." All are from *John 19:29*. Several authors use "lips." Ellen White's eyewitness view of the events are always more definite.

[143] For the last two sentences to this point, a loose paraphrase, Hanna, p. 742; "dread" is also used in Farrar, p. 658. Verbatim carried over from **3***SP* **164.3**.

[144] Use of *Mark 15:34*, as in Fleetwood, p. 365. "Scorn" is used in Hanna, p. 742. Highlighted from *RH* **12-28-1897**.

[145] A beautiful adaptation of Fleetwood, p. 362 (see context in Chapter 7), built upon the Biblical expressions "upon the cross," *John 19:31*; "stripes," *Isa. 53:5*; "nail" and "hands," *John 20:25*; "feet," *Luke 24:39*; "the tree," *1 Peter 2:24*; "crown of thorns" and "head," *Matt. 27:29*; and "drops" of "blood," *Luke 22:44*. Phrasing is from **3***SP* **162.2**. Ellen White frequently used the phrase "the spotless son of God."

[146] A paraphrase with alterations and additions, using the expression "hiding of His Father's face," March, *WHJ* 316. ±Flavel, p. 147, and Kitto, p. 423, use similar expressions. Ellen White used the expression "hiding of His Father's face" in *PH169* 14.3 and *2T* 214.2 (91% of *2T* 200–215 is from *PH*169; both were printed in 1869). She also used it much later in an address to the General Conference 11-17-1883. Phrase "opens the gates of paradise" is used in Hanna, p. 719, though Ellen White assimilated the phrase "the gates of paradise" for a sermon in *2SAT* 33.1.

[147] The last clause, a loose paraphrase, adapting the words of March, *WHJ* 317. Thought gem carried over from **3***SP* **162.2**.

[148] Beginning with "darkness" and including "had settled" to this point, a loose paraphrase, Fleetwood, p. 363.

world, was withdrawing His beams from[149] the once favored city of Jerusalem. The fierce lightnings of God's wrath were directed against the fated city. {*DA* 756.1}

Suddenly the gloom lifted from the cross, and in clear, trumpet-like tones,[150] that seemed to resound throughout creation, Jesus cried, "It is finished." "Father, into Thy hands I commend My spirit."[151] A light encircled the cross, and the face of the Saviour shone with a glory like the sun. He then bowed His head upon His breast, and died.[152] {*DA* 756.2}

Amid the awful darkness, apparently forsaken of God, Christ had drained the last dregs in the cup of human woe.[153] In those dreadful hours He had relied upon the evidence of His Father's acceptance heretofore given Him. He was acquainted with the character of His Father; He understood His justice, His mercy, and His great love.[154] By faith He rested in Him whom it had ever been His joy to obey.[155] And as in submission He committed Himself to God, the sense of the loss of His Father's favor was withdrawn.[156] By faith, Christ was victor.[157] {*DA* 756.3}

Never before had the earth witnessed such a scene. The multitude stood paralyzed, and with bated breath gazed upon the Saviour. Again darkness settled upon the earth, and a hoarse rumbling, like heavy thunder, was heard. There was a violent earthquake. The people were shaken together in heaps.[158] The wildest confusion and consternation ensued. In the surrounding mountains, rocks were rent asunder,[159] and went crashing down into the plains. Sepulchers were broken open, and the dead were cast out of their tombs.[160] Creation seemed to be shivering to atoms. Priests, rulers, soldiers, executioners, and people, mute with terror, lay prostrate upon the ground. {*DA* 756.4}

When the loud cry, "It is finished," came from the lips of Christ, the priests were officiating in the temple. It was the hour of the evening sacrifice.[161] The lamb representing Christ had been

---

[149] A very close verbatim, Fleetwood, p. 363, "the Sun of righteousness was withdrawing his beams, not only from the promised land, but from the whole world ..." Another close verbatim is Barnes, 1*NG* 331, "the Sun of righteousness was withdrawing his beams for a time." A loose paraphrase, Kitto, p. 422, "At length the sun refused any longer to behold such wickedness." Verbatim phrases and imagery from *Mal. 4:2* and *John 8:12* are carried over from 3*SP* 167.1.

[150] Hanna, p. 741, refers to the "gloom" that "had hung around the scene." Phrasing carried over from 3*SP* 165.1.

[151] Verbatim use of Jesus' words in *John 19:30* and *Luke 23:46* as in Fleetwood, pp. 366, 367, and in most source works.

[152] A verbatim, expanded paraphrase of *John 19:30*, Farrar, p. 660, "He bowed His head upon His breast." This is a very common expression. ±Ingraham, p. 410, has "a supernatural glory shone around him." Sentences are carried over from 3*SP* 165.3.

[153] A similar thought, built on Jesus' use of cup in His Gethsemane prayer of *Matt. 26:39*, using the words "drained," "dregs," "the cup," is in Hanna, p. 736. A closer paraphrase, using the words "the last dregs" and "cup," but not "drained" is in ±Adams (1878), p. 334. The highlighted near verbatim was carried over from *PH169* (1869) 10.3.

[154] The near verbatim was carried over from *PH169* 10.3, "The Redeemer of the world now relies upon the evidences which had hitherto strengthened him. That his Father accepted his labors, and was pleased with his work."

[155] From "In those dreadful hours" to this point, a similar thought, ±Nicoll, p. 312, "His faith does not fail ..." ±Bennett, p. 480, says "divinity was still present, supporting the humanity to bear and to merit"; highlighted is from *PH169* 10.3 and *BEcho* 9-15-1892.

[156] A similar thought, Hanna, p. 739.

[157] For the last two sentences, a very loose paraphrase, Pentecost, *BS '88*, p. 190, and ±Ellicott, p. 323.

[158] Farrar, p. 661, refers to the earthquake in *Matt. 27:51, 54*, as does ±Ingraham, p. 410. The description of the fearful end, the crowd being paralyzed, and the shivering of creation are unique to Ellen White's eyewitness description of this event.

[159] Kitto, p. 423, uses "rocks were rent asunder"; similar expressions in Jones, p. 394, and Farrar, p. 661; a very loose paraphrase, ±Clark, p. 289; "rocks rent" is from *Matt. 27:51*; other authors use "rent asunder" for the veil.

[160] A very loose paraphrase, ±Ingraham, p. 410, "The ground still continued to rock, and the sepulchres of the kings, with the tombs of ancient prophets, were riven by vast chasms, and the green earth was strewn with the bones and bodies of the dead."

[161] Two sentences, a loose paraphrase, Hanna, p. 750. Edersheim, *LTJM* (1886) 611 and *The Temple* (1874), p. 256 and pp. 242, 243, discuss "the evening sacrifice." ±Burrell (1892), p. 236, has "this being the hour of the evening sacrifice ..." though the source work has previously been unused and is not listed as being in the Ellen G. White libraries, and *Ezra 9:5* has "the evening sacrifice" and *Dan. 9:21* has "the time of the evening oblation."

---

brought to be slain. Clothed in his significant and beautiful dress, the priest stood with lifted knife, as did Abraham when he was about to slay his son. With intense interest the people were looking on. But the earth trembles and quakes; for the Lord Himself draws near. With a rending noise the inner veil of the temple is torn from top to bottom by an unseen hand,[162] throwing open to the gaze of the multitude a place once filled with the presence of God. In this place the Shekinah had dwelt. Here God had manifested His glory above the mercy seat. No one but the high priest ever lifted the veil separating this apartment «from the rest of the temple».[163] He entered in once a year to make «an atonement for the sins of the» people.[164] But lo, this veil is rent in twain. The most holy place of the earthly sanctuary is no longer sacred.[165] {DA 756.5}

All is terror and confusion. The priest is about to slay the victim; but the knife drops from his nerveless hand,[166] and the lamb escapes. Type has met antitype in the death of God's Son.[167] The great sacrifice has been made.[168] The way into the holiest is laid open. A new and living way is prepared for all.[169] No longer need sinful, sorrowing humanity await the coming of the high priest. Henceforth to officiate as priest and advocate in the heaven of heavens.[170] It was as if a living voice had spoken to the worshipers: There is now an end to all sacrifices and offerings for sin.[171] The Son of God is come according to His word, "Lo, I come (in the volume of the Book it is written of Me,) to do Thy will, O God."[172] "By His own blood" He entereth "in once into the holy place, having obtained eternal redemption for us."[173] Heb. 10:7; 9:12. {DA 757.1}

---

[162] Hanna, pp. 750, 751, may have the closest parallel—"How strange, how awful to the ministering priests, standing before that veil, to feel the earth tremble beneath their feet, and to see the strong veil grasped, as if by two unseen hands of superhuman strength, and torn down in the middle from top to bottom . . ." Jones, p. 394; ±Cumming, *LLL* 487; ±Burrell (1892), p. 236; and Melvill, *GL* 862, are all paraphrases of *Matt. 27:51*. 3SP 166.2 has "Suddenly they felt the earth tremble beneath them, and the vail of the temple, a strong, rich drapery that had been changed yearly, was rent in twain from top to bottom by the same bloodless hand that wrote the words of doom upon the walls of Belshazzar's palace. The most holy place, that had been sacredly entered by human feet only once a year, was revealed to the common gaze."

[163] A paraphrase of *Heb. 9:7*, Melvill, *GL* 862, "Once in the year, the high priest alone, and with many significant rites, passed this boundary, and thus prefigured the entry of Christ as our intercessor into heaven; but at all other times, and for all other persons, an entrance within the veil was prohibited . . ." Matthew Henry, p. 338, has "The veil kept people off from drawing near to the most holy place, where the *Shechinah* was." Verbatim phrase "from the rest of the temple" is used in ±Ellicott, p. 323, fn. 3.

[164] Verbatim phrase from ±Adams (1878), p. 330, which is based on "to make an atonement for the children of Israel for all their sins once a year" of *Lev. 16:34*. Edersheim, *LTJM* 612, describes the priest entering "once a year" to make "atonement," though their entrance "only once a year" was noted earlier in 3SP 166.2; Edersheim, *LTJM* 610, uses the "rending" sound; a similar thought by ±Patton (1880), p. 207.

[165] Words "veil" and "rent in twain," from *Mark 15:38* and *Matt. 27:51*. Hanna, p. 751, and ±Deems, p. 676, use the word "sacred" though not in saying that the Most Holy Place was "no longer sacred."

[166] Phrase "falls/drops from his nerveless hand" is used by several authors outside source works at <www.google.books.com>.

[167] The phrase "type met Antitype in the death of Christ" was part of Ellen White's vocabulary as is evident from her use of it in sermons in *RH* 7-15-1890 and 1SAT 233.3, and in *YI* 5-1-1873. Melvill, *GL* 863 has a similar expression, "type has given place to antitype."

[168] ±Bennett, p. 494, makes the same point by quoting *Heb. 9:24–26*; ±Nicoll, p. 321, says: "The great sacrifice for the sins of the whole world was offered." Hanna, p. 768, has "the pouring out of his soul in the great sacrifice for sin."

[169] Beginning with "Type has met antitype," a similar thought, ±Clark, p. 290; starting with "The great sacrifice" to this point, a similar thought, ±Bennett, p. 494 (quoting *Heb. 9:24–26*); Neander, pp. 421, 422; ±Burrell (1892), p. 236; Matthew Henry, p. 337; ±Macduff, *BTS* 378. "Laid open" is in ±Deems, p. 676; Pentecost, *BS '88*, p. 190; ±Cumming, *LLL* 488; and ±SR-Mt 374. Hanna, p. 751, provides perhaps the closest parallel, from two phrases in reverse order. The first is a close paraphrase, based on "a new and living way" of *Heb. 10:19, 20* and the second is a near verbatim, based on "the way into the holiest" of *Heb. 9:8*.

[170] Verbatim phrase in same context, Bennett, p. 494.

[171] A loose paraphrase, ±Cumming, *LLL* 488, and ±SR-Mt 374, recognize "an end" to "sacrifices."

[172] Highlighted from the beginning of the paragraph to this point is from MS 111, 1897 in 12MR 416.3.

[173] Highlighted is from MS 101, 1897 in 12MR 392.4.

Insights from her earliest "eyewitness" account

 Limited in what it covers of the earthly life of Jesus, *Spiritual Gifts* was largely overlooked in tracing parallels to the "sources." Its inclusion in our investigation in this book has enabled us to make the pleasant discovery that certain wordings in *The Desire of Ages*, which were assumed to derive from other authors, are actually Mrs. White's own thoughts and expressions from her earlier narrative. As we have noted in the footnotes of the last two chapters, there is noticeable *verbal similarity*—and even more *conceptual continuity*—between many phrases in *The Desire of Ages* and phrases in *Spiritual Gifts* and in periodical articles that predate the sources. This discovery demonstrates that Ellen White already had an overview of the life of Christ in mind and had written out a great many of its details before she made use of any of the "sources." Such a discovery should not surprise us, for she mentioned in a letter early in 1889 that "the betrayal, trial, and crucifixion of Jesus" had passed before her point by point (Ltr. 14, 1889 in 4*BIO* 382.6), and the account of the crucifixion in *Spiritual Gifts* itself indicates that it was written by an "eyewitness," who had seen, not only that which is described in Scripture, but also that which would not have been seen by the natural eye—the spiritual activities behind the scenes. Following the moving account of Jesus' crucifixion, Ellen White wrote in *Spiritual Gifts*: "*I beheld* the angelic host watching with untold interest the resting place of JESUS" (1*SG* 64.1, emphasis supplied). We have also noted instances in which the wording of Ellen White's comments in the "Sufferings of Christ" (*PH169*, printed in 1869) and in *The Spirit of Prophecy*, vol. 3 (printed November 1877), which form the foundation for her description of events in the "closing scenes" of the Saviour's earthly life, predate many of the supposed source works.

In complaining about Mrs. White's use of sources, Walter Rea begrudgingly observed:

> Perhaps one of the hardest charges to meet and refute is that Ellen wrote what she had seen first in vision, and that she used the words, thoughts, and arrangement of others only because they said what she wanted to say and did not have the ability to say. —Walter Rea, *The White Lie*, p. 222.

Actually it wasn't Mrs. White's inability as a writer, but the exalted nature of her message that demanded the best language available. Over the years, Ellen White was quick to adopt certain descriptions of Biblical truth because they were in harmony with what she had previously been shown in vision.[174] Even Walter Rea acknowledged the consistency of what she borrowed with what she had previously written:

> The color of the new threads did not clash with the ultimate pattern of the fabric being woven through the years. —Walter Rea, *The White Lie*, p. 92.

This is certainly true of the descriptions she adapted in presenting the "eyewitness" account of Jesus' life, death, and resurrection she had been given. Ellen White was drawn to certain works because they were in line with what she wanted to say, not so she would know what to say.

· · · · · · · · · ·

In our next chapter, we will evaluate Mrs. White's use of sources in Chapters 77 and 78 of *The Desire of Ages* and draw some general conclusions about Ellen White's literary practices.

---

[174] This is reflected in her comment on her readiness to accept the messages of Jones and Waggoner concerning righteousness by faith: "I have said to myself, It is because God has presented it to me in vision that I see it so clearly, and they cannot see it because they have never had it presented to them as I have. And when another presented it, every fiber of my heart said, Amen." —MS 5, 1889, p. 10, sermon, Rome, New York, June 19, 1889, in 5*MR* 219.1.

Pictured above are paragraphs from MS 111, 1897, written in one of Ellen White's "scratch books"[1] especially for *The Desire of Ages*. This manuscript supplied wording for the last paragraphs of Chapter 78. Ellen White wrote this manuscript quickly—not always capitalizing, dotting "i"s, or crossing "t"s, but, with care, the words can still be deciphered:[2]

> But all is terror and confusion. The priest's hand is upraised, ready to plunge [the knife] to the heart of the victim, but the knife dropped from the nerveless hand. The lamb, no longer fettered, escapes and is free.

---

[1] In her diary entry for Dec. 20, 1890, Ellen White wrote: "I see that there are many things to be done. I must jot them down in scratch books and transfer them" (*The Ellen G. White 1888 Materials*, p. 767, par. 3).

[2] The cursory nature of her writing she describes in a letter to her son Edson: "I cannot write unless the Holy Spirit helps me. Sometimes I cannot write at all. Then again, I am aroused at eleven, twelve, and one o'clock; and I can write as fast as my hand can move over the paper." —Ltr. 11, 1903, Jan. 5, in 3*SM* 49.1.

CHAPTER 7
Evaluating Ellen White's Use of Sources

We begin our appraisal of literary sources in Chapters 77 and 78 of *The Desire of Ages* with a note on the materials Ellen White produced specifically for those chapters.

The role of "fresh matter" in the composition of the book

Ellen White wrote numerous original manuscripts on topics and events in the life of Christ (which they called "matter") to provide Marian Davis with material to complete certain chapters of *The Desire of Ages*. For Chapter 77 of *The Desire of Ages*, she wrote at least eight different new manuscripts (e.g. MS 129, 1897 in Chapter 1). We have in our possession, for the preparation of this book, the transcribed copies of these manuscripts—45 typewritten, double-spaced, 8½" x 11" pages—complete with handwritten additions. The topics of these pages include the trials before Pilate and Herod, Pilate's wife's dream, and Christ's final condemnation before Pilate. In looking over these manuscripts, we note that a number of paragraphs and sentences were selected for use in *The Desire of Ages*. Though Ellen White does include some phrasing from the books that she has read in some of these manuscripts, an impartial reading leaves one with the sense that they are free-flowing accounts of "what she had actually seen in vision."[1] She does not write as if she had an open book before her. Any borrowed language melts into her own eyewitness narrative.

For *The Desire of Ages*, Chapter 78, there are 43 pages of material, made up of nine manuscripts and one letter. "The Penitent Thief" appears to have been a key topic for Mrs. White, since she writes on this subject in three of the documents. MS 111, 1897 has several pages that were used (with slight changes and deletions) in the final paragraphs of *The Desire of Ages*, Chapter 78. One sentence from the typewritten transcription of the manuscript is of particular intrigue:

> The priest is about to plunge his knife to the heart of the victim, but the knife drops from his nerveless hand, and the lamb, no longer fettered, escapes.

Observe the same sentence as simplified on page 757 of *The Desire of Ages*:

> The priest is about to slay the victim; but the knife drops from his nerveless hand, and the lamb escapes.

In either its original or simplified form, the sentence dramatically portrays the end of the sacrificial system. If it was Marian Davis who suggested the change, she certainly knew how to simplify Ellen White's wording without disturbing the kernel thought! Without a doubt, simplicity in presenting divine truth was one of the guiding principles in the composition of *The Desire of Ages*.[2]

---

[1] Walter F. Specht, *The Literary Relationship Between The Desire of Ages, by Ellen G. White and The Life of Christ, by William Hanna*, part II (Loma Linda University, 1979), p. 28.

[2] The compactness and readability of *The Desire of Ages* is owing, in part, to the editorial skill of Marian Davis, who made it a priority "to begin both chapters and paragraphs with short sentences, *and indeed to simplify wherever possible, to drop out every needless word . . .*" —Ltr. Marian Davis to W. C. White, April 11, 1897, from Sunnyside in *Exhibits* #67.

William Hanna's *Life of Christ*

By contrast, the other works on the life of Christ of this era were generally longer and their sentence structure was more complex. William Hanna's *Life of Christ*, which appears to have been one of Ellen White's favorite reference works on this subject, is a case in point. Even though *The Desire of Ages* often expands on the spiritual lessons of scenes that other works overlook, the chapters in Hanna that cover the same topics as *The Desire of Ages*, Chapters 77 and 78, are about three times the length!

What correspondence do we find between Hanna and *The Desire of Ages*? Since Ellen White first wrote on the life of Christ in the 1850s, Hanna's work, published in 1863, would have been available to her by the time she expanded her account in the 1870s in the *Spirit of Prophecy* volumes and in the 1890s in *The Desire of Ages*. Carefully scanning *Spirit of Prophecy*, vol. 3, Chapter 9, and *The Desire of Ages*, Chapter 77, author Marcella Anderson found 143 parallels to Hanna's *Life of Christ*—58 in 3*SP* and 85 in *DA*. This would indicate that wording from Hanna was first added in 3*SP*. Even with its approximately eight and a half percent greater length than the corresponding chapter in 3*SP*, Chapter 77 of *DA* has only a slightly higher percentage of parallels. We can correlate this higher percentage with parallels from Hanna in *DA* that are not in 3*SP*. Thus we conclude that Hanna was consulted again in the preparation of new materials for *DA*. In Chapter 78, Marcella found about 57 parallels for the corresponding chapters in Hanna's *Life of Christ*. These were mostly *simple* to *loose paraphrases*. In all, Hanna's *Life of Christ* is connected with about 57% of all the footnoted parallels in Chapter 77 and about 37% of those in Chapter 78. In what way did Ellen White use Hanna's work? Only in the rarest of instances does she use a near verbatim thought gem from Hanna (e.g., *DA* 173.3 and Hanna, p. 134, about "the necessity of the new birth"). The majority of the common phrases are from Scripture. That the literary parallels between Hanna and *The Desire of Ages* ranged from *simple* to *loose paraphrase* would indicate that Ellen White was adapting a few thoughts and phrases here and there from Hanna to help provide structure and details for the *Desire of Ages* narrative. Analysis of these parallels led Marcella, in her research, to significant conclusions about the way Ellen White used Hanna's material in these chapters. We quote from her Life of Christ Research Project notes:

How did Ellen White use Hanna's life of Christ in The Desire of Ages?

> [I] have done everything to find parallels between *DA* and Hanna's *The Life of Christ* for this section [Chaps. 77 and 78] that I have [done] on my assigned *DA* Chapters 10 and 75, short of actual paragraph-indexing. *Spirit of Prophecy*, Vol. 3, was also used in finding parallels. Apparently Ellen White used many words or phrases from Hanna, but more often than not she used those words or phrases in a different sense than he did, or completely rephrased. [I] have indicated what I felt is loosely paraphrased by vertical dashed lines along the margins. . . .
>
> In *DA*, for the respective chapters, I did not discover that Ellen White borrowed Hanna's "free handling" of Scripture. She quoted from the Gospel of Mark more than he did. Obviously she would have used (and did use) many of the same passages of Scripture, but the quoting of texts from the narrative in the gospel for the respective stories seems justifiable and therefore should not be considered as borrowing. . . .
>
> Extrabiblical insights unique to *DA* (over Hanna, March, or Jones): 731:1+, 3 ([the] mob like wild beasts and Herod seeking to humiliate Jesus; another scene intruding itself; 732:1 (Pilate's wife's dream, even including the 2nd coming of Jesus); 733:1b (history & characteristics of Barabbas); 733:2 (last part: demons in the crowd); 734:2+ (comments made in ridicule of Jesus; Satan's part; a perfect offering of the Lamb of God); 738:4f (answer of Caiaphas and its significance); 742:3 (Simon's reaction to bearing the cross); 744 (scene at

Calvary, Christ's calmness); 745:4f (the significance of the inscription above the head of Jesus); 746:4f (Satan with his angels in human form at the cross); 749:3 (history of the penitent thief); 751:1 (scene as Jesus speaks to the penitent thief); 753:1+ (guilt pressing upon Jesus; Satan's fierce temptations); 754:1+ (God veils last sufferings of His Son; the last moments, nameless terror upon the throng); 756:1, 3 (fearful end; crowd paralyzed; creation shivering).[3]

Summing up the differences between Hanna and *The Desire of Ages*, Chapters 77 and 78—besides the difference in total length—(1) Ellen White used Hanna's words in an adapted sense, (2) she did not follow Hanna's unique use of Scripture, and (3) she gives many details of the story not discussed by Hanna or the other sources.[4] These unique details argue against the assertion that she simply took the *conjectures* of the sources and turned them into *certainties*.[5] She has had "eyewitness" views of the Biblical scene and describes what others cannot, as Arthur White notes:

> She gives details found in neither the Bible nor other authors, indicating she primarily has seen in vision that which she was describing. —"Ellen G. White and Her Writings," *Adventist Review*, November 27, 1980, p. 8.[6]

Other major sources of parallels[7]

After Hanna, the next most frequent sources of parallels in Chapters 77 and 78 were Farrar, Jones, and Edersheim. Judging from the way Edersheim expresses certain ideas, it would seem possible that he consulted Jones and Farrar as sources, though his "life of Christ" is written in a different style than theirs. In the Life of Christ Research Project, Dr. Veltman and his assistants often found more than one author using similar language to present many of the aspects of the life of Christ. Duplication of sources was even more noticeable in our analysis of *DA*, Chapters 77 and 78. It is for this reason that it is so difficult to give a percentage of use for each possible source work and for the overall borrowing of the two chapters. Nevertheless, the weight of evidence points to four authors' works as major source works for the two chapters: *The Life of Christ* by William Hanna; *The Life of Christ* by Frederic W. Farrar; *Life-Scenes from the Four Gospels* by George Jones; and *The Life and Times of Jesus the Messiah* by Alfred Edersheim. (These works were in Ellen White's office or personal libraries at the time of her death.) The best example of a unique wording in Chapter 77 from Edersheim can be found on page 739 of *The Desire of Ages* (and is referred to later in this chapter). Most of the second full paragraph on the page appears to be a loose paraphrase of Edersheim's wording, though the tightest of parallels is in the sentence, "From land to land throughout the world, from century to century, dead, dead in trespasses and sins!" It's a sentence that would not, for the length of the phrasing that it borrows, require quotation marks or footnoting.

---

[3] Marcella Anderson, unpublished typewritten comments, 8-25-1981 (filed with the *DA* research materials at Pacific Union College). The number after the colon (e.g. 742:3) is not for the paragraph number, but for the relative position on the page. In the actual report, a decimal was used (e.g. 50.9), as we see in the example from Fleetwood in Appendix B.

[4] James White wrote: "In her published works there are many things set forth which cannot be found in other books, and yet they are so clear and beautiful that the unprejudiced mind grasps them at once as truth. . . ." —*Life Sketches of James and Ellen White* (Battle Creek, Mich.: Seventh-day Adventist Publ. Assn., 1880), pp. 328, 329. His wife's incorporation of "thought gems" from her reading either before or after the 1880 statement does not negate its correctness.

[5] Walter Rea, "The Making of a Prophet: How Ellen White Turned Fiction into 'Truth'," *Adventist Currents*, March 1987, at <www.ellenwhiteexposed.com/rea/fiction.htm>.

[6] Arthur White gives many additional examples of unique details in her life of Christ writings in a document at <www.whiteestate.org/vault/Inspiration.html>.

[7] Fred Veltman arbitrarily defined a "*major* source work" as a work supplying more than ten literary parallels per *DA* chapter and a "*minor* source work" as a work supplying ten or less. Distinguishing a work as either "major" and "minor" does not, however, help in determining whether a source had parallels that are highly "recognizable."

Minor sources of parallels

Recognizing how difficult it is to prove literary dependency, we can tentatively add a few other potential contributors of wording for these chapters. These minor sources (less than 10 parallels per chapter each) include Fleetwood's *The Life of Our Lord and Saviour Jesus Christ* (for Chaps. 77 and 78), Daniel March's *Walks and Homes of Jesus* and Ingraham's *The Prince of the House of David* (for Chap. 78). Other than the unexceptional use of many of the same Scriptures, the most recognizable gleaning from Fleetwood is found in the first half of paragraph one of *DA* 755, shown later in this chapter. The most recognizable gleaning from March is also given later in this chapter. The only notable parallel from Ingraham was the phrase «the greatest criminal of the three». Though the footnotes for *DA* 744.1, 2 point out parallel expressions between Ingraham and 1*SG*, Ingraham was not the source of her view of the crucifixion because her depiction differs from his in essential details.

For Chapter 78, the following possible source works were cited six or more times—Neander, Kitto, Geikie, Lange, Rufus W. Clark, William Smith's *New Testament History*, James Bennett, and George Pentecost's *Bible Studies from the Old and New Testaments . . . for 1888*. What makes their being sources less certain is that their parallels are duplicated by other source works. The only striking parallels to Geikie are "stripped to the waist" and the commonly used phrase "robe of mockery." If Mrs. White did have Geikie's *Life and Words of Christ*, published by November 1877, before she used these phrases in 3*SP*,[8] it would make no difference for marking and footnoting, for they fall short of the five-word threshold. Two other striking parallels—3*SP* 147.1 with Neander, p. 417, and *DA* 730.3 with Kitto, p. 413—turned out to be based on Ellen White's own expressions in *Spiritual Gifts*, vol. 1. Of the eight source works listed above, Lange, Clark, Smith, and Bennett aren't even listed in the inventory of Ellen White's libraries (though other works of Lange, Clark, and Smith are). It is possible that Deems was also a minor source for Chapters 77 and 78, however, there is no record that Ellen White ever owned his work and his work does give indication of dependence on Hanna.

One should bear in mind that a number of the source works have only been cited because they express their points in nearly the same way or because they have many of the same verbatim words as *The Desire of Ages*. If we would count only the parallels with the highest level of certainty, a great number of parallels in each chapter would be eliminated, and the rate of literary dependency for *The Desire of Ages* would be lowered.

 ## How should we describe Ellen White's use of sources?

One description of Ellen White's use of sources is "copying."

> Mrs. White's copying from others was not a necessity, but was done chiefly to conserve time and in the interests of brevity and forcefulness. She acted without knowledge of the literary standards that would count a moderate use of others' writings as unfair or worthy of condemnation. —W. C. White and D. E. Robinson, "Brief Statements Regarding the Writings of Ellen G. White," p. 11.

> Ellen White maintained extensive diaries or journals. Not only did she (generally) keep daily records but often she amplified her thoughts, seemingly without any particular reason except to let her mind flow out on paper. These entries included both personal impressions

---

[8] *The Publishers' Weekly*, November 17, 1877 announced the publication of Geikie's *Life and Works of Christ* in two volumes. The publication of 3*SP* was announced in *RH* 2-14-1878, though "on Sabbath morning, August 18 [1877], a portion of the manuscript for *Spirit of Prophecy*, volume 3, on the trial, crucifixion, resurrection, and ascension of Christ" was read (3*BIO* 67.2) and, on November 4, Ellen White wrote Willie and Mary, "We received proofs of my matter, Spirit of Prophecy" (Ltr. 34, 1877).

and thoughts from her reading. At such times, without any attempt to organize under specific headings, Mrs. White copied or paraphrased those items from her extensive reading[9] that she wanted to remember. From these journals her editorial assistants would gather material for periodical articles. As time passed, many of these early jottings became part of her published books. —Herbert E. Douglass, *Messenger of the Lord*, p. 456 (cf. Veltman, *LCRP* 904, 944).

Except for a few scattered phrases in *Sketches from the Life of Paul* and the historical material in *The Great Controversy*[10] (covered by the description of White and Robinson) and for the very few scattered near verbatim gems of thought in her writings she adapted from her reading as "she was ever seeking for more beautiful phraseology and for more perfect and exact language"[11] (covered by the description of Douglass), the description doesn't fit the literary parallels in her writings. To say that she "copied" implies that she put little thought into the transfer of material from one page to another. However, almost all the parallels in Ellen White's writings are either partly or almost entirely adapted. Even many of the sentences that were classified as "verbatim" in the *LCRP* contain original elements (see Appendix B). One could say that Ellen White "copied" in the sense that she imitated portions of Daniel March, John Harris and Henry Melvill as she put her own thoughts into words. However, that isn't what most people mean by *copying*. (The most readable of these authors is Daniel March, who does say things *well*, even if he doesn't always say them *right*.)

Another description of her use of sources is "borrowing."

> Ellen White knew what she was *borrowing* and did not borrow material mindlessly, simply to fill a page. She interacted with the material . . . —Denis Fortin, "Ellen G. White as a Writer: Case Studies in the Issue of Literary Borrowing."[12]

In the field of literature, the term "borrowing" is frequently employed to describe the unattributed and unacknowledged—but legitimate—use of the wording of one writer by another.

---

[9] "You ask regarding the reading habits of my Mother. Sister White was a very industrious woman, and when not engaged to the full extent of her strength in traveling, or speaking, or in writing testimonies and books, she spent a portion of her time in reading and in study. Of course the Bible came first. After that such books as D'Aubigne's *History of the Reformation*, Martyn's *History of the Reformation*, and later she read a little in Wylie, but not much. She also read various books on the life of Christ—Fleetwood's, Farrar's, Geikie's, Lightfoot's, and [Samuel] Andrew's [sic], and later she read from Hanna; but I do not think she ever read Edersheim. [He may not be sure, but evidence from MS 95, 1897 indicates that she did read Edersheim.] She had in her library and occasionally read from Conybeare and Howson's life of Paul, and Farrar's life of Paul. She also read from the best religious papers. How did she get them? She used to ask the editors of the Review and [the] Signs to pass over to her their exchanges [publishers of periodicals frequently "exchanged" editions of their magazines at no cost], when they were done with them; and for years when she was in middle age and vigorous she would read an hour or two each day after completing a good day's work in writing. As a result of this reading she found many precious articles, which she recommended for publication in the Review; more often she found good things to read to the family. Furthermore she cut out hundreds of articles and pasted them into scrapbooks, thinking they would be useful in days to come." —Ltr. W. C. White to L. E. Froom, Feb. 14, 1926, cited in *Ministry*, June 1982, p. 6. Beginning in early 1876, many of the character-building stories she had gathered as far back as the 1850s were republished in the "Home Circle," a department of the *Signs* (3BIO 52ff) and later in *Sabbath Readings for the Home Circle* and in *Scrapbook Stories: from Ellen G. White's Scrapbooks* (1949). Writing to her children about "a piece" she was working on "for the *[Health] Reformer*," Ellen White said: "Do not neglect to send my selections for I want them to use. Send my scrap books also." —Ltr. 25, 1877, Oct. 16, from Oakland. Four of the original 12–15 scrapbooks are at the White Estate.

[10] Regarding the absence of footnotes in these books, W. C. White noted that this was due to his "lack of experience in the publishing work," *LP* (1883) and the *GC* (1884) being the first of his mother's books to be issued after his father's death (Ltr. W. C. White to M. N. Campbell, July 30, 1907, in F. D. Nichol, *Ellen G. White and Her Critics*, pp. 449, 450). In his defense, careful comparison of Ellen White's and Conybeare and Howson's books on the life of Paul has revealed that only minimal *verbatim* "descriptive" and "historical" material (2.9181%) was integrated into *LP*. Verbatim material is usually less than 5 consecutive words. See David Conklin's analysis of the literary similarity of Ellen G. White's *Sketches from the Life of Paul* as compared with Conybeare and Howson's *The Life and Epistles of St. Paul* at <www.ellenwhite.info/conybeare-howson-cleveland-a.htm.>.

[11] Robert W. Olson, "Ellen G. White's Use of Uninspired Sources," p. 7.

[12] Available at <www.andrews.edu/~fortind/EGWWhite-Conybeare.htm>, emphasis supplied.

This term is used because, when a few words are borrowed for a new literary piece, they are still available to the original writer. They aren't like a car or a cell phone that can only be used by one person at a time. Though not wanting to call attention to the human side of her writing—either of herself or of her sources of language— Mrs. White was always mindful of the rights of others and adjusted her attribution through the years in keeping with changing societal expectations.[13]

There is one other description of Ellen White's use of sources, and that description comes from Ellen White herself. In an article entitled, "Truth to Be Rescued From Error," she wrote:

> ... Gems of thought are to be *gathered* up and *redeemed* from their companionship with error; for by their misplacement in the association of error, the Author of truth has been dishonored. The precious gems of the righteousness of Christ, and truths of divine origin, are to be carefully searched out and placed in their proper setting, to shine with heavenly brilliancy amid the moral darkness of the world. Let the bright jewels of truth which God gave to man, to adorn and exalt his name, be carefully rescued from the rubbish of error, where they have been claimed by those who have been transgressors of the law, and have served the purposes of the great deceiver on account of their connection with error. Let the gems of divine light be reset in the framework of the gospel. Let nothing be lost of the precious light that comes from the throne of God. It has been misapplied, and cast aside as worthless; but it is heaven-sent, and each gem is to become the property of God's people and find its true position in the framework of truth. Precious jewels of light are to be collected, and by the aid of the Holy Spirit they are to be fitted into the gospel system. ... Jesus has said, "Gather up the fragments ... that nothing be lost." — *Review and Herald*, Oct. 23, 1894, emphasis supplied.

Such a use of sources she saw as being in line with Christ's rescue of gems of truth:

> Christ was the originator of all the ancient gems of truth. Through the work of the enemy these truths had been displaced. They had been disconnected from their true position, and placed in the framework of error. ... Christ rescued them from the rubbish of error, gave them a new, vital force, and commanded them to shine as jewels, and stand fast forever. Christ Himself could use any of these old truths without borrowing the smallest particle, for He had originated them all.[14] —Ellen G. White, MS 25, 1890, written from Battle Creek, Jan. 7–9, 1890 (in *E. G. White 1888 Materials*, p. 524).

W. C. White commented on the guidance his mother was promised in *gathering* gems of truth:

> In the early days of her work, Mother was promised wisdom, in the selection from the writings of others, that would enable her to select the gems of truth from the rubbish of error. —W. C. White to E. E. Andross, June 18, 1920.[15]

---

[13] In response to the question about whether her borrowing was an infringement on others' rights, Mrs. White asked: "'Who has been injured?' No injustice or injury could be named. Nevertheless, she gave instruction that, lest anyone should be offended or led to stumble over the fact that passages from historians had been used without credit, in future editions of her book *Great Controversy*, a faithful effort should be made to search out those passages that had been copied from historians which had not been enclosed in quotation marks, and that quotation marks should be inserted wherever they could be used. This instruction was conscientiously followed." —"Brief Statements Regarding the Writings of Ellen G. White" (1933), p. 8.

[14] See BIBLICAL PARALLEL 4 in Chapter 9.

[15] White Estate Correspondence File, cited by Robert W. Olson in "Ellen G. White's Use of Historical Sources in *The Great Controversy*," *Adventist Review*, Feb. 23, 1984. W. C. White went on to say: "We have all seen this fulfilled, and yet when she told me of this, she admonished me not to tell it to others." He believed her reason for this was that it might lead some of the brethren to claim too much for her writings and use them as a means of settling matters of history, which her writings were not intended to do.

Ellen White was a rapid reader and had a very retentive memory. The revelations which she had received enabled her to grip subjects regarding which she read in a vigorous way. This enabled her to select and appropriate that which was true and to discard that which was erroneous or doubtful. —W. C. White, 3*SM* 462.

In the days of antiquity, Solomon had similarly gathered pearls of wisdom from various unnamed sources in the ancient world (see Prov. 1:1; 10:1; and 25:1).

> And moreover, because the preacher was wise, he still taught the people knowledge; yea, he gave good heed, and sought out, and set in order many proverbs. The preacher sought *to find out acceptable words*: and that which was written was upright, even *words of truth*. —Solomon, Ecclesiastes 12:9, 10, emphasis supplied.

> Can an inspired writer gather gems of truth from other writers?

In the same way, the Spirit of inspiration led Mrs. White to glean "thought gems" and vocabulary from her reading to help her in faithfully communicating the truths which God had given her to share. Some "thought gems" required very little adapting (such as Beecher and Boyd in *DA*, Chap. 1). Others required considerably more. Walter F. Specht observes:

> Mrs. White was very selective in any expressions she *borrowed*, and did not hesitate to correct or improve them.[16]

Ellen White's use of recognizable parallels

The following exhibit of recognizable parallels from *The Desire of Ages* backs up Specht's observation. In each example, the passage from the source work is listed first, followed by the corresponding passage from Mrs. White. To many readers of Ellen White the wording of the first gem will sound strangely familiar. It was originally part of a chapter on Christ's crucifixion, entitled "Jerusalem," in Daniel March's *Walks and Homes of Jesus*.

Capturing the elegance of Daniel March

March: "Nevertheless it will do us all good, frequently and solemnly to review the closing scenes in the Saviour's earthly life. Amid all the material and worldly passions, by which we are beset and tempted, we shall learn many salutary lessons, by going back in memory, and spending a thoughtful hour, in the endeavor to strengthen our faith and quicken our love at the foot of the cross. What then are the lessons which the divine Passion, the infinite sacrifice, the true and redemptive Cross of Christ is fitted to teach? . . .

"First of all we may learn that lesson which is the beginning of life and peace to weary souls, the lesson of penitence at the foot of the cross." —*Walks and Homes of Jesus*, pp. 313, 314.

Ellen White: "It would be well for us to spend a thoughtful hour each day in contemplation of the life of Christ. *We should take it point by point, and let the imagination grasp each scene, especially the closing ones.* As we thus dwell upon His great sacrifice for us, our confidence in Him will be more constant, our love will be quickened, and we shall be more deeply imbued with His spirit. If we would be saved at last, we must learn the lesson of penitence and humiliation «at the foot of the cross»." —*The Desire of Ages*, p. 83, emphasis supplied.

Don't you like what Ellen White does with March's words? It is simple elegance and much more memorable than the original! This gem was first cut, polished, and reset for a testimony

---

[16] Walter F. Specht, *The Literary Relationship Between The Desire of Ages, by Ellen G. White and The Life of Christ, by William Hanna* (Loma Linda University, 1979), p. 17, emphasis supplied.

about the consecration of ministers in *Testimonies for the Church* (1880), vol. 4, p. 374. Later, it was reset in *The Desire of Ages* chapter on Jesus' first Passover visit. There it emphasizes the importance of never losing sight of Jesus. Mrs. White's simplified rearrangement of March's quotation encourages the reader to do something that March did not do—let the imagination grasp each scene in the life of Christ—the very thing that *The Desire of Ages* was written to help the reader do! Notice that the only verbatim phrase of sufficient length to require footnoting would be the very common phrase "at the foot of the cross."

March: "But the love of Jesus is infinitely more generous, patient and self-denying than a mother's love. He has been more deeply afflicted by our ingratitude and disobedience than any mother ever was by the misconduct of her child. He has longed and labored for our eternal salvation more earnestly than any human parent ever did for the welfare of an only son.
"As we stand and gaze by faith upon the cross of Jesus, every expression of his agonized countenance, every drop of blood flowing from his many wounds, every convulsion with which the torture of crucifixion shakes his frame, every groan which the hiding of his Father's face extorts from his troubled soul, seems to say to us, 'It is for thee that these pangs are borne. It is that thou mayest be forgiven that I consent to have all shames and crimes imputed to me. It is to blot out the record of thy dark and dreadful iniquity that my blood is shed. The grave shall close over me with its horror of great darkness that I may spoil the dominions of death and unbar the gates of life for thee. I submit to all this shame and agony because I have loved thee with an everlasting love [Jer. 31:3], and I could not rest till I had brought back thy wayward and wandering soul to God.'" —*Walks and Homes of Jesus*, pp. 316, 317.

Ellen White: "My love for you has been more «self-denying than a mother's love». It was that I might blot out your dark record of iniquity, *and put the cup of salvation to your lips, that I suffered the death of the cross, bearing the weight and curse of your guilt.* The pangs of death, and the horrors of the darkness of the tomb, I endured, that I might conquer him who had the power of death, unbar the prison house, and open for you the gates of life. I submitted to shame and agony because I loved you with an infinite love, and would bring back my wayward, wandering sheep to the paradise of God, to the tree of life. . . ." —*Testimonies for the Church* (1880), vol. 4, p. 387, emphasis supplied.

Ellen White: "And all that He endured—the blood drops that flowed from His head, His hands, His feet, the agony that racked His frame, and the unutterable anguish that filled His soul at «the hiding of His Father's face»—speaks to each child of humanity, declaring, It is for thee that the Son of God consents to bear this burden of guilt; for thee He spoils the domain of death, and opens the gates of Paradise. *He who stilled the angry waves and walked the foam-capped billows, who made devils tremble and disease flee, who opened blind eyes and called forth the dead to life, —offers Himself upon* the cross *as a sacrifice, and this from love to thee.*" —*The Desire of Ages*, p. 755, via 3SP 162.2, emphasis supplied.

Should anyone be surprised that Ellen White, a devoted mother, would be taken with the beauty of this thought gem, which compares the love of God with the love of a mother, or that she should adapt its touching imagery again and again over the years?[17] In Ellen White's adaptation, she enhances the literary impact of the thought by repeating "for thee" and "to thee" and by adding, in the last sentence, what Gladys King-Taylor calls a "splendid example of the three rhythmic stages of sentence structure" with the "gradual rise from *He* to *life*, level progress from *offers* to *sacrifice*, and the cadence at the close" (*Literary Beauty of Ellen G. White's Writings*, pp. 118–120).

---

[17] Ellen White's earliest use of the gem, in *3SP* (1878) 162.2f, included "it is for love . . . thee," "blood drops," "hiding of His Father's face," and "gates," but not "more self-denying than a mother's love," "blot out," "record," "dark," "iniquity," "wayward," "wandering," and "pangs." *Present Truth* 2-4-1886 has the same parallels as *3SP*, but also uses "pang." Ellen White used "more self-denying than a mother's love" in *RH* 5-3-1881, *ST* 6-19-1884, and *RH* 11-15-1887.

Recasting the vocabulary of George Jones

Jones: "He saw their purpose: and saw the calm and dignified face before him, the noble expression of features, the grandeur even yet marked upon that brow. How unlike a culprit! How strange that such a person should be brought before him as a malefactor to be put to death! He looked on the countenance of the crowd of accusers ... They were dark, scowling faces, though their owners stood in robes of office around the bound individual before him, whose features expressed even then only benignity and kindness, mingled with calmness and resignation." —*Life-Scenes from the Four Gospels*, p. 373.

Ellen White: "Pilate beheld . . . . a serene and noble countenance and dignified bearing. . . . He discovered no trace of crime in his face . . .

"Pilate was filled with sympathy and amazement as he beheld the uncomplaining patience of Jesus. Gentleness and resignation were expressed in every feature; there was no cowardly weakness in his manner, but the strength and dignity of long-suffering. . . ." —*The Spirit of Prophecy*, vol. 3, pp. 129, 143.

Ellen White: "On His face he saw no sign of guilt, no expression of fear, no boldness or defiance. He saw a man of calm and dignified bearing, whose countenance bore not the marks of a criminal, but the signature of heaven. . . . He read the purposes of the priests." —*The Desire of Ages*, pp. 724, 725.

Jones: "The governor was startled and amazed; it was a new aspect in the affair; for hitherto they had been urging it upon him on political grounds. The strange dignity of the accused had before impressed him; —his calmness, truly like that of a God while all were raging around him for his destruction; —the majesty which no mocking could put down." —*Life-Scenes from the Four Gospels*, p. 379.

Ellen White: "Pilate was startled, . . . but he had an indistinct faith in God and in beings superior to humanity." —*The Desire of Ages*, p. 736, via 3SP 144.3.

"He who could have driven that mob in terror from His sight by the flashing forth of His divine majesty—submitted with perfect calmness to the coarsest insult and outrage. . . . As their cruelty degraded His torturers below humanity into the likeness of Satan, so did His meekness and patience exalt Jesus above humanity, and prove His kinship to God." —*The Desire of Ages*, p. 734, via 3SP 139.1.

Whether Ellen White actually used Jones's words is hard to know, but, if she did—judge for yourself—do they not fit in perfectly with her own narrative?

Adapting the imagery of Alfred Edersheim

Edersheim: "Since the Paschal Supper Jesus had not tasted either food or drink. After the deep emotion of that Feast, with all of holiest institution which it included; after the anticipated betrayal of Judas, and after the farewell to His disciples, He had passed into Gethsemane. There for hours, alone—since His nearest disciples could not watch with Him even one hour—the deep waters had rolled up to His soul. He had drunk of them, immersed, almost perished in them. There had he agonised in mortal conflict, till the great drops of blood forced themselves on His Brow. There had He been delivered up, while they all had fled. To Annas, to Caiaphas, to Pilate, to Herod, and again to Pilate; from indignity to indignity, from torture to torture, had He been hurried all that livelong night, all that morning. All throughout He had borne Himself with a Divine Majesty, which had awakened alike the deeper feelings of Pilate and the infuriated hatred of the Jews. . . . Unrefreshed by food or sleep, after the terrible events of that night and morning, while His pallid Face bore the blood-marks from the crown of thorns, His mangled Body was unable to bear the weight of the Cross. . . . It was the Divine strength of His pity and love which issued in His Human weakness." — *The Life and Times of Jesus the Messiah*, vol. 2, pp. 586, 587.

Ellen White: "The Saviour's burden was too heavy for Him in His weak and suffering condition. Since the Passover supper with His disciples, He had taken neither food nor drink. He had agonized in the garden of Gethsemane in conflict *with satanic agencies.* He had endured the anguish of the betrayal, and had seen His disciples forsake Him and flee. He had been taken to Annas, then to Caiaphas, and then to Pilate. From Pilate He had been sent to Herod, then sent again to Pilate. From insult to renewed insult, from mockery to mockery, twice tortured by the scourge, —all that night *there had been scene after scene of a character to try the soul of man to the uttermost. Christ had not failed. He had spoken no word but that tended to glorify God.* All through the disgraceful farce of a trial «He had borne Himself with» firmness and dignity. But when after the second scourging the cross was laid upon Him, human nature could bear no more. He fell fainting beneath the burden." —*The Desire of Ages,* pp. 741, 742, via MS 95, 1897, emphasis supplied.

Edersheim: "The Mishnah tells us, that, after the solemn washing of hands of the elders and their disclaimer of guilt, priests responded with this prayer: 'Forgive it to Thy people Israel, whom Thou hast redeemed, O Lord, and lay not innocent blood upon Thy people Israel!' But here, in answer to Pilate's words, came back that deep, hoarse cry: 'His Blood be upon us,' and—God help us! —'on our children!' Some thirty years later, and on that very spot, was judgment pronounced against some of the best in Jerusalem; and among the 3,600 victims of the Governor's fury, of whom not a few were scourged and crucified right over against the Praetorium, were many of the noblest of the citizens of Jerusalem. A few years more, and hundreds of crosses bore Jewish *mangled bodies* within sight of Jerusalem. And still have these wanderers seemed to bear, from century to century, and from land to land, that burden of blood; and still does it seem to weigh 'on us and our children.'" —*The Life and Times of Jesus the Messiah,* vol. 2, p. 578.

"With this cry Judaism was, in the person of its representatives guilty of denial of God, of blasphemy, of apostasy. *It committed suicide; and, ever since, has its dead body been carried in show* from land to land, and from century, to century; to be dead, and to remain dead, till He come a second time, Who is the Resurrection and the Life!" —*The Life and Times of Jesus the Messiah,* vol. 2, p. 581, emphasis supplied.

Ellen White: "Looking upon the smitten Lamb of God, the Jews had cried, 'His blood be on us, and on our children.' That awful cry *ascended to the throne of God.* That sentence, pronounced upon themselves, was written in heaven. *That prayer was heard.* The blood of the Son of God was upon their children and their children's children, a perpetual curse.

"Terribly was it realized in the destruction of Jerusalem. *Terribly has it been manifested in the condition of the* Jewish *nation* for eighteen hundred years, —a *branch severed from the vine, a dead, fruitless branch,* to be gathered up and burned. From land to land throughout the world, from century to century, dead, dead in trespasses and sins! *Terribly will that prayer be fulfilled* in the great judgment day. When Christ shall come to the earth again, *not as a prisoner surrounded by a rabble will men see Him.*" —*The Desire of Ages,* p. 739, emphasis supplied.

Ellen White makes her own statement with key phrases from Edersheim, avoiding the more gruesome aspects of his imagery, anchoring her statements in the imagery of Scripture (John 15:1–5; Eph. 2:1), and framing the cry of the people as a "prayer" that went up before God.

Simplifying the descriptiveness of Frederic Farrar

Farrar: "Both he [Pilate] and the people almost simultaneously bethought themselves that it had always been a Paschal boon to liberate at the feast some condemned prisoner. He offered, therefore, to make the acquittal of Jesus an act not of imperious justice, but of artificial grace." —*Life of Christ,* p. 629.

Ellen White: Pilate was forced to action. He now bethought himself of a custom which might serve to secure Christ's release. It was customary at this feast to release some one prisoner whom the people might choose. *This custom was of pagan invention*; there was not a shadow of justice in it." —*The Desire of Ages*, p. 733, emphasis supplied.

Though several authors mention this "custom," it is the use of the archaic "bethought" that points to Farrar as the source. Only Ellen White declares it to be "of pagan invention." Her use of "justice" is to say that the pagan custom was unjust. Farrar's used it to say that Pilate was trying to circumvent the judicial process.

Farrar: ". . . 'His blood be on us and on our children.' . . . Before the dread sacrifice was consummated, Judas died in the horrors of a loathsome suicide. Caiaphas was deposed the year following. Herod died in infamy and exile. Stripped of his Procuratorship very shortly afterwards, on the very charges he had tried by a wicked concession to avoid, Pilate, wearied out with misfortunes, died in suicide and banishment, leaving behind him an execrated name." —*Life of Christ*, p. 639.

Ellen White: "Pilate yielded to the demands of the mob. Rather than risk losing his position, he delivered Jesus up to be crucified. But in spite of his precautions, the very thing he dreaded afterward came upon him. His honors were stripped from him, he was cast down from his high office, and, stung by remorse and wounded pride, not long after the crucifixion he ended his own life. . . .

"When Pilate declared himself innocent of the blood of Christ, Caiaphas answered defiantly, 'His blood be on us, and on our children.'" —*The Desire of Ages*, p. 738, via 3*SP* 146.

Ellen White's simplified paraphrase does contain a few recognizable verbatim words, but notice that, though "dread" and "dreaded" are marked as a parallel, they carry very different meanings—one describing Jesus' death and the other Pilate's loss of position. Only Ellen White identifies Caiaphas as the one who made the statement.

Farrar: "It could have been no darkness of any natural eclipse, for the Paschal moon was at the full; . . . [*skipping three sentences*] Its later stages seem to have thrilled alike the guilty and the innocent with emotions of dread and horror. [*skipping one sentence*] What Jesus suffered then for us men and our salvation we cannot know, for during those three hours He hung upon His cross in silence and darkness; or, if He spoke, there were none there to record His words. . . ." —*Life of Christ*, p. 657.

Ellen White: "There was no eclipse or other natural cause for this darkness, which was as deep as midnight without moon or stars. . . . At the ninth hour the darkness lifted from the people, but still enveloped the Saviour. *It was a symbol of the agony and horror that weighed upon His heart.*" —*The Desire of Ages*, pp. 753, 754, via 3*SP* 163.2.

Only Ellen White speaks of the darkness as a symbol of that which weighed upon Jesus' heart.

Farrar: "At that moment the veil of the Temple was rent in twain from the top to the bottom. An earthquake shook the earth and split the rocks . . . Even the multitude, utterly sobered from their furious excitement and frantic rage, began to be weighed down with a guilty consciousness that the scene which they had witnessed had in it something more awful than they could have conceived, and as they returned to Jerusalem they wailed, and beat upon their breasts." —*Life of Christ*, pp. 660, 661.

Ellen White: ". . . they felt guilty of doing a great wrong. No jest nor mocking laughter was heard in the midst of that fearful gloom; and when it was lifted, they solemnly made their way to their homes, awe-struck and conscience-smitten. . . ." —*The Spirit of Prophecy*, vol. 3, p. 169.

Ellen White: "*After a while some whispered that Jesus would now come down from the cross.* Some attempted to grope their way back to the city, beating their breasts and wailing in fear. . . . With a rending noise the inner veil of the temple is torn from top to bottom by an unseen hand. . . . But lo, this veil is rent in twain." —*The Desire of Ages*, pp. 754, 757, via 3*SP* 164.2.

Ellen White uses several of Farrar's words, but her simpler and more definite sentences are easier to understand, and she includes a unique eyewitness detail not found in Farrar. Most of the parallels in this passage are either paraphrased or verbatim wording from Scripture.

Condensing the potency of John Fleetwood

Fleetwood: "Take one view of thy dying Saviour breathing out his spirit upon the cross! Behold his unspotted flesh lacerated with stripes, by which thou art healed! See his hands extended and nailed to the cross, —those beneficent hands which were incessantly stretched out to unloose thy heavy burdens and to impart blessings of every kind! Behold his feet riveted to the accursed tree and nails, —those feet which always went about doing good and traveled far and near to spread the glad tidings of everlasting salvation! View his tender temples encircled with a wreath of thorns, which shoot their keen afflicting points into his blessed head, —that head which was ever meditating peace to poor, lost, and undone sinners and spent many a wakeful night in ardent prayer for their happiness!" —*Life of Christ*, p. 362.

Ellen White: "The spotless son of God hung upon the cross, His flesh lacerated with stripes; those hands so often reached out in blessing, nailed to the wooden bars; those feet so tireless on ministries of love, spiked to the tree; that royal head pierced by the crown of thorns; *those quivering lips shaped to the cry of woe.*" —*The Desire of Ages*, p. 755, via 3*SP* 162.2, emphasis supplied.

Ellen White tightly adapts Fleetwood's potent contrast of the loving ministry of Jesus with the horror of His crucifixion, adding her own vivid imagery. Both writers utilize Scriptural wording.

Condensing, adapting, and correcting "thought gems" outside *The Desire of Ages*

The following are a few other examples of "thought gems" outside *The Desire of Ages* that illustrate Ellen White's condensing of thought, adapting of language, and correcting of theology. We begin with the earliest identified of these.

Larkin B. Coles: "Flesh-eating is certainly not NECESSARY to health or strength, as every candid mind must see. If it be used, it must be a matter of fancy, and not of necessity. [*skipping 12½ sentences*] it excites the animal passions. [*skipping nine sentences*] When we increase the proportion of our animal nature, we oppress the intellectual. [*skipping two sentences*] . . . the use of flesh tends to create a grossness of body and spirit." —*Philosophy of Health* (1848), pp. 64, 66, 67.

Ellen White: "Yet we do not hesitate to say that flesh meat is not necessary for health or strength. If used it is because a depraved appetite craves it. Its use excites the animal propensities to increased activity and strengthens the animal passions. When the animal propensities are increased, the intellectual and moral powers are decreased. The use of the flesh of animals tends to cause a grossness of body and benumbs the fine sensibilities of the mind." —*Testimonies for the Church*, vol. 2 (1868), p. 63.

Anyone reading Ellen White's *How to Live* series would have known the source of this "gem." It was gleaned from three pages of the same book that was excerpted with credits by the Whites to illustrate the harmony between "what the Lord had revealed" to Ellen White and the cutting-edge health writings of the day. (See explanation from *Review and Herald*, Oct. 8, 1867, in Chapter 8.)

Daniel March: "*We must not defer our obedience* till every shadow of uncertainty and every possibility of *mistake* is removed. The doubt that demands perfect knowledge will never yield to faith, for faith rests upon *probability*, not demonstration. *There is no scientific ground of faith, simply because what has become science is taken out of the sphere of faith.* We must obey the voice of duty when there are many other voices crying against it, and it requires earnest heed to distinguish the one which speaks for God. . . ." —*Night Scenes in the Bible*, pp. 201, 202, emphasis supplied.

Ellen White: "*If you refuse to believe* until «every shadow of uncertainty and every possibility of» *doubt* is removed you will never believe. «The doubt that demands perfect knowledge will never yield to faith». Faith rests upon *evidence*, not demonstration. The Lord requires us to «obey the voice of duty, when there are» other voices all around us urging us to pursue an opposite course. It requires earnest attention from us to distinguish the voice which speaks from God." —*Testimonies for the Church*, vol. 5 (1882), p. 69, emphasis supplied.

Note that March writes about waiting to *obey* while Ellen White writes about refusing to *believe*. Note also the significant changes she made in using "doubt" rather than "mistake" and "evidence" rather than "probability." Yes, Mrs. White has adapted this thought gem (which she first used in Ltr. 22, 1872), but has she not also improved upon it as well?

Daniel March: "This most surpassing revelation of the divine love, in the incarnation and suffering of the Son of God, is all that can give us peace and triumph in the last and utmost trial. Take the cross from Christianity and it is as if the sun were taken from the day and the stars from the night. Without the cross we have no Father in heaven, to draw us to himself with the relentings and compassions of a father's heart; . . . Without the cross, the powers of darkness are unconquerable, the punishment of sin is inevitable, there is nothing before us but a fearful looking for of judgment and fiery indignation which shall devour and destroy.

"The cross alone can give us hope and victory in the last and utmost trial. . . .

"At the foot of the cross, the penitent and believing soul has reached the highest elevation, above all the foes of his peace, and he thence looks forth a king and a conqueror, upon a subject world." —*Walks and Homes of Jesus*, pp. 335, 336, 339.

Ellen White: "Christ's death shows God's great love for man. It is the pledge of our salvation. To remove the cross from the Christian would be like blotting out the sun. The cross brings us near to God, reconciling us to him. Jehovah looks upon it with the relenting compassion of a Father's love. *He looks upon the suffering his Son endured in order to save the race from eternal death, and he accepts us in the Beloved.*

"Without the cross, man could have no connection with the Father. On it hangs our every hope. *In view of it the Christian may advance with the steps of* a conqueror; for from it streams the light of the Saviour's love. When the sinner reaches the cross, and looks up to the One who died to save him, he may rejoice with fullness of joy; for his sins are pardoned. Kneeling at the cross, he has reached the highest place to which man can attain. . . . Through the cross we learn that our Heavenly Father loves us with an infinite and everlasting love." —*Review and Herald*, April 29, 1902 (later used in *The Acts of the Apostles* [1911], pp. 209, 210), emphasis supplied.

The difference may be subtle, but Ellen White corrects the implication that God might have loved us less without the cross. She points out that the cross is simply the means by which a loving Father showed us He has always loved us. She also draws attention to the Christian's active advance as "a conqueror." How would one mark and footnote this unique adaptation of March?

Henry Melvill: ". . . never does this Gospel put on an aspect of greater loveliness, than when it addresses itself to the outcast and the destitute . . . But then it is that the Gospel appears under its most radiant form, when it enters the hovel of the peasant, and lights up that hovel with gladness, and fans the cheek of the sick man with angels' wings, and causes the crust of bread and the cruse of water to be received as a banquet of luxury . . . that he whom his fellow-men have loathed and abandoned, rises into the dignity of a being whom the Almighty delighted to honor . . . But he is lifted above the world, and sits in heavenly places with Christ: he has none of the treasures of the earth, but the pearl of great price he hath made his own." —*Sermons*, vol. 1 (1853), p. 173.

Ellen White: "«Never does the gospel put on an aspect of greater loveliness than when it» is brought to the most needy and destitute regions. Then it is that its light shines forth with the clearest radiance and the greatest power. Truth from the word of God «enters the hovel of the peasant»; rays from the Sun of righteousness light up the rude cottage of the poor, bringing gladness to the sick and suffering. Angels of God are there, and the simple faith shown makes «the crust of bread and the» cup of water a banquet. . . . Those who have been loathed and abandoned are *through faith and pardon* raised to the dignity of sons and daughters of God. Lifted above the world, they sit in heavenly places in Christ. They may have no earthly treasure, but they have found the pearl of great price." —*Testimonies for the Church*, vol. 7 (1902), p. 226, emphasis supplied.

Mrs. White omits the phrase "fans the cheek of the sick man with angels' wings," for, though poetic, it is not accurate. Notice also that she enhances and corrects Melvill's imagery theologically—it is "the Sun of righteousness" (Mal. 4:2) who lights up the hovel of the peasant, the "loathed and abandoned" are raised "through faith and pardon" as "sons . . . of God" John 1:12; and they sit "in Christ" (Eph. 2:6), not merely "with" Him.

Friedrich W. Krummacher: ". . . But we have a God, my friends, who always knows exactly, and much better than we do, what is good and necessary for his children; and, in truth, he never leads them otherwise than they would wish him to lead them, if they were able to see as clearly into their hearts and necessities as he does. But we very seldom know what is good for us; and therefore the ways by which God leads us are generally mysterious and obscure, just because the *why* and the *wherefore* are concealed from us. . . . This is the way of our gracious God. We must venture upon His Word." —*Elijah the Tishbite*, pp. 20, 21.

Ellen White: "The whys and wherefores are often concealed from you, and yet speak the words I shall give you however painful it may be to you. The ways God leads His people are generally mysterious. You have asked for God's way. You have your supplications answered. God knows better than you what is good and essential for His children. «He never leads them otherwise than they would wish Him to lead them if they were able to see as clearly» as He does their necessities and *what they must do to establish characters that will fit them for the heavenly courts above*. The people whom God is leading «must venture upon His word.»" —MS 29, 1890, Nov. 21, transcribed from "Diary, p. 321" in Ron Graybill, *E. G. White's Literary Work: An Update*, Appendix C.[18]

Almon Underwood: "Another requisite of prevailing prayer, is faith. He that cometh unto God, must believe that he is, and that he is a rewarder of those who diligently seek him. [*skipping nine sentences*] You are not to expect it to come in a particular way, nor necessarily at just such a time." —*God's Will Known and Done* (1860), p. 291.

Ellen White: "Another element of prevailing prayer is faith. 'He that cometh to God must believe that He is, and that He is a rewarder of them that diligently seek Him.' Hebrews 11:6. . . .

---

[18] Before using this thought gem in her diary, Ellen White had already used it in *Signs of the Times*, May 25, 1888: "He always knows much better than we do, just what is necessary for the good of his children, and he leads us as we would choose to be led if we could discern our own hearts and see our necessities and perils, as God sees them." (A better known adaptation of the thought gem is "God never leads His children otherwise than they would choose to be led, *if they could see the end from the beginning, and discern the glory of the purpose which they are fulfilling as co-workers with Him*." —*The Desire of Ages*, p. 224, emphasis supplied.) The adaptation of the gem she made in her diary was to "repeat in finite words" (*Gospel Workers*, p. 94) the encouragement given her by the angel about delivering God's messages though she didn't understand God's purpose. Nowhere in her published writings does she indicate that these were the exact words of her angel guide. That she had used the description before explains why she would think to use it to describe the message from the angel. That her words could involve a reconstruction of what she was told is seen in her testimony on another occasion: "I cannot write the exact words as He spoke them. I will try my best to give you the import of them." —Ltr. 8, 1888 in 8*MR* 431.1 (or *TSB* 160) as cited by Ron Graybill, "The 'I saw' parallels in Ellen White's writings," *Adventist Review*, July 29, 1982 at <www.adventistarchives.org/doc_info.asp?DocID=9673>.

COLOR CODING: Scripture verbatim «5 consecutive» paraphrase

But to claim that prayer will always be answered in the very way and for the particular thing that we desire *is presumption.*" —*Steps to Christ,* p. 96 (first used in *ST* 8-21-1884), emphasis supplied.

Ellen White contrasts faith and presumption—a difference not addressed by Underwood.

Edward Bickersteth: "It is a key to open the storehouse of all God's treasury to us; as by knocking we enter into the place where we desire to go, so by prayer we obtain all the blessings which we require." —*A Treatise on Prayer* (1850), p. 12.

Ellen White: "Prayer is the key in the hand of faith to unlock heaven's storehouse, where are treasured the boundless resources of Omnipotence." —*Steps to Christ,* pp. 94, 95.

Is Ellen White's statement not better worded and more memorable than that of Bickersteth? As James Russell Lowell once insightfully observed:

> Though old the thought and oft exprest
> 'Tis his at last who says it best.[19]

What conclusions can we draw from the colorized text?

Though there are other recognizable parallels scattered throughout the rest of Ellen White's writings,[20] the sentences we have just reviewed are some of the more recognizable, and the evidence that we have amassed is now sufficient to allow us to draw some conclusions about what the markings in *The Desire of Ages* tell us *conclusively* about Ellen White's literary borrowing.[21]

RED. Like the maples in an autumn landscape, the splash of red in these exhibits stands out more vividly than the other more predominant colors and, in a few instances, signals Ellen White's borrowing of a nearly exact quotation or a well-worded phrase. More often, however, red merely draws attention to *some of the same isolated words she used as another writer* in making her point. When the similarity of parallels is so unexceptional and the selection of a source work is largely a matter of noting which source has the most parallel verbatim words, the correlation of isolated verbatim words to sources may suggest dependency where none actually exists.

Some have suggested that future editions of *The Desire of Ages* use quotation marks and footnotes to designate borrowed words, but this would prove problematic since very few of the verbatim parallels reach the five-word threshold for marking, and many of these are either so unremarkable or self evident that they would not need footnoting. Even if *The Desire of Ages* should acknowledge literary borrowing, what would it say? *Select isolated sentences and phrasing have been adapted from other life of Christ works, which have also been consulted to provide structure to chapters and occasional historical facts.*

BLUE. The presence of blue merely tells us that Ellen White has followed the narrative of another work on the life of Christ. In some cases, the parallels have been quite similar. Even by modern standards, however, the paraphrasing of isolated sentences from another author does not require quotation marks or footnoting. In other cases, the looseness of similarity with the supposed source has left us wondering if she wasn't actually making the same point without any real dependence on the designated source.

Many verbatim and paraphrased words are marked with heavy underscoring, indicating that they were paralleled by more than one source. Among the works on the life of Christ, there does seem to be something of a "common pool" of vocabulary for telling the redemption story. The writers talk of

---

[19] Quoted by Olson in "Ellen G. White's Use of Uninspired Sources," p. 6.

[20] Such as the phrase "original, unborrowed, underived" in *DA* 530.3 from *SR-Jn* 6 to describe the life in Christ (John 1:4).

[21] This summary on the colorization of the text was inspired by the reaction of author Kevin Morgan's son, Adam.

the "weak" and "vacillating" Pilate, of Jesus' answering "not a word," of the "curiosity" of Herod and Pilate, of Pilate's wife's "warning," of the condemnation of Jesus as an "innocent man," of the "burden of the cross," of the "robber and murderer" Barabbas, of the "place of execution," of the "inscription" in Hebrew, Greek, and Latin, of the "stupefying potion" offered Jesus, of those "at the foot of the cross," of the "penitent thief," and of Jesus' "ignominious death." Should drawing from such a common pool of language be considered literary theft by any reasonable standard?

GREEN. The prominence of the color of living things tells us that Ellen White used a lot of Bible verses and Biblical language, which may or may not have been suggested by the works of other authors. Much of Ellen White's verbatim borrowing is nested within phrasing that a source borrowed from *Scripture*, showing that Ellen White sometimes borrowed a few words from another author in making her own Scriptural paraphrase. Should any of these instances be condemned as literary theft?

YELLOW. This sunshiny color has drawn our attention to phrases from Mrs. White's fresh manuscripts, used in *The Desire of Ages*, which are closer than the wording of the "sources." Does this closer wording in her free-flowing accounts not point to a mechanism other than the picking out of words here and there from the sources to improve her writing? From his correlation of verbatim wording in Ellen White's pre-*DA* manuscripts and the sources, Dr. Fred Veltman concluded:

> Ellen White used the writings of others consciously and intentionally. The literary parallels are not the result of accident or photographic memory. —Veltman, *Ministry*, Dec. 1990, p. 11.

That Ellen White "consciously and intentionally" used the writings of others does not mean that she *copied* every isolated parallel verbatim word as she wrote, for, unless she copied whole paragraphs of material with only minor alteration, the use of source works for the selection of isolated words would have made the process of writing so excruciatingly slow that Ellen White could never have written the thousands of pages of manuscript she wrote for *The Desire of Ages* or the estimated 25,000,000 words in her letters and journals. It seems more reasonable to conclude that a great many of the isolated verbatim words are *vocabulary* that Ellen White assimilated from her extensive reading. Does not the later appearance of many of these same verbatim words and phrases in her unscripted sermons and in her writings on unrelated topics validate this conclusion? On certain occasions she did read a previously written testimony to a congregation, but the vast majority of her public speaking was without notes (which is why it required secretaries to take down her sermons in shorthand to be edited for periodical articles). Describing her public presentations, she wrote: "I speak the words given me by a power higher than human power, and I cannot, if I would, recall one sentence" (MS 22, 1890 in 1*MR* 28.3). From other evidence it seems reasonable to conclude that parallel verbatim wording was introduced by a previous composition—either of Mrs. White or of another writer—being used *as a storyline guide,*[22] *in providing structure for her narrative,* or *in jogging her memory about what she had seen in vision.*[23] The phrases from 3*SP* that appear in MS

---

[22] "The great events occurring in the life of our Lord were presented to her in panoramic scenes as also were other portions of the *Great Controversy*. In a few of these scenes chronology and geography were clearly presented, but in the greater part of the revelation the flashlight scenes, which were exceedingly vivid, and the conversations and the controversies, which she heard and was able to narrate, were not marked geographically or chronologically, and *she was left to study the Bible and history, and the writings of men who had presented the life of our Lord to get the chronological and geographical connection.*" —W. C. White, 3*SM* 459, 460, emphasis supplied. (For example, *GC,* Chap. 1, has verbatim words that correlate with Macduff's *Memories of Olivet*, Chap. 12.)

[23] W. C. White writes: "Another purpose served by the reading of history and the *Life of Our Lord* [Hanna] and the *Life of Paul* [Conybeare and Howson], was that in so doing there was brought vividly to her mind scenes presented clearly in vision, but which were through the lapse of years and her strenuous ministry, dimmed in her memory. Many times in the reading of Hanna, Farrar, or Fleetwood, she would run on to a description of *a scene which had been vividly presented to her,* but forgotten, and which she was able to describe in more detail than that which she had read." —Ltr. to L. E. Froom, Jan. 8, 1928 in 3*SM* 460.1, 2, emphasis supplied. He also writes: "It was remarkable that in her reading and scanning of books that her mind was directed to the most helpful books

129, 1897 (see Chapter 1) give evidence that Ellen White used her own composition in writing out her "eyewitness" account of the trial before Herod. Verbatim parallels to Fleetwood in 1*RL* (see Appendix B, EXHIBIT G) give evidence that she used Fleetwood's life of Christ in writing out her own "eyewitness" account of Christ's temptation. Verbatim parallels to Farrar in the first seven paragraphs of MS 51, 1897 give evidence of a similar purpose in *DA*, Chapter 75 (see *LCRP* 553, 555, 564). These examples and the patchwork of other highlighting colors are consistent with the testimony of Marian Davis and W. C. White about Ellen White's use of sources and her own "matter."

To assert that Ellen White "copied and borrowed almost everything" (Walter Rea, *Chicago Tribune*, Nov. 23, 1980 in Robert W. Olson, *101 Questions*, p. 79) or that *The Desire of Ages* was "drawn largely from other writers" (*The White Lie*, p. 72) overlooks the uniqueness of what Ellen White wrote on the "greatest of subjects" (*YI* 8-31-1887). Focusing solely on *similarity*, Dr. Rea's 1982 appraisal of Ellen White's use of sources missed her *originality* in those very statements. Distilling similar material (at times without proper ellipses to indicate when wording had been omitted), his two-column exhibits conveyed the false impression that Ellen White copied paragraph after paragraph from page after page. This false impression was compounded by the inclusion of excerpts from Ellen White's writings, which may treat the same subject as another writer, but contain little or no parallel verbatim wording. When the full text of the two works are included and marked for display (as in *The Prophet and Her Critics* by Leonard Brand and Don S. McMahon, which compares parallel chapters of *Prophets and Kings* and *Night Scenes in the Bible*), the exhibit creates quite a different impression—the borrowing is seen to be very sparse and the similar material to be carefully adapted into an original treatment of the subject.

The truth is that, whether Ellen White used Biblical descriptions, assimilated language, adapted gems of thought, or words and phrases absorbed from her use of sources as storyline guides, one thing is certain—her finished product is clearly her own, and she has done her readers a great service in *identifying, improving, and making more memorable* some of the most effective language available for telling the "story of Jesus' love."

 ## Why didn't Ellen White call attention to her sources?

Though Ellen White sometimes refers to books she has read, she doesn't call attention in *The Desire of Ages* to sources other than Scripture. And why is this? As the preface to *The Desire of Ages* points out, the book was written, not for scholars or skeptics, but "to present the love of God" so "all may partake" (*DA* 14). Thus Ellen White patterns her book after the sermonic March and Hanna[24] and not after the heavily annotated Andrews and Edersheim. Like her contemporary Frank Gunsaulus, she *avoided that which would be construed as a display of learning,*[25] and, like her

---

and to the most helpful passages contained in those books. Occasionally she would mention to father, and in my presence, her experience in being led to examine a book which she had never looked into before, and her experience in opening it to certain passages that *helped her in describing that which she had seen and wished to present.*" —3*SM* 463.2, emphasis supplied.

[24] "By means of the best critical helps, the writer was, in the first instance, at pains to read aright and harmonize the accounts given by the different evangelists. Out of them he has endeavored to construct a continuous and expanded narrative, intended to bring out, as vividly as possible, not only the sequence of the incidents, but the characters, motives, and feelings of the different actors and spectators in the events described. He has refrained from all critical or doctrinal discussions as alien from the object he had in view; nor *has he thought it necessary to burden the following pages with references to all the authorities consulted.* The English reader will find in the writings of Alford, Stier, or Ellicott, the warrant for most of those readings of the original and inspired records upon which the following narrative is based." —William Hanna, *The Life of Christ*, preface, p. 7, note, emphasis supplied.

[25] "A long list, indeed, would they furnish, if I were to supply the names of the authors and the books which I have freely drawn upon, and all other means employed by me, in writing this book. To make such an acknowledgment in the form of a catalogue, would expose me justly to the charge of pedantry [*pedantry* is "an undue display of learning"]. . . . he who was seriously determined to make any account of Jesus Christ must have previously acquainted himself with the results of the exploration, exegetical inquiry, thinking

spiritual forebear Methodist John Wesley, she avoided that which would "divert the mind of the reader from keeping close to the point in view, and receiving what was spoken only according to its own intrinsic value."[26] She wanted nothing to *take away from the self-validating nature of divine truth in the writings themselves*,[27] which "are so clear and beautiful that the unprejudiced mind grasps them at once as truth,"[28] as the preface to the first in his Redemption series points out:

> One thing in particular will impress the reader, that the writer of these little books presents many beautiful thoughts which are not expressed in other writings of the kind. And these thoughts are so very natural in their connections with the subject, so simple, plain, and beautiful, that the reader will often inquire why he has not before thought of them. —Publishers, *Redemption; or the First Advent of Christ, with His Life and Ministry* [1RL], preface, p. 8.

She wanted nothing to "make of none effect the testimonies of the Spirit of God" (*MR926* 55.1), nothing to empty "the messages of their power,"[29] and nothing to dismiss the inspiration of what God had given in counsel.[30] Mrs. White could hardly recommend to her readers[31] the mixture of Truth and Falsehood in the sources—as helpful as they might be in expressing truth. As an example, consider the following list of statements taken from works of John Cumming:

From *The Life and Lessons of Our Lord*:
1. At death is "the immediate entrance of the soul into its destiny"(p. 464). .... **F**[32]
2. However, there is "no purgatory to enter" (p. 465). ....**T**
3. "There is . . . conclusive evidence that the soul does not sleep after death" (p. 465). .... **F**[33]
4. "All Scripture assures us that instant death is instant glory" (p. 466). .... **F**[34]

---

and faith of many of the ablest men who have ever toiled with the greatest of subjects." —Frank W. Gunsaulus, *The Man of Galilee: A Biographical Study of The Life of Jesus Christ*, (1899), preface.

[26] "It was a doubt with me for some time, whether I should not subjoin to every note I received from them the name of the author from whom it was taken; especially considering I had transcribed some, and abridged many more, almost in the words of the author. But upon farther consideration, I resolved to name none, that nothing might divert the mind of the reader from keeping close to the point in view, and receiving what was spoken only according to its own intrinsic value." —John Wesley, *Explanatory Notes Upon the New Testament*, Preface, p. v. (With the exception of *GC*, Wesley's transcribing and abridging of sources certainly exceeded Ellen White's rare adaptation of a near verbatim sentence or incorporation of a verbatim word or phrase.)

[27] In the second of two book introductions she wrote herself (the first being the preface to *Spiritual Gifts*, vol. 4a), written just four years before launching work on the life of Christ revision, Ellen White gives the reason she did not clutter the pages of her works with references to sources: "In some cases where a historian has so grouped together events as to afford, in brief, a comprehensive view of the subject, or has summarized details in a convenient way, his words have been quoted; but except in a few instances no specific credit has been given, since they are *not quoted for the purpose of citing that writer as authority*, but *because his statement affords a ready and forcible presentation of the subject*." —"Author's Preface," *GC* (1888), p. h., emphasis supplied.

[28] James White, *Life Sketches of James and Ellen White* (1880), p. 328.

[29] Fred Veltman, *LCRP*, Introduction, p. 172.

[30] Ron Graybill, *E. G. White's Literary Work: An Update*. An edited and annotated transcript of a tape recording of morning worship talks given at the General Conference of Seventh-day Adventists, Nov. 15–19, 1981, p. 23.

[31] A sermon from which Ellen White adapted 35% of an article—the highest percentage for any of her compositions (see W. H. Johns, *Ministry*, June 1982)—could not be recommended to readers because it falsely taught that "the soul . . . rushes into the body" at the resurrection (Henry Melvill, "The First Prophecy," *Sermons*, vol. 1 [1853], p. 18). In her *RH* 7-18-1882 article, "The First Prophecy," Ellen White drew from 11 of Melvill's 41 paragraphs (seven very lightly) for 43 out of 124 of her sentences (five using the same Scripture). Though there are many striking words and phrases among these sentences (11 phrases have five or more consecutive words), judging from her having written previously on the subject (*RH* 2-24-1874) and from most of the parallel sentences being loose paraphrase, it would seem that she used Melvill's sermon as a guide for her article because she found it consistent with her understanding of the subject and containing language she could adapt to express what God gave her to communicate.

[32] The reward of life everlasting for those who sleep in Christ will be given at the second coming (Rev. 22:12; 1 Thes. 4:16).

[33] "Sleep" is the uniform description of death throughout Scripture (Psa. 13:3; Luke 8:42; John 11:11; 1 Thes. 4:14).

[34] There is but one verse that can be construed to say this—2 Cor. 5:8, but 1 Cor. 15:54 says glory comes at the resurrection.

5. Participation in baptism and the Lord's Supper is not essential to salvation, but it is the believer's duty and privilege if circumstances afford them (p. 467). .... **T**
6. "It is Christ's prerogative alone to forgive and absolve from sin" (p. 468). .... **T**

From *Sabbath Evening Readings on the New Testament. John*:
7. Nothing is mentioned in Scripture that Lazarus witnessed scenes after death (p. 192; p. 277 adds that there is perfect silence in Scripture about any such accounts). .... **T**

From *Occasional Discourses*, vol. II:
8. The soul (at least of the believer in Christ) is immortal (p. 233). .... **F**[35]

From *Foreshadows. Lectures on our Lord's Miracles*:
9. At the marriage feast at Cana, Christ turned water to fermented wine (p. 13). .... **F**[36]
10. The resurrection "in Christ" is a living reality; at the resurrection loved ones are to be re-united (p. 282ff). .... **T**
11. At the resurrection there will be "perfect recognition" of those we have known (p. 282ff). .... **T**
12. "Our dead do live" in "spirit-land" (p. 282ff). .... **F**[37]
13. It is gross idolatry to pray to the departed saints-spirits (p. 282ff). .... **T**
14. There is only one Mediator, Christ Jesus (p. 282ff). .... **T**

From *The Great Tribulation; or, Things Coming on the Earth*, Second Series:
15. Christ is sitting on His throne; there is no more propitiatory sacrifice (p. 244). .... **T**

From *The Daily Life; or Precepts and Prescriptions for Christian Living*:
16. Jesus "pleads before the throne our Prince and our Intercessor; and he will come again in intolerable glory and receive us to himself, that where he is there may we be also" (p. 239). .... **T**

From *The End: or, The Proximate Signs of the Close of this Dispensation*:
17. As a sign of the End, the Jewish race would be both restored to their ancient land as well as converted to "the knowledge and enjoyment of the Gospel of Christ" (p. 141). .... **F**[38]

From *Minor Works*, First Series:
18. Romish traditions and so-called miracles are not in harmony with the Gospel (Part I). .... **T**
19. Christ crucified is the sum and substance of Christianity (Part II). .... **T**
20. There is an absolute necessity of professed believers in Christ being baptized with the Holy Ghost; Joel 2 is yet to have a glorious fulfillment (Part III). .... **T**
21. There is not a changing of the old nature to a new, but an implanting in the midst of the old nature "a powerful, a conquering, and a dominant new" (p. 76). .... **T**
22. The Holy Spirit leads to Christ (Part III). .... **T**

From *Minor Works*, Second Series:
23. The natural heart, before regeneration by the Holy Spirit, is enmity to God (Part II). .... **T**
24. Our peace comes from our being justified by faith in Christ—faith that lays hold upon what Christ *has done*, i.e., His "finished sacrifice" (Part II). .... **T**[39]

From *Minor Works*, Third Series:
25. Infants are to be baptized, signifying a dedication on the part of the parents. .... **F**[40]

---

[35] God only has immortality (1 Tim. 6:16); humans put on immortality at the resurrection (1 Cor. 15:52–54).

[36] The Greek word *oinos* does not designate whether juice is fermented or unfermented; what Jesus made was made fresh that very day.

[37] Though having commended His *spirit* to the Father, Jesus told Mary that *He* was not yet ascended to the Father.

[38] Hebrews 11:5 says Abraham desired a better country, a heavenly one.

[39] Cumming has no concept of the "holy places" of heaven (Heb. 9:23, 24) or of Christ's ministry in the Holy of Holies.

[40] An infant cannot believe (Mark 16:16), but it can be given or "dedicated" to the Lord, as were children in Scripture.

26. Baptism is not a transformation of the nature, but is symbolic of that change (Part II). .... **T**
27. Baptism is a seal that God will fulfill His promises to the new son or daughter in Christ (Part II). .... **T**

From *The Great Tribulation; or, Things Coming on the Earth*, First Series:

28. Regarding the outpouring of the Holy Spirit, there is yet to be a "great and copious baptism that is to prepare a people for the coming of the Lord" (p. 130). .... **T**[41]

From *Signs of the Times; or, Present, Past and Future*:

29. Elijah from the "realms of glory" and "clothed with its beauty" will literally come to herald Christ's second advent, even as did John the Baptist before the first (p. 187). .... **F**[42]
30. The second advent of Christ clearly will be personal and premillenial (p. 188). .... **T**
31. That advent will not be a secret rapture known only to a few, but a worldwide event to be witnessed by all (p. 177). .... **T**
32. Papal Rome is equivalent to the Apostasy and the Antichrist of Scripture. .... **T**

From *The Great Preparation; or, Redemption Draweth Nigh*, Second Series:

33. Babylon (Rev. 14 and 18) is essentially Papal Rome (p. 283ff). .... **F**[43]
34. Her sins are exceeding many (and he enumerates them) (Lecture XXXV). .... **T**
35. "God's people are justified, through faith in the righteousness of Christ and in that alone" (p. 293). . **T**
36. Rev. 18:4 constitutes the warning cry that precedes the "nearing and final desolation of the great Apostasy . . ." (p. 283). .... **T**

From *Voices of the Night*:

37. The Christian is to hate sectarianism and pray for and love all that love Jesus (p. 117). .... **T**
38. God's true people may be found in all denominations (p. 118). .... **T**
39. Conversion is not to be halfway work; thus justification is realized (p. 322). .... **T**

From *Prophetic Studies; or, Lectures on the Book of Daniel*:

40. Papal Rome is predicted in Daniel, 2 Thessalonians, and Revelation. .... **T**
41. Babylon (Papal Rome) is now (1853) drinking of the cup of the indignation of God, and "all her boasted triumphs are but the installments, as it were, or foretokens of her speedy downfall" (p. 245). **F**[44]
42. Not all in this world will be eternally saved. .... **T**
43. The atonement of Christ and God's holy law are very exalted; by contrast sin is exceedingly grievous. .... **T**
44. The Sacrificial atonement of Jesus Christ at Calvary was primarily substitutionary, —he writes: "Jesus died, not an example how the good should meekly suffer, but an atonement by which the sins of the guilty might be forgiven" (p. 359). .... **T**[45]

From *The Church Before the Flood*:

45. Jesus "assigned the first day of the week to be the Christian Sabbath" (p. 75). .... **F**[46]

Ellen White had good reason for not burdening her pages with references, but the question remains, "Should her gathering of gems and assimilation of language without specific mention of sources be classified as *plagiarism*?" We will address this fundamental question in our next chapter.

---

[41] Cumming does not connect the latter rain with the call out of Babylon in Rev. 18:4.

[42] Cumming misses the point that, though not literally Elijah, John the Baptist fulfilled the prophecy about the sending of Elijah before the coming of Messiah (Mal. 4:5).

[43] Babylon includes papal Rome, but the woman in scarlet of Revelation has daughters (Rev. 17:5).

[44] In 1853, she had not yet been restored from her "deadly wound" (Rev. 13:3).

[45] Cumming misses what Hebrews 12 teaches about Christ's life being our example. As Ellen White wrote, "His life was as complete as a pattern, as his death was complete as a sacrifice." —*Signs of the Times*, May 16, 1895.

[46] Jesus declared Himself "Lord of the Sabbath" (Mark 2:27); he made no declaration about a new day of worship.

CHAPTER **8**

Issues of Legality, Ethics, and Integrity

"Well gentlemen, it should not surprise us to hear of Walter Rea's discoveries. We all know the problems with the writings of Ellen G. White."

So spoke the professor in his pastoral leadership class. It was October 23, 1980, at Pacific Union College, Angwin, California. That very morning, under the headline "Plagiarism Found in Prophet Books,"[1] the *Los Angeles Times* had announced: "Former SDA minister finds E. G. White to have plagiarized, and therefore concludes she was a fraud. She took material from other authors without giving them credit." The class was filled with young men in their late teens and early twenties. Without hesitation 22-year-old Bill Emmet raised his hand and addressed his teacher.

"Elder Waverly, I'm a new Adventist and have fallen in love with the Spirit of Prophecy writings. Could you tell us what's wrong with what she's written?"

The professor, enraged, slammed himself against the chalkboard in pretended shock, and the reader is left to imagine the dialog that ensued.[2]

Was the headline correct? Did Ellen White plagiarize?

 What is plagiarism?

In one way or another, every one of us who writes or speaks, borrows from others language and ways of presenting our thoughts. If we didn't, no one would ever understand us. However, this kind of assimilation from others to express ourselves does not constitute *plagiarism* or "literary theft." *To plagiarize*, according to Webster, one must "take ideas, writings, etc. from [another] and pass them off as one's own." In his classic work, *Plagiarism and Originality*, Alexander Lindey wrote: "Copying someone else's story or play or song, intact or with inconsequential changes, and adding one's name to the result constitute a simple illustration of plagiarism."[3] None of Ellen White's books used a source in this way, though Arthur L. White describes an instance in which one of hers was:

> The book Education was, in the year 1912, published by the Minister of Education of Serbia. His name was Raja R. Radosavlyevish. He held degrees of Doctor of Philosophy, Master and Doctor of Pedagogy, and was a graduate of Columbia University. He published the book Education in its entirety in the Serbian language while he was serving as Minister of Education of his country. His name appears on the title page. He signed a foreword to the book, stating the need and he was pleased to fulfill this need. From that point on, the book is Education from first to last. . . . comparing it paragraph by paragraph, I find all the Scripture texts used in Education appearing in their rightful places in the Serbian book and the lengths of the paragraphs are corresponding. I am led to believe that he translated the

---

[1] John Dart, "Plagiarism found in Prophet Books," *Los Angeles Times*, October 23, 1980, pp. 1, 3, 21.

[2] Although this is an actual incident, the names are pseudonyms. Incident used by permission.

[3] Alexander Lindey, *Plagiarism and Originality* (New York: Harper & Brothers Publishers, 1952), p. 2.

whole book and put it out as his work. . . . Our brethren considered that there would be little to be gained by attempting to do anything about it.[4]

A slightly less obvious form of literary borrowing that would still be considered plagiarism occurs whenever a writer borrows heavily from a single source (as opposed to many sources), paraphrases much of that one source's material, uses whole verbatim sentences from it, follows its format, and gives evidence of obvious dependence upon its subject matter.[5] None of Ellen White's works borrowed from a single source in this way. It should be noted that not all borrowing of literary material is plagiarism. "We must be careful," Lindey warned, "not to confuse borrowing with theft. There is a world of difference between the winnowings of a Dante and the outright looting of a Stendahl. . . . every instance of borrowing must be assessed in its time and place."[6]

Though nearly self evident, these are not the definitions most people have in mind today when they think of plagiarism. Most today think of plagiarism in terms of its academic definition:

> Academic plagiarism occurs when a writer repeatedly uses more than four words from a printed source without the use of quotation marks and a precise reference to the original source in a work presented as the author's own research and scholarship.[7]

It should be pointed out that, though many have assumed otherwise, such a definition would not have been used in the nineteenth century when the concept of literary borrowing was not so rigidly defined.[8] A comment made by John Cumming (one of the authors of the source works analyzed for borrowing in the Life of Christ Research Project) humorously illustrates this point:

> In the course of my lecturing on this parable, I received a note from a hearer, complaining I had not acknowledged my obligations to Trench. The answer is, Trench and I are both very deeply indebted to Olshausen.[9]

---

[4] Arthur L. White in a letter to Dr. A. N. Nelson, 1961. Q & A File Number 43-C-51. *RH* 9-6-1864 (vol. 24, no. 15) calls attention to an entire poem (minus one of its verses), written by Annie Smith, that was printed under the name of Luthera B. Weaver.

[5] Walter Rea asserted that Mrs. White was heavily dependent upon Hanna for *The Desire of Ages*, citing Walter Specht's study as support, Rea writes: "he had found that the copying from Hanna had begun at the beginning and ended at the ending" (*The White Lie*, 1982, p. 90). But Specht's report says no such thing. On the contrary, Specht demonstrates Ellen White's independence, pointing to the criteria of Alfred M. Perry for determining literary dependence:

"1. Resemblance of the contents: telling the same stories. 2. Resemblance in continuity: telling the stories in the same order. 3. Similar sentence and word order: telling the stories in the same way. 4. Extensive agreement (50 percent to 60 per cent) in the words used. 5. Agreement in using unusual words or harsh construction." —Alfred M. Perry, "The Growth of the Gospels," *Interpreter's Bible*, vol. 7, p. 62, in Walter F. Specht, *The Literary Relationship Between The Desire of Ages, by Ellen G. White and The Life of Christ, by William Hanna*, pp. 1, 2.

On criteria *one* and *two*, Specht notes that Hanna and Ellen White tell the same stories in generally the same order since they are following the Gospels, but Ellen White sometimes rearranges topics and covers topics not in Hanna. On criteria *three*, he notes the difference in their sentence length—Hanna tended to use "long and involved sentences" while Ellen White tended to use much shorter ones. On criteria *four*, he notes that there is not "extensive agreement" between Hanna and White—her wording is often linked to multiple works, not the 50–60% from a single work as required by Perry. On criteria *five*, he notes that many of the unique constructions in both Hanna and Ellen White come from the King James Bible.

[6] Lindey, p. 63.

[7] Definition taken from the Web Page of Professor Irving Hexham, Department of Religious Studies, University of Calgary (Calgary, Alberta, Canada) at <www.ucalgary.ca/~hexham/study/plag.html>.

[8] "One can detect a proliferating concern with plagiarism in the mid-nineteenth century. . . . American writers of the antebellum period were attempting to work out the limitations and the possibilities of proprietary authorship . . ." —Ellen Weinauer, "Plagiarism and the Proprietary Self: Policing the Boundaries of Authorship in Herman Melville's 'Hawthorne and His Mosses'," *American Literature*, vol. 69, no. 4 (1997): pp. 700, 712.

[9] *Cumming's Minor Works*, Second Series (1854), p. 130. Cf. Dr. Hermann Olshausen, 1796–1839. *Biblical commentary on the New Testament*, translated by David Fosdick, Jr. (New York: Sheldon, Blakeman & Co., 1857–58), 6 vols.

In comparing Ellen White's writings to the possible source works in the Life of Christ Research Project, we discovered that at least two of the major source work authors—John Harris and Daniel March—did not indicate when they had consulted other writers. Even though the originality of these two works was not the focus of our study, we did sometimes notice striking similarity of phrasing between their writings and other writings of the same genre.

Even Ellen White's noted nineteenth century critic, D. M. Canright, who denounced her for copying "her subject matter without credit or sign of quotation,"[10] apparently felt no obligation to give credit to Moses Hull for the use of his title[11] and large amounts of his material, including numerous nearly verbatim pages from Hull's book in Canright's expanded revision of *The Bible from Heaven*.[12] (The books to which he referred as being without "sign of quotation" were *Sketches from the Life of Paul* and *The Great Controversy*, the latter being the fourth in the series of *Spirit of Prophecy* volumes.)

Dudley M. Canright

Why didn't Mrs. White use quotation marks in these earlier books? W. C. White explains: "Mrs. White made no effort to conceal the fact that she had copied from other writers, statements that exactly suited her purpose. And in her handwritten manuscripts, most of the passages that she had copied word for word, were enclosed in quotation marks. But there were also many passages that were paraphrased. . . . Much time would be required to study each passage and mark it consistently."

---

[10] D. M. Canright, *Seventh-Day Adventism Renounced* (1889), p. 139. Some have called attention to the statement of A. G. Daniells at the 1919 Bible Conference: ". . . we got Conybeare and Howson [for *LP*], and we got Wylie's 'History of the Reformation,' [for *GC* (1888)] and we read word for word, page after page, and no quotations, no credit . . ." ("Inspiration of the Spirit of Prophecy as Related to the Inspiration of the Bible," *Spectrum*, vol. 10, no. 1, p. 52). For *LP*, this doesn't mean that there was page after page of cut-and-paste material. F. D. Nichol documents only 7% of *LP* being from Conybeare and Howson, 4% from Farrar's *The Life and Work of St. Paul* (which quoted from Conybeare and Howson without noting the fact), and an additional 1.85% of loose paraphrases (F. D. Nichol, *Ellen G. White and Her Critics*, pp. 424, 425). Very little of the parallel material would require quotation marks (see <www.ellenwhite.info/conybeare-howson-cleveland-a.htm>). The only footnoted references in the 1884 and 1888 editions of *GC* referred to Scripture—an indication of what the author intended to emphasize. Canright was not entirely correct. There were quotation marks, and an observant reader should have noticed the quotation marks within quotation marks and the *ellipses* inside *quotation marks*, which were used to denote omitted portions of dialogue. Both of these show that she was using historical sources and not hiding the fact (e.g., 4*SP* 83, 92, 96, 108, 115, 125). To clear up any doubt about her use of sources for *descriptiveness* rather than *authority*, Mrs. White included an explanatory statement in the Author's Preface of the 1888 revision of *GC*. Expanded by materials inspired by her stay in Europe, the 1888 revision came off the press in February of 1889 before the debates with Canright in March.

[11] Some have accused Ellen White of plagiarizing *The Great Controversy Between Christ and Satan* from H. L. Hastings' *The Great Controversy Between God and Man. Its Origin Progress and End*. While the titles are similar, there is significant difference in the "scope, purpose, and content" of the two books (Warren H. Johns, "Literary Thief or God's Messenger?" *Ministry*, June 1982, pp. 13, 14). A careful comparison of the two revealed only a few inconsequential similarities and no mention in Hastings' book of the very core of the great controversy theme—the fall of Lucifer from heaven of Isaiah 14; Ezekiel 28; and Revelation 12.

[12] Canright rewrote Moses Hull's 1863 book, *The Bible from Heaven*, expanding it by 108 pages. Using whole verbatim pages from the earlier book without mention of Hull, Canright published the new book in 1878 under the same title. (See Francis D. Nichol, *Ellen G. White and Her Critics*, pp. 407, 408.) Canright's defense of his actions was that he wasn't a prophet, that he was merely expanding a work that had been disgraced by the author's apostasy to spiritualism, and that he "claimed no originality in the book" (*Healdsburg Enterprise*, March 20, 1889). On the last point, Canright's preface for the book implies otherwise. The book was written "after extensive reading and careful thought upon the subject." W. C. White wrote: "When tracts and pamphlets were published, the expositions of truth therein presented, frequently represented the results of united, concerted study, and the forms of expression by the several writers were very similar and sometimes identical. All felt that the truths to be presented were *common property* and wherever one could help another or get help from another in the expression of Biblical truths, it was considered right to do so. Consequently, there were many excellent statements of present truth copied by one writer from another. And no man said that aught which he wrote was exclusively his own." —"Brief Statements Regarding the Writings of Ellen White" (1933), p. 7, emphasis supplied. It is only Canright's double standard that makes his actions reprehensible. Ellen White's use of material in *GC* from James White, Uriah Smith, and J. N. Andrews, without attribution falls into this same category of use and is explained by Ellen White's statement in the "Author's Preface" of the 1888 revision of *GC*: "In narrating the experience and views of those carrying forward the work of reform in our own time, similar use has occasionally been made of their published works" (*GC* h).

To expedite the release of these books, "it was decided to leave out quotation marks entirely," and she was "advised to leave out the quotation marks and did so. But afterward, when presented with the fact that this was considered unfair to the people from whom she had made quotations, she said to have them in by all means."[13]

In time, attitudes about literary rights changed radically.[14] By the beginning of the twentieth century, a writer—even one with a recognizable name and respected ability—was lucky if he or she wasn't accused of plagiary some time in his or her career. The "Who's Who" of the accused included such notables as Henry Wadsworth Longfellow, Harriet Beecher Stowe, Rudyard Kipling, Edgar Allen Poe, Cunningham Geikie, and even William Shakespeare. To this flurry of accusations, one anonymous writer responded:

> We are getting weary of this cry of plagiarism. . . . the outcry of theft does not proceed, as a rule, from those whose thunder has been stolen, but from people who have no thunder that is worth stealing. It is the easiest form of criticism to accuse a man of want of originality, and it is one that commends itself especially to little minds. —"The Cry of Plagiarism," *The Spectator* (Feb. 28, 1891), p. 306.

In legal terms, did Ellen White make "fair use" of others' writings?

In the June 1982 issue of *Ministry* magazine, associate editor Warren H. Johns reported on a 27-page opinion by attorney Vincent L. Ramik[15] on Ellen White's use of sources. Attorney Ramik performed his study at the behest of the General Conference of Seventh-day Adventists. His "unequivocal" finding dealt with both plagiary and copyright infringement:

> Based upon our review of the facts and legal precedents . . . Ellen White was not a plagiarist, and her works did not constitute copyright infringement/piracy.[16]

In preparation for his report to the General Conference, Attorney Ramik spent more than 300 hours researching approximately 1000 American legal cases relevant to the times and practices of Ellen G. White and reading *The Great Controversy* as well as portions of her other works. Regarding *content* and the propriety of using the materials of others, Ramik said:

> Nowhere have we found the books of Ellen G. White to be virtually the "same plan and character throughout" as those of her predecessors. Nor have we found, or have the critics made reference to, any intention of Ellen White to supersede . . . [other authors] in the market with the same class of readers and purchasers. . . . Moreover, so long as the materials were selected from a variety of sources and were "arranged and combined with certain passages of the text of the original work, and in a manner showing the exercise of discretion, skill, learning, experience, and judgment," the use was "fair." . . .[17]

Vincent L. Ramik

---

[13] "Brief Statements Regarding the Writings of Ellen G. White," p. 10, and letter from W. C. White to J. C. Stevens, July 25, 1919, W. C. White Letterbook #129 in Robert W. Olson, "Ellen G. White's Use of Uninspired Sources," April 10, 1980, p. 13, with commas added to the original.

[14] "The more readers and writers revered 'originality' as an absolute artistic virtue, the more the spectre of guilt floated over the 'influenced' writer's horizon." —David Carpenter, "Hoovering to Byzantium," found online at <www.dccarpenter.com/hoovering.htm>.

[15] Attorney Ramik was senior partner of Diller, Ramik & Wight, Ltd., a firm specializing in patent, trademark, and copyright cases. The 27-page report is now available in 17 pages at <www.whiteestate.org/issues/ramik.html>.

[16] Vincent L. Ramik quoted in Roger W. Coon, Victor Cooper, et al. Interview with Vincent L. Ramik, attorney, "Ellen White's Use of Sources," *Adventist Review*, Sept. 17, 1981, p. 2.

[17] Ramik, p. 2.

In elaborating on the 27-page Ramik report, Warren H. Johns summarized the five essentials of the "legal definition of plagiarism or literary piracy":

1. Motive: Was there any intent to deceive?

2. Extent or scope: Did the author rely heavily upon a single source?

3. Style: Did the author make only "colorable alterations"?

4. Content: Has the theme, framework, or structure of a prior work been taken over?

5. Infringement: Have the profits resulting from the sale of the older book been diminished by the sale of the new? [See notes on sales in Appendix A.]

The charge of plagiarism cannot be leveled by taking just one of these five essentials in isolation; it must involve a combination of all. . . .

Not one of her books is based solely upon one previously published work.[18]

Regarding *motive* and the intent to deceive or cover up—the first of the five essentials in literary theft—Warren H. Johns called attention to five clarifying facts:

Fact No. 1: . . . Let her own words speak: "I am just as dependent upon the Spirit of the Lord in relating or writing the vision as in having the vision." —*Selected Messages*, book 3, p. 48. . . . If the Spirit was such an indispensable part of her writing, and if, as we have seen, her writing involved using other sources, then God's Spirit must have been a directing force in the choice and adaptation of those sources. . . . This thought is further expanded by W. C. White and D. E. Robinson: "She was told that in the reading of religious books and journals, she would find precious gems of truth expressed in acceptable language, and that she would be given help from heaven to recognize these and to separate them from the rubbish of error with which she would sometimes find them associated." —"Brief Statements Regarding the Writings of Ellen G. White," 1933, p. 5, published as an insert in the *Adventist Review*, June 4, 1981. . . .

Fact No. 2: On occasion, Ellen White did her research into other sources in full view of others. According to W. C. White, her son, she was granted, along with her husband, a writing room on the second floor of the brick Review and Herald building. That room contained the library, from which she "made selection of books which she considered profitable to read" (*Selected Messages*, book 3, p. 463). . . .

According to W. C. White, who worked very closely with his mother, she would often spend an hour or two of reading during daylight hours after having completed a hard day's work of writing. (W. C. White letter to L. E. Froom, Feb. 14, 1926). Much of her reading was done in the open.

Fact No. 3: Ellen White freely loaned her books— books that presumably she would need, sooner or later, in her research. It would seem inexplicable for her to do so if she were attempting to conceal the fact of her borrowing from these very sources. . . .

The Review and Herald Publishing building, Battle Creek, Michigan

Fact No. 4: Ellen White made no attempt to conceal from her helpers the fact that she relied upon available books for her research and writing. When working on *The Great Controversy* in Basel, Switzerland, her assistants made good use of J. N. Andrews' extensive library (see *Selected Messages*, book 3, p. 439). . . .[19]

---

[18] Warren H. Johns, *Ministry*, June 1982, p. 13.

Fact No. 5: Ellen White recommended to the general Seventh-day Adventist church membership the very books from which she was drawing selected material in writing her books and testimonies.[20]

As an example, when Ellen White published *Sketches from the Life of Paul* in June of 1883 as a supplement to the 1883/1884 Sabbath School lessons on Acts already in progress,[21] Conybeare and Howson's larger work on the life of Paul was being sold by the Review office and had been twice recommended by Ellen White.[22] That she would be "stealing" from the very book she was recommending makes no sense unless one assumes that she had such a poor memory that she forgot which book she had "copied" from or that she thought SDA readers were so illiterate that they would never read the larger work being sold through the Review office. Both assumptions are ludicrous.[23]

Attorney Ramik's legal opinion, which relates most specifically to the use of sources in *The Great Controversy*, also applies to *The Desire of Ages*, for the purpose of the book, its style, additional content, and adapted borrowed phrasing all unite to create a unique literary work that is like no other. In the legal sense, Ellen White's use of sources in *The Desire of Ages* was certainly fair.

---

[19] Warren H. Johns mentions in his article *The Young Lady's Counsellor* by Daniel Wise, from which Ellen White quoted in the *Health Reformer*, July 1873, p. 221, and Conybeare and Howson's *The Life and Epistles of the Apostle Paul*. Mrs. White kept no secret about her use of sources, openly requesting books from her library for her writing: "Will you please get and mail the covered book *History of Paul*, and put in a red-covered book, [Smith's] *Bible Antiquities*—[a] sort of Bible dictionary. . . . Take special pains to send the books I desire. There is one old book bought in Oakland—[Melvill's] *Sermons*; also another book, *Old Worthies of the Old Testament*. You look over my books and send all I shall really need." —Ltr. 52, 1878, Nov. 8, to Mary White from Grand Prairie, Texas (3*BIO* 103.2). She requested or mentioned a number of other resources in letters to various recipients. Among these were "some histories of the Bible" for "the order of events" (Ltr. 38, 1885 in 3*SM* 122.1); *How to Be a Man* (Ltr. 23, 1861 [7-26]); *The Martyrs of Spain* (Ltr. 1a, 1868 [1-19]); the missionary paper *Woman's Friend* (MS 2, 1874); that they "need not send" Daniel March's *Walks and Homes of Jesus* (Ltr. 27a, 1876 [5-22] in *Exhibits* #27) as she worked on 2*SP* while traveling by train from Oakland to Kansas; *Jewish Antiquities*, a Bible dictionary, and Daniel March's *Night Scenes of the Bible* (Ltr. 60, 1878 [12-8]) after reading proofs for 3*SP* in November; *Antiquities of the Bible* or *Jewish Antiquities* (Ltr. 62, 1878 [12-19] and Ltr. 40, 1886 [4-4]); Cumming's *Signs of Christ's Coming* (Ltr. 4, 1879) and *Signs of the Times* (Ltr. 6, 1879 [1-6]); *History of Paul's Life* (Ltr. 45a, 1880); a book by Harriet Beecher Stowe; selections from *Mother's Duties* and *Home Influences* (Ltr. 45c, 1880 [11-7]); *Eminent Men of Michigan* (Ltr. 28, 1882 [Sept.]); *The Giant Cities of Bashan* (Ltr. 45, 1886 [5-12]); and *Barnes' Notes* and Horace Mann (Ltr. 243, 1899 [6-5] and Ltr. 189, 1900 in 4*BIO* 448).

[20] W. H. Johns, *Ministry*, June 1982, pp. 14, 15.

[21] The advantages of this work over the *Life and Epistles of St. Paul* of Conybeare and Howson (which was not under copyright in America) were its brevity (334 vs. 764 pages) and its additional insights from Ellen White (approximately 36% of *Sketches from the Life of Paul* came from the *Redemption* pamphlets 7 and 8 on Paul and 3*SP*, published in 1878). *Sketches from the Life of Paul* eventually went out of print (at what point is uncertain since it was still advertised in *The Signs of the Times* until 1885). Eleven years after 1885, Mrs. White was voicing her desire to enlarge the book. "We will have two volumes of the life of Christ and a small book upon the parables, ... but *the lives of the disciples and apostles is yet to be prepared.*" —Ltr. 140, 1896 (Jan. 23), emphasis supplied. (See also Ltr. 102b, 1899 in 4*BIO* 449.6, which mentions taking up "the New Testament history from the ascension of Christ to Revelation" and Ltr. 70, 1903 in 5*BIO* 261.4, in which she mentions "a book on *The Acts of the Apostles*.") Later she wrote: "I think that a new edition of *The Life of Paul* should be published. I shall make some additions to this book, however, before it is republished." —Ltr. 150, 1903, in the preface of the facsimile edition of *LP*. Due to intervening book projects, it wasn't until 1911 that *The Acts of the Apostles* (25% of which came from *LP*) was published.

[22] In *ST* 2-22-1883 (3*BIO* 215.4), she wrote: "The Life of St. Paul by Conybeare and Howson, I regard as a book of great merit, and one of rare usefulness to the earnest student of the New Testament history." Prior to this, she had noted: "Many of our people already have the *Life of Christ* [by Geikie]. *The Life of Paul*, now offered for sale at this office, is *another* useful and deeply interesting work which should be widely circulated" (*RH* 12-26-1882, emphasis supplied).

[23] A reporter, who listened to Ellen White's description of her visit to Europe, referred to her "remarkable memory of details" ("Mrs. Ellen G. White's Able Address. A Characteristic and Eloquent Discourse by This Remarkable Lady," *Battle Creek Daily Journal*, Oct. 5, 1887, quoted in White, 4*BIO* 375). Ellen White had an excellent memory, and she wrote to people who had no TV or radio to fill their leisure time—a fact that is highlighted by another of her recommendations: "Provide something to be read during these long winter evenings. For those who can procure it, D'Aubigne's *History of the Reformation* will be both interesting and profitable" (*RH* 12-26-1882). She wrote this just prior to 4*SP* (*GC* 1884 edition).

Did Ellen White deny that she borrowed?

For many people, the question is not whether Mrs. White broke any law, but whether she violated the reader's *trust*. "... her borrowing may have been perfectly legal, it may have been perfectly ethical, but if she denied that she did something that she, in fact, did [do], then we have a problem with her integrity."[24] Mrs. White made six explicit "denials" regarding sources. (Implicit denials through her claims of divine inspiration will be covered in Chapter 9.)

Her **first two** denials have to do with her early health writings. In response to the question, "Did you receive your views upon health reform [May 21, 1863] before visiting the Health Institute at Dansville, N. Y., or before you had read works on the subject?" Ellen White wrote:

> I did not read any works upon health until I had written Spiritual Gifts, Vols. iii and iv, Appeal to Mothers,[25] and had sketched out most of my six articles in the six numbers of "How to Live." I did not know that such a paper existed as the Laws of Life, published at Dansville, N.Y. I had not heard of the several works upon health, written by Dr. J. C. Jackson, and other publications at Dansville, at the time I had the view named above. I did not know that such works existed until September, 1863, when in Boston, Mass., my husband saw them advertised in a periodical called the Voice of the Prophets, published by Eld. J. V. Himes. My husband ordered the works from Dansville and received them at Topsham Maine. His business gave him no time to peruse them, and as I determined not to read them until I had written out my views, the books remained in their wrappers. —*Review and Herald*, Oct. 8, 1867, p. 260.

> That which I have written in regard to health was not taken from books or papers. . . . My views were written independent of books or of the opinions of others. —MS 7, 1867 in 3SM 282.3.

She explains further that, after writing out her views, she collected materials from various health works for the series *How to Live*. Her explanation was virtually without challenge until the discovery of a single parallel statement to *Spiritual Gifts* in Dr. John C. Gunn's popular medical handbook:

> Taking "day by day," not "daily bread," but <u>a poison of</u> a <u>most deceitful and malignant kind, that sends its exciting and paralyzing influence into every nerve of the body</u>; and Nature, no longer able to bear this deadly narcotic, bows down under its paralyzing influence. —Dr. John C. Gunn, *Domestic Physician* (1857), pp. 367, 368.

Gunn's statement paralleled *Spiritual Gifts* (Aug. 1864), vol. 4a, p. 128, which reads:

> "Tobacco is <u>a poison of</u> the <u>most deceitful and malignant kind,</u> <u>having an exciting, then a paralyzing influence upon the nerves of the body</u>. It is all the more dangerous because its effects upon the system are so slow, and at first scarcely perceivable. . . ."

---

[24] Ron Graybill, *E. G. White's Literary Work: An Update* (Nov. 15–19, 1981), pp. 1, 2. Paul K. Conkin writes in *American Originals: Homemade Varieties of Christianity* (Chapel Hill, NC: University of North Carolina Press, 1997), p. 137: "Few have challenged her character or integrity . . . Her writings reveal a becoming tenderness or softness. Even when most apocalyptic or most harsh in her judgments of the apostasies and the moral lapses of the modern age, she still emphasized a God of love . . ."

[25] *Spiritual Gifts*, Vol. 3, which she mentions, does not deal directly with health. Though *Appeal to Mothers*, p. 9, has significant parallel phrasing, given in the order of Jackson's *The Sexual Organism and Its Healthful Management*, pp. 75–76, the book deals largely with a single subject not outlined as part of her 1863 health reform vision in *Spiritual Gifts*, vol. 4a. That subject is "secret vice." See MS 1, 1863 in 3SM 279.2–280.4 for Ellen White's description of the contents of the vision. She writes: "My first writing of the vision was *the substance* of the matter contained in Volume IV and in How to Live." —3SM 281.1, emphasis supplied.

To make sense of the anomaly created by this discovery, one must consider carefully what her 1867 statements deny. Does not the specific mention of the "publications at Dansville" and the "works from Dansville" indicate which works she meant when she said she "did not read any works on health" before writing out what God revealed to her and that she did not mean that she had not read *anything at all* on health?[26] Is it reasonable to assume that a conscientious mother of three would have read nothing at all to aid her in the care of her family—including Gunn's popular book (considered a bit "behind the times"), displayed with the family Bible on thousands of parlor tables across America? The similarity of her statement certainly suggests an acquaintance with Gunn's lament against liquor *and* tobacco, which Ellen White could have adapted for her own statement on tobacco, printed in mid-August 1864. However, the paraphrasing in her statement, the fact that she goes on to mention twice that tobacco is a "slow poison" (something that doesn't come from Gunn), and that nothing else in her description ties to Gunn's book could just as well indicate that she learned of the statement by word of mouth, perhaps as she, in 1863, "talked freely with Dr. Lay[27] and many others upon the things which had been shown . . . in reference to health" (3*SM* 282.2). Whether from her reading or by word of mouth, there is good evidence that her anti-tobacco views were, as she said, "written independent of books or of the opinions of others." In contrast to Gunn, who allowed for the medicinal use of tobacco (*Domestic Physician*, p. 935) and who referred to its limited use as "comparatively harmless" (p. 368), Ellen White warned: "I have seen in vision that tobacco was a filthy weed, and that it must be laid aside or given up. If it is used as a medicine, go to God, He is the great Physician, and those that use the filthy weed for medicine greatly dishonor God" (Ltr. 5, 1851; 5*MR* 377). Moreover, her description of the effects of nicotine, tobacco's active agent, is more pharmacologically correct than Gunn's—tobacco first excites, *then* it depresses.

Dr. H. S. Lay

Interestingly, Gunn did not originate the statement, but merely conflated two earlier statements—one from Pastor B. I. Lane's *The Mysteries of Tobacco* (1845), p. 94, which came from the *Sixth Report of the American Temperance Society* (1833), p. 59—"Taking 'day by day,' not 'daily bread,' but a poison of a most deceitful and malignant kind . . . ," and one from Larkin B. Coles' *The Beauties and Deformities of Tobacco-Using* (1851), p. 22, quoted in the *Review and Herald* of May 24, 1864—". . . instead of a healthy vital force pervading the nervous system,—there is found the deadly narcotic power of this poison, sending its exciting and paralyzing influence into every nerve of the body."

A **third** statement that is taken as a denial came in response to a question sent to Ellen White about Mrs. White's description of the proper length of a woman's dress at a time in which it was fashionable for dresses to drag the ground. Mrs. White had given three descriptions—"an inch or two above the filth of the streets," "somewhat below the top of

---

[26] When the White's sons were infected with deadly diphtheria, Ellen White was able to nurse them to health with hydrotherapy treatments James "chanced to see" (Spalding, *Origin and History of Seventh-day Adventists*, vol. 1, p. 343) in one of the "exchanges," which came to the Review and Herald office—the *Yates County Chronicle* of Penn Yan, New York, or some journal quoting it" (2*BIO* 13.5). With her strong stance against tobacco, she likely had also read temperance materials prior to the 1863 Otsego, Michigan vision on health.

[27] "Just before I came to the Conference I had a talk with Dr. Lay, and he told me of how he heard the first instruction about health reform away back in 1860 and especially in 1863. While he was riding in a carriage with Brother and Sister White, she related what had been presented to her upon the subject of health reform, and laid out the principles which have stood the test of all these years—a whole generation." —Dr. John Harvey Kellogg, *General Conference Daily Bulletin*, March 8, 1897, p. 309; cited in D. E. Robinson, *The Story of Our Health Message*, pp. 83, 84. Ellen White's statements in *Spiritual Gifts*, vol. 4a, were not published until mid-August 1864, before she visited Dansville with her husband for three weeks in September. Dr. Lay did not join the staff at Jackson's Dansville health institute until the summer of 1864.

the boot," and "about nine inches from the floor." Mrs. White's clarifying response might have been long since forgotten had it not been interpreted beyond its natural sense. Mrs. White had written:

> Although I am as dependent upon the Spirit of the Lord in writing my views as I am in receiving them, yet the words I employ in describing what I have seen are my own, unless they be those spoken to me by an angel, which I always enclose in marks of quotation. As I wrote upon the subject of dress, the view of those three companies revived in my mind as plain as when I was viewing them in vision; but I was left to describe the length of the proper dress in my own language as best I could. —*Review and Herald*, Oct. 8, 1867.

Mrs. White was not denying use of wording from outside sources in expressing what she had seen, but merely stating that, except for the words of angels, the content of the vision was not given to her in *auditory* form. God left it to her to put in words *what she had seen*, just as He did for the Apostle John. John was told, in Revelation 1:11, "What thou *seest* write," *not* "Write the *words* I give you" (and John apparently borrowed from the book of Enoch to put what he saw into words, see Chap. 9).

In a **fourth** denial, Ellen White pointed to God as the authority behind her messages. Robert Olson explains: "On March 28, 1882, Ellen White sent a very pointed letter to the church at Battle Creek, Michigan. [5*T* 45–62.] Some of the members there, resenting her strictures, accused her of basing her reproofs on unfounded gossip. Ellen White responded with another letter in which she asserted that what she had written three months earlier was not just human opinion. She declared: 'You might say that this communication was only a letter. Yes, it was a letter, but prompted by the Spirit of God, to bring before your minds things that had been shown me. In these letters which I write, in the testimonies I bear, I am presenting to you that which the Lord has presented to me. I do not write one article in the paper expressing merely my own ideas. They are what God has opened before me in vision—the precious rays of light shining from the throne.' [5*T* 67.] Ellen White was not, in this statement, ruling out the idea that some of her testimonies might contain passages gleaned from her reading. Rather, she was affirming her deep conviction that her messages of reproof bore the signet of Heaven. Just a little farther on in the letter she says, 'I was told to gather up the light that had been given me and let its rays shine forth to God's people.' "This light was found, not only in her own letters and manuscripts, but in the writings of others as well."[28]

Ellen White's **fifth** denial about sources came on February 18, 1887 in a letter addressed to A. T. Jones and E. J. Waggoner. Church leaders were taking sides over the meaning of the law in Galatians. To reassure Jones and Waggoner that her views of the matter came from God and not from the opinions of men, Mrs. White wrote:

> I have not been in the habit of reading any doctrinal articles in the paper [the *Review and Herald*], that my mind should not have any understanding of anyone's ideas and views, and that not a mold of any man's theories should have any connection with that which I write. —Ltr. 37, 1887 in 3*SM* 63.4.

The language of her statement regarding not being "in the habit" indicates that she was not issuing an absolute denial for all times. Just "two months later she wrote G. I. Butler, one of the other parties in the dispute, that she had just read a doctrinal statement of his and was 'pained' by it."[29]

The **sixth** of Ellen White's denials has the most to do with *The Desire of Ages* and the charge of plagiarism. On June 25, 1897, Ellen White wrote to Fannie Bolton:

---

[28] Robert W. Olson, "Ellen White's Denials," *Ministry*, February 1991, p. 16.

[29] Robert W. Olson, citing *Ellen G. White 1888 Materials*, vol. 1, p. 32.

> Your words regarding me and my writings are false, and I must say that you know them to be false. Nevertheless, those unacquainted with you take your words as being the words of one who knows. Because you have been acquainted with me, and connected with me, you can state what you please, and you think that your tracks are so covered that they will never be discovered. But my writings have not stopped. They go out as I have written them. No words of my copyists are put in the place of my own words. This is a testimony that cannot be controverted. My articles speak for themselves. —*MR926* 77.6.

What was she denying? She was denying Miss Bolton's charge that she merely picked out items from her reading and handed it over to her assistants to dress up for publication.

> Brother McCullagh has reported your words of information given him from house to house, saying that I have very little to do in getting out the books purported to come from my pen, that I had picked out all I had written from other books, and that those who prepared my articles, yourself in particular, made that matter that was published. This is the way you became my adversary. —Ltr. 25, 1897 to Fannie Bolton, April 11, 1897 in *MR926* 74.4.

The evidence of Mrs. White's denial spoke for itself. Even though Fannie Bolton was no longer working for Mrs. White, Mrs. White was still producing articles for Church periodicals.

So why would Miss Bolton make such a claim? The answer is that, having been a correspondent for the Chicago *Daily Inter Ocean* before working for Mrs. White, Miss Bolton became dissatisfied with the anonymity of transcribing Mrs. White's letters and preparing her periodical articles for publication, and, therefore, took credit for writing she had corrected for spelling, grammar, and syntax from Mrs. White's pen (see Chapter 1 of this book). Contrarily, Mrs. White took no credit for originating what she wrote, but recognized that the messages she put into words came from God:

> Sister White is not the originator of these books. They contain the instruction that during her life-work God has been giving her. They contain the precious, comforting light that God has graciously given His servant to be given to the world. From their pages this light is to shine into the hearts of men and women, leading them to the Saviour. —*Review and Herald*, Jan. 20, 1903.

Whom did Ellen White consider to be the source of her messages?

With such a perspective on the source of her writings, is there any wonder why, before giving credit to sources became a public concern, Ellen White chose to only draw attention to Scripture in the footnotes of the 1884 and 1888 editions of *The Great Controversy*?

· · · · · · · · · ·

Having dealt with (1) the *legal* standard of plagiarism—Mrs. White did not violate any of the laws of her time; (2) the question of whether or not her borrowing was *ethical*—it was acceptable for authors of this era and genre of literature to borrow as she did; (3) and the question of *integrity*—Mrs. White does not deny having read other works, but recommended some of these very works and called for the gathering of gems as she had done; we move on, in our next chapter, to consider whether Mrs. White's writings measure up to the *standard of inspiration* established in Scripture.

CHAPTER 9

The Litmus Test of Inspiration

> Mrs. White moved me! In all candor, she moved me. . . . And I think her writings should move anyone, unless he is permanently biased and is unswayable.
>
> —Vincent L. Ramik.[1]

For many people, "inspiration" is not something that can be defined. It is just something that is felt or perceived. Because a piece of literature moves them or conveys deep meaning, they consider it inspired. Such people don't generally question the process of inspiration. Their interest is in enjoying inspiration's benefits.

For others, the label "divinely inspired" can only be attached to a writer's work if it passes the highest possible standard—some type of *verbal dictation by God.*[2] In support of this standard, they cite Paul's statement, "All scripture is given by inspiration of God . . ." (2 Tim. 3:16). Unfortunately, these same people will often have difficulty explaining what this description means. Paul's statement literally reads, "All Scripture is *God-breathed.*" So how does God *breathe* Scripture? In one sense the phrase can certainly refer to the supernatural revelations that God has given to mankind through prophets in visions and dreams. God's Word declares: "Surely the Lord GOD will do nothing, but he revealeth his secret unto his servants the prophets" (Amos 3:7). God himself says, "Hear now my words: If there be a prophet among you, I the LORD will make myself known unto him in a vision, and will speak unto him in a dream" (Num. 12:6). Such a view of inspiration is limited, however, in that it assumes that all "God-breathed" Scripture came by *direct dictation* from the Holy Spirit. As we shall see in this chapter, such a notion does not adequately describe the process of divine inspiration—either for the writers of the Bible or for Ellen White. There is, in fact, another Biblical description of inspiration that allows for more than just visions and dreams. Peter wrote: ". . . holy men of God spake as they were moved by the Holy Ghost" (2 Peter 1:21). So what do the movings of the Spirit in inspired writings look like—especially when God does not dictate every word for the inspired writer?

God works through human individuality.

"We have this treasure in earthen vessels . . ." (2 Cor. 4:7). Paul is here describing "the light of the knowledge of God" showcased in the lives of believers. This light was first reflected "in the face of Jesus Christ" when He took on humanity (2 Cor. 4:6). In becoming flesh and dwelling among us, Jesus was declaring who God is (John 1:14, 18). "He was the Word of God— God's thought made audible" (*Desire of Ages*, p. 19). Jesus was Immanuel— "*God with us*" (Matt. 1:23; John 1:14). He was God's "treasure" in an "earthen vessel," a mysterious union of the human and the divine. Is there not a beautiful parallel here to God's written word? As Jesus, in coming to our earth, "clothed" His divinity with humanity, so

Does God dictate His messages to inspired writers word for word?

---

[1] Quoted in *Adventist Review*, September 17, 1981, p. 3.

[2] For a recent Adventist exposition on this subject, see Fernando Canale, "Revelation and Inspiration," in *Understanding Scripture: An Adventist Approach*, George W. Reid, ed. *Biblical Research Institute Studies*, vol. 1 (Silver Spring, MD: Biblical Research Institute, General Conference of Seventh-day Adventists, 2005), pp. 47–74.

were the thoughts of divinity "clothed," if you will, in the words and language of humanity in the Holy Scriptures. The oracles of God, committed to the various writers of Scripture in visions, dreams, or through promptings of the Holy Spirit, were penned by these same writers in their own words, flavored by their own personalities and experiences. Thus the individuality of each writer comes through. The reader recognizes that Jeremiah was a weeping prophet; that David in the Psalms was a shepherd of sheep; that Solomon in the Proverbs was indeed wise and that later, in Ecclesiastes, he had finally gained true wisdom as he returned to the Lord after years of apostasy; that John in his epistles exuded the love of God; that Matthew the former tax collector had become enamored with the teachings of Jesus; and that Paul, in his several epistles written for different audiences, was both a devoted pastor and a reflective theologian.

This view of inspiration is well summarized by Ellen White's statement adapted from the words of Calvin Stowe:[3]

> It is not the words of the Bible that are inspired, but the men that were inspired. Inspiration acts not on the man's words or his expressions but on the man himself, who, under the influence of the Holy Ghost, is imbued with thoughts. But the words receive the impress of the individual mind. The divine mind is diffused. The divine mind and will is combined with the human mind and will; thus the utterances of the man are the word of God. —MS 24, 1886, written by Mrs. White, while in Europe, in her April 1886 journal entry in 1SM 21.2.

Dependence on the Spirit of God

What marks the writings of the Bible writers as divinely inspired is the utter dependence of the writer on the Spirit of God to express that which God has given him to communicate. Without the inspiration of *God's Spirit*, the human writer never could have delivered that which constitutes *God's message*. Through human language in the Bible we hear the thoughts of God expressed as accurately as the human agent was able to communicate them. We find the same dependence on the Spirit in faithfully communicating God's message with Ellen White.

> Before I stand on my feet, I have no thought of speaking as plainly as I do. But the Spirit of God rests upon me with power, and I cannot but speak the words given me. I dare not withhold one word of the testimony. I speak the words given me by a power higher than human power, and I cannot if I would, recall one sentence.

---

[3] Though her journal entry was not published until 1951, when F. D. Nichol included it in "Appendix M" of *Ellen G. White and Her Critics*, pp. 655, 656, Ellen White's adaptation of Calvin E. Stowe's statement epitomizes her view of inspiration—a view she articulated in the Author's Preface of the 1888 edition of *The Great Controversy*. Regarding the writings of Calvin Stowe, David Neff wrote: "We have evidence of her writing most of the ideas which are common to her and Dr. Stowe at a time prior to the writing of this manuscript [MS 24, 1886]. Some of these writings antedate any possible awareness on her part of Stowe's book." —David Neff, "Ellen White's Theological and Literary Indebtedness to Calvin Stowe," revised 1979, p. 19. Borrowing from Stowe's *wording*, Ellen White's definition of inspiration is actually a contrast to Stowe's *subjective view* of inspiration, as a comparison of the two statements will show:

"It is not the words of the Bible that were inspired, *it is not the thoughts of the Bible that were inspired*; it is the men who wrote the Bible that were inspired. Inspiration acts not on the man's words, *not on the man's thoughts*, but on the man himself; so that he, *by his own spontaneity, under the impulse of the Holy Ghost, conceives* certain thoughts and gives utterance to them in certain words, both the words and the thoughts receiving the peculiar impress of the mind which conceived and uttered them, and being in fact just as really his own, as they could have been if there had been no inspiration at all in the case. . . . Inspiration generally is a purifying, and an elevation, and an intensification of the human intellect subjectively, rather than an objective suggestion and communication; though suggestion and communication are not excluded. The Divine mind is, as it were, so diffused through the human, and the human mind is so interpenetrated with the Divine, that for the time being the utterances of the man are the word of God." —Calvin Stowe, *Origin and History Of the Books of the Bible* (1867), pp. 19, 20, wording that differs conceptually italicized.

COLOR CODING: verbatim paraphrase

> In the night season the Lord gives me instruction, in symbols, and then explains their meaning. He gives me the word, and I dare not refuse to give it to the people. The love of Christ, and, I venture to add, the love of souls constrains me, and I cannot hold my peace. —MS 22, 1890, pp. 11, 12 (Diary, Jan. 10, 1890) in 1*MR* 28.4.

When Ellen White was first called to deliver reproofs to individuals, she initially tried to soften the messages, but was told that she was to declare to others what the Lord had revealed to her (2*SG* 62). From that point on she could write:

> I have faithfully written out the warnings that God has given me. They have been printed in books, yet I cannot forbear. I must write these same things over and over. I ask not to be relieved. As long as the Lord spares my life, I must continue to bear these earnest messages. —MS 21, 1910 in 3*SM* 50.1.

> It is utterly false that I have ever intimated I could have a vision when I pleased. There is not a shade of truth in this. I have never said I could throw myself into visions when I pleased, for this is simply impossible. I have felt for years that if I could have my choice and please God as well, I would rather die than have a vision, for every vision places me under great responsibility to bear testimonies of reproof and of warning, which has ever been against my feelings, causing me affliction of soul which is inexpressible. Never have I coveted my position, and yet I dare not resist the Spirit of God and seek an easier position. —Ltr. 2, 1874, To J. N. Loughborough, August 24, 1874 in 8*MR* 238.4.

She considered the words she wrote to be the message of God because it was the Spirit of God who guided her in what to say and in how to say it.

> The lips of a speaker may move under the inspiration of the Holy Spirit. Thus the words of God find utterance in warnings, in appeals, in reproof, in correction in righteousness. This power is not in the speaker. It is a power put within him by God, that he may be enabled to reach those who are dead in trespasses and sins, and arouse them from their spiritual death to receive life from God. —Ltr. 21, 1897 in 2*MR* 30.3.

At times she wrote out a testimony under the inspiration of God, but delayed its delivery until the Spirit impressed her to send it.

> The Lord did help and bless me in a signal manner during the conference in Melbourne. I labored before I entered it very hard giving personal testimonies which I had written out one year before, but could not feel clear to send them. I thought of the words of Christ, "I have many things to say unto you but ye cannot bear them now." When I enclosed the communication already to mail, it seemed that a voice spoke to me saying, "Not yet, not yet, they will not receive your testimony."

> Prior to the conference I saw the persons in responsible positions, and labored with one man three hours, reading that which I had held so long. He said, "Sister White, had you sent that to me I would not have received it; but the Lord has moved upon you to move discreetly; for three nights past I dreamed that the Lord had shown my case to Sister White, and she had a message for me." The man had not a religious experience. He was bound up in Free Masonry. —Ltr. 39, 1893, Mar. 20, from Napier, New Zealand, to Dear Brother and Sister M in 20*MR* 157.1.[4]

She also looked to God for help in expressing her thoughts while writing:

---

[4] For more on the testimony for the man "bound up in Free Masonry," N. D. Faulkhead, see 4*BIO* 49–56.

I have all faith in God. . . . He works at my right hand and at my left. While I am writing out important matter, He is beside me, helping me. He lays out my work before me, and when I am puzzled for a fit word with which to express my thought, He brings it clearly and distinctly to my mind. I feel that every time I ask, even while I am still speaking, He responds, "Here am I" (Ltr. 127, 1902 in 2*MR* 156.6).

Ellen White's dependence on God did not substitute for her reading to improve her writing skills or doing research to put God's revelations in their proper context.

She does assert: "In these letters which I write, in the testimonies I bear, I am presenting to you that which the Lord has presented to me." —*Testimonies*, vol. 5, p. 67. But she is not thereby denying that she used other sources in writing out her views. The very testimony in which she makes this statement has nearly one third of its material taken from March's *Night Scenes in the Bible* and Krummacher's *Elijah the Tishbite*.[5] Ellen White consistently gives credit where credit is due—to God the author of all truth. To declare the divine source of her writings is not to deny the human; neither is an acknowledgment of the human side of her writings a denial of the divine.

> "Ellen White consistently gives credit where credit is due—to God the author of all truth."
>
> Warren H. Johns

All truth is composed of a unique blend of the human and the divine. If truth were only divine in its utterance, it would be so far beyond the finite minds of men that it would find its sole abode in the mind of the Infinite. If truth were only human in its expression, it would have no power to lift man from himself to his Creator.[6]

Mrs. White never claimed that every word she ever wrote was verbally dictated from on high. A man once wrote her saying: "I was led to conclude and most firmly believe that *every* word that you ever spoke in public or private, that every letter you wrote under *any* and *all* circumstances, was as inspired as the ten commandments," Ellen White responded that neither she nor "the pioneers in our cause have made such claims." Then she pointed to a description of Biblical inspiration she had included in the "Author's Preface" for the 1888 *Great Controversy*:

The Bible points to God as its Author; yet it was written by human hands; and in the varied style of its different books it presents the characteristics of the several writers. The truths revealed are all "given by inspiration of God" (2 Tim. 3:16); yet they are expressed in the words of men. The Infinite One by his Holy Spirit had shed light into the minds and hearts of his servants. He has given dreams and visions, symbols and

---

[5] **Daniel March** (*Night Scenes*, pp. 201, 202) helped her describe the response of faith in 5*T* 69 (see comparison in Chapter 7 of this book). **Friedrich Krummacher** helped her describe the forbearance of God at the half-heartedness of His people: "Brethren, who knows what our own churches have still to experience? We are at present evidently under Divine forbearance; can any one of us say how long it will last? It cannot be expressed how much mercy has already been expended upon us. Yet how many are there who really thank God, and are heartily devoted to his service? How would it be, if the Lord were suddenly to remove all his true children from the [222] midst of us, and leave the impenitent to themselves? Would our population suffer a very perceptible decrease? Or is not the case with ourselves, as it is every where else; that the little flock of Israel amongst the Canaanites is like a drop in the ocean, and like the little stars, which, in a tempestuous night, twinkle only here and there among the black and stormy clouds. Are not a great part of our people dead? Yes, though many of them hear the sound of the word of life. . . ." —*Elijah the Tishbite*, pp. 221, 222.

Ellen White: "I have been shown that unbelief in the testimonies has been steadily increasing as the people backslide from God. It is all through our ranks, all over the field. But few know what our churches are to experience. I saw that at present we are under divine forbearance, but no one can say how long this will continue. No one knows how great the mercy that has been exercised toward us. But few are heartily devoted to God. There are only a few who, like the stars in a tempestuous night, shine here and there among the clouds. . . . It may be that erelong all prophesyings among us will be at an end, and the voice which has stirred the people may no longer disturb their carnal slumbers." —5*T* 76.1, 77.1.

[6] Warren H. Johns, "Literary Thief or God's Messenger?" *Ministry*, June 1982, pp. 15, 16.

COLOR CODING: verbatim paraphrase

figures; and those to whom the truth was thus revealed, have themselves embodied the thought in human language.

The ten commandments were spoken by God himself, and were written by his own hand. They are of divine, and not of human, composition. But the Bible, with its God-given truths expressed in the language of men, represents a union of the divine and the human. Such a union existed in the nature of Christ, who was the Son of God and the Son of man. Thus it is true of the Bible, as it was of Christ that 'the Word was made flesh, and dwelt among us.' John 1:14.

Written in different ages, by men who differed widely in rank and occupation and in mental and spiritual endowments, the books of the Bible present a wide contrast in style, as well as a diversity in the nature of the subjects unfolded. Different forms of expression are employed by different writers; often the same truth is more strikingly presented by one than by another. And as several writers present a subject under varied aspects and relations, there may appear, to the superficial, careless, or prejudiced reader, to be discrepancy or contradiction, where the thoughtful, reverent student, with clearer insight, discerns the underlying harmony. —"Author's Preface," *The Great Controversy* (1888), pp. c and d.

Can an inspired writer use literary sources?

Robert W. Olson, past director of the Ellen G. White Estate, puts Mrs. White's literary borrowing in perspective in an article that addresses the larger question of whether an inspired writer can legitimately use sources—whether or not they are inspired.

Did Ellen White's literary borrowings in any degree dilute her claim to inspiration? This is a vital question. Some of the things she wrote were not original with her. Neither were they supernaturally provided by means of divine revelation. Does this mean that some of her writings were not inspired? In other words, Is originality a test of inspiration? . . .

First, a few definitions: By "originality" we mean that the prophet was the first person to say it. By "revelation" we mean that the prophet received his information in a vision, a dream, or some other supernatural source. By "inspiration" we mean that the prophet wrote under the direct guidance and control of the Holy Spirit.

In the Scriptures we find a number of examples which indicate that a prophet's writing need not have been original and need not have come by special revelation in order to have been inspired.[7]

Though God says: "Behold, I am against the prophets, saith the Lord, that steal my words every one from his neighbor" (Jer. 23:30), there is nothing wrong with one prophet borrowing from another. God's concern about those who were stealing the words of His prophets was not their *use*, but their *abuse*. He was against these so-called prophets because they prophesied "false dreams," using the words of His prophets to cause His "people to err by their lies" (Jer. 23:32). If this were not the case, His words would condemn any Bible writer who used the words of another Bible writer without giving credit. There are many examples in the Bible of writers borrowing from "his neighbor" without identifying the source. We find, in 2 Kings 18:17–20:21, an example of borrowing in which all but two verses of the passage were borrowed from Isaiah 36:1–39:8. Another notable borrowing between authors in the Old Testament is Micah 4:1–3, which is almost

---

[7] Robert W. Olson, "Ellen G. White's Use of Uninspired Sources," p. 16.

identical to Isaiah 2:2–4. In the New Testament, there is also extensive borrowing among inspired writers. Matthew and Luke borrowed 91% of the wording of Mark; Peter borrowed from Jude (or vice versa)—all without identifying their sources. Notice the similarity between Peter and Jude.

BIBLICAL PARALLEL 1.	Parallels between Peter and Jude
Jude. 4 For there are certain men crept in unawares, who were before of old ordained to this condemnation, ungodly men, turning the grace of our God into lasciviousness, and denying the only Lord God, and our Lord Jesus Christ. 6 And the angels which kept not their first estate, but left their own habitation, he hath reserved in everlasting chains under darkness unto the judgment of the great day. 7 Even as Sodom and Gomorrha, and the cities about them in like manner, giving themselves over to fornication, and going after strange flesh*, are set forth for an example, suffering the vengeance of eternal fire.† 8 Likewise also these *filthy* dreamers defile the flesh, despise dominion, and speak evil of dignities. 9 Yet Michael the archangel, when contending with the devil he disputed about the body of Moses, durst not bring against him a railing accusation, but said, The Lord rebuke thee. 10 But these speak evil of those things which they know not: but what they know naturally, as brute beasts, in those things they corrupt themselves. 11 Woe unto them! for they have gone in the way of Cain, and ran greedily after the error of Balaam for reward, and perished in the gainsaying of Core. 12 These are spots in your feasts of charity, when they feast with you, feeding themselves without fear: clouds *they are* without water, carried about of winds; trees whose fruit withereth, without fruit, twice dead, plucked up by the roots 13 Raging waves of the sea, foaming out their own shame; wandering stars, to whom is reserved the blackness of darkness for ever. 16 These are murmurers, complainers, walking after their own lusts; and their mouth speaketh great swelling *words*, having men's persons in admiration because of advantage. 18 How that they told you there should be mockers in the last time, who should walk after their own ungodly lusts.	**2 Peter 2.** 1 But there were false prophets also among the people, even as there shall be false teachers among you, who privily shall bring in damnable heresies, even denying the Lord that bought them, and bring upon themselves swift destruction. 4 For if God spared not the angels that sinned, but cast *them* down to hell, and delivered *them* into chains of darkness, to be reserved unto judgment; 6 And turning the cities of Sodom and Gomorrha into ashes† condemned *them* with an overthrow, making *them* an ensample unto those that after should live ungodly; 7 And delivered just Lot, vexed with the filthy conversation of the wicked* 10 But chiefly them that walk after the flesh in the lust of uncleanness, and despise government. Presumptuous *are they*, self-willed, they are not afraid to speak evil of dignities. 11 Whereas angels, which are greater in power and might, bring not railing accusation against them before the Lord. 12 But these, as natural brute beasts, made to be taken and destroyed, speak evil of the things that they understand not; and shall utterly perish in their own corruption; 13 And shall receive the reward of unrighteousness, *as* they that count it pleasure to riot in the day time. Spots *they are* and blemishes, sporting themselves with their own deceivings while they feast with you; 15 Which have forsaken the right way, and are gone astray, following the way of Balaam *the son* of Bosor, who loved the wages of unrighteousness; 17 These are wells without water, clouds that are carried with a tempest; to whom the mist of darkness is reserved for ever. 18 For when they speak great swelling *words* of vanity, they allure through the lusts of the flesh, *through much* wantonness, those that were clean escaped from them who live in error. 3:3 Knowing this first, that there shall come in the last days scoffers, walking after their own lusts,

COLOR CODING: verbatim paraphrase

We also find that Paul borrowed from pagan writers for expressions in his epistles and in the book of Acts. In commenting on "For we are his offspring," A. T. Robertson lists several:

> Aratus of Soli in Cilicia (ab. B.C. 270) has these very words in his *Ta Phainomena* and Cleanthes, Stoic philosopher (300–220 B.C.) in his *Hymn to Zeus* has *Ek sou gar genos esmen.* In I Cor. 15:33 Paul quotes from Menander [the comic poet, who probably took it from Euripides, cf. Socrates, *Ecclesiastical History*, 3.16.] and in Titus 1:12 from Epimenides [ab. B.C. 600]. J. Rendel Harris claims that he finds allusions in Paul's Epistles to Pindar, Aristophanes, and other Greek writers. There is no reason in the world why Paul should not have acquaintance with Greek literature, though one need not strain a point to prove it. Paul, of course, knew that the words were written of Zeus (Jupiter), not of Jehovah, but he applies the idea in them to his point just made that all men are the offspring of God. —A. T. Robertson, *Word Pictures in the New Testament*, vol. 3, p. 289.

BIBLICAL PARALLEL 2.	Paul's borrowing from pagan authors

Menander: "Evil communications corrupt good manners."
  Aratus: "For we are also his offspring."
  Cleanthes: "For out of him we are offspring."
  Epimenides: "They fashioned a tomb for thee, O holy and high one—The Cretans, always liars, evil beasts, idle bellies! But thou art not dead; thou livest and abidest for ever; For in thee we live and move and have our being,"
	Paul, 1 Cor. 15:33: "Be not deceived: evil communications corrupt good manners."
	  Acts 17:28: "For in him we live, and move, and have our being; as certain also of your own poets have said, For we are also his offspring."
	  Titus 1:12: "One of themselves, *even* a prophet of their own, said, The Cretians *are* alway liars, evil beasts, slow bellies."

Paul also apparently borrowed conceptually from a first-century B.C. book of the Apocrypha. Compare Romans 1:20 with Wisdom 13:5–8 (RSV), which reads: "From the greatness and beauty of created things comes a corresponding perception of their Creator.... Yet again, not even they are to be excused; for if they had the power to know so much that they could investigate the world, how did they fail to find sooner the Lord of these things?" Then compare Romans 9:21 with Wisdom 15:7 (RSV), which reads: "For when a potter kneads the soft earth and laboriously molds each vessel for our service, he fashions out of the same clay both the vessels that serve clean uses and those for contrary uses, making all in like manner; but which shall be the use of each of these the worker in clay decides."[8] (Compare also Eph. 6:13–17 with Wisdom 5:17–20, and Rom. 1:22, 23 with Wisdom 12:24.)

One could overlook Paul's anonymous use of a few sayings of ancient poets if they were all that was ever borrowed in Scripture, but they obviously were not.[9] We return to Robert Olson's article:

---

[8] Tim Crosby, "Does Inspired Mean Original?" *Ministry*, February 1986, p. 5, accessed at <www.adventistarchives.org/docs/MIN/MIN1986-02/index.djvu?djvuopts&page=5>.

[9] Biblical borrowing from extra-biblical sources might seem minimal as compared to Ellen White's lengthier use as in her adaptation of Calvin Stowe's essay on inspiration. A more apt comparison to Ellen White's use of Stowe would be Jude's use of Enoch. Like Jude, Ellen White was no more dependent for *theology* in using the uninspired words of Stowe than was Jude in using the words of the pseudepigraphical First Enoch. Each borrowed enough to declare the truth. (The many unbiblical teachings of the Book of Enoch that Jude did not borrow can be readily seen in *The Old Testament Pseudepigrapha*, vol. 1, edited by James H. Charlesworth.) An even better comparison would be the lengthier borrowing by Bible writers of material from their own inspired contemporaries (such as Jude borrowing from Peter or Micah from Isaiah). Yet, such a comparison is limited in that Ellen White did not have any *inspired* contemporaries from whom to borrow. All that was available to her, besides the Scriptures, were the doctrinally flawed writings of other Christian authors. Most of these she could not conscientiously recommend, although she did recommend books she thought beneficial to her reading audience—such as Wylie's history of Protestantism, D'Aubigne's history of the Reformation, Geikie's life of Christ, and Conybeare and Howson's life of Paul.

Jude penned several lines which are practically identical with a passage in a pseudepigraphal book known to have been in circulation in the century before Christ. . . .

We do not question the inspiration of Jude 14, 15, even though someone else wrote it before Jude did. Jude 9 is also apparently taken from an earlier non-canonical source . . . .[10]

Based on the similarity of phrasing between the two, it would appear that John the Revelator also used the pseudepigraphal book of Enoch since more than 80 of the 404 verses in Revelation show some literary relationship to the book of Enoch.[11] That's a literary dependency rate of 19.8%.

BIBLICAL PARALLEL 3.	New Testament borrowing from the Book of Enoch
Book of Enoch. Behold, he will arrive with a million of the holy ones in order to execute judgment upon all. He will destroy the wicked ones and censure all flesh on account of everything that they have done, that which the sinners and the wicked ones committed against him. —1 Enoch 1:9.	**Jude 14.** And Enoch also, the seventh from Adam, prophesied of these, saying, Behold, the Lord cometh with ten thousands of his saints, 15 To execute judgment upon all, and to convince all that are ungodly among them of all their ungodly deeds which they have ungodly committed, and of all their hard *speeches* which ungodly sinners have spoken against him.
And I saw . . . and as I looked, behold, a star fell down from heaven. —1 Enoch 86:1.	**Revelation.** I saw a star fall from heaven unto the earth —Rev. 9:1.
We have grown rich and accumulated goods. —1 Enoch 97:8.	I am rich, and increased with goods —Rev. 3:17.
The horse shall walk through the blood of sinners up to his chest.—1 Enoch 100:3.	Blood came out of the winepress, even unto the horse bridles —Rev. 14:20.
The names of [the sinners] shall be blotted out from the Book of life and the books of the Holy One.—1 Enoch 108:3.	I will not blot out his name out of the book of life —Rev. 3:5.
The first heaven shall depart and pass away; a new heaven shall appear; and all the powers of heaven shall shine forever sevenfold. —1 Enoch 91:16.	And I saw a new heaven and a new earth: for the first heaven and the first earth were passed away; and there was no more sea. —Rev. 21:1.

Robert Olson concludes his article with one final example:

Luke did considerable investigation in available sources before writing his gospel. He says:

Inasmuch as many have undertaken to compile an account of the things accomplished among us . . . it seemed fitting for me as well, having investigated everything carefully from the beginning, to write it out for you in consecutive order, most excellent Theophilus, so that you might know the exact truth about the things you have been taught. — Luke 1:1, 3, 4, NASB.

---

[10] Olson, p. 17. About the source of *Jude 9*, "Yet Michael the archangel, when contending with the devil he disputed about the body of Moses, durst not bring against him a railing accusation, but said, The Lord rebuke thee," Richard Bauckham writes: "There is widespread agreement that Jude's source in v 9 was the lost ending of the work preserved for us only in Latin translation, in the incomplete and rather poor text of a sixth-century manuscript in Milan, a work sometimes known as the *As. Mos. [Assumption of Moses]*, but more appropriately known as the *T. Mos. [Testament of Moses]*." —R. J. Bauckham, *Word Biblical Commentary* on Jude, (Word Books, 1983), p. 67.

[11] For more examples, see Crosby, p. 6.

COLOR CODING: verbatim paraphrase

Luke did not acquire his information through visions or dreams but through his own research. [The same could be said for some of Ellen White's information as well.] Yet while material in the gospel of Luke was not given by divine revelation it was nonetheless written under divine inspiration. . . .

The answer, then, to our question—Did Ellen White's literary borrowings in any degree dilute her claim to inspiration? —is No. That is, the answer is no unless we insist on one standard for the Bible prophets and a different standard for Ellen White. *If it was proper for the Biblical prophets to use uninspired sources at times, we can hardly fault Ellen White for following their example.*[12]

Even elements of Jesus' teachings can be considered as adaptations of earlier teachers. Parts of the Lord's Prayer are found in the Old Testament and in ritual Jewish prayers, known as *Ha-Kaddish*.[13] Around 180 B.C., Ben-Sira wrote against repetition in prayers, declared that old wine is more desirable than new, called for forgiving one's neighbor before receiving forgiveness, and described the rich man who decides to enjoy his goods, not knowing "when his time will come" (compare Sirach 7:14; 9:10; 28:2; and 11:18, 19 with Matt. 6:7, 8; Luke 5:39; Matt. 6:14; and Luke 12:16–21). The earlier-written Story of Ahikar also has similarities to the teachings of Jesus.[14]

BIBLICAL PARALLEL 4.	**Jesus' statements compared to those of earlier writers**
Earlier writer. What is hateful to you, do not do to your neighbor; that is the whole Torah, while the rest is the commentary thereof. —Hillel (30–10 B.C.). (See also Tobit 4:16.)	**Jesus.** Therefore all things whatsoever ye would that men should do to you, do ye even so to them: for this is the law and the prophets. —Matt. 7:12.
I was beset with hunger, and the Lord Himself nourished me. I was alone, and God comforted me: I was sick, and the Lord visited me: I was in prison, and my God showed favour unto me: in bonds, and He released me. —Testament of Joseph 1:5, 6.	For I was an hungred, and ye gave me meat: I was thirsty, and ye gave me drink: I was a stranger, and ye took me in: Naked, and ye clothed me: I was sick, and ye visited me: I was in prison, and ye came unto me. —Matt. 25:35, 36.
Come unto me, ye unlearned, and lodge in my school. . . . Put your necks under her yoke, and let your souls receive instruction; it is to be found close by. See with your eyes that I have labored little, and found for myself much rest. —Ben-Sira, Sirach 51:23–27.	Come unto me, all ye that labour and are heavy laden, and I will give you rest. Take my yoke upon you, and learn of me; for I am meek and lowly in heart: and ye shall find rest unto your souls. —Matt. 11:28, 29.
Father, I have sinned unto thee. Forgive me, and I will be to thee a slave henceforth for ever. —Ahikar 8:24 (Armenian).	I will arise and go to my father, and will say unto him, Father, I have sinned against heaven, and before thee, And am no more worthy to be called thy son: make me as one of thy hired servants. —Luke 15:18, 19.

Such a list of parallels may be poorly received because people assume that the words Jesus used came directly from "the mouth of God" (Matt. 4:4) and not through any contemporary sources. However, the similarity of Jesus' literary devices to those of His earlier contemporaries would suggest that the Saviour did borrow wording and figures of speech that His audience would readily understand. However, His unique turn of phrase in the parallels shows that He used the expressions of

---

[12] Olson, pp. 18, 19, emphasis supplied.

[13] *Seventh-day Adventist Bible Commentary*, vol. 5, p. 346.

[14] Crosby, p. 4.

others for His own purposes. To Renan's contention that, because certain teachings of Jesus were similar to those of Hillel, Jesus was Hillel's "pupil and plagiarist," Frederic Farrar responded:

> The originality of Jesus, even to those who regard Him as a mere human teacher, consists in this—that His words have touched the hearts of all men in all ages, and have regenerated the moral life of the world. Who but a pedant[15] in art would impugn the originality of Michael Angelo because his Pietà is said to have resembled a statue of Signorelli; or of Raphael, because his earlier works betray the influence of Perugino? Who but an ignoramus would detract from the greatness of Milton because his *Paradise Lost* offers some points of similarity to the *Adam* of Battista Andreini? (Frederic Farrar, *Life of Christ* [1877], vol. 2, p. 454).

No doubt, the intimation that Biblical writers borrowed at all may be troubling to some—particularly if they have assumed that writers of Scripture got all their messages through direct divine "dictation." But the evidence shows that God did not always give Bible writers the very words to use. There are sources of information in Scripture besides God's "whisperings." Paul learned of conditions in Corinth and Colossae from Titus and Epaphras (2 Cor. 7:7; Col. 1:4, 7). Old Testament chroniclers incorporated information from non-canonical royal histories (1 Kings 11:4; 14:19, and 29 mention the Acts of Solomon, the Book of the Acts of the Kings of Israel, and the Book of the Acts of the Kings of Judah). Solomon gathered pearls of wisdom from various unnamed sources in the ancient world. Luke constructed his account of the life of Christ from various unnamed sources, including the Gospel of Mark. Jesus employed the literary devices of His culture. John put what was shown him in vision into his own words (some of which he must have derived from prior reading). Inspired writings were also edited by technical help. Peter, Paul, and John employed an *amanuensis* or "secretary," who not only took dictation, but were responsible for spelling and grammar.[16] Nonetheless, all their writings included in the Scriptures are inspired. They are the Word of the LORD, and any borrowing of wording in their composition has only to do with the *literary form* they chose to use and not with the *truthfulness of their message*.

> All scripture is given by inspiration of God, and is profitable for doctrine, for reproof, for correction, for instruction in righteousness. That the man of God may be perfect, throughly furnished unto all good works. —2 Timothy 3:16, 17.

Our confidence in the inspiration of each Bible writer need not be shaken if we recognize that the communication of divine truth does not begin with the *words* of man, but with the *thoughts* of God! Whenever Scripture speaks to those with "ears to hear" (Mark 7:16), we are not hearing the word of Euripides or Ben-Sira or even of Paul or John, but the Word of the living God, spoken in human language to reach the human heart! The message is more than the words used to communicate it.

> We have also a more *sure word* of prophecy; whereunto *ye do well that ye take heed*, as unto a light that shineth in a dark place, until the day dawn, and the day star arise in your hearts: . . . *For the prophecy came not in old time by the will of man: but holy men of God spake as they were moved by the Holy Ghost.* —2 Peter 1:19, 21, emphasis supplied.

---

[15] A pedant is "a person who makes a tedious show of dull learning." —*The New Lexicon Webster's Dictionary of the English Language*, p. 739.

[16] See 1 Peter 5:12 for Peter; Romans 16:22 for Paul; and, for John, consider the difference in style between his gospel and the Revelation. This difference would seem to indicate that he had help in writing his gospel, but not in the Revelation—a "letter" written from isolated Patmos.

Paul did not derive his authority for his statements from Epimenides or Aratus. Neither did Jude derive his authority from First Enoch. In each case, the inspired writer merely used the words of an earlier writer because his words were what were needed to express God's truth clearly, bringing it home to the human heart[17] in harmony with previously revealed truth.

To the law and to the testimony: if they speak not according to this word, it is because there is no light in them. —Isaiah 8:20.

What inspiration is and what it is not

Warren H. Johns wrote three articles in *Ministry* dealing with inspiration, plagiarism, Mrs. White's use of sources, and her authority as a "prophet." In the third of these, he summarized what inspiration is, in contrast to the mistaken idea of inspiration held by many.

> "There is no new thing under the sun. Is there any thing whereof it may be said, See, this is new? It hath been already of old time, which was before us."
> —Solomon, Ecclesiastes 1:9, 10.

1. *Inspiration is not [to] be equated with originality....* We have consistently maintained that none of our distinctive doctrines originated with Ellen White. That means that all such truths were spelled out by others prior to her speaking and writing on the subject....

2. *Inspiration does not involve the dictation of divinely chosen words.* "The writers of the Bible were God's penmen, not His pen," says Ellen White....

3. *Inspiration is not diminished by the use of uninspired sources....* Is the golden rule less inspired than the rest of the Sermon on the Mount because Christ adapted it from rabbinic sources? Paul occasionally drew upon some of the inter-testamental books ... Does this mean that Paul's writings are less inspired in the places he used sources ...?

4. *Inspiration is affected by outside human influences.* If a message from God must be incarnated in human form before it can become intelligible to man, then that message will inevitably be shaped according to the messenger's thought patterns, culture, environment, background, training, personality, and reading habits.... Influence, when under divine supervision, becomes an asset, not a liability. As the divinely called messenger reads widely from a variety of sources he becomes better attuned to the needs of his age, and he adapts the language of his messages into a form that will greatly increase their impact and effectiveness....

5. *Inspiration goes beyond what has been presented in vision, and sometimes stands independent of visions.* Seventh-day Adventists have been given no mandate to find vision sources for everything that Ellen White has written while under inspiration.... Ellen White points out that what she writes apart from any specific vision is just as much inspired as that which has a vision for its basis (*Testimonies*, vol. 5, pp. 683–691).

6. *Inspiration provides the narrative for those portions of visions that were symbolic or that lacked a narrative.* Ellen White herself often describes her visions as "scenes," "views," or "representations" (*Testimonies*, vol. 1, p. 659; *Gospel Workers*, p. 94; *The Great Controversy*, pp. x, xi; *Spiritual Gifts*, vol. 2, p. 292; *Selected Messages*, book 3, pp. 51, 56). The emphasis seems usually to be more on the visual than the auditory, although in some cases the auditory is present. Even in those cases where the auditory

---

[17] Ellen G. White, *The Great Controversy*, p. xii.

portion of the vision is present, Ellen White is given the liberty to write it out in her own words (*Gospel Workers*, p. 94). . . .

7. *Inspiration must include divine guidance in the selection of sources.* . . . The question of infallibility versus fallibility in the inspired writings hinges upon one's concept of inspiration. If one is firmly convinced that the very words of God were dictated to the prophet, then the writings must be infallible because God never makes a mistake in what He says.[18] Ellen White avoids making such claims. "In regard to infallibility, I never claimed it; God alone is infallible. His word is true, and in Him is no variableness, or shadow of turning." —*Selected Messages*, book 1, p. 37. . . . She consistently pointed to Scripture as one's final authority. . . ."[19]

How do Ellen White's writings relate to Scripture?[20]

Closing her remarks to the delegates of the 1909 General Conference session, Ellen White lifted her Bible and uttered words that echoed the emphasis of her lifelong ministry:

I commend unto you this Book.[21]

These were her last words before a General Conference session. She was 81. Throughout her long career of writing and preaching, Ellen White upheld the Protestant principle of *sola scriptura*. Yet, in so doing, she recognized that the principle of *sola scriptura* does not deny its own provisions for the gift of prophecy. In her earliest book, she showed the relation of the Protestant principle to the prophetic gift:

I recommend to you, dear reader, the Word of God as the rule of your faith and practice. By that Word we are to be judged. God has, in that Word, promised to give visions in the "*last days*"; not for a new rule of faith, but for the comfort of his people, and to correct those who err from Bible truth. —*Early Writings*, p. 78 (first written in *A Sketch of the Christian Experience and Views of Ellen G. White*, 1851, p. 64).

As Paul wrote in 1 Corinthians 14:3, the prophetic gift was given to the Church for "edification, exhortation, and comfort." To *edify* means to "build up" by teaching. To *exhort* means to call to a higher standard—the higher standard of Scripture. To *comfort* means to give hope through pain and loss. These objectives are precisely what Ellen White's early visions did for the Adventist believers following the Great Disappointment of 1844 and what her writings do for us today. "The *Testimonies* were not given to take the place of the Bible" (*Testimonies*, vol. 5, p. 663), but "to bring the minds of His people to His word, to give them a clearer understanding of it" (*Testimonies*, vol. 4, p. 246). "Additional truth is not brought out; but God has through the

---

[18] Refining this idea, we should note that the message of the Bible is *infallible* and true, but not *inerrant*. Minor discrepancies in Biblical accounts sometimes do occur. Num. 10:29 describes Hobab as Moses' *brother-in-law*, while Judges 4:11 identifies him as his *father-in-law*. 1 Sam. 16:10 identifies David as the *eighth* son of Jesse, while 1 Chr. 2:15 identifies him as the *seventh*. (Could these possibly be copyists' errors?) Matt. 27:9, 10 connects a prophecy with Jeremiah, though the words cited actually come from Zech. 11:12, 13, which may have come "bundled" (to use the language of computer software) with Jeremiah and thereby been thought a part of it. Luke 19:1 has Jesus healing a blind man *before entering* Jericho, Matt. 20:29 and Mark 10:46 have him healing the man *upon leaving* the city. Stephen says "threescore and fifteen souls" went down into Egypt (Acts 7:14), Gen. 46:27 has "threescore and ten." The Gospels report different superscriptions over Jesus' cross. These minor variances in accounts affect neither the *truthfulness* nor the *reliability* of Scripture. They only demonstrate that the Bible describes real events, recounted and written down by real human beings!

[19] W. H. Johns, *Ministry*, June 1982, pp. 17–19, quoting Ltr. 10, 1895 (from 1*SM* 37.4).

[20] See <www.whiteestate.org/issues/scripsda.html> for a summary statement on this topic.

[21] Reported by William A. Spicer, *The Spirit of Prophecy in the Advent Movement*, p. 30 in 6*BIO* 197.5.

Testimonies simplified the great truths already given and in His own chosen way brought them before the people to awaken and impress the mind with them, that all may be left without excuse" (*Testimonies*, vol. 5, p. 665). For Ellen White, the Bible was much more than a book of culturally-conditioned ethics.

> It is one thing to treat the Bible as a book of good moral instruction, to be heeded so far as is consistent with the spirit of the times and our position in the world; it is another thing to regard it as it really is—the word of the living God, the word that is our life, the word that is to mold our actions, our words, and our thoughts. To hold God's word as anything less than this is to reject it. —Ellen G. White, *Education*, p. 260.

In contrast to Joseph Smith, who called himself "God's Oracle," Ellen White never set herself up as the final arbiter of Biblical interpretation.[22] She wrote:

> Little heed is given to the Bible, and the Lord has given a lesser light to lead men and women to the greater light. —*Colporteur Ministry*, p. 125 (from *Review and Herald*, Jan. 20, 1903).

> How are Ellen White's writings a "lesser light"?

As "a lesser light" (and not "*the* lesser light") Ellen White's role was to lead to "the greater light" of the Scriptures, which, in turn, testify of Jesus (John 5:39).

> We receive Christ through His word, and the Holy Spirit is given to open the word of God to our understanding, and bring home its truth to our hearts. —Ellen G. White, *Thoughts from the Mount of Blessing*, p. 112.

If all we ever needed to understand the Scriptures was to read them, then what role would there be for preaching? Like a telescope, good preaching simply helps the hearer "see" what already exists. Preaching no more adds to Scripture than a telescope adds stars to the sky. It just makes the Scriptures plain. As a "preacher" in print, Ellen White's goal was to make the Scriptures plain.

> This is my work—to open the Scriptures to others as God has opened them to me. —Ellen G. White, *Testimonies for the Church*, vol. 8 (1904), p. 236.

> I wish all to understand that my confidence in the light that God has given stands firm, because I know that the Holy Spirit's power magnified the truth, and made it honorable, saying: "This is the way, walk ye in it." In my books, the truth is stated, barricaded by a "Thus saith the Lord." —Ellen G. White, Ltr. 90, 1906 in *Colporteur Ministry*, p. 126.

Every messenger in the Bible who was guided by the Holy Spirit was a "lesser light" to direct fallen human beings to Jesus, the *greatest light* of all (John 1:9; 8:12; 9:5)!

> The prophet John . . . was the lesser light, which was to be followed by a greater. The mind of John was illuminated by the Holy Spirit, that he might shed light upon his people; but no other light ever has shone or ever will shine so clearly upon fallen man as that which emanated from the teaching and example of Jesus. . . . And [John] was not permitted to see the result of his own labors. It was not his privilege to be with Christ and witness the

---

[22] On Joseph Smith's claim to be "God's Oracle," see *Journal of Discourses*, vol. 2, preface. It may be helpful to contrast Ellen White's claim that "the Bible is the only rule of faith and doctrine" (*RH* 7-17-1888), with claims made regarding Joseph Smith, whose writings the Church of Jesus Christ of Latter-day Saints hold as above the Bible. Mormon scholar Stephen E. Robinson writes that the visions and revelations of Joseph Smith "form the foundation of LDS doctrine. . . . For Latter-day Saints the highest authority in religious matters is continuing revelation from God given through the living Apostles and prophets of his Church, beginning with Joseph Smith and continuing to the present leadership." —*Encyclopedia of Mormonism*, Vol. 1, p. 401 at <www.lightplanet.com/mormon/faq/faq_doctrine.htm>.

manifestation of divine power attending the greater light. —Ellen G. White, *The Desire of Ages*, p. 220.

Nowhere shall we find anything that will help our spiritual life as will a study of the life of Christ. And as we seek to walk in His footsteps, there will come to us a supply of divine grace such as sustained Him under every circumstance. —Ellen G. White, *Review and Herald*, Jan. 6, 1910.

In giving us His Word, God has put us in possession of every truth essential for our salvation. The storehouse of the unsearchable riches of Christ is open to heart and hand. . . . When the life of Christ and the character of His mission are dwelt upon, rays of light will shine forth, and at every fresh attempt to discover truth, something that has never yet been unfolded will be revealed. —Ellen G. White, *Signs of the Times*, April 18, 1900.

In a certain sense, every true believer is a *lesser light* (Matt. 5:14) with the privilege and responsibility of directing others to the *greater light* of Jesus!

For a moment [Christ] looked into futurity, and heard the voices proclaiming in all parts of the earth, "Behold the Lamb of God, which taketh away the sin of the world" (John 1:29). —Ellen G. White, *DA* 622.2.

When God's people humble the soul before him, individually seeking his Holy Spirit with all the heart, there will be heard from human lips such a testimony as is represented in this scripture, "After these things I saw another angel come down from heaven, having great power and the earth was lightened with his glory." There will be faces aglow with the love of God; there will be lips touched with holy fire, saying, "The blood of Jesus Christ his Son cleanseth us from all sin." —Ellen G. White, Ltr. 25b, 1892 in *E. G. White 1888 Materials*, p. 1007.

"'*Christ—The Way of Life*' is a linear pictorial depiction of the plan of salvation. An early version, brought to the attention of Seventh-day Adventists by Dr. M. G. Kellogg in the 1860s, showed as its centerpiece a tree from whose branches hung the Ten Commandments. James and Ellen White liked the general motif, but in 1881 they commissioned New York City artist Thomas Moran to redraw the illustration with the crucified Christ in the center, as more in harmony with Seventh-day Adventist theology, which finds salvation in Christ rather than in the Ten Commandments." —Roger W. Coon, "Look a Little Higher" (Silver Spring, MD: Ellen G. White Estate, Inc., 1990), pp. 16, 17.

In upholding the Bible as the standard for doctrines and the motivation for lifestyle change, Ellen White insisted:

> God will have a people upon the earth to maintain the Bible, and the Bible only, as the standard of all doctrines and the basis of all reforms. —*The Great Controversy*, p. 595.

Why would God need to give additional light?

God gives additional light to intensify the light He has already given. Had the ancient people of God obeyed His law of Ten Commandments in all its implications from the heart (Deut. 4:8, 9; 5:29), there would have been little need for the additional instructions in judgments, statutes, and ordinances written out by God's servant, Moses (cf. *PP* 364.2). Likewise, had modern spiritual Israel had a heart to study and obey the teachings of the Scriptures, the counsels in the *Testimonies* would not have been required. Describing a certain meeting she saw in a dream, Ellen White wrote:

> I took the precious Bible and surrounded it with the several *Testimonies for the Church*, given for the people of God. Here, said I, the cases of nearly all are met. The sins they are to shun are pointed out. The counsel that they desire can be found here, given for other cases situated similarly to themselves. God has been pleased to give you line upon line and precept upon precept. But there are not many of you that really know what is contained in the *Testimonies*. You are not familiar with the Scriptures. If you had made God's word your study, with a desire to reach the Bible standard and attain to Christian perfection, you would not have needed the *Testimonies*. It is because you have neglected to acquaint yourselves with God's inspired Book that He has sought to reach you by simple, direct testimonies, calling your attention to the words of inspiration which you had neglected to obey, and urging you to fashion your lives in accordance with its pure and elevated teachings. —*Testimonies for the Church*, vol. 5, pp. 664, 665.

Had believers understood this relationship, they would never have misconstrued one of Ellen White's own statements to justify their neglect of God's counsels:

> I do not ask you to take my words. Lay Sister White to one side. Do not quote my words again as long as you live until you can obey the Bible. When you make the Bible your food, your meat and your drink, when you make its principles the elements of your character, you will know better how to receive counsel from God. I exalt the precious Word before you today. Do not repeat what I have said, saying, "Sister White said this," and, "Sister White said that." Find out what the Lord God of Israel says, and then do what He commands. —MS 43, 1901, p. 10, in 2*SM* 33.1, a talk presented by Ellen White in the Battle Creek College library just prior to the General Conference session, April 1, 1901.

In a statement she made later that same year, Ellen White clarified what she had meant:

> These are not the words of Sister White, but the words of the Lord, and His messenger has given them to me to give to you. God calls upon you to no longer work at cross purposes with Him. —Ltr. 73, 1901, written July 7, 1901, from St. Helena, Calif., "To those who occupy responsible positions in Battle Creek" in 13*MR* 222.2.

Ellen White did not want God's people to blindly follow her counsels without understanding the underlying principles for those counsels in God's Word. The testimonies which God gave Ellen White were to direct the attention of His people to the most important—and often overlooked—messages of the Bible which guide our lives and testify of Jesus.

> The Bible must be your counselor. Study it and the testimonies God has given; for they never contradict His Word. —Ltr. 106, 1907 (March 19, 1907) in 3*SM* 32.3.

As Ellen White had written in *The Great Controversy*:

> The Spirit was not given—nor can it ever be bestowed—to supersede the Bible; for the Scriptures explicitly state that the word of God is the standard by which all teaching and experience must be tested. —*The Great Controversy* (1888), p. e.

> None but those who have fortified the mind with the truths of the Bible will stand through the last great conflict. —*The Great Controversy* (1888), p. 593.

The integrating factor

In the Introduction to *The Great Controversy*, Ellen White calls attention to the grand and central theme that pervades every book in the *Conflict of the Ages* series—including the one subtitled *The Conflict of the Ages Illustrated in the Life of Christ.*

> It is not so much the object of this book to present new truths concerning the struggles of former times, as to bring out facts and principles which have a bearing on coming events. Yet viewed as a part of the controversy between the forces of light and darkness, all these records of the past are seen to have a new significance; and through them a light is cast upon the future, illumining the pathway of those who, like the reformers of past ages, will be called, even at the peril of all earthly good, to witness "for the word of God, and for the testimony of Jesus Christ."

> To unfold the scenes of the great controversy between truth and error; to reveal the wiles of Satan, and the means by which he may be successfully resisted; to present a satisfactory solution of the great problem of evil, shedding such a light upon the origin and the final disposition of sin as to make fully manifest the justice and benevolence of God in all His dealings with his creatures; and to show the holy, unchanging nature of His law, is the object of this book. That through its influence souls may be delivered from the power of darkness, and become "partakers of the inheritance of the saints in light," to the praise of Him who loved us, and gave himself for us, is the earnest prayer of the writer. —*The Great Controversy* (1888), p. h.

Regarding the final volume in this series, she wrote:

> *Great Controversy* should be very widely circulated. It contains the story of the past, the present, and the future. In its outline of the closing scenes of this earth's history, it bears a powerful testimony in behalf of the truth. I am more anxious to see a wide circulation for this book than for any others I have written; for in *The Great Controversy*, the last message of warning to the world is given more distinctly than in any of my other books. —Ltr. 281, 1905 (reprinted in *Review and Herald*, April 8, 1954).

Because the theme of the great controversy enables the student of the Bible to see more clearly the spiritual battle between Christ and Satan, it is the "key that will unlock to him the whole treasure house of God's word" (*Education*, p. 126).

> The Bible is its own expositor. Scripture is to be compared with scripture. The student should learn to view the word as a whole, and to see the relation of its parts. He should gain a knowledge of its grand central theme, of God's original purpose for the world, of the rise of the great controversy, and of the work of redemption. He should understand the nature of the two principals that are contending for supremacy, and should learn to trace their working through the records of history and prophecy, to the great consummation. He should see how this controversy enters into every phase of human experience; how in every act of life he himself reveals the one or the other of the

two antagonistic motives; and how, whether he will or not, he is even now deciding upon which side of the controversy he will be found —Ellen G. White, *Education*, p. 190.

Calvin . . . Luther, Schleiermacher, Barth, Brunner, Bultmann . . . saw certain basic truths—none was the integrating factor of *The Great Controversy* theme. Some saw more of the fullness of God's character than others—and their theologies reflected their view. Compare the picture of God that Luther, Calvin, or Wesley saw—and then note how their pictures of God informed their theologies.[23]

Divinely ordained authority

At issue for most people is not whether Ellen White made a proper use of sources, but whether or not her writings should be accorded spiritual authority in their lives. It was this issue of authority that caused many men of influence to part ways with the Seventh-day Adventist Church and its teachings. In summarizing the departure of Canright, Hull, and several others from the Seventh-day Adventist Church, Arthur W. Spalding declares:

In all these cases, as in various others since, the chief point of attack by the mutineers was the Spirit of prophecy in Ellen G. White. It always arose out of a rebellion against reproof and counsel, either in personal or in doctrinal matters.[24]

As Warren H. Johns has pointed out, we need the God-given guidance she provides:

Ellen White's authority does not reside within herself; it is not centered in a mere person. It is a derived authority. It is God-given and Bible-centered. Her authority, while less than that of Scripture, is higher than each of us as individuals. God has given her special insights into spiritual things, insights that we do not possess or that we possess only faintly. To reject her authority is to substitute our wisdom for a wisdom higher than ours.[25]

As God called Moses with duties beyond those of a prophet to be His messenger to lead Israel into Canaan, so did God provide a formative leader whose roles would be more diverse than that of a prophet for His last-day people, headed toward the heavenly Canaan. She wrote:

Early in my youth I was asked several times, Are you a prophet? I have ever responded, I am the Lord's messenger. . . . Why have I not claimed to be a prophet? — Because in these days many who boldly claim that they are prophets are a reproach to the cause of Christ; and because my work includes much more than the word "prophet" signifies. . . .[26]

To claim to be a prophetess is something that I have never done. If others call me by that name, I have no controversy with them. But my work has covered so many lines that I cannot call myself other than a messenger, sent to bear a message from the

---

[23] "Off the Back Burner," Segment 14, in a General Conference of SDAs retirees communiqué, June 1996.

[24] Arthur W. Spalding, *Origin and History of Seventh-day Adventists*, vol. 1, pp. 230, 231.

[25] W. H. Johns, *Ministry*, June 1982, p. 19.

[26] There are many fully inspired non-canonical prophets listed in Scripture, such as Jasher (Joshua 10:13; 2 Sam. 1:18), Nathan and Gad (1 Chr. 29:29), Shemaiah (2 Chr. 12:15), Iddo (2 Chr. 12:15; 9:29), Ahijah (2 Chr. 9:29), Oded (2 Chr. 15:8), Jehu (2 Chr. 20:34), John the Baptist (Matt. 11:9–14), and Agabus (Acts 11:28; 21:10). See also those who prophesied in Acts 19:6; 21:9. Though not a canonical prophet, Ellen White does pass the tests of a prophet. She (a) spoke in harmony with Biblical truth (Isa. 8:20), (b) upheld Jesus as the divine son of God and the center of our faith (1 John 4:2; John 12:32), (c) bore fruits of righteousness (Matt. 7:20), and (d) prophesied that which has come to pass (Deut. 18:22) except when the prophecy was conditioned upon the response of its recipient (Jer. 28:9; Jonah 3:4).

Lord to His people, and to take up work in any line that He points out. —Ellen G. White, *Review and Herald*, July 26, 1906.

As the children of Israel, who were headed for an earthly Canaan, often murmured against Moses and rebelled against his leading and the authority of God, so has modern Israel, headed for the heavenly Canaan, complained against their God-given guide.

> Satan's snares are laid for us as verily as they were laid for the children of Israel just prior to their entrance into the land of Canaan. We are repeating the history of that people. —Ellen G. White, *Testimonies for the Church*, vol. 5, p. 160.

In the same way that Moses was laid to rest before Israel entered the Promised Land, so has it been that Ellen White was laid to rest before the entrance of God's people into the heavenly Canaan. However, just as Moses' sage words continued to guide ancient Israel after his death, so have the counsels of God through Ellen White continued to warn, guide, nurture and bless God's last-day people whenever those words have been heeded. Responding to the question of what would happen when her living witness would cease at her death, Ellen White answered:

> "The books that she has written will not die. They are a living witness to what saith the Scriptures . . ." —Ltr. 55, 1905, "To Elder O. A. Olsen," Jan. 30, 1905, in 1*MR* 141.1.[27]

Heavenly guidance to arrive safely home

Let us not forget that it was the loving heavenly Father himself who determined that His end-time people would need the additional guidance of the prophetic "testimony of Jesus" to guide them safely through the perils of the last days (Rev. 12:17; 19:10). ". . . Till we all come in the unity of the faith, and of the knowledge of the Son of God, unto a perfect man, unto the measure of the stature of the fulness of Christ" (Ephesians 4:13) tells us that the objective of the gift of prophecy has not yet been fulfilled.

> The Bible is like a high seas chart by which a pilot guides a ship to its destination. As we study the prophecies of the Bible which predict Christ's second coming and witness the fulfillment of these divine forecasts, our confidence in Bible prophecy, and in the Bible itself, is strengthened. Seventh-day Adventists believe that, as God's remnant church nears the heavenly harbor, God has given it a harbor map to help guide it safely past the dangerous shoals and reefs that lie before us. . . . Just as the harbor map agrees with the high seas chart at every significant point, so do Ellen White and her writings agree with the Bible at every significant point.[28]

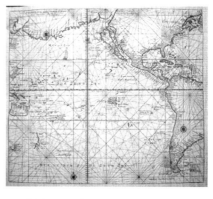

A high seas chart of the Pacific Ocean

. . . .

In our final chapter, we will hear the authors' closing statements.

---

[27] She also wrote: "Abundant light has been given to our people in these last days. Whether or not my life is spared, my writings will constantly speak, and their work will go forward as long as time shall last" (Ltr. 371, 1907 in 3*SM* 76).

[28] Donald E. Mansell, *The Coming Conflict and the Overcomer's Reward*, Introduction, pp. 13, 14, adapted by permission of author.

CHAPTER 10
Closing Statements

Though it had long been Ellen White's great desire to tell the story of Jesus' love, she wrote on a variety of other subjects during her many years of ministry. Among these subjects are how to find and maintain a personal relationship with Christ, how to teach religion in the home and educate the youth for now and eternity, and how to maintain optimum physical health.[1]

It is in relation to physical health that we find an interesting statement that relates to the matter of "literary borrowing" in *The Desire of Ages*. It is a thought that was expressed by the late Dr. Clive M. McCay, Ph.D., Professor of Nutrition at Cornell University as he assessed Mrs. White's views on nutrition. Dr. McCay came to know about these views through a graduate student of his named Helen Chen, who gave him a copy of *Counsels on Diet and Foods* in 1955. This is his testimony.

"How would she know?"

Among the thousand historical acquaintances in my files, one of the most worth-while is Ellen G. White. As near as one can judge by the evidence of modern nutritional science, her extensive writings on the subject of nutrition, and health in general, are correct in their conclusions. This is doubly remarkable: Not only was most of her writing done at a time when a bewildering array of new health views—good and bad—were being promoted but the modern science of nutrition, which helps us to check on views and theories, had not yet been born. Even more singular, Mrs. White had no technical training in nutrition, or in any subdivision of science that deals with health. In fact, because of her frail health from childhood she completed only a part of grammar school education.[2]

Well before the birth of Mrs. White there were a few Americans protesting the bad diet, the smoking, and the drinking. Even from early antiquity there had been groups outside the Jewish traditions that subscribed to vegetarianism. Sylvester Graham, who was born in 1794, stirred the young American nation with his lectures advocating vegetarianism, the improvement of bread, the abolishment of alcoholic beverages, and more healthful living. He had much influence during the first half of the nineteenth century, but left no permanent group of followers. The vegetarian church was founded in Philadelphia in 1817, but it soon disbanded.

About 1840 the Shakers stopped the use of pork, strong drink, and tobacco. Many turned to vegetarianism. . . . But the Shakers reached their peak about 1850 and have now—thanks to their celibate views—almost perished.[3]

To sum up the discussion: Every modern specialist in nutrition whose life is dedicated to human welfare must be impressed in four respects by the writings and leadership of Ellen G. White.

---

[1] In *Steps to Christ, Christ's Object Lessons, The Sanctified Life;* in *The Adventist Home, Child Guidance, A Solemn Appeal,* and *Education;* and in *The Ministry of Healing, Counsels on Diet and Foods,* and *Counsels on Health,* respectively.

[2] Clive M. McCay, Ph.D., "A Nutrition Authority Discusses Mrs. E. G. White," *RH* 2-12-1959, p. 16.

[3] McCay, February 19, 1959, p. 6.

In the first place, her basic concepts about the relation between diet and health have been verified to an unusual degree by scientific advances of the past decades. Someone may attempt to explain this remarkable fact by saying: "Mrs. White simply borrowed her ideas from others." But how would she know which ideas to borrow and which to reject out of the bewildering array of theories and health teachings current in the nineteenth century? She would have had to be a most amazing person, with knowledge beyond her times, in order to do this successfully!

In the second place, everyone who attempts to teach nutrition can hardly conceive of a leadership such as that of Mrs. White that was able to induce a substantial number of people to improve their diets.

In the third place, one can only speculate about the large number of sufferers during the past century who could have had improved health if they had accepted the teachings of Mrs. White. . . .

In spite of the fact that the works of Mrs. White were written long before the advent of modern scientific nutrition, no better over-all guide is available today.[4]

The work of a modern prophet projected

We may speculate about the possible sources of words in *The Desire of Ages*, but we cannot help but marvel at the wisdom that enabled Ellen White to adapt and improve on what she obviously did "borrow" from the works of other Christian writers. Amazingly, her literary gathering from other writers to produce *The Desire of Ages* was hypothetically described by one of her contemporaries, John Harris, in his preface to *The Great Teacher*:

> Suppose, for example, an inspired prophet were now to appear in the church, to add a supplement to the canonical books—what a Babel of opinions would he find existing on almost every theological subject! —and how highly probable is it that his ministry would consist, *or even seem to consist*, in the mere selection and ratification of such of these opinions as accorded with the mind of God. *Absolute originality would seem to be almost impossible.* The inventive mind of man has already bodied forth speculative opinions in almost every conceivable form; . . . *leaving little more, even to a divine messenger, than the office of taking some of these opinions, and impressing them with the seal of heaven.* —Harris, *TGT*, preface, xxxiii-xxxiv, emphasis supplied.

Ellen White had an education that few others have been privileged to enjoy, which enabled her to speak and write with authority.

A personal note

As I think back over the years as to how the priceless gift of the counsels of Ellen White has blessed my family and myself, I am filled with thanksgiving and praise. My grandparents, maternal and paternal, were stirred with the spirit of the three angels' messages and of the Testimonies "which God in His providence has linked with the work of the third angel's message from its very rise" (5T 654.2).

My maternal grandparents, Elder and Mrs. W. C. Hankins, were missionaries to the southern part of China for nineteen years (1905–1924). Granddad Hankins had a distinct remembrance of the 1888 General Conference held in Minneapolis, and of seeing, on occasion, "the servant of the Lord," Ellen White.

---

[4] McCay, February 26, 1959, p. 10.

On my late husband's side of the family, his maternal grandfather, Elder Arthur Swain Hickox, was a young minister in Australia whose first wife died (and his marriage to his second wife, Carrie Gribble, was celebrated in Ellen White's home). While Elder Hickox had been struggling with his bereavement, his little daughter Lillian was left with relatives in America. When the time came for her to rejoin her father, she was sent by boat with trustworthy custodians to Australia. Upon arriving, she was fully expecting to be met by her father, but was met by Elder Willie White instead. Lillian was so disappointed that she began to bawl. The stewardess who had her in charge offered to keep her for a time in one of the ship's cabins, but W. C. White told her that Lillian's father was too far away to make the trip to get her, and he himself would have to take her. Lillian cried her heart out for awhile, but in time she had a happy reunion with her father.

When Lillian Hickox was nearly nine years old, Sister White visited the family. Mrs. White recorded her remembrances and impressions of the occasion:

> We took dinner at the Mission in Hamilton, and in the afternoon we drove to the place where Brother Hickox is laboring, about three miles off. We had a very profitable interview, and a precious season of prayer. Brother and Sister Hickox have two nice children, a girl of nine and an adopted boy of five. During our praying season, the little girl knelt by her father and the boy by his mother, and everyone, even the little boy, took part in prayer.

> Just before we left, the little girl came up to me, and putting her arm about me, said, "I do like to have you here, Sister White, and I am sorry you cannot stay longer." Such words were as music in my ears, for I could not have had a higher compliment given me than to hear such an expression from a child. The light and joy of the Lord was expressed in the face of the nine year old girl.

Thinking back over the past years that I have intermittently worked on the manuscript for this book, I could tell of a number of difficulties that have had to be met and overcome. Nonetheless, the delight of being able to hold communion with such elevating, inspiring themes about the Saviour has far outweighed the mention of any setback. Many times I have been led to seek the Lord most earnestly on my knees. Through it all, this has been my chief resource—

> In His name [Christ's disciples] were to present their petitions to the Father, and they would receive answer. . . . Christ's name was to be their watchword, their badge of distinction, their bond of union, the authority for their course of action, and the source of their success. —Ellen G. White, *The Acts of the Apostles*, p. 28 (adapted from *TGT* 66).

E. MARCELLA ANDERSON KING

We rest our case.

Critics of Ellen White have charged that she plagiarized or "copied" from others in *The Desire of Ages* from start to finish. Though technically speaking she did very little word-for-word "copying" from the writings of others, those who try to dismiss this charge of the critics by emphasizing that she "only borrowed a little" are really missing the point. For the critics, "borrowing" equals *stealing*, and it doesn't matter how little one does, it is still wrong to steal—especially for one who claimed inspiration.

What the critics may not have stopped to consider is that, though originality of expression is at the heart of the plagiarism charge, *total* originality is not a prerequisite for communicating messages from God. The inspired writers Luke and Solomon gathered from others without identifying their sources; Matthew and Luke almost picked Mark's Gospel clean in composing their own Gospels; Jude, in his epistle, and John, in the Revelation, used the language of the apocryphal book of Enoch; Paul built on extrabiblical authors and learned of conditions in the churches from human messengers. What made them inspired writers was not the source of their words, but the source of the messages they communicated. Inspiration is more than words. Like the writers of Scripture, Ellen White drew for her writings from various sources—she received direct revelations, she studied the Scriptures and reference works, she assimilated vocabulary and adapted choice phrasing from her reading—though, all the while, she looked to God to guide her in what she was to write. She submitted to the Holy Spirit—like the virgin Mary (in Luke 1:38)—and depended on the Holy Spirit to help her faithfully communicate what God revealed, whether through visions or through other means. It was submission to God that qualified her to be a messenger, not her giftedness as a writer.

Though *The Desire of Ages* is certainly well written, *writing ability* and *uniqueness of expression* should not be made the final test of whether or not it is divinely inspired. Mrs. White's concern over the wording of the book was not so that we would praise her for her literary skill, but so that we would not be diverted from the book's great object—a life-changing encounter with Jesus! (See the preface to *DA*.) As a faithful "life of Christ," *The Desire of Ages* was written in conformity to the outline of the Gospels. It was not a novel that could follow the whims of the author's imagination (unlike many works of Christian fiction written today). Imagination was not what guided Ellen White in its writing. Her earlier recounting of the life and passion of Christ in *Spiritual Gifts* attests to this fact. She wrote: "I saw," "I heard," "I was shown." Nonetheless, she was not satisfied with that first simple writing. A subject as exalted as the life of Christ deserved better! In the 1870s and again in the 1890s, she applied herself to the task of telling the story again, but more fully and with greater expressiveness, and, even though she adapted the wording of others to tell the story, her own originality comes through.

My own view of *originality* was forever indelibly stamped by the pronouncement of my college English teacher as she returned a research paper that I had put together for Freshman Comp. Having been instructed to write an "original" report on some subject, I racked my brain to come up with something that had never been written before. However, as Solomon wisely proclaimed: "There is nothing new under the sun" (Eccl. 1:9). Resigned to the impossibility of my assignment, I turned in a paper on a subject that I had drawn from several different sources. As the teacher was returning the graded papers to the members of the class, she said to me: "Now that's original!" I was flabbergasted! What had I done? I had used *un*-original sources with *un*-original words to reach an *original* conclusion that was different in its net effect from any of the sources I had researched. As the evidence in this book has shown, Ellen White's writing in *The Desire of Ages* was far more than the "warming over" of any other "Life of Christ" that she read before completing the book.

Though the charge of plagiarism implies a lack of originality, a work should not be considered un-original because the author has used the same Scripture as another author or has paraphrased another author's paraphrase of Scripture, using a few of the same words. Neither should it be considered un-original because the author has used the same words as another writer to state a self-evident Biblical fact, such as Jesus was "with the Father before the world was," or because the author has stated the same truth as another writer in different words. A work is not un-original because the writer has read another person's treatment of a subject to gain vocabulary for his or her own original statement or because the writer has adapted a sentence or two from another author's entire book or chapter, using it in a different context, or has used *two* verbatim words out of another author's sentence of *36 words*. (These are actual examples from Ellen White's borrowing, and they are well within the bounds of the law and of the accepted literary practice of other authors who wrote on the life of Christ.)

The real problem with Ellen White's borrowing is not originality of expression, but one's presuppositions about inspiration. Had Ellen White not claimed divine inspiration, her use of other works would be called *good research.* Had she not worked through an assistant, her compositions would be seen as *good writing.*[5] Had there been no similarity between her words and the words of others, her memorable expressions would be described as *quite impressive.* Yet, as we now know, inspired writers *can* do research and *can* use literary help; they were able to use expressions from earlier writers without imbibing false theology.

Thus, if we can lay aside our pre-conceived notions about *inspiration, literary help,* and *originality,* we just might find that Ellen White's book *is* good research, good writing, and really quite impressive—not because we handicap Ellen White's writing for her lack of formal education or her writing in spite of poor health, but because her book presents one consistent message that holds the attention, touches the heart, and lifts up Jesus like no other book in its class! If we spend all our time on the technicalities of *how it was produced,* we may miss out on the blessing of *what it says!*[6]

> When a person looks merely at the mechanics of her writing it may seem that some of Ellen White's writing is to be attributed to human sources. But when we search what she has written looking for truth, we hear the voice of God speaking to our hearts.[7]

Professor H. C. Lacey, who was well aware of the process of the composition of *The Desire of Ages,* could affirm without reserve:

> I gladly and with all my heart accept *The Desire of Ages* as an inspired book; indeed I regard it as the most spiritual Life of Christ, outside the Gospels, ever given to His Church.[8]

Even though there are parallel elements and parallel language between Ellen White's account of the life of Christ and those of other writers, no one person has exclusive rights to the particulars of Jesus' earthly life, and Ellen White's unique focus on the conflict of the ages and the unique eyewitness details that she includes in telling the story, make it plain that she has had a view of the scenes of Jesus' life that the other writers on the life of Christ did not have.[9] Under the guidance of the Holy Spirit and the editorial efforts of Marian Davis, Ellen White was able to give voice to the great longing of her heart—to tell "the story of Jesus' love." It is the prayer of this author that the evidence in this book has strengthened your confidence in the inspiration of the messages sent through her and that your love for Christ and faith in Him will grow each day as you use the spiritual resource of *The Desire of Ages* to assist you in taking a "thoughtful hour" to contemplate the scenes in our Saviour's earthly life.

KEVIN L. MORGAN

---

[5] Those who have never written a book may not realize how much effort and research are required. It takes much more than simply putting one's thoughts on paper from the first blank page until the last. Good writing is the long but satisfying process of finding just the right word and transition to unite every major point of one's subject into a harmonious whole.

[6] Vincent L. Ramik makes a similar point: "I believe that the critics have missed the boat badly by focusing upon Mrs. White's *writings,* instead of focusing upon the *messages* in Mrs. White's writings." —Ramik, *Adventist Review,* Sept. 17, 1981, p. 3.

[7] Paul A. Gordon, "Why Did Ellen G. White Borrow?" (Ellen G. White Estate, May 1981), p. 13.

[8] Ltr. to Samuel Kaplan, an Adventist minister in New York, July 24, 1936, in *Exhibits* #90.

[9] The evidence we have reviewed from the writing of *The Desire of Ages* is consistent with James White's claims about the uniqueness of his wife's writings, as witnessed by their unique focus and details which could not have come from the other writers—even though James died 17 years before its publication; it is consistent with W. C. White's testimony about the care of his mother's literary assistants in using Ellen White's own words in her manuscripts and Ellen White's use of the writings of others to jog her memory about what she had seen in vision and to relate the story in its proper order.

APPENDIX A
Characterizations of the "Lives of Christ"

Because the charge of plagiarism implies that an author's work is unnecessary in that a plagiarized work duplicates previously published material, the following summaries and samples of the major life of Christ volumes, available at the time of the publication of *The Desire of Ages* (1898), are included for the reader's comparison.[1] Samples are marked for their literary parallels with the *DA* text and followed by the reference for the *DA* parallel (e.g. Hanna, *The Life of Christ*, p. 684 ‖ *DA* 728.2).

John Fleetwood. *Life of our Lord* (1767)

- Reprinted in different editions well into the nineteenth century
- Apologetic motif with a faithfulness to the gospel accounts so strict that it came across as a harmony of the Gospels written in the author's own prose
- Favorite stylistic device was the extended paraphrase, which mingled Jesus' words with his own narrative of situations and events
- Took the account of the Gospels literally
- Sources were Scripture and a few references to Josephus (Pals, pp. 22, 23).

> An example of some of the best writing of Fleetwood is in Chapter 8.
> On the Web at <http://books.google.com/books?hl=en&id=_-k2AAAAMAAJ&dq>.

John Harris. *The Great Teacher* (1836)

- Vivid imagery, though often tedious by current standards of prose
- Dealt with the authority, originality, spirituality, tenderness and benevolence, and practicality of Jesus' teaching
- Introductory essay by Heman Humphrey dealt with the mystery of the incarnation.

The Great Commission (1854)

- Treated the growth and development of the Church
- Essays develop slowly
- Neither book lists its sources.

Samples of both books are in the footnotes of Chapter 4.
The Great Teacher on the Web at <http://books.google.com/books?id=QPc2AAAAMAAJ>.
The Great Commission on the Web at <http://books.google.com/books?id=2GECAAAAYAAJ>.

Octavius Winslow (1855). *The Glory of the Redeemer in His Person and Work* (1855).

- In overtly sermonic style he exalts the sublimity of redemption.
- His ornate language eventually becomes wearisome.

Samples of the writing of Winslow are in the footnotes of Chapter 4.
Selections on the Web at <www.gracegems.org/W/glory.htm>.

---

[1] Dr. Fred Veltman directed us to Daniel L. Pals' book, *The Victorian "Lives" of Jesus* (San Antonio, TX: Trinity University Press, 1982), which provided several summaries in this Appendix as noted.

J. H. Ingraham. *The Prince of the House of David* (1855/1859 Pals)

- A religious novel to prove the divinity of Christ, depicting the life and death of Christ through the letters of a young Jewish woman to her father
- The author fills in details and invents story lines and characters in colorful language
- The book sold more than a million copies and was still in print until 1975.

Sample: By this time, the people, who were dragging Jesus to death, were got out of the gate, where a cross of heavy cypress was obtained by the Centurion, from a yard near the lodge, wherein stood several new crosses, awaiting whatsoever victims Roman justice might, from day to day, condemn to death. Two others were also brought out, and laid upon the shoulders of two men, the lieutenants of Barabbas, who were also that day to be crucified. The released Barabbas was himself present, and the most active, in laying the cross upon the back of the already faint and drooping Jesus. —Ingraham, *The Prince of the House of David: or, Three Years in the Holy City* (1859), p. 390.

On the Web at <http://quod.lib.umich.edu/t/text/text-idx?c=moa;idno=AAN0532>.

C. J. Ellicott. *Historical Lectures on the Life of Christ* (1863)

- Provided scholarship that improved on the older harmonies
- Made use of German philology, exegetical science, and works on travel in Palestine
- Target audience was the scholar and the general reader, though he fell short of his mark by writing more as an apologist than as a historian
- The *Lectures* reached six editions by 1876, but "excited no wide-spread public interest" (Pals, pp. 31, 32)
- Reprinted in the Michigan Historical Reprint Series, December 2005.

Sample: Was there to be no outward sign, no visible token that earth and heaven were sympathizing in the agonies of Him by whose hands they had been made and fashioned? No, verily, it could not be. If one Evangelist, as we have already observed, tells us that on the night of the Lord's birth a heavenly brightness and glory shone forth amid the gloom, three inspired witnesses now tell us that a pall of darkness was spread over the whole land from the sixth to the ninth hour. But while they thus specially notice the interval, it may be observed that they maintain the most solemn reserve as to the incidents by which it was marked. Though full and explicit as to the circumstances of the agony in the garden, they are here profoundly silent. The mysteries of those hours of darkness, when with the sufferings of the agonized body mingled the sufferings of the sacred soul, the struggles with sinking nature, the accumulating pressure of the burden of a world's sin, the momently more and more embittered foretastings of that which was its wages and its penalty, the clinging desperation of the last assaults of Satan and his mustered hosts, the withdrawal and darkening of the Paternal presence, —mysteries such as these, so deep and so dread, it was not meet that even the tongues of Apostles should be moved to speak of, or the pens of Evangelists to record. —Ellicott, *Historical Lectures on the Life of Christ*, pp. 320, 321 || DA 753.1.

On the Web at <http://books.google.com/books?id=1RVdZvOTeyQC&dq>.

Joseph Ernest Renan. *Vie de Jesus* (1863)

- The controversial historical-critical life of Christ, unquestionably a work of literary genius, captivating "the reading public, if not the scholarly community, of Europe"
- The *Vie* passed swiftly through countless editions and new printings
- The author was an Orientalist at the College de France who once intended to be a priest but lost his faith by reading German critical theology
- Dismissed the traditional supernaturalist view of the Scriptures, though holding the "flawed" gospel record as historical
- In his portrayal, Jesus "was crucified outside the city, a martyr to the fabrications of his own restless, ever more fanatical mind" (Pals, pp. 32–34).

COLOR CODING: verbatim paraphrase

Sample: The life of Jesus, to the historian, ends with his last sigh. But so deep was the trace which he had left in the hearts of his disciples and of a few devoted women, that, for weeks to come, he was to them living and consoling. Had his body been taken away, or did enthusiasm, always credulous, afterwards generate the mass of accounts by which faith in the resurrection was sought to be established? This, for want of peremptory evidence, we shall never know. We may say, however, that the strong imagination of Mary Magdalene here enacted a principal part. Divine power of love! sacred moments in which the passion of a hallucinated woman gives to the world a resurrected God! —Renan, *The Life of Jesus* (1864), p. 357.

On the Web at <http://books.google.com/books?id=B_oWAAAAIAAJ&dq>.

William Hanna. *The Life of Christ* (1863) and *The Life of our Lord upon Earth* (1869)

- Follow-up to 1862 popular semi-devotional history, *The Last Day of our Lord's Passion*
- Written in direct response to Renan's *Vie de Jesus* (Hanna, pp. 7–12)
- Combined "strands of history, geography, and a fair measure of free speculation"
- Constructed "a continuous and expanded narrative" from the Gospels, bringing out the characters, motives, and feelings of the different actors and spectators in the events described
- Refrained from all critical and doctrinal discussions, his purpose was to reassure
- Composed originally as sermons, the work contained leftover "repetitions and interpolations" and was "exceedingly long" (Pals, pp. 69–71)
- Intentionally chose not "to burden the following pages with references to all the authorities consulted," referring the reader only to Alford, Stier, and Ellicott.

Sample: Herod, the king of Galilee, happened at this very time to be in Jerusalem. Pilate will send the case to him; and thus get the responsibility of deciding it shifted, from his own shoulders, by laying it upon one who not only may be quite willing to assume it, but may regard as a compliment the reference of the case to his adjudication. There was a misunderstanding between the two—the Roman procurator and the Galilean king—which the sending of Jesus to the latter for trial might serve to heal. Pilate had done something to displease Herod—something, in all likelihood, in the very way of interfering with what Herod regarded as his rights, and the rights of his subjects. Some Galileans had been up lately at Jerusalem, offering sacrifice there. There had been a riot, which Pilate had promptly and summarily quelled; but in doing so he had mingled the blood of some of these Galileans with their sacrifices—cut them down without inquiring whose subjects they were, or what right they might have to demand a trial in one or other of the Herodian courts. For this, or some such fancied interference with his jurisdiction, Herod had taken offence at Pilate. The recognition of his jurisdiction, then, by sending to him for trial such a notorious person as Jesus, would be the very kind of compliment most soothing to his kingly vanity. Herod recognized and appreciated the compliment; and whatever else Pilate lost by the line of conduct he pursued that day, he as least gained this—he got the quarrel between himself and Herod healed. —Hanna, *The Life of Christ*, p. 684 ‖ *DA* 728.2.

On the Web at <http://quod.lib.umich.edu/cgi/t/text/text-idx?c=moa;cc=moa;view=toc;idno=AGA2387.0001.001>.

George Jones. *Life-Scenes from the Four Gospels* (1865)

- His earlier book *Excursions to Cairo, Jerusalem, Damascus and Balbec, from the United States Ship Delaware, During Her Recent Cruise, with an Attempt to Discriminate Between Truth and Error in Regard to the Sacred Places of the Holy City* was inspired by Jones's visit to the Holy Land as a navy chaplain, thirty years before.[2]
- Compared to Hanna, the 'parallels' in Jones to *The Desire of Ages* seem rather sparse.
- With some of the verbatim words and phrases being exactly the same as from Hanna, there could be a link of dependency, even though Jones has his own distinctive style.[3]

---

[2] From Schramer, James, and Donald Ross, eds. *Dictionary of Literary Biography, vol. 183: American Travel Writers, 1776–1864* (Detroit: Gale Research, 1997).

[3] Marcella Anderson's notes, September 15, 1981.

Sample: There stood near to the cross a group,—a singular one it was amid that scene of scoffing, and malice, and triumph at Christ's sufferings;—for the faces and actions of these persons gave demonstration how deeply they sympathized with the <u>sufferer</u>. They were his mother; her sister, wife of Cleophas; Mary Magdalene; and the faithful John. Best love is ever bravest; and these loved the most. They stood there, true to him, their souls writhing under those tauntings and those scornful insulting cries. They looked toward the cross; and they there saw the <u>marks of</u> agony; the anguish apparent in his face, and in the spasms and convulsions of his body;—that face so <u>gentle</u> and calm, and so God-like always, but now clouded with the pain which expressed itself in <u>every</u> line and <u>feature</u>;—the eyes now bloodshot;—the brow and form wounded and bloody;—the languor of <u>exhaustion</u> stealing over the limbs and frame. Not one word, however, of complaint from him; his eyes still showed love to them and to all. His voice and tone when he spoke, were now as always, in kindness and <u>love</u>. —Jones, *Life-Scenes from the Four Gospels* (1865) p. 389 ‖ *DA* 735.4; 735.1.

On the Web at <www.archive.org/details/lifescenesfromfo00jonerich>.

Daniel March. *Walks and Homes of Jesus* (1866); *Night Scenes in the Bible* (1868 under title *Night Unto Night*; 1872, reprinted by Kregel Publications in 1972); and *Days of the Son of Man* (1882)

- Absolutely beautiful prose, though sometimes wordy.
- Include narrative, geographical description, and exhortation, but list no sources.
- Object to "look upon our Lord as he was seen by the men of his time, and to combine with that view the more mature and instructed impressions which spring from faith in his redeeming work and his divine nature" (*Walks and Homes*, p. 3).
- Rich in perceptive lessons from the cross of Calvary
- Say little about the value of Christ's life on earth, His intercessions in heaven, or the relation of the cross and the broken sacred law
- Do not list authorities nor footnote borrowed phrasing.

Samples of March's writing are in Chapter 7.

Walks and Homes of Jesus on the Web at <www.archive.org/details/walkshomesofjesu00marcrich>; *Days of the Son of Man* at <http://books.google.com/books?id=1yEWAAAAYAAJ>.

Frederic William Farrar. *Life of Christ* (1874)

- A world-class scholar writing "in rich, colorful, eminently readable and engaging style"
- Exceeded thirty editions and 100,000 in sales and was published into the 1890s
- It was "the work of a believer."
- "Farrar readily supplied motives, occasions, reasons, and reactions for the interested parties. He had too a flair for the dramatic, which came to his aid especially in passages like the passion narrative."
- His "ornate, effusive prose" is described in the words of the critic of the *London Quarterly*: "the style glitters a little too much" (Pals, pp. 78–84).
- "So influential was Farrar's *The Life of Christ* . . . that from 1874 to the end of the century almost every successful British Life was to draw heavily upon the model shaped by Farrar" (Kissinger, *The Lives of Jesus: A History and Bibliography*, p. 30).
- Farrar's *Life of Christ* was reprinted in the Michigan Historical Reprint Series in 2002.

Sample: We have caught glimpses of this Herod Antipas before, and I do not know that all History, in its gallery of portraits, contains a much more despicable figure than this wretched, dissolute Idumæan Sadducee—this petty princeling drowned in debauchery and blood. To him was addressed the sole purely contemptuous expression that Jesus is ever recorded to have used. Superstition and incredulity usually go together; avowed atheists have yet believed in augury, and men who do not believe in God will believe in ghosts. Antipas was rejoiced beyond all things to see Jesus. <u>He had long</u> <u>been wanting</u> to see Him because of the rumours he had heard; and this murderer of the prophets hoped that Jesus would, in compliment to royalty, amuse by some <u>miracle</u> his gaping <u>curiosity</u>. He harangued and <u>questioned</u> <u>Him</u> <u>in many words</u>, but gained not so much as one syllable in reply. Our Lord confronted all his ribald questions with the majesty of silence. —Farrar, *The Life of Christ* (1874), p. 627f || *DA* 728.3, 729.2.

On the Web at <http://books.google.com/books?id=MnMOAAAAYAAJ>.

Cunningham Geikie. *The Life and Words of Christ* (1877)

- That Geikie and Farrar's books were similar was evident even on a superficial comparison. "Both were two-volume works whose prefatory lists of sources disclosed virtually identical research: earlier Lives and New Testament commentaries (both English and foreign), with special stress on conservative scholarship, travelogues from the Orient, and some of the newer German studies of late-Jewish literature . . .
- "What gave the work its element of novelty was the painstaking care with which Geikie filled in the historical scene and context. With the attention to fine detail manifest . . . he sketched the history, economy, religion, society, and thought of Judea in the time of Christ. Like Farrar, he was a scholar of the "extensive" sort, a specialist in no single subject, but a skillful expositor with a capacity to understand his authorities, absorb their researches, and convey the results to his readers in lucid prose.
- "For political background Geikie drew on Tacitus, Suetonius, and Josephus, as well as the books of the Maccabees, to fill in both the imperial and local scene. Along with Farrar he was one of the first in Britain to appreciate the significance of Jewish intertestamentary literature, not merely the Apocrypha, but also the more recently explored apocalyptic and pseudepigraphical literature. . . .
- "His prose was more direct, more suited to strictly historical narrative and more resistant of the temptation to indulge in heavy moralizing or devotional reflections.
- "Like most others who followed Farrar, he occasionally fell to supplying motives and seemed at times to know his characters too well. . . .
- "An extremely successful book, it enjoyed new editions and impressive sales well into the first decade of the twentieth century, achieving a circulation second only, it would seem, to Farrar's Life" (Pals, pp. 94–97). Republished by Gardners Books Ltd. in 2007
- Includes a list of authorities.

Sample: Roman citizens were still exempted, by various laws, from this agonizing and painful punishment, which was employed sometimes to elicit confessions, sometimes as a substitute for execution, and, at others, as the first step in capital sentences. It was in full use in the provinces, and lawless governors did not scruple to enforce it even on Roman citizens, in spite of its acknowledged illegality. Jesus was now seized by some of the soldiers standing, near, and after being stripped to the waist, was bound in a stooping posture, His hands behind His back, to a post, or block, near the tribunal. He was then beaten at the pleasure of the soldiers, with knots of rope, or plaited leather thongs, armed at the ends with acorn-shaped drops of lead, or small, sharp-pointed bones. —Geikie, *The Life and Words of Christ*, p. 547 || *DA* 735.4.

On the Web at <http://books.google.com/books?id=NFmYDrVFODIC>.

James Stalker. *Life of Jesus Christ* (1879)

- Smaller than Farrar and Geikie—only 154 pages long—it often differs from Ellen White's recounting of the story
- "It was designed chiefly for instructional purposes in Sunday school classes, yet it attracted an audience well beyond the church classroom.
- "Stalker's purpose was not to present a piece of definitive scholarship, but to offer a sort of introductory sketch—a clear historical outline of Jesus' life and character as well as of the course of his ministry.

- "Under this limitation he naturally was forced to dispense with the luxuriant descriptive passages and historical digressions that found a place in long works. . . . This simple retelling of the life of Christ with an accent on the basic beliefs of orthodox theology won and held a large readership" (Pals, pp. 98, 99).
- Stalker's book has been reprinted by Jernigan Press, Atlanta, Georgia, 1984.

Sample: There was nothing a Roman governor dreaded so much as a complaint against him sent by his subjects to the emperor. At this time it was specially perilous; for the imperial throne was occupied by a morbid and suspicious tyrant, who delighted in disgracing his own servants, and would kindle in a moment at the whisper of any of his subordinates favoring a pretender to royal power. Pilate knew too well that his administration could not bear inspection, for it had been cruel and corrupt in the extreme. Nothing is able so peremptorily to forbid a man to do the good he would do as the evil of his past life. This was the blast of temptation which finally swept Pilate off his feet, just when he had made up his mind to obey his conscience. He was no hero, who would obey his convictions at any cost. He was a thorough man of the world, and saw at once that he must surrender Jesus to their will. —Stalker, *Life of Jesus Christ*, pp. 140, 141 ‖ *DA* 737.4.

On the Web at <http://books.google.com/books?id=ztoOAAAAIAAJ&dq>.

Alfred Edersheim. *Life and Times of Jesus the Messiah* (1886)

- "Written by a converted Jewish emigré . . . the two-volume *Life and Times* was a monument to Edersheim's industry, patience, intimate knowledge of the ancient Jewish world, and deep preoccupation with the life of Christ. . . .
- "Although Edersheim insisted that his notes had been pared to a minimum, his book was crowded at every turn with quotations from the Talmud and explanations of minute features of Jewish life. There were passages on eating habits and crops, on exports and commerce, on clothing and domestic life, on the Jewish religious sects and their history, teaching, and practice, on the Essenes and the apocalyptic writers, on Jewish magic, medicaments, and angelology, on Hillel and Shammai and their schools, on Philo and the Hellenistic Jews, Persia and the Babylonian Jews, Herod and the Roman occupation, the Midrash, Haggadah, and Halakah, on temple rites and legal practice, the synagogue, the Sanhedrin, and all the previous and subsequent misfortunes of ancient Judaism" (Pals, pp. 104, 105).
- Includes a list of authorities
- Two volumes in one was released in an updated edition by Hendrickson in 1992.

A sample of *Edersheim*'s writing is found in Chapter 7.
Available on the Web at <http://books.google.com/books?id=hKMHAAAAQAAJ>.

Samuel Andrews. *Life of Our Lord Upon Earth* (1891/1862)

- "Another work which won approval from critics was Samuel Andrews'. This was an unpretentious study, which did not claim to be a definitive Life of Christ.
- "As a kind of gospel handbook, halfway between a Life and a harmony, it supplied summaries of recent scholarship on the gospels and, revealingly, a good deal of ancient Jewish history and geography—the stuff of historical romance—which testifies to the growing interest in such things manifested by readers" (Pals, p. 61).
- Includes a list of authorities
- *Life of Our Lord* was last reprinted by Zondervan in 1954.

Sample: At this moment, about to give sentence, Pilate could not give up the poor satisfaction of mocking the Jews in what he knew well to be a tender point—their Messianic hopes. He cries out, "Behold your king." His contemptuous words only bring back the fierce response, "Away with Him; crucify Him." Still more bitterly he repeats, "Shall I crucify your king?" The answer of the chief priests, for the people are not said to have joined in it, "We have no king but Cæsar," was an open renunciation of their allegiance to Jehovah, and of the covenant which He had made with the house of David, (2 Sam. vii. 12.) Thus had the Jews been led, step by step, not only to reject their Messiah, to prefer a robber and murderer before Him, to insist mercilessly that He should be put to a most shameful death, but even to accept and openly proclaim the Roman emperor as their king. This was the culminating point of national apostasy. —Andrews, *Life of Our Lord*, p. 541 ‖ *DA* 737.6, 738.5.

1891 edition on the Web at <http://books.google.com/books?id=g8YOAAAAIAAJ>.

Ellen G. White. *The Desire of Ages* (1898)

- "With the aid of her literary assistants, she built out of the common quarry of stone not a replica of another's work but rather a customized literary composition that reflects the particular faith and Christian hope that she was called to share . . ."[4]

- ". . . a distinct character of Ellen White's work on the life of Christ is in the stress given to . . . 'spiritual realities.' [p. 929] . . . Ellen White writes as if she is dealing with realities, whether on earth or beyond the world we see. The reader is not left to imagine anything except what it would have been like to have been in Palestine in the time of Jesus and to have faced the realities she is describing. [p. 930] [She] stayed with the main storyline and with the essential elements of the background and characterizations. The reader of the DA is hardly ever conscious of the text itself or impressed with the literary skill of the author. One is caught up with the narrative and its meaning and appeal. This cannot always be said of the sources she used . . . The fingerprint of Ellen White may be found in the devotional, moral, or Christian appeals or lessons which may be expected anywhere in the chapter, but are often placed at the end. [p. 931]. . . . We should not forget that Ellen White's *main objective* for revising her earlier work on the life of Christ was to prepare a work to be sold by colporteurs in the interest of *bringing people to Jesus Christ*."[5]

  > "The reader. . . is caught up with the narrative and its meaning and appeal."
  >
  > Dr. Fred Veltman

- "... it is the purpose of this book so to present the blessed Redeemer as to help the reader to come to Him face to face, heart to heart, and find in Him, even as did the disciples of old, Jesus the Mighty One, who saves 'to the uttermost,' and transforms to His own divine image all those who come unto God by Him. Yet how impossible it is to reveal His life! It is like attempting to put upon canvas the living rainbow; into characters of black and white the sweetest music" (Publishers, "Preface," *The Desire of Ages*, p. 14).

1898 edition on the Web at <http://books.google.com/books?id=ntsOAAAAIAAJ>.

---

[4] Dr. Fred Veltman, *Ministry*, December 1990, p. 15.

[5] Dr. Fred Veltman's comments in the "Full Report of the Life of Christ Research Project," pp. 928–931, emphasis supplied. In a list of future writing projects, Ellen White wrote: "We are now deciding to spend this winter and next summer in preparing books. First, I get articles prepared for *Signs*. 2. I get out articles for private testimony, health institutions. 3. Get out testimony No. 30. 4. Letters to her children by a mother. 5. [*Spirit of Prophecy*] vol. 4 [i.e., the 1884 edition of *GC*]. 6. Life of Christ, both books. The most sharp and interesting matter in one large book for canvassers to use for public sale." —Ltr. 43, 1880 in 3*BIO* 148.8. "Since these books are sent out without explanation as to the authority by which the author speaks, it was thought best to avoid, as far as we could, statements for which the Bible seems to furnish no proof, or which to the ordinary reader appear to contradict the Bible. Better to give the reader what they will accept and profit by than to excite criticism and questioning that will lead them to discredit the whole." —Marian Davis to J. E. White, Dec. 22, 1895, in *Exhibits* #61.

APPENDIX B

A Brief Sketch of the Life of Christ Research Project (1980–1988)

When Dr. Fred Veltman launched the original Life of Christ Research Project, his objective was not to prove or disprove the charges of plagiarism per se, but to analyze how much use Ellen White made of source works in the production of *The Desire of Ages*. In setting up the project, Dr. Veltman faced a monumental task. How was he to obtain the probable source works that were no longer all in one place? Of the 1200 works in the private and office libraries of Ellen White at the time of her death, perhaps 75 of them relate to the four Gospels in some way. Approximately 50 more were devotional, inspirational books (including sermons) that could contain material relating to certain portions of *The Desire of Ages*. To perform a thorough evaluation of possible sources, Dr. Veltman would need to obtain as many of these as possible—first at the White Estate Office and then at libraries across the country. The search was on!

> How exhaustive was the scope of the investigation?

Obtaining 40 works of the most familiar authors—which included William Hanna, Daniel March, John Harris, George Jones, Alfred Edersheim, Frederic W. Farrar, Robert Boyd, John R. Macduff, Andrew Murray, Samuel J. Andrews, and Cunningham Geikie—was only the beginning. Over the span of the next eight years, the researchers would obtain and search through more than 500 works! It was the duty of Marcella Anderson (now Marcella King), Dr. Veltman's research assistant, to peruse each volume and pick out the portions relating to *The Desire of Ages* chapters under investigation. (Those who would suggest that there were likely many more sources of parallels than those identified are simply unaware of the exhaustive nature of this investigation!)

With this kind of comprehensive study, it soon became apparent that a thorough investigation of all 87 chapters of *The Desire of Ages* would simply not be feasible under the time and financial constraints of the project. It was decided that a carefully selected representative number of chapters would work just as well in making valid generalizations about the book. Because Walter Rea had asserted that longer chapters would be found to have more borrowing than shorter ones, Dr. Veltman

Marcella Anderson

divided the book into three groups, according to length: 29 long chapters; 29 short chapters; and 29 middle-length ones. From each of these three categories, five chapters were randomly selected by two professors of the Pacific Union College Mathematics Department, Dr. Richard Rockwell and Dr. A. Keith Anderson. Chapters 3, 13, 46, 56, and 83 were selected from the short chapters; Chapters 10, 14, 37, 72, and 75 from the long chapters; and Chapters 24, 39, 53, 76, and 84 from the middle-length chapters. Since Walter Rea had also asserted that the earlier "life of Christ" treatises by Ellen White had a smaller percentage of borrowing than *The Desire of Ages*, Dr. Veltman decided to perform the research necessary to settle this issue as well. (Both of Dr. Rea's assertions were proved false.)

To further conserve resources, Dr. Veltman recruited volunteer readers. Each volunteer was assigned one or two chapters of *The Desire of Ages*, plus Chapter 75, which was the control chapter that insured consistent application of method. In addition to their assigned *DA* chapters, each volunteer was to read the portions of the possible source works relating to those chapters. Reports from their reading were compiled under each respective *Desire of Ages* chapter, whether or not source parallels had been found. The readers' goal was to find as many literary parallels as possible between the source works and the *Desire of Ages* chapters. If any book did not yield parallels to *The Desire of Ages*, it could be ruled out as a source work.

As we discussed in Chapter 1 of this book, Ellen White made use of literary helpers in producing her books and articles for church journals. *The Desire of Ages* was a revision of the life of Christ accounts in *Spirit of Prophecy*, vols. 2 and 3, published in the 1870s, with additional materials written by Mrs. White. In order to find materials of Mrs. White that had been used in *The Desire of Ages*, Dr. Veltman and Marcella King combed through Ellen White's periodical articles, her books published before 1898 (*The Desire of Ages* having been published late that year), her personal diaries and letters, her handwritten manuscripts and transcripts, and her later manuscripts on the life of Christ. However, they did not make use of the *Spiritual Gifts* (vol. 1 and 4a) life of Christ material. Dr. Veltman was granted free access to the E. G. White files at the White Estate. From these files he brought back reams of unpublished materials. Marcella Anderson reviewed these manuscripts and catalogued them according to the chapters of *The Desire of Ages*, retyping the most pertinent portions that had to do with Ellen White's writings on the life of Christ, her use of literary helpers and writing methods, and the issues of inspiration and revelation. If the work of Ellen White were to be isolated from that of her editors, it would be necessary to have her handwritten supporting manuscripts. Though only Chapters 14, 24, and 75 of *The Desire of Ages* had any handwritten documentary support, the chapters in *Spirit of Prophecy*, vols. 2 and 3, upon which Chapters 3, 10, 13, and 14 of *The Desire of Ages* were built, all had corresponding handwritten manuscripts. These supportive manuscripts, which related to the fifteen research chapters, were not sent out to the volunteer readers, but were examined for source parallels by Dr. Veltman, Dr. J. Paul Stauffer (part-time researcher), and Marcella Anderson.

Evaluation of sources and source parallels

In order to assign a relative numeric value to the level of literary dependency of each chapter, Dr. Veltman determined that sentences (and not words) would be the basic unit of evaluation. Each sentence would be assigned a number according to its relative level of dependency from zero to seven—(**0**) for *strict independent* and *Bible quotations*, (**1**) for *partial independent*, (**2**) for *Bible used same as in source*, (**3**) for *loose paraphrase*, (**4**) for *simple paraphrase* (the largest category), (**5**) for *strict paraphrase*, (**6**) for *not so strict verbatim* (the smallest category), and (**7**) for *strict verbatim*. With each sentence being assigned a number, an average level of literary dependency could be calculated and the literary dependency of the rest of the book could be reliably projected.

Dr. Veltman arbitrarily designated each work that was demonstrated to have parallel material to *The Desire of Ages* as either a major or minor source. "Major" meant that a work had more than ten sentences that paralleled material in a given *Desire of Ages* chapter; "minor" meant it had less than ten. Based on these criteria, there were ten major source works that Ellen White likely consulted for the 15 chapters of *The Desire of Ages* covered in the research project, a major source work tending to dominate in each of the chapters. The major sources are, in order of descending use in the chapters: *The Life of Christ* by William Hanna; *Night Scenes in the Bible* by Daniel March; *The Great Teacher* by John Harris; *The Life of Christ* by Frederic Farrar; *Walks and Homes of Jesus* by Daniel March; *Life-Scenes from the Four Gospels* by George Jones; *The Life and Times of Jesus the Messiah* by Alfred Edersheim; *The Prince of the House of David* by J. H. Ingraham; *Salvation by Christ* by Francis Wayland; and *Sabbath Evening Readings on the New Testament, St. John* by John Cumming.

Because color coding was not available for the Life of Christ Research Project report (verbatim and near verbatim words were boldfaced and similar wording was underlined), the following color-coded exhibit of dependent sentences has been provided to help the reader better visualize the differences between designations. It should be noted that none of the 2624 sentences in the 15 random chapters covered in the Life of Christ Research Project were rated as **V1** "strict verbatims" and that six of the 15 chapters—10, 13, 53, 56, 72, and 76—did not have any **V2** "verbatims" with "slight modification of word forms, incidental word substitutions or punctuation changes." This looser definition of "verbatim" sometimes included sentences that stretch the limits of the term "verbatim," and leave one wondering how quotation marks could have been used.

How many "verbatims" were located in *The Desire of Ages*?

EXHIBIT A. MODIFIED VERBATIM—**V2**, rated **6** for literary dependency—*29* sentences in *LCRP*	
Chapter 3 (One **V2** out of 130 sentence units)	
DA 34.4: "The fullness of the time had come."	John Harris, *The Great Teacher*, p. 49: "When, in the fulness of time, the eternal Son came forth from the bosom of the Father, he descended to a region of spiritual darkness."
Perhaps this should have been identified as a **B2**, since the quotation follows Gal. 4:4 more closely than Harris: "But when the fulness of the time was come . . ."	
Chapter 14 (Five **V2**s out of 250 sentence units)	
DA 138.4: "Again the face of the prophet was lighted up with glory from the Unseen, as he cried, 'Behold the Lamb of God!'"	George Jones, *Life-Scenes from the Four Gospels*, p. 96: "On the following day, while two of John's disciples were standing near by, Jesus came, in sight, and the Baptist's face again took the glow of inspiration, as he cried: 'Behold the Lamb of God!'"
This "verbatim" is more of a strict paraphrase of the original, with the words of John taken from John 1:29, "The next day John seeth Jesus coming unto him, and saith, Behold the Lamb of God, which taketh away the sin of the world."	
DA 138.4: "The words thrilled the hearts of the disciples."	Jones, *LSFG* 96: "The two disciples, how they were thrilled by the words!"
Here Ellen White adapts Jones's expanded paraphrase of John 1:37: "And the two disciples heard him speak, and they followed Jesus," possibly conflating the word "heart" from a similar description in Luke 24:32: ". . . Did not our heart burn within us, while he talked with us by the way, and while he opened to us the scriptures?"	
DA 140.3: "Philip entered into no controversy." *Four verbatim words from two sentences of more than 36 words.*	Henry Melvill, *The Golden Lectures*, p. 81: "The reply of Philip is every way observable. He entered on no controversy, he attempted no discussion; he felt that the means which had been effectual with himself were most likely to be effectual with Nathanael; . . ."
DA 142.4: "If you believe on Me as such, your faith shall be quickened." *Eight verbatim words out of 99 in the source.*	William Hanna, *Life of Christ*, p. 108a: "Believe what that sign was meant to confirm; believe in me as the lamb of God, the Saviour of the world, the baptizer with the Holy Ghost, and your eye of faith shall be quickened . . ."
DA 142.4: "I have opened them to you." *Two more verbatim words out of the same 99-word sentence in the source.*	Hanna, *LC* 108b: ". . . and you shall see those heavens standing continually open above my head—opened by me for you . . ."

Chapter 24 (One **V2** out of 153 sentence units)	
DA 240.1: "They hurried him to the brow of a precipice, intending to cast him down headlong."	Daniel March, *Walks and Homes of Jesus*, p. 61: ". . . they hurry him forth to the brow of a precipice, near by the synagogue, that they may cast him down headlong."

Ellen White adapts March's paraphrase of Luke 4:29, "And rose up, and thrust him out of the city, and led him unto the brow of the hill whereon their city was built, that they might cast him down headlong." Hanna, p. 171, also has "to the brow of a precipice" and "hurrying him to the brow of the hill."

Chapter 37 (Five **V2**s out of 217 sentence units)	
DA 350.3: "Where He had passed, the objects of His compassion were rejoicing in health, and «making trial of their new-found powers»." *Eleven verbatim words out of 53.*	Harris, *TGT* 343: "Where he had passed, the restored might be seen, making trial of their new-found powers; listeners, formed into groups to hear the tale of healing; and the delighted objects of his compassion, rehearsing, with earnestness, what had passed, imitating his tones, and even trying to convey an idea of his condescending ways."
DA 350.3: "«His voice was the first sound» that many had ever heard, «His name the first word they had» ever spoken, His face the first they ever looked upon."	Harris, *TGT* 343: "His voice was the first sound which many of them heard; his name the first word they had pronounced, his blessed form the first sight they had ever beheld." *Ten verbatim words out of 52.*
DA 350.3: "As He passed through the towns and cities He was like a vital current, diffusing life and joy wherever He went."	Harris, *TGT* 343: "He went through the land like a current of vital air, an element of life, diffusing health and joy wherever he appeared."
DA 352.2: "And «more than angels are in» the ranks." *Six verbatim words out of 59.*	Harris, *TGT* xliv: ". . . he reminds them that they struggle for an invisible world, that they fight in the fellowship . . . with all the children of light, that more than angels are in their ranks."
DA 353.1: "Every soul was precious in His eyes." *In context:* "Christ Himself did not suppress one word of truth, but He spoke it always in love. He exercised the greatest tact, and thoughtful, kind attention in His intercourse with the people. He was never rude, never needlessly spoke a severe word, «never gave needless pain to a sensitive» soul. He did not censure human weakness. . . . Every soul was precious in His eyes."	James R. Miller, *Week-Day Religion*, p. 187: "Every scrap of humanity was sacred and precious in his eyes." *In context:* "A true appreciation of the story of the teachings of the gospel will reveal the fact that our Lord himself exercised the most beautiful and thoughtful tact in all his mingling among the people. He was utterly incapable of rudeness. He never needlessly spoke a harsh word. He never gave needless pain to a sensitive heart. He was most considerate of human weakness. He was most gentle toward all human sorrow. He never suppressed the truth, but he uttered it always in love. . . . Every scrap of humanity was sacred and precious in his eyes. He bore himself always in the attitude of tenderest regard for every one."

Note the difference between "He was utterly incapable of rudeness" and "He was never rude," between "scrap of humanity" and "soul," and between "sacred and precious" and "precious." This quotation expands on the metaphoric explanation of Jesus' demeanor in Matt. 12:20, "A bruised reed shall he not break, and smoking flax shall he not quench, till he send forth judgment unto victory."

Chapter 39 (One **V2** out of 158 sentence units)	
DA 369.1: "We are not to plunge into difficulties, neglecting the means God has provided, and misusing the faculties He has given us."	±Francis Wayland, *Salvation by Christ*, p. 246: "When we plunge ourselves into difficulty, by a neglect of the means or by a misuse of the faculties which God has bestowed upon us, it is to be expected that he will leave us to our own devices."

Chapter 46 (Two **V2**s out of 89 sentence units)	
DA 419.1: "The Saviour and his disciples have spent the day in traveling and teaching, and the mountain climb adds to their weariness."	March, *WHJ* 150: "He has spent the day in travel and in teaching, and this mountain climb at night adds a heavy weight to weariness that demanded rest before the evening came."
DA 419.3: "The disciples do not venture to ask Christ «whither He is going, or for what purpose»."	March, *WHJ* 151: "They do not ask him whither he is going, or for what purpose, he leads them away to the solitude of the mountain—just as night is setting in, and they all need repose and protection in the homes which they have left behind."
Chapter 75 (Six **V2**s out of 351 sentences)	
DA 698.3: "Christ was to be tried formally before the Sanhedrin; but before Annas He was subjected to a preliminary trial." *Fifteen verbatim words out of 58.*	Hanna, *LC* 663: "It was in this hall, and before Annas, that Jesus was subjected to that preliminary informal examination recorded in the eighteenth chapter of the gospel of St. John, ver. 19–24. He was to be formally tried, with show at least of law, before the Sanhedrim, the highest of the Jewish courts; but this could not be done at once."
DA 699.2: "Their own rules declared that every man should be treated as innocent until proved guilty." *Twelve verbatim words out of 56.*	Frederic Farrar, *Life of Christ*, p. 615: "But He would not repeat it, in spite of their insistence, because He knew that it was open to their wilful misinterpretation, and because they were acting in flagrant violation of their own express rules and traditions, which demanded, that every arraigned criminal should be regarded and treated as innocent until his guilt was actually proved."
DA 700.3: "And He «suffered in proportion to the perfection of His holiness» and His hatred for sin." *Twelve verbatim words out of 100.*	Harris, *TGT* 340: "... 'he *suffered*, being tempted,'— suffered in proportion to the perfection of his holiness, and the depth of his aversion to sin; but though his residence in an atmosphere of sin was revolting to his purity, though the presence of depravity made his continuance here a perpetual sacrifice, his love induced him to submit ..."
DA 704.0: "Of all the throng He alone was calm and serene."	±J. H. Ingraham, *The Prince of the House of David*, p. 349 (listed as being on p. 360 in the *LCRP* because of the edition used): "He alone, of all that countless host, he alone was calm—serene—fearless!"
DA 706.1: "Caiaphas was desperate." *Two verbatim words out of 44.*	John Kitto, *Daily Bible Illustrations*, p. 408: "On this Caiaphas became desperate, and adopted a resource which our own rules of evidence would declare most infamous, and which was also wholly adverse to the first principles of Mosaic jurisprudence and the like of which occurs in no circumstance of Hebrew history."
DA 706.4: "There was a time to be silent, and a time to speak."	Joseph Hall, *Scripture History; or Contemplations on the Historical Passages of the Old and New Testaments*, p. 575: "There is a time to speak, and a time to keep silence."
Both are paraphrases of Ecclesiastes 3:7, second part. Perhaps the *LCRP* should have set up a separate category for Biblical paraphrase.	

Chapter 83 (Four **V2**s out of 116 sentence units)

DA 800.2: "During the journey the sun had gone down, and before the travelers reached their place of rest, the laborers in the fields had left their work."	Daniel March, *Night Scenes*, p. 417: "The sun has gone down behind the gray hill-tops, and the shadows of evening have begun to deepen in the narrow valleys, and the laborers have left the terraced orchards and vineyards on the hill-sides before the two travelers reach their home . . ."
DA 800.3: "Christ never forces His company upon anyone."	March, *NS* 418: "He never forces himself upon any."
DA 800.4: "Now He puts forth His hands to bless the food."	March, *NS* 418, 419: "When bread, the simple fare of the poor, was set before them, he put forth his hands to bless it."
That this occurred as He blessed the food is found in Luke 24:30.	
DA 800.4: "The disciples start back in astonishment."	March, *NS* 419: "But what now so suddenly startles the wondering disciples?"
More of a simple paraphrase than a verbatim.	

Chapter 84 (Four **V2**s out of 138 sentence units)

DA 802.2: "Every eye is fastened upon the Stranger."	March, *NS* 422: "Every eye is fixed upon the stranger."
DA 802.2: "No footstep has been heard."	March, *NS* 422: "No sound of entering footsteps has been heard."
DA 805.2: "The Holy Spirit was not yet fully manifested; for Christ had not yet been glorified."	Hanna, *LC* 806, "The Holy Ghost was not yet in his fulness given, because that Jesus was not yet glorified."
A strict paraphrase of Hanna's loose quoting of John 7:39: "But this spake he of the Spirit, which they that believe on him should receive: for the Holy Ghost was not yet given; because that Jesus was not yet glorified."	
DA 807.3: "The doubting disciple knew that none of his companions had seen Jesus for a week."	Hanna, *LC* 817: "Thomas knew that for seven days none of the disciples had seen the Lord."
More of a strict paraphrase than a verbatim, based on details presented in John 20:24, 26.	

For all other categories, only the first instance will be listed.

EXHIBIT B.	**STRICT PARAPHRASE—P1**, rated **5** for literary dependency—*183* sentences

DA 104.3: "In his manner and dress he resembled the prophet Elijah." *The phrase "singular appearance" of Jones was used in the previous sentence in DA.*	Jones, *LSFG* 3: ". . . a large gathering of excited people around a man of singular appearance, who was making a most wonderful announcement, and was engaging in a baptismal rite of startling significance. He was a gaunt ascetic; in his dress and manner, and in his authoritative language, reminding all who saw and heard him of the old prophet; and indeed, in his appearance so much resembling Elijah, that the query was immediately started in every man's mind, whether he was not actually that prophet risen from the dead."
Like "modified verbatims," "strict paraphrases" can also be the extraction of a phrase or two from a much longer sentence. In this case, Jones's speculation makes no sense. These people weren't living when Elijah walked the earth!	

COLOR CODING: Scripture verbatim «5 consecutive» paraphrase

EXHIBIT C.	SIMPLE PARAPHRASE—P2, rated **4** for literary dependency—*256* sentences
DA 32.2: "One language was widely spoken, and was everywhere recognized as the language of literature."	±E. W. Thayer, *Sketches from the Life of Jesus, Historical and Doctrinal*, p. 21, par. 3: "When we further consider that there was, as it were, one universal language, superseding by its copiousness and fulness all others, —the language of literature, of cultivation, of the arts, and of trade and commerce,—we easily—see that the whole world had almost become one family; . . ."

In this example it is the uniqueness of the phrase "the language of literature" that suggests literary dependency. The differences between strict and simple paraphrases are that the simple paraphrase does not follow the same order and that the simple paraphrase often adds an original thought.

EXHIBIT D.	LOOSE PARAPHRASE—P3, rated **3** for literary dependency—*93* sentences
DA 32.2: "The nations were united under one government."	±Thayer, *SLJ* 21.2: "While the dominion of Rome so oppressed the nations; it yet unified the world, and harmonized it into the semblance of one family."

Though Ellen White may express the same general idea as Thayer, without the previously identified verbatim phrase, "language of literature," it would be difficult to certify that she derived her wording from Thayer.

EXHIBIT E.	SOURCE BIBLE—B1, rated **2** for literary dependency—*84* sentences
DA 32.4: "In 'the region and shadow of death,' men sat unsolaced [Matt. 4:16]."	Harris, *TGT* 51: ". . . what must have been the wishes and aspirations of those who, with a keen perception of their exigence [i.e., urgency], were sitting in darkness and the shadow of death?"

One might question the uniqueness of quoting Matthew 4:16 in a chapter describing the condition of the people at the coming of Christ. Other **B1**s were more striking than this.

EXHIBIT F.	PARTIAL INDEPENDENT—I2, rated **1** for literary dependency—*178* sentences
DA 31.2: "From the days of Enoch the promise was repeated through patriarchs and prophets, keeping alive the hope of appearing, and yet He came not."	William Kennedy, *Messianic Prophecy, and the Life of Christ*, p. 174: "We remember the Patriarch's remark, that 'Judah's sceptre should not depart till Shiloh come;' we remember the promise of an eternal dominion to the family of David: and still more vividly shines, the vision of Daniel."

Only one significant verbatim word—"promise." Ellen White refers to Enoch, while Kennedy refers to the prophecy of Gen. 49:10. (Later sentences in both *DA* and Kennedy do mention Daniel's prophecy.)

To these *178* partial independent sentences, we can add *1612* "strictly independent" sentences and 189 Bible quotations for a total of *1979* sentences showing virtual independence from the sources— 75% of the total *2624* sentence units. There were examples of greater similarity when it came to pre-*DA* materials, as the following comparison illustrates for the reader. (Though the parallels with 1*RL* certify Fleetwood as a source for *DA*, none of its parallels were included in the *DA* text.)

COLOR CODING: Scripture verbatim «5 consecutive» paraphrase

EXHIBIT G. **PRE-*DA* PARALLELS**—*Redemption Leaflets*, no. 1, and Fleetwood's *Life of Christ*	
1*RL* 4/48.[1] *Satan reasoned with Christ* thus: If the words spoken after his baptism were indeed the words of God, that he was the Son of God, he need not bear the sensations of hunger; he could give him proofs of his divinity by showing his power in changing the stones of that barren wilderness into bread: "If thou be the Son of God, command that these stones be made bread." (**P2**—paraphrasing Matt. 4:3) [*skipping one independent sentence*]	Fleetwood,[2] *LC* 50.9+ But, at the expiration of the forty days, when the blessed Jesus had endured the keenest hunger, the tempter, to make proof of the divinity of his mission, insolently demanded why he bore the sensations of hunger, since, if he was the Son of God, he must have power to change the stones of that dreary wilderness into bread.
1*RL* 6/48. *Christ meets Scripture with Scripture,* by citing the words of Moses, "Man shall not live by bread alone; but by every word that proceedeth out of the mouth of God." (**B1**) [*skipping two independent sentences*]	Fleetwood, *LC* 51.3 But our blessed Saviour repelled his device, by citing the words of Moses, which implied, that God, whenever it seemed good in his sight, could, by extraordinary means, provide for the support of the human race. "Man shall not live by bread alone, but by every word of God."
1*RL* 9/48. Being defeated here, Satan tries another device. (**P1**—implied by Matt. 4:5) [*skipping three independent sentences*]	Fleetwood, *LC* 51.5 Satan, being defeated in his effort, took him to the top of a very high mountain, and, thinking to work on him by another artifice ...
1*RL* 13/49. Satan, by an insulting taunt, urged Christ to prove his mission by casting himself down from the high eminence whereon he had placed him, *declaring that God had promised that angels should bear him up.* (**P2**—an expanded paraphrase of Matt. 4:6 and Luke 4:9) [*skipping 14 independent sentences about presumption*]	Fleetwood, *LC* 52.2 ... by a taunt of insolence, urged him to prove the truth of his mission by casting himself down from thence, citing, as an encouragement for him to comply with his desire a text from the Psalms:
1*RL* 28/50. This presumptuous blasphemy, and insult to Jehovah, excited the indignation of Christ, and led him to exercise his divine authority, and command Satan in an authoritative, dignified manner to desist. (**P1**)	Fleetwood, *LC* 51.9 This blasphemy, as well as insolence, incited the blessed Jesus to exert his divine authority and command him, in a peremptory manner, to desist.

Summary of literarily dependent sentences

From an evaluation of the various parallels found in pre–*DA* materials and in the *DA* text itself, based on the criteria and methods described above, Dr. Veltman gave the following summary:

> For those looking for some percentage of dependency I think it is safe to say that about 31 percent of the DA text measured some degree of literary dependency and about 61 percent registered independence. The rest represents the use of Scripture.[3]

> The rate of dependency ... averages out at 3.33 or at the level of Loose Paraphrase when viewing the degree of dependency for dependent sentences.... When looking at the average dependency rate for an entire chapter, including the independent sentences, the rate drops to 1.12 or about the level of Partial Independence.[4]

---

[1] *LCRP* 147. In *LCRP* notation, the numbers before the "/"are *sentence* numbers in a work, and after it are *page* numbers.

[2] Hanna was used in a similar way in 2*RL*. Recall W. C. White's statement about her "reading of Hanna ... or Fleetwood" to jog her memory and enable her to write "more in detail" (as witnessed by italicized phrases) than her source (3*SM* 460.2).

[3] Fred Veltman, *LCRP* 941.

[4] *LCRP* 882, 883. The rating of "loose paraphrase" means one word or more of parallel, though not necessarily verbatim.

In other words, "there are twice as many independent sentences as there are dependent sentences"[5] and most of the sentences designated as having verbal similarity followed their "sources" loosely with some additional original thought. (The reader should be reminded that the 31 percent of literary dependence was based on the marking of all sentences that bore any resemblance to the "sources"—*no matter how faint*—including the **2**s of *source Bible* sentences and the **1**s of *partially independent* sentences. Many dependent sentences had only a single significant verbatim word.[6] Several of these single verbatim words were only Biblical names.[7] Other dependent sentences did not have a single word that was identical with the alleged source except for common words like "of," "the," "and," or "but."[8] Still other dependent sentences were more strikingly similar to Scripture than to the alleged sources.[9])

From the largest dependent category of sentences to the smallest, there is evidence of originality of expression and thought on Mrs. White's part. As Dr. Veltman has stated: "There is no question that she used sources but she was selective. She evidently was governed by her own purposes and priorities. The sources were her slaves, never her masters"[10] We might also add that those "purposes and priorities" were under the Holy Spirit's direction.

Source work summary for the *LCRP*

For the 15 selected chapters from *The Desire of Ages* in the Life of Christ Research Project, the volunteer readers found ten different major source works from nine authors and 23 minor source works from 20 authors. *Two* of the ten major source works and *eight* of the 23 minor source works do not appear in the list of books in Ellen White's libraries. However, the two unlisted major source authors and four of the unlisted minor source authors have other works that do appear, slightly increasing the likelihood of their actually being sources.

In reviewing the chapters outside the 15, the volunteer readers ended up—unofficially— covering every chapter in the book. In the course of their reading, they located many parallels to the remaining 72 chapters. These parallels were not included in the Life of Christ Research Project report because, without sufficient time to consistently treat the chapters in which they were found, the inclusion of isolated parallels would have distorted the analysis and conclusions of the project.

For those who would like to pursue further research in *DA* chapters outside the 15 of the Life of Christ Research Project, we recommend several source works and *DA* chapters as possessing recognizable parallels. These include John R. Macduff, *Memories of Olivet* for *DA* Chapters 49, 64, 74, and 87; Hugh Macmillan, *Our Lord's Three Raisings from the Dead* for *DA* Chapter 58; George F. Pentecost, ±*The Birth and Boyhood of Jesus* for *DA* Chapter 8; Phillip Bennett Power, *The "I Wills" of Christ* for *DA* Chapter 27; and James A. Wylie, *Scenes from the Bible* for *DA* Chapters 57 and 74. (Chapters with located parallels outside those in the *LCRP* are noted in the APPENDIX C.)

---

[5] *LCRP* 883.

[6] Some examples are *LCRP* 10 (DA34/32 "darkness," rated **I2**), 11 (DA36/33 "inspiration," rated **P3**; DA40/33 "expectations"/ "expected," rated **I2**), 12 (DA44/33 "bigotry," rated **P3**; DA46/33 "Interpreter" rated **P3**; DA47/34 "types," rated **I2**), 23 (DA99/36 "beheld," rated **P3**), 25 (DA107/36 "demon(s)" rated **P3**), 72 (DA8/97 "presence," rated **P3**), 74 (DA21/98 "forgets"/"forgot," rated **P3**), 79 (DA61/100 "surrounding," rated **I2**), 83 (DA97/102 "ascetic," rated **P2**; DA99/102 "retreat," rated **P3**).

[7] Examples: *LCRP* 6 (DA8/31 "Daniel," rated **I2**), 74 (DA19/98 "Zacharias," rated **I2**), and 86 (DA121/103 "Isaiah," rated **I2**).

[8] Examples: *LCRP* 9 (DA29/32, rated **I2**), 25 (DA109/36, rated **P3**), 30 (DA124/37, rated **P3**), 72 (DA10/97, rated **I2**), 74 (DA20/98, rated **I2**), and 83 (DA98/102, rated **P3**). We would like to express our appreciation to David J. Conklin for locating the above examples in the *LCRP*.

[9] Examples: *LCRP* 12 (DA50/34 Mal. 3:1, not a **P3**) and 14 (DA65/34 Gal. 4:4, not a **V2**).

[10] Veltman, p. 933.

APPENDIX C
Bibliography of Source Works

The possible sources of literary parallels are listed in this bibliography, followed in curly brackets by their SOURCE RATING for *The Desire of Ages* and their EGW LIBRARY designation. The SOURCE RATING is divided in three: the *first* (e.g. {X/s^{37}/-/Lib=O}) for *DA*, Chaps. 1, 2, 77, and 78; the *second* (e.g. {X/s^{37}/-/Lib=O}) for the 15 chapters of the *LCRP*; and the *third* (e.g. {X/s^{37}/-/Lib=O}) for all other chapters found to contain parallels.[1] Superscript numbers designate the *DA* chapter in which parallels were found (e.g. {X/s^{37}/-/Lib=O}). If boldfaced (e.g. s^{75}), the chapter contains seven or more parallels; if italicized (e.g. s^{37}), it contains at least one clearly recognizable parallel.[2] Page location(s) for this book follow the entry in brackets (e.g. [127]). Counting those with a fairly high degree of certainty, Ellen White used about 50 of these as at least a minor source of wording.

SOURCE RATING codes:

S   Major <u>S</u>ource for *The Desire of Ages* text (with listing of more than ten identified literary parallels)

s   Minor literary <u>s</u>ource for one or more of these same chapters (with listing of ten or less identified literary parallels)

Q   <u>Q</u>uestionable source with only a hint of allusion or a duplicate of other sources; additional evidence required (see below)

X   Ruled out as a contributor to the particular chapters under evaluation

PRE   A source for a <u>pre</u>-*DA* composition that was used in the *DA* text.

EGW LIBRARY codes as evidence of availability to Ellen White:

±   Less likely as a source work because it is not listed in the Ellen G. White library inventory

P   From inventory of EGW <u>P</u>rivate library (listed as "A" in Inventory of EGW Private and Office Libraries)

O   From inventory of EGW <u>O</u>ffice library (listed as "B" in Inventory of EGW Private and Office Libraries)

C   Listed in C. C. <u>C</u>risler's collection, purchased by Ellen White from Crisler just two years before her death

H   Contains Ellen White's <u>h</u>andwritten signature

U   <u>U</u>ninventoried works that Ellen White likely used because of the *recognizability* of parallels

R   <u>R</u>eferenced in connection with the preparation of Ellen White's compositions in at least one of the following ways:

  · mentioned by Ellen White or Marian Davis (like Conybeare and Howson, D'Aubigne, and Geikie)
  · requested by Ellen White (like March's *WHJ* and *NS*, Melvill, Barnes, and Cumming)
  · recalled by W. C. White as a source (like Hanna, Farrar, Fleetwood, Geikie, Lightfoot, and Andrews)
  · cited in an Ellen G. White publication (like Coles' *Philosophy of Health* in *How to Live*)

D   <u>D</u>ifferent work from the same author in EGW libraries, suggesting she could have had access to the work

ADDITIONAL CRITERIA for certifying Ellen White's use of a particular work:

· Is the parallel in the chapter (or underlying pre-*DA* composition) clearly *recognizable* and *significant*?

· If not, does the chapter (or underlying pre-*DA* composition) have a *pattern of verbatim words* from a source?

· Is the parallel *unique to a single source* or is it common to many sources?

· Was the parallel phrasing predated by similar phrasing in an EGW composition printed before the supposed source?

· Do markings in the source work correspond to the literary parallel (as with the bookmark stain in Underwood for *Steps to Christ* and the lines in the margins of MacDuff's *Memories of Olivet* for the *GC*)?

· If questionable, was the literary source *listed in one of Ellen White's libraries*, and is there evidence that it was acquired by Mrs. White before the time of writing?

· Or were there *recognizable parallels* from the same source *in other chapters or compositions*?

· Were parallel verbatim words *taken from Scripture* or *are they a paraphrase of Scripture*?

---

[1] Parallels outside the chapter exhibits of this book and the LCRP were compiled from the findings of Marcella Anderson King and the volunteer readers of the *LCRP*, Walter Rea's *The White Lie*, Tim Poirier's "Project Surprise," David J. Conklin, and Kevin L. Morgan.

[2] Most of the parallels in the source works—whether *major*, *minor*, *questionable*—would require no quotation marks or footnotes since they are either predated by Ellen White's own earlier similar phrasing, fail the five or more consecutive verbatim word test (this includes many *highly recognizable* parallels), or are so self-evident or unremarkable that footnoting would be superfluous. Our thanks to David J. Conklin for his exhibits at <http://dedication.www3.50megs.com/David/index.html> which helped in identifying the more recognizable parallels in the *LCRP* report.

Abbott, John S. C. *The History of Christianity: Consisting of the Life and Teachings of Jesus of Nazareth; the Adventures of Paul and the Apostles; and the Most Interesting Events in the Progress of Christianity, from the Earliest Period to the Present Time* (Boston: B. B. Russell, 1872), 504 pp. {Q^{77} ^{78}/X/-/Lib=O} [65, 96, 99, 105]

Abbott, Lyman. *A Life of Christ Founded on the Four Gospels and Illustrated by Reference to the Manners, Customs, Religious Beliefs, and Political Institutions of His Times* (New York: Harper & Brothers, Franklin Square, 1882), 534 pp. {X/X/-/Lib±}

――――. *Jesus of Nazareth: His Life and Teachings; Founded on the Four Gospels and Illustrated by Reference to the Manners, Customs, Religious Beliefs, and Political Institutions of His Times* (New York: Harper and Bros., 1869), 522 pp. {Q/X/-/Lib±}

Adams, Charles C. *Life of our Lord Jesus* (New York: No. 11 Bible House. Charles F. Roper, 1878), 407 pp. {Q^{77} ^{78}/X/-/Lib±D}

Adams, Nehemiah. *Christ a Friend: Thirteen Discourses* (Boston: John P. Jewett & Co., 1856), 290 pp. {X/X/-/Lib±}

Anderson, John L. *The Messiah: A Narrative of the Life and Death, Resurrection and Ascension of our Lord; in the Chronological Order of the Four Gospels* (London: John Murray, 1864), 830 pp. {Q^{77} ^{78}/X/-/Lib±}

Andrews, Samuel J. *The Life of our Lord upon the Earth Considered in its Historical, Chronological, and Geographical Relations* (New York: Charles Scribner's Sons, 1862, 1891), 651 pp. {Q^{1} ^{77} ^{78}/s^{75}/-/Lib=O, R} [32, 39, 49, 64, 65, 82, 83, 84, 87, 89, 90, 93, 98, 103, 105, 108, 129, 171–173, 182]

Angus, Joseph. *Christ Our Life: in its Origin, Law, and End* (Philadelphia: American Baptist Publication Society, 1853), 336 pp. {Q^{77} ^{78}/X/-/Lib±} [73, 87, 97–99]

Balfern, W. P. *Glimpses of Jesus; or, Christ Exalted in the Affections of His People*, 2nd ed. (New York: Sheldon, Blakeman & Co., 1858), 259 pp. {Q^{78}/X/-/Lib±} [106]

Barnes, Albert. *The Atonement, Relations to Law and Moral Government* (Philadelphia: Parry & McMillan, successors to A. Hart, late Carey & Hart, 1859), 358 pp. {X/X/-/Lib±D}

――――. *Notes, Explanatory and Practical, on the Gospels: Designed for Sunday School Teachers and Bible Classes*, vol. I (New York: Harper & Brothers, 1860; c. 1832), 414 pp. {Q^{78}/X/-/Lib=P, R} [99, 109, 138, 182]

――――. *Notes, Explanatory and Practical, on the Gospels: Designed for Sunday School Teachers and Bible Classes* vol. II (New York: Harper & Brothers, 1854; c. 1832), 413 pp. {Q^{77} ^{78}/X/-/Lib=P, R} [85, 86, 99, 138, 182]

Beecher, Charles. *Redeemer and Redeemed, an Investigation of the Atonement and of Eternal Judgment* (Boston: Lee & Shepard, 1864), 357 pp. {s^{1} PRE-s^{1}/X/s^{79}/Lib=O, H} [55–57, 119]

Beecher, Henry Ward. *The Life of Jesus, the Christ*, vol. 2 (New York: J. B. Ford and Co., 1871), 510 pp. (republished Kessinger Publ., 2007). {Q^{78}/X/-/Lib±D} [97]

――――. "The Sifting of Peter by Satan." In *Remarkable Characters and Places of the Holy Land: Comprising an Account of Patriarchs, Judges, Prophets, Apostles, Women, Warriors, Poets, and Kings* … edited by Charles W. Elliott (Hartford, Conn.: J. B. Burr & Co., 1867), pp. 521–532. {X/X/-/Lib±D}

Bennett, James. *Lectures on the History of Jesus Christ*, 2 vols., 2nd ed. (London: F. Westley & A. H. Davis, 1828), 602 pp. and 627 pp., respectively. {Q^{77} ^{78}/s^{75}/-/Lib±} [64, 76, 77, 96, 103, 104, 109, 110, 116]

Bickersteth, Edward Henry. *The Rock of Ages, or Scripture Testimony to the One Eternal Godhead of the Father, and of the Son, and of the Holy Ghost*, new, revised ed. (Philadelphia: Presbyterian Board of Publication, 1890–1899?) [also published under the title *Trinity* (Grand Rapids, MI: Kregel Publications, 1959)], 182 pp. {X/X/-/Lib±D}

――――. *A Treatise on Prayer* (American Tract Society, 1850), 332 pp. {X/X/-/Lib±U} [127]

Bliss, Sylvester. *Memoirs of William Miller* (Boston: Published by Joshua V. Himes, 1853), 426 pp. {Q^{77}/X/-/Lib±} [81]

Blunt, Henry. *Lectures upon the History of our Lord and Saviour Jesus Christ: Delivered during Lent, 1833, at the Church of the Holy Trinity, Upper Chelsea*, Part I, 10th ed. (London: J. Hatchard & Son; Piccadilly: Hamilton, Adams & Co., 1843), 293 pp. {Q^{78}/X/-/Lib±D} [100]

Bonar, Horatius. *Family Sermons* (a later 1954 ed.: *Fifty-two Sermons*); (London: James Nisbet & Co., 1863), 464 pp. {X/X/-/Lib±D}

――――. *Light and Truth: or, Bible Thoughts and Themes. The Gospels* (London: James Nisbet & Co., 1874), 422 pp. {Q^{77}/X/-/Lib±D} [88, 99]

Boyd, Robert. *The World's Hope; or, the Rock of Ages* (Chicago, etc.: H. S. Goodspeed & Co., 1873), 700 pp. {s^{1} ^{77} PRE-s^{1}/s^{72} PRE-s^{72}/s^{18}/Lib=P, O} [55–58, 66, 69, 76, 119, 173]

Burrell, David James. *The Gospel of Gladness* (New York: American Tract Society, 1892), 318 pp. {Q^{78}/X/-/Lib±} [109, 110]

Clark, Rufus W. *The True Prince of the Tribe of Judah; or, Life Scenes of the Messiah* (Boston: Albert Colby & Co., 1860), 355 pp. {Q^{77} ^{78}/X/-/Lib±D} [64, 66, 68, 72, 81, 83, 84, 89, 97, 99, 100, 105, 109, 110, 116]

Coles, Larkin B. *The Beauties and Deformities of Tobacco-Using; or, Its Ludicrous and Its Solemn Realities* (Boston: Brown, Taggard, & Chase, 1851), 144 pp. {-/-/-/Lib=P, H} [140]

――――. *Philosophy of Health: Natural Principles of Health and Cure* (Boston: Brown, Taggard, & Chase, 1860), 312 pp. {-/-/-/Lib= P, H} [124, 182]

Conybeare, William John, and J. S. Howson, *The Life and Epistles of the Apostle Paul* (New York: T. Y. Crowell, no date), 764 pp. {-/-/-/Lib= P, O, M} [117, 128, 135, 138, 149, 182]

Crosby, Howard. *Jesus: His Life and Work as Narrated by the Four Evangelists* (New York: University Publ. Co., 1871), 551 pp. {Q^{78}/X/-/Lib±D} [100]

Cumming, John. *The Church Before the Flood* (London: Arthur Hall, Virtue, & Co., 1853), 608 pp. {X/s^{72}/Q^{21} ^{29}/Lib±D} [132]

――――. *Cumming's Minor Works*. First Series (Philadelphia: Lindsay & Blakiston, 1854), 3 vols., 127 pp., 130 pp., 123 pp., respectively. {X/X/-/Lib±D} [131]

――――. *Cumming's Minor Works*. Second Series (Philadelphia: Lindsay & Blakiston, 1854), 3 vols., 90 pp., 184 pp., 132 pp., respectively. {X/X/-/Lib±D} [131, 134]

——. *Cumming's Minor Works*. Third Series (Philadelphia: Lindsay & Blakiston, 1855), 91 pp., 83 pp., 198 pp., respectively. {X/s^{72}/-/Lib±D} [131, 132]

——. *The Daily Life; or Precepts and Prescriptions for Christian Living* (Boston: John P. Jewett & Co., 1855), 279 pp. {X/X/-/Lib=P} [131]

——. *The End: or, The Proximate Signs of the Close of this Dispensation* (London: John Farquhar Shaw, 1855), 458 pp. {X/X/-/Lib=P, O, R} [131, 138?, 182?]

——. *Foreshadows. Lectures on our Lord's Miracles* (Philadelphia: Lindsay and Blakiston, 1854), 378 pp. {X/s^{39}/-/Lib±D} [131]

——. *The Great Preparation; or, Redemption Draweth Nigh*. First Series (New York: Rudd & Carleton, 1860), 259 pp. {X/X/-/Lib±D}

——. *The Great Preparation; or, Redemption Draweth Nigh*. Second Series (New York: Rudd & Carleton, 1861), 323 pp. {X/X/-/Lib±D} [132]

——. *The Great Tribulation; or, Things Coming on the Earth,* First Series; . . . Second Series (New York: Rudd & Carleton; London: Richard Bentley, 1860), 290 pp. and 305 pp., respectively. {X/X/s^{69}/Lib±D} [132]

——. *The Life and Lessons of Our Lord, Unfolded and Illustrated*, new ed. (London: John F. Shaw & Co., 1880), 616 pp. {Q$^{77\ 78}$/-/ s^3 Q$^{5\ 6\ 37}$/Lib±U} [85, 101, 110, 130, 131]

——. *Occasional Discourses*, 2 vols., 3rd ed. (London: Arthur Hall, Virtue & Co., 1848), 360 pp. (in Vol. 2). {X/X/-/Lib±D} [130]

——. *Prophetic Studies; or, Lectures on the Book of Daniel* (London: Arthur Hall, Virtue & Co., 1853), 500 pp. {Q^1/X/-/Lib=O, H} [55–57]

——. *Sabbath Evening Readings on the New Testament. St. John*. (Boston: John P. Jewett & Co.; Cleveland, Ohio: Jewett, Proctor, & Worthington, 1856), 464 pp. {Q^{77} ^{78}/S^{39} PRE-s^{39}/S^{58} s^{62}/Lib=P, H} [89, 97, 99, 100, 131, 175]

——. *Sabbath Evening Readings on the New Testament. St. Luke*. (London: Arthur Hall, Virtue & Co. 25, Paternoster Row, 1855), 538 pp. {Q$^{77\ 78}$/X/-/Lib±D} [66–68, 72, 76, 80, 82, 97]

——. *Sabbath Evening Readings on the New Testament. St. Mark*. (London: Arthur Hall, Virtue & Co., 1853), 266 pp. {Q^{78}/X/-/Lib±D} [101, 104]

——. *Sabbath Evening Readings on the New Testament. St. Matthew*. (Boston: John P. Jewett & Co.; Cleveland, Ohio: Jewett, Proctor, & Worthington, 1855), 423 pp. {Q^{78}/s$^{37\ 46}$/-/Lib±D} [110]

——. *Signs of the Times; or, Present, Past and Future* (Philadelphia: Lindsay & Blakiston, 1855), 288 pp. {X/X/-/Lib±R} [132, 138, 182]

——. *Voices of the Night*, enlarged ed. [early ed., Boston: John P. Jewett & Co., 1854]; (London: Virtue, Hall, & Virtue, 1854), 470 pp. {X/X/-/Lib±D} [132]

Cuyler, Theodore Ledyard. *Right to the Point. Spare Minute Series* (selected from the writings of Theodore L. Cuyler by Mary Storrs Haynes, with an Introduction by Newman Hall); (Boston: D. Lothrop & Co., 1884), 266 pp. {X/X/s^{36}/Lib=P}

D'Aubigne, J. H. Merle. *History of the Reformation of the Sixteenth Century*, Revised (NY: R. Carter & Bros., 1853), tr. H. White. {-/-/-/Lib=P} [24, 117, 138, 149, 182]

Deems, Charles F. *Who Was Jesus?* (New York: J. Howard Brown, 1880), 756 pp. [same book, under the title *The Light of the Nations* (New York: Gay Brothers & Co., 1884)] {Q$^{77\ 78}$/s$^{72\ 75}$/-/Lib±} [66, 69, 73, 74, 76, 79, 82, 84–86, 90, 97, 101, 110, 116]

Didon, Father Henri. *Jesus Christ*, 2 vols. (London: Kegan Paul, Trench, Trubner, & Co., Ltd., 1893), 493 pp. and 481 pp., respectively. {Q$^{77\ 78}$/X/-/Lib±} [69, 72, 74, 84, 87, 90, 96, 100, 103]

Dods, Marcus. *The Gospel of St. John*, 2 vols. edited by W. Robertson Nicoll for *The Expositor's Bible* (New York: Hodder & Stoughton, 1891, 1892, or George H. Doran Co., 1900), 388 pp. and 427 pp., respectively. {X/s^{76}/-/Lib=O}

Edersheim, Alfred. *The Life and Times of Jesus the Messiah*, 2 vols. (New York: E. R. Herrick & Co., 1886), 696 pp. and 828 pp., respectively. {S$^{77\ 78}$ s^1/s^{76} s$^{10\ 72\ 75}$/s$^{5\ 12}$ ^{66}/Lib=O} [32, 54, 56, 57, 64, 69, 74, 81, 82, 86, 88, 93, 94–96, 98, 100, 101, 103, 104, 109, 110, 115, 117, 121, 122, 129, 171, 173, 175]

——. *Sketches of Jewish Social Life in the Days of Christ* (London: The Religious Tract Society, 1876), 342 pp. {X/X/s^{23}/Lib±D}

——. *The Temple: Its Ministry and Services as They Were at the Time of Jesus Christ* (New York: Hodder & Stoughton, 1874), 414 pp. {Q^{78}/X/-/Lib=O} [109]

Ellicott, C. J. *Historical Lectures on the Life of our Lord Jesus Christ, Being the Hulsean Lectures for the Year 1859. With Notes, Critical, Historical, and Explanatory* (Boston: Gould & Lincoln, 1863), 382 pp. {Q$^{77\ 78}$/X/-/Lib±D} [93, 106, 107, 109, 110, 167, 168]

Ewald, Heinrich. *The Life of Jesus Christ*, translated and edited by Octavius Glover (Cambridge: Deighton, Bell, & Co., 1865), 364 pp. {Q^{77}/X/-/Lib±D} [93]

Farrar, Frederic W. *The Life of Christ* (New York: Hurst & Co., 1874), 752 pp. {S$^{77\ 78}$/S^{75} s$^{14\ 39\ 72\ 76}$ PRE-S^{75}/s$^{15\ 16}$/Lib=P, R} [29, 32, 64–66, 68–72, 74, 75, 77–82, 86, 87, 89–93, 95–100, 102, 103, 105, 107, 108, 109, 115, 117, 122–124, 128, 129, 135, 152, 169, 170, 173, 174, 177, 182]

Farrar, Frederic W. *The Life and Work of St. Paul* (London: Casell, Peter, Galpin and Co., n.d), 2 vols., 678 and 668 pp. {-/-/-/Lib=O} [117, 135]

Flavel, John. *The Whole Works of John Flavel*, 2 vols. (London, etc.: John Nicholson, 1716), 684 pp. and 752 pp., respectively. {Q^1 $^{77\ 78}$/X/-/Lib±D} [56, 72, 79, 83, 92, 108]

Fleetwood, John. *The Life of our Lord and Saviour Jesus Christ: Containing a Full and Accurate History from His Taking upon Himself our Nature to His Crucifixion, Resurrection and Ascension, Together with the Lives, Transactions, and Sufferings of His Holy Evangelists, Apostles, and other Primitive Martyrs. Also, A History of the Jews* (Philadelphia: J. W. Bradley, 1860), 541 pp. {s$^{77\ 78}$/s$^{10\ 14\ 46}$ PRE-S^{10} S$^{13\ 46}$/ Q^5 ^{75}/Lib=P, R} [29, 32, 64, 71, 82–84, 89, 90, 92, 98, 99, 100, 101, 107–109, 115–117, 124, 128, 129, 166, 179, 180, 182]

Foote, A. L. R. *Closing Scenes in the Life of Christ; Being Sequel to "Incidents in the Life of our Saviour"* (London: James Nisbet and Co., 1862), 320 pp. {Q^{78}/X/-/Lib±} [106]

Geikie, Cunningham. *The Life and Words of Christ* (London: Henry S. King and Co., 1877 [1883 EGW lib.]), 2nd vol., 670 pp. $\{Q^{77\ 78}/s^{10\ 53\ 56\ 72\ 75}$ PRE-$S^{10}/Q^5\ s^{57\ 75}$/Lib=P, R} [32, 40, 85, 90, 98–101, 104, 108, 116, 117, 136, 138, 149, 170, 173, 182]

Gray, Andrew. "The Cause, Symptoms, and Cure, of Indifference to Religion," *The Scotch Preacher: or, A Collection of Sermons* (Edinburgh: T. Cadell, T. Longman, and J. Dickson, 1779), 338 pp. {-/-/-/Lib±} [92]

Greenhough, J. G. *The Apostles of our Lord* (London: Hodder & Stoughton, 1904), 278 pp. $\{X/X/s^{30}$/Lib=O}

Gunn, John C. *Gunn's Domestic Physician* or *Home Book of Health* (Cincinnati, Ohio: Moore, Wilstach, Keys, 1857), 791 pp. {-/-/-/Lib±} [139, 140]

Gunsaulus, Frank Wakely. *The Man of Galilee: A Biographical Study of The Life of Jesus Christ* (Philadelphia: J. H. Moore Company, 1899), 682 pp. {-/-/-/Lib±} [129, 130]

Hall, Joseph. *Scripture History; or Contemplations on the Historical Passages of the Old and New Testaments*, abridged by George Henry Glasse (New York: American Tract Society, no date), 516 pp.; (London: T. Nelson and Sons, 1860), 602 pp. $\{Q^{78}/s^{75}$/-/Lib=P} [95, 97, 106, 177]

Halsey, Le Roy J. *The Beauty of Immanuel, His Name Shall Be Called Wonderful* (Philadelphia: Presbyterian Board of Publication, 1860), 204 pp. $\{Q^{78}/X$/-/Lib±D} [106]

Hanna, William. *The Life of Christ* (New York: American Tract Society, 1863), 861 pp. As published in six volumes, it was also called *The Life of our Lord upon Earth* (1869). $\{S^{77\ 78}\ s^1/S^{14\ 24\ 37\ 53\ 72\ 75\ 83\ 84}\ s^{10\ 13\ 39\ 46\ 76}$ PRE-$S^{10\ 13\ 37\ 75\ 83\ 84}\ s^{24\ 39\ 46\ 53\ 72}/S^{5\ 11\ 19\ 54\ 80\ 85\ 86}\ s^{6\ 7\ 11\ 15\ 16\ 17\ 20\ 27\ 28\ 29\ 35\ 36\ 40\ 41\ 45\ 47\ 48\ 58\ 59\ 63\ 65\ 66\ 67\ 71\ 76\ 81\ 82\ 80\ 87}$/Lib=O, H, R} [9, 19, 29, 32, 49, 52, 55, 57, 63–77, 79–110, 114, 115, 117, 128, 129, 134, 168, 169, 173–175, 177, 178, 182]

Harris, John. *The Great Commission: or, the Christian Church Constituted and Charged to Convey the Gospel to the World* (with an introductory essay by William R. Williams); (Boston: Gould & Lincoln, 1854), 396 pp. $\{s^1/X$/-/Lib=P, O, C} [50, 51, 56, 57, 135, 166, 173]

———. *The Great Teacher: Characteristics of our Lord's Ministry* (with an introductory essay by Heman Humphrey); (Amherst: J. S. & C. Adams, 1836), 444 pp. $\{S^{1\ 77}\ s^{2\ 78}$ PRE-$s^1/S^{3\ 37\ 75}$ PRE-$S^{3\ 13}\ s^{37}/s^{5\ 12\ 21\ 24\ 31\ 33\ 41\ 50\ 51\ 52\ 55\ 61\ 66\ 71\ 73\ 79\ 81\ 86}$/Lib=O, C, H} [49, 51–58, 60–62, 92, 106, 117, 135, 162, 163, 166, 167, 173, 174, 175, 176, 177, 179]

Hastings, Horace Lorenzo. *The Great Controversy Between God and Man* (Boston: H. L. Hastings, 1858), 167 pp. {-/-/-/Lib±D} [135]

Henry, Matthew. *An Exposition of the Old and New Testaments: Wherein each Chapter Is Summed Up in its Contents; the Sacred Text Inserted at Large . . . with Practical Remarks and Observations*, vol. V, edited by George Burder & Joseph Hughes (Philadelphia: Towar & Hogan, 1828), 960 pp. $\{Q^{78}/X$/-/Lib=P} [97, 101, 104, 106, 107, 110]

Humphrey, Heman, D.D., in an introductory essay in *The Great Teacher* by John Harris (Amherst: J. S. & C. Adams, 1836), pp. ix–xviii. $\{s^1$ PRE-s^1/X/-/Lib=D} [52, 55–57, 166]

Ingraham, J. H. *The Prince of the House of David; or, Three Years in the Holy City* (New York: Pudney & Russell Publishers, 1855), 456 pp. $\{s^{77\ 78}$ PRE-$s^{78}/S^{75}\ s^{14\ 76}$/-/Lib±U, D} [68, 78, 80, 81, 83, 94, 96, 98, 99, 100, 104, 107–109, 116, 167, 175, 177]

Jones, George. *Life-Scenes from the Four Gospels*, 3rd ed. (Philadelphia: J. C. Garrigues & Co., 1868), 443 pp. $\{S^{77\ 78}/S^{14}\ s^{10\ 72\ 75}/s^{19}$/Lib=P, H} [57, 64–66, 68, 70–72, 74, 75, 81, 83–93, 96–98, 100, 102, 104–107, 109, 110, 114, 115, 121, 168, 169, 173–175, 178]

Kennedy, William S. *Messianic Prophecy, and the Life of Christ*, 2nd ed. (Andover: Warren F. Draper; Boston: Gould & Lincoln; New York: John Wiley; Philadelphia: Smith, English & Co., 1860), 484 pp. $\{Q^{78}/s^3$/-/Lib=O} [97, 100, 179]

Kirk, Edward Norris. *Lectures on the Parables of our Saviour* (New York: R. Craighead, 1857), 506 pp. $\{X/X/s^{73}$/Lib=O, C, H}

Kitto, John. *Daily Bible Illustrations: Being Original Readings for a Year on subjects from Sacred History, Biography, Geography, Antiquities, and Theology*. Vol. VII: *The Life and Death of our Lord* (New York: Robert Carter & Brothers, 1881 [also, an 1853 ed.]), 433 pp. $\{Q^{77\ 78}/s^{10\ 75}$/-/Lib=O, C} [64, 65, 67, 68, 74, 76, 77, 82, 83, 84, 87, 89, 90, 93, 96–98, 100, 101, 104, 105, 108, 109, 116, 177]

———. *The Suffering Saviour; or, Meditations on the Last Days of Christ*, translated by Samuel Jackson (New York: Robert Carter & Brothers, 1855), 474 pp. $\{X/s^{75}$/-/Lib±D}

Krummacher, Friedrich Wilhelm. *Elijah the Tishbite* (New York: American Tract Society, no date) 458 pp. $\{X/X/s^{22}$/Lib=P, O, C} [126, 146]

Lane, Benjamin Ingersol. *The Mysteries of Tobacco* (New York: Wiley and Putnam, 1845), 185 pp. {-/-/-/Lib±} [140]

Lange, Johann P. *The Life of the Lord Jesus Christ: A Complete Critical Examination of the Origin, Contents, and Connection of the Gospels*, 4 vols., edited, with additional notes, by Marcus Dods (Edinburgh: T. & T. Clark, 1872), 544 pp., 504 pp., 512 pp., 502 pp., respectively. $\{Q^{78}/s^{53\ 72}$/-/Lib±D} [95–98, 100, 102, 103, 105, 116]

Leask, W. *The Footsteps of Messiah: Review of Passages in the History of Jesus Christ* (New York and Philadelphia: William S. Martien, 1847), 351 pp. $\{X/X$/-/Lib±}

Lightfoot, J. B. *On a Fresh Revision of the English New Testament* (London and New York: Macmillan & Co., 1872), 259 pp. $\{Q/X$/-/Lib=O, C, M?} [117, 182]

Macduff, John Ross. *Brighter than the Sun; or, Christ the Light of the World, a Life of Our Lord* (New York: Robert Carter & Brothers, 1878), 433 pp. $\{Q^{78}/X$/-/Lib±D} [95, 96, 98, 105, 110, 173]

———. *Memories of Olivet* (New York: Robert Carter & Brothers, 1868), 373 pp. $\{Q^{78}/X/S^{49\ 64\ 74\ 87}\ s^{51\ 63\ 67}$/Lib=P, O, C} [106, 128, 173, 181, 182]

———. *Sunsets on the Hebrew Mountains* (London: James Nisbet & Co., 1869), 317 pp. (reprinted St. Paul: D.D. Merrill, 1980) $\{X/X/s^{79}$/Lib=P, H} [173]

Mackenzie, W. Douglas. *The Revelation of the Christ. Familiar Studies in the Life of Jesus* (London: The Sunday School Union, 1896), 303 pp. {Q$^{77\,78}$/X/-/Lib±} [85, 88, 101]

Macmillan, Hugh. *Our Lord's Three Raisings from the Dead* (Glasgow: James Maclehose, 1876), 338 pp. {X/X/S^{58} s^{32}/Lib=P, O, H} [181]

March, Daniel. *Days of the Son of Man* (Philadelphia: J. C. McCurdy & Co., 1882), 685 pp. {X/s^{24}/s$^{4\,79\,86}$/Lib±U} [169]

——. *Night Scenes in the Bible* (Philadelphia &c.: Ziegler & McCurdy, 1872), 544 pp. {X/S$^{83\,84}$ PRE-S$^{83\,84}$/s$^{10\,16\,17\,25\,26\,40\,49\,74\,85}$/Lib=O, R} [62, 117, 124, 125, 129, 138, 146, 169, 173, 174, 178, 182]

——. *Our Father's House, or, The Unwritten Word* (Philadelphia: Zieglar and McCurdy, 1870), 560 pp. {X/X/Q$^{26\,55}$/Lib=O}

——. *Walks and Homes of Jesus* (Philadelphia: Presbyterian Publication Committee, 1866), 339 pp. {s^{78}/S$^{24\,46}$ s$^{39\,72\,75}$ PRE-S$^{24\,46\,75}$ s$^{39\,72}$/S$^{4\,21\,26}$ s$^{7\,8\,12\,40\,41\,45\,47\,49\,63}$/Lib=O, R} [2, 93, 103, 108, 114, 116, 117, 119, 120, 125, 129, 138, 169, 173, 176, 177, 182]

Melvill, Henry. *The Preacher in Print. Second Series. The Golden Lectures*, Vol. 1 (London: James Paul, 1, Chapter House Court, 1851). {s^{56}/s^{14}/-/Lib=O, C} [99, 110]

——. *The Golden Lectures, forty-six sermons delivered at St. Margaret's Church, Lothbury, on Tuesday mornings, from January 3, to December 26, 1854*, 7 vols. From *The Preacher in Print, second series* (London: James Paul, 1851–1857). {X/X/-/Lib=O, C}

——. *Sermons by Henry Melvill*, 3rd ed., enlarged, edited by C. P. McIlvaine (New York: Stanford & Swords, 1853, 1844), 561 pp. {s^1 Q^{77}/s^{14} PRE-S$^{13\,14}$/s$^{12\,21\,52}$/Lib=P, O, R} [52, 53, 55, 56, 57, 62, 92, 117, 125, 126, 130, 138, 175, 182]

——. *Sermons by Henry Melvill*, 2 vols., edited by C. P. McIlvaine (New York: Stanford & Swords, 1850), 416 pp. and 382 pp., respectively {X/-/-/Lib±D}

Miller, James R. *Week-Day Religion* (Philadelphia: Presbyterian Board of Publication, 1880), 315 pp. {X/s^{37}/-/Lib=O} [176, 177]

Neander, Augustus. *The Life of Jesus Christ in its Historical Connexion and Historical Development* (New York: Harper & Bros., 1848), 450 pp. {s$^{77\,78}$/X/-/Lib=O, C} [68, 70, 74, 77, 81, 84, 87, 89, 91, 98–101, 103, 107, 110, 116]

Nevin, Alfred. *The Parables of Jesus* (Philadelphia: Presbyterian Board of Publication, 1881), 503 pp. {X/X/-/Lib=P}

Nevin, John W. *A Summary of the Biblical Antiquities; for the Use of Schools, Bible-Classes and Families;* (Philadelphia: American Sunday-School Union, 1849), 447 pp. {Q^2/X/-/Lib±} [59]

Nicoll, W. Robertson. *The Incarnate Saviour. A Life of Jesus Christ.* (Edinburgh: T. & T. Clark, 1881), 388 pp. {Q$^{77\,78}$/s^{46}/-/Lib±} [84, 99, 102, 103, 109, 110]

Parker, Joseph. *Ecce Deus: Essays on the Life and Doctrine of Jesus Christ, with Controversial Notes on "Ecce Homo"* (Edinburgh: T. & T. Clark, 1867), 338 pp. {Q^1/X/-/Lib±} [50, 56, 57]

Patton, William. *Jesus of Nazareth: Who was He? And What Is He Now?* (New York: American Tract Society, 1880), 320 pp. {Q^{78}/X/-/Lib±} [110]

Pentecost, George F. *Bible Studies from the Old and New Testaments Covering the International Sunday-School Lessons for 1888* (New York and Chicago: A. S. Barnes & Co., 1887), 343 pp. {s$^{77\,78}$/s^{72}/-/Lib=O, C} [66, 69, 89, 95, 96, 101, 104, 106, 109, 110, 116]

——. *Bible Studies from the Old and New Testaments Covering the International Sunday-School Lessons for 1889* (New York and Chicago: A. S. Barnes & Co., 1888), 403 pp. {Q$^{77\,78}$/s$^{37\,39\,72}$/-/Lib=O, C} [99]

——. *Bible Studies from the New Testament Covering the International Sunday-School Lessons for 1890* (New York and Chicago: A. S. Barnes & Co., 1889), 391 pp. {X/X/-/Lib=O, C}

——. *Bible Studies from the Old and New Testaments Covering the International Sunday-School Lessons for 1892* (New York and Chicago: A. S. Barnes & Co., 1891), 416 pp. {X/X/-/Lib=O, C}

——. *The Birth and Boyhood of Jesus* (New York: American Tract Society, 1896), 399 pp. {Q^{77}/X/S^8/Lib±D} [181]

——. *Israel's Apostasy and Studies from the Gospel of St. John Covering International Sunday-School Lessons for 1891* (New York and Chicago: A. S. Barnes & Co., 1890), 405 pp. {Q^{77}/X/-/Lib=O, C} [84, 87, 88]

Plumer, William S. *The Rock of our Salvation: A Treatise Respecting the Natures, Person, Offices, Work, Sufferings, and Glory of Jesus Christ* (New York: The American Tract Society, 1867), 519 pp.; republished by Sprinkle Publications and Hess Publications, 1995. {Q^{77}/X/-/Lib±U} [93]

Porter, Josias L. *The Giant Cities of Bashan; and Syria's Holy Places* (New York: Thomas Nelson & Sons, 1883), 377 pp. {X/X/s$^{26\,30\,63}$/Lib=O, C, R} [138]

Power, Philip Bennett. *The "I Wills" of Christ; Being Thoughts upon Some of the Passages in Which the words "I Will" Are Used by the Lord Jesus Christ* (Edinburgh: Religious Tract Society; London: William Macintosh, 1866), 382 pp. {X/X/S^{27}/Lib=P} [181]

Pressensé, Edmond Dehault de. *Jesus Christ: His Times, Life and Work* (London: Jackson, Walford, & Hodder, 1866), 560 pp. {Q^{77}/X/-/Lib±D} [89, 91]

Renan, M. Ernest. *The Life of Jesus* (Garden City, New York: Dolphin Books, Doubleday & Co., Inc., 1863), 317 pp. {X/X/-/Lib±} [89, 101, 152, 167, 168]

Robinson, Thomas. *Scripture Characters: or, a Practical Improvement of the Principal Histories in the Old and New Testaments*, 2 vols. (London: Henry G. Bohn, 1849), 701 pp. and 716 pp., respectively. {Q^{77}/X/-/Lib=O} [64, 84, 93]

Schauffler, W. G. *Meditations on the Last Days of Christ; Together with Eight Meditations on the Seventeenth Chapter of John* (London: Sampson Low, Son & Co.; Cleveland, Ohio: Jewett et al; Boston: J. P. Jewett & Co., 1853), 439 pp. {Q^{78}/X/-/Lib±} [96]

Simons, Michael Laird, ed. *Evenings with Moody and Sankey: Comprising Sermons and Addresses at their Great Revival Meetings ...* (Philadelphia: Henry T. Coates & Co., 1877), 296 pp. {Q^{78}/X/-/Lib±D} [95]

Sixth Report of the American Temperance Society (1833), 112 pp. {-/-/-/Lib±} [140]

Smith, Hannah Whitall. *The Christian's Secret of a Happy Life* (New York, Chicago, Toronto: Fleming H. Revell Co., 1883, 1888), 250 pp. {X/Q/-/Lib±U}

Smith, William, ed. *A Dictionary of the Bible Comprising its Antiquities, Biography, Geography and Natural History* (New York, Chicago, Toronto: Flaming H. Revell Co., no date) 778 pp. {X/s^{76}/s^{12}/Lib=P, O, C, R} [138]

———, ed. *The New Testament History. With an Introduction, Connecting the History of the Old and New Testaments* (New York: Harper & Brothers, 1876), 780 pp. {Q^{78}/X/-/Lib±D} [96, 98, 99, 100, 105, 107]

Stalker, James. *The Life of Jesus Christ*, new, revised edition (New York, Chicago, Toronto: Flaming H. Revell Co., 1880), 167 pp. {Q$^{77\,78}$/X/-/Lib±D} [89, 96, 98, 170, 171]

Stanford, Charles. *The Evening of our Lord's Ministry Being Preludes to 'Voices from Calvary'* (London: The Religious Tract Society, 1886), 331 pp. {Q^{77}/X/-/Lib±} [82]

———. *From Calvary to Olivet. Being a Sequel to 'Voices from Calvary'* (London: The Religious Tract Society, 1893), 352 pp. {Q^{78}/X/-/Lib±} [101]

Strickland, William P. *The Light of the Temple* (Cincinnati: J. Ernst, 1854), 288 pp. {Q$^{77\,78}$/X/-/Lib=O, H} [96]

Stowe, Calvin. *Origin and History Of the Books of the Bible, Both the Canonical and the Apocryphal, Designed to Show What the Bible Is Not, What It Is, and How to Use It* (Hartford, CT: Hartford Publ. Co., 1867), 583 pp. {-/-/-/Lib=O} [144, 149]

Talmage, T. DeWitt. *From Manger To Throne: A New Life Of Jesus The Christ, A History Of Palestine And Its People* (Philadelphia, PA: Historical Publ. Co., 1889) 544 pp. {Q^{77}/X/-/Lib±} [82]

Taylor, Jeremy. *The History of the Life and Death of Jesus Christ*, new, revised ed. (London: Routledge, Warne, and Routledge, 1860, 1856), 714 pp. {Q$^{77\,78}$/X/-/Lib=O} [85, 104]

Thayer, E. W. *Sketches from the Life of Jesus, Historical and Doctrinal* (Chicago and New York: Fleming H. Revell Co., 1891), 548 pp. {Q^{77}/s^{376}/-/Lib±} [57, 66, 90, 179]

Thompson, Joseph P. *Jesus of Nazareth: His Life for the Young* (Boston: James R. Osgood & Co., 1876), 438 pp. {Q^{78}/X/-/Lib±} [99]

Trench, Richard Chenevix. *Notes on the Parables of Our Lord* (New York: D. Appleton & Co., 1855), 425 pp. {X/X/-/Lib=P, O, C}

———. *Sermons Preached in Westminster Abbey* (New York: W. J. Widdleton, 1860), 368 pp. {Q^{78}/X/-/Lib±D}

———. *Studies in the Gospels*, 3rd ed., revised (London: Macmillan & Co., 1874; first printing, 1867), 335 pp. {Q$^{77\,78}$/X/-/Lib±D} [68, 82, 97, 102, 134]

Underwood, Almon. *Millennial Experience; or, God's Will Known and Done* (Boston: Henry Hoyt, 1860), 379 pp. {Lib=P, O, H} [126, 127, 182]

Walker, James Barr. *Philosophy of the Plan of Salvation* (Cincinnati: George L. Weed, 1845), 239 pp. {X/X/Q^{15}/Lib±}

Wayland, Francis. *Salvation by Christ. A Series of Discourses on Some of the Most Important Doctrines of the Gospel* (Boston: Gould & Lincoln, 1859), 386 pp. {X/S^{39}/-/Lib±} [175, 176]

Weiss, Bernhard. *The Life of Christ*, 3 vols., translated by M. G. Hope (Edinburgh: T. & T. Clark, 1892 [vol. 3], 1894 [vols. 1 and 2]), 393 pp., 403 pp., and 428 pp., respectively. {Q$^{77\,78}$/X/-/Lib±} [83, 86, 96]

Williams, Henry W. *The Incarnate Son of God: or, the History of the Life and Ministry of the Redeemer, Arranged, Generally, according to Greswell's Harmony of the Gospels; with a Concise View of the Mediatorial Economy* (London: J. Mason, 1853), 384 pp. {Q^{78}/X/-/Lib±} [106, 107]

Winslow, Octavius. *The Glory of the Redeemer in His Person and Work* (Philadelphia: Lindsay & Blakiston, 1855), 419 pp. {S^{1} s$^{77\,78}$/PRE-S^{13}/-/Lib=P} [49–54, 56, 57, 83, 105, 166, 167]

Wright, Paul. *The New and Complete Life of Our Blessed Lord and Saviour Jesus Christ: That Great Example as Well as Saviour of Mankind* (Mill-Hill, NJ: Daniel Fenton, 1810), 498 pp. {Q^{77}/X/-/Lib±} [92]

Wylie, James A. *Scenes from the Bible* (Glasgow and London: William Collins, Sons, & Co., 1867), 352 pp. {Q^{78}/X/S$^{57\,74}$ s^{73}/Lib=P} [97, 99, 107, 181]

Wylie, James A. *History of Protestantism* (London: Casell and Co., n.d), 3 vols. {-/-/-/Lib=P, O, C} [8, 23, 24, 117, 135, 149]

APPENDIX D
Bibliography of Reference Works

Listed below are the works quoted in this book (other than the source works in Appendix C and unpublished EGW manuscripts, documents, and letters), followed in brackets by their page location(s) in this book (e.g. [114, 115]).

Anderson, E. Marcella. unpublished typewritten comments on source work by William Hanna, 2 pp.; filed with "Life of Christ Research Project materials," Aug. 25, 1981. [114, 115]

Ballenger, Edward S. *The Gathering Call*, Sept. 1932, pp. 16–22. [38]

Bauckham, Richard J. *Word Biblical Commentary*, vol. 50, 2 Peter, Jude (Word Books, 1983), 377 pp. [150]

Brand, Leonard and Don S. McMahon. *The Prophet and Her Critics* (Nampa, ID: Pacific Press Publ. Assn., 2005), 127 pp. [48, 129]

Butler, Jonathan. *Spectrum*, vol. 12, no. 4, pp. 44–48. [9]

Canale, Fernando. "Revelation and Inspiration," in *Understanding Scripture: An Adventist Approach*, George W. Reid, ed. *Biblical Research Institute Studies*, vol. 1 (Silver Spring, MD: Biblical Research Institute, General Conference of Seventh-day Adventists, 2005), pp. 47–74. [143]

Canright, Dudley M. *The Bible from Heaven: A Summary of Plain Arguments for the Bible and Christianity* (Battle Creek, MI: S.D.A. Publ. Assn., c. 1878), 300 pp. [135]

"Mrs. E. G. White and Her Revelations," *Michigan Christian Advocate*, Oct. 8, 1887. [8]

———. *Seventh-Day Adventism Renounced* (New York: Fleming H. Revell Co. 1889), 14th ed., 417 pp. [8, 135]

Carpenter, David. "Hoovering to Byzantium," found online at <www.dccarpenter.com/hoovering.htm>. [136]

Charlesworth, James, ed. *The Old Testament Pseudepigrapha*, vol. 1 (Garden City, NY: Doubleday & Co., Inc., 1983), 995 pp. [149]

Conkin, Paul K. *American Originals: Homemade Varieties of Christianity* (Chapel Hill, NC: University of North Carolina Press, 1997), 354 pp. [139]

Coon, Roger. *A Gift of Light* (Hagerstown, MD: Review and Herald Publ. Assn., 1983, 1998), 63 pp. [7]

———. "A 'Testimony' from the 'Other Side,'" *Perspective Digest*, vol. 2, no. 2., pp. 30, 31. [7]

———. "Look a Little Higher" (Silver Spring, MD: Ellen G. White Estate, Inc., 1990), 32 pp. [156]

Coon, Roger W. Victor Cooper, et al. Interview with Vincent L. Ramik, attorney, "Ellen White's Use of Sources," *Adventist Review* (Washington, DC), Sept. 17, 1981 pp. 3–6. [136]

Cottrell, Raymond F. *The Literary Relationship Between The Desire of Ages, by Ellen G. White and The Life of Christ, by William Hanna*, part I, (Nov. 1, 1979), 39 pp. [12]

Crosby, Tim. "Does Inspired Mean Original?" *Ministry*, February 1986, pp. 4–7. [149–151]

"The Cry of Plagiarism," *The Spectator*, Feb. 28, 1891, pp. 305–306. [136]

Dart, John. "Plagiarism found in Prophet Books," *Los Angeles Times*, October 23, 1980, pp. 1, 3, 21. [133]

Douglass, Herbert E. *Messenger of the Lord: The Prophetic Ministry of Ellen G. White* (Nampa, ID: Pacific Press Publ. Assn., 1998), 586 pp. [116, 117]

Fortin, Denis. "Ellen G. White as a Writer: Case Studies in the Issue of Literary Borrowing," at <www.andrews.edu/~fortind/EGWWhite-Conybeare.htm>. [117]

Gordon, Paul A. "Why Did Ellen G. White Borrow?" (Ellen G. White Estate, May 1981), 13 pp. [165]

Graybill, Ron. *E. G. White's Literary Work: An Update*. An edited and annotated transcript of a tape recording of presentations made in the morning worship services at the General Conference of Seventh-day Adventists, Nov. 15–19, 1981), 45 pp. [126, 130, 139]

———. "The 'I saw' parallels in Ellen White's writings," *Adventist Review*, July 29, 1982, pp. 4–6. [126]

Graybill, Ron, and Robert W. Olson, compilers. "Exhibits Relating to the Writing of The Desire of Ages," White Estate Document File #508. [*Exhibits*], (Washington, DC, E. G. White Estate, May 23, 1979) at <www.whiteestate.org/issues/DA-HOW/DA-How.html>. [12, 16, 18, 19, 25–27, 29, 31–34, 36–38, 40–46, 49, 51, 113, 138, 165, 172]

Hackleman, Douglas. "GC Committee Studies Ellen White's Sources," *Spectrum*, Vol. 10, No. 4 (March 1980). [8]

Hexham, Irving. Department of Religious Studies, University of Calgary (Calgary, Alberta, Canada) at <www.ucalgary.ca/~hexham/study/plag.html>. [47, 134]

Hoyt, Frederick G. "The Specter of Plagiarism Haunting Adventism" (San Diego Adventist Forum, August 12, 2006). 64 pp. [11]

"Inspiration of the Spirit of Prophecy as Related to the Inspiration of the Bible, August 1, 1919," *Spectrum*, vol. 10, no. 1, pp. 44–57. [135]

"Is Mrs. E. G. White a Plagiarist," *Healdsburg Enterprise*, March 20, 1889. [8, 135]

Johns, Warren, Ron Graybill, Tim Poirier, compilers. *A Bibliography of Ellen G. White's Private and Office Libraries*, Third Revised Edition (Silver Spring, MD: Ellen G. White Estate, April 1993), 70 pp. [57]

Johns, Warren H. "Ellen White: Prophet or Plagiarist?"; "Literary Thief or God's Messenger?"; "Human Thoughts or Divine Truths?" *Ministry* (Washington, D.C., June 1982), pp. 5–18. [117, 130, 135–138, 146, 154, 159]

Kellogg, John Harvey. *General Conference Daily Bulletin*, March 8, 1897, p. 309. [140]

King-Taylor, Gladys. *Literary Beauty of Ellen G. White's Writings* (Mountain View, CA: Pacific Press Publ. Assn., 1953), 124 pp. [96, 104–106, 120]

Kissinger, Warren S. *The Lives of Jesus: A History and Bibliography* (New York: Garland Publ., Inc., 1985), 230 pp. [169]

Le Vayer, La Mothe in Mary Moss. "No Plagiarism," *New York Times* (Jan. 6, 1906): BR6. [12]

Lindey, Alexander. *Plagiarism and Originality* (New York: Harper & Brothers Publishers, 1952) 366 pp. [133, 134]

Lloyd, Ernest. *Scrapbook Stories: from Ellen G. White's Scrapbooks* (Mountain View, CA: Pacific Press Publ. Assn., 1949), 96 pp. [117]

Mansell, Donald Ernest and Vesta West Mansell. *The Coming Conflict and the Overcomer's Reward* (Nampa Idaho: Mansell & McCoy Publications, 2005), 631 pp. [160]

Mazzeo, Tilar J. *Plagiarism and Literary Property in the Romantic Period* (Philadelphia: University of Pennsylvania Press, 2007), 236 pp. [12]

McAdams, Donald R. "Ellen G. White and the Protestant Historians" (unpublished manuscript, Andrews University, March 1974, revised 1977), 244 pp. [8]

McMahon, Don S. *Acquired or Inspired? Exploring the Origins of the Adventist Lifestyle* (Victoria, Australia: Signs Publ. Co., 2005), 150 pp. [8]

McCay, Clive M., Ph.D. "A Nutrition Authority Discusses Mrs. E. G. White," *Review and Herald*, Feb. 12, 19, 26, 1959 (Review and Herald Publ. Assn., Takoma Park, Washington, D.C.), a reprint of 8 pages. [161, 162]

Neff, David. "Ellen White's Theological and Literary Indebtedness to Calvin Stowe" (revised 1979), 22 pp. [144]

The New Lexicon Webster's Dictionary of the English Language (New York: Lexicon Publication, Inc., 1988), 1149 pp. plus encyclopedic supplements.

Nichol, Francis D. *Ellen G. White and Her Critics* (Washington, DC, Review and Herald Publ. Assn., 1951), 703 pp. [8, 9, 117, 135, 144]

Numbers, Ron. *Prophetess of Health: A Study of Ellen G. White* (New York: Harper and Row, 1976), 271 pp. [8]

"Off the Back Burner," Segment 14, in a General Conference of SDAs retirees' communiqué of June 1996. [159]

Olson, Robert W. *One Hundred and One Questions on the Sanctuary and on Ellen White [101 Questions]* (Washington, D. C.: March 1981), 111 pp. [129]

———. "Ellen G. White's Use of Historical Sources in *The Great Controversy*," *Adventist Review*, Feb. 23, 1984, pp. 3–5. [118]

———. "Ellen G. White's Use of Uninspired Sources" (Washington, DC, Ellen G. White Estate, April 10, 1980), 19 pp. [81, 117, 127, 136, 147, 150, 151]

———. "Ellen White's Denials," *Ministry*, Feb. 1991, p. 15–18. [141]

Pals, Daniel L. *The Victorian "Lives" of Jesus* (San Antonio, TX: Trinity University Press, 1982), 223 pp. [166–171]

Perry, Alfred M. "The Growth of the Gospels," *Interpreter's Bible*, vol. 7, p. 62, in Walter F. Specht, *The Literary Relationship Between The Desire of Ages, by Ellen G. White and The Life of Christ, by William Hanna*, part II (Loma Linda University: unpublished paper, 1979), p. 2. [134]

Pickle, Bob. *A Response to the Video: Seventh-day Adventism: The Spirit Behind the Church* (Halstad, MN: Pickle Publ. Co., 2002). [8]

The Publishers' Weekly (New York: F. Leipold, 1878), Jan. 2, 1873–Dec. 28, 1878. [117]

Rea, Walter. *The White Lie* (Turlock, California: M&R Publications, 1982), 409 pp. [8, 9, 11, 54, 57, 111, 129, 134]

———. "The Making of a Prophet: How Ellen White Turned Fiction into 'Truth'," *Adventist Currents*, March 1987 at <www.ellenwhiteexposed.com/rea/fiction.htm>. [115]

Review of *The White Lie* in *Forward* (San Juan Capistrano, CA: 1982), vol. 5, no. 1. [9]

Robertson, Archibald Thomas. *Word Pictures* in the New Testament (Nashville: Sunday School Board of the Southern Baptist Convention, 1930–1933), vol. 3, 477 pp. [149]

Robinson, D. E. in "How the E. G. White Books Were Written—5," *Ministry*, Feb. 1980, pp. 12–14. [25, 26, 34]

Robinson, D. E. *The Story of Our Health Message* (Nashville: Southern Publ. Association, 1943, 1955, 1965), 445 pp. [140]

Robinson, Stephen E. *Encyclopedia of Mormonism* (New York: Macmillan Publ. Co., Inc., 1992), 5 vols., 1850 pp. [155]

Sabbath Readings for the Home Circle (Washington, D.C.: Review and Herald Publ. Assn., no date), 400 pp. [117]

Schramer, James, and Donald Ross, eds. *Dictionary of Literary Biography, vol. 183: American Travel Writers, 1776–1864* (Detroit: Gale Research, 1997). 418 pp. [168]

Seventh-day Adventism: The Spirit Behind the Church (Hemet, CA: Jeremiah Films, 1999) video. [13]

Seventh-day Adventist Bible Commentary, Francis D. Nichol, editor (Review and Herald Publ. Assn., Washington, D.C., 1956, 1980), vol. 5. [151]

Seventh-day Adventist Encyclopedia, Don F. Neufeld, editor (Review and Herald Publ. Assn., Washington, D.C., 1996), vol. 10, 966 pp. [8]

Spalding, Arthur W. *Origin and History of Seventh-day Adventists* (Washington, DC: Review and Herald Publ. Assn., 1961), vol. 1, 415 pp. [7, 140, 159]

Specht, Walter F. *The Literary Relationship Between The Desire of Ages, by Ellen G. White and The Life of Christ, by William Hanna*, part II (Loma Linda University: unpublished paper, 1979), 83 pp. [113, 119, 134]

Veltman, Fred. "Full Report of the Life of Christ Research Project," (Angwin, California, November 1988), 2,222 pp. typewritten. [8, 9, 11–13, 29, 41, 48, 57, 58, 62, 117, 129, 130, 173–186]

———. "*The Desire of Ages* Project: the data," *Ministry*, October 1990, pp. 4–7 and "*The Desire of Ages* Project: the conclusions," *Ministry*, December 1990, pp. 11–15. [11, 12, 128, 172]

Weinauer, Ellen. "Plagiarism and the Proprietary Self: Policing the Boundaries of Authorship in Herman Melville's 'Hawthorne and His Mosses'," *American Literature*, 69/4 (1997): pp. 700, 712. [134]

Wesley, John. *Explanatory Notes Upon the New Testament* (New York: J. Soule and T. Mason for the Methodist Episcopal Church in the United States, 1818), 766 pp. [130]

White, Arthur L. "Ellen G. White and Her Writings," *Adventist Review*, Nov. 27, 1980, pp. 7–9. [115]

———. "The Ellen G. White Historical Writings," *Adventist Review*, Aug. 2, 9, 16, and 23, 1979 at <www.whiteestate.org/issues/inspiration.html>. [13, 46, 115]

———. *Ellen G. White: The Australian Years, 1891–1900 [4BIO]* (Washington, DC, Hagerstown, MD: Review and Herald Publ. Assn., 1983), 472 pp. [16, 25, 26, 37, 40, 43, 45, 46, 78, 111, 138, 145]

———. *Ellen G. White: The Early Elmshaven Years, 1900–1905 [5BIO]* (Washington, DC, Hagerstown, MD: Review and Herald Publ. Assn., 1981), 428 pp. [138]

————. *Ellen G. White: The Lonely Years, 1876–1891* [3*BIO*] (Washington, DC, Hagerstown, MD: Review and Herald Publ. Assn., 1984), 509 pp. [8, 19, 21–25, 32, 116, 118, 138, 172]

————. *Ellen G. White: The Progressive Years, 1862–1876* [2*BIO*] (Washington, DC, Hagerstown, MD: Review and Herald Publ. Assn., 1986), 512 pp. [17, 18, 62, 140]

White, Ellen G. *The Acts of the Apostles* (Mountain View, CA: Pacific Press Publ. Assn., 1911), 633 pp. [125, 138, 139, 163]

————. *The Adventist Home* (Hagerstown, MD: Review and Herald Publ. Assn., 1952, 1980), 583 pp. [161]

————. *Appeal to Mothers* (Battle Creek, MI: S. D. A. Publ. Assn., 1952, 1864), 34 (of 64) pp. [139]

————. "At the Iowa and Kansas Camp-Meeting," article by W. C. White, but largely quoting E. G. White, *Advent Review & Sabbath Herald*, Jan. 6, 1910 (Washington, DC: Review and Herald Publ. Assn.), p. 8. [156]

————. *Child Guidance* (Washington, D.C.: Review and Herald Publ. Assn., 1954), 616 pp. [161]

————. "Child Life of Jesus," *The Signs of the Times*, July 30, 1896. [52]

————. "Child Life of Jesus," *The Youth's Instructor*, Nov. 21, 1895. [52]

————. "The Child Samuel," *Bible Echo*, June 18, 1894. [50]

————. "Christ and Nicodemus," *The Signs of the Times*, April 18, 1900 (Oakland, CA: Pacific Press Pub.), p. 244. [156]

————. "Christ Our Sacrifice," *Advent Review & Sabbath Herald*, Sept. 21, 1886. [38]

————. "Christ Seeks the Lost through Human Agents," *The Signs of the Times*, Jan. 1, 1894. [60]

————. "Christ the Center of the Message," *Advent Review & Sabbath Herald*, March 20, 1894. [60]

————. "The Christian's Calling Honorable," *The Signs of the Times*, April 8, 1889. [94]

————. "The Christian's Privilege," *Advent Review & Sabbath Herald*, Nov. 15, 1887. [120]

————. "Christ's Comforting Assurance," *The Signs of the Times*, June 17, 1889. [94]

————. "Christ's Mission to the World," *The Signs of the Times*, June 27, 1892. [51]

————. *Christ's Object Lessons* (Washington, D.C.: Review and Herald Publ. Assn., 1900, 1941), 436 pp. [34, 43, 44, 161]

————. "Christ's Victory Gained Through Pain and Death," *The Signs of the Times*, March 26, 1894. [82]

————. *Colporteur Ministry* (Mountain View, CA: Pacific Press Publ. Assn., 1953), 176 pp. [46, 155]

————. "Conditions of Prevailing Prayer," *The Signs of the Times*, Aug. 21, 1884. [127]

————. "Conflicts and Victories of the Church," Ltr. 25b, 1892, Manuscript Release No. 1200, originally published in the *Paulson Collection*, pp. 145–147; now in *Ellen G. White 1888 Materials*, vol. 3 (Washington, DC: The Ellen G. White Estate), 452 pp. [156]

————. "Continue in the Son and in the Father," *The Signs of the Times*, July 4, 1895. [49]

————. *Counsels on Diet and Foods* [CDF; a compilation from her writings], (Review and Herald Publ. Assn., Takoma Park, Washington, D.C., 1938), 511 pp. [161]

————. *Counsels on Health* (Mountain View, CA: Pacific Press Publ. Assn., 1923, 1957), 687 pp. [161]

————. *The Desire of Ages* [DA] (Mountain View, CA: Pacific Press Publ. Assn., 1898, 1940), 863 pp. [7–181]

————. "The Duty of Paying Tithes and Offerings," *Advent Review & Sabbath Herald*, Dec. 17, 1889. [55]

————. *Early Writings* of Ellen G. White [EW] (Washington, D.C.: Review and Herald Publ. Assn., 1882, 1945), 324 pp. [14, 16, 154]

————. *Education* (Pacific Press Publ. Assn., Mountain View, California, 1903, 1942), 320 pp. [133, 155, 158, 159, 161]

————. *The Ellen G. White 1888 Materials* (Washington, D.C.: The Ellen G. White Estate, 1988), vol. 3, 452 pp. [112, 118, 141, 156]

————. "Even your Sanctification," *The Signs of the Times*, Oct. 11, 1899. [54]

————. "Evidence of Genuine Faith," *Advent Review & Sabbath Herald*, March 6, 1888. [106]

————. "Faith the Christian's Privilege," *The Signs of the Times*, June 19, 1884. [120]

————. "The First Advent of Christ," *Advent Review & Sabbath Herald*, Dec. 17, 1872, and Dec. 24, 1872. [49, 51, 53, 61, 62, 101]

————. "The First Prophecy," *Advent Review & Sabbath Herald*, July 18, 1882. [130]

————. *Fundamentals of Christian Education* [FE] (Nashville, TN: Southern Pub. Assn., 1923). 576 pp. [29]

————. "The Gift of God's Grace," *The Youth's Instructor*, July 29, 1897. [59]

————. "God Made Manifest in Christ," *The Signs of the Times*, Jan. 20, 1890. [53]

————. *Gospel Workers* (Mountain View, CA: Pacific Press Publ. Assn., 1915, 1948), 519 pp. [126, 153, 154]

————. "Go to Work To-Day in My Vineyard," *Advent Review & Sabbath Herald*, April 9, 1889. [78, 96]

————. "The Great Controversy," *Advent Review & Sabbath Herald*, Sept. 7, 1897. [55]

————. *The Great Controversy Between Christ and Satan* (Mountain View, CA: Pacific Press Publ. Assn., 1888, 1911), 722 pp., 718 pp. [8, 16, 24, 118, 128, 130, 135, 136, 138, 142, 144, 146, 147, 153, 157, 158, 172, 182]

————. "Grow in Grace," *The Youth's Instructor*, June 28, 1894. [49]

————. "He Was Wounded for Our Transgressions," *Advent Review & Sabbath Herald*, Dec. 28, 1897. [102, 108]

————. "Holiday Gifts," *Advent Review & Sabbath Herald*, Dec. 26, 1882. [138]

————. "Importance of Education" (Address before the Battle Creek College Teachers and Students at Gen. Conf., Nov. 15, 1883), *Advent Review & Sabbath Herald*, Aug. 19, 1884. [50]

————. "The Law from Sinai," *The Signs of the Times*, March 7, 1878. [106]

————. "Led By the Spirit," *Advent Review & Sabbath Herald*, Jan. 4, 1887. [69]

————. Ltr. 281, 1905, reprinted in *Review and Herald* (Washington, DC), April 8, 1954. [158]

————. "The Life of Christ," *Advent Review & Sabbath Herald*, Dec. 31, 1872. [53, 62]

————. "The Life of Christ," Nos. 3, 6, and 12, *The Youth's Instructor*, Feb. 1, 1873; May 1, 1873; March 1, 1874. [52, 59, 110]

————. "The Love of God," *The Signs of the Times*, Nov. 25, 1889. [86, 106]

————. *Manuscript Release* No. 926, "The Fannie Bolton Story" [*MR926*] (E. G. White Estate, April 1982). [26, 36, 130, 142]

————. *Manuscript Releases*, vol. 1 [*1MR*] (Washington, DC, E. G. White Estate, 1981), 398 pp. [128, 145, 160]

————. *Manuscript Releases*, vol. 2 [*2MR*] (Washington, DC, E. G. White Estate, 1987), 349 pp. [51, 146]

————. *Manuscript Releases*, vol. 5 [*5MR*] (Silver Spring, MD, E. G. White Estate, 1990), 455 pp. [111, 140]

————. *Manuscript Releases*, vol. 7 [*7MR*] (Silver Spring, MD, E. G. White Estate, 1990), 424 pp. [25]

————. *Manuscript Releases*, vol. 8 [*8MR*] (Silver Spring, MD, E. G. White Estate, 1990), 457 pp. [126, 145]

————. *Manuscript Releases*, vol. 10 [*10MR*] (Silver Spring, MD, E. G. White Estate, 1990), 393 pp. [18]

————. *Manuscript Releases*, vol. 11 [*11MR*] (Silver Spring, MD, E. G. White Estate, 1990), 392 pp. [40]

————. *Manuscript Releases*, vol. 12 [*12MR*] (Silver Spring, MD. E. G. White Estate, 1990), 421 pp. [52, 55, 88, 95, 101, 107, 110]

————. *Manuscript Releases*, vol. 13 [*13MR*] (Silver Spring, MD, E. G. White Estate, 1990), 410 pp. [157]

————. *Manuscript Releases*, vol. 14 [*14MR*] (Silver Spring, MD, E. G. White Estate, 1990), 353 pp. [35, 38, 39]

————. *Manuscript Releases*, vol. 15 [*15MR*] (Silver Spring, MD, E. G. White Estate, 1990), 370 pp. [14]

————. *Manuscript Releases*, vol. 17 [*17MR*] (Silver Spring, MD, E. G. White Estate, 1990), 361 pp. [54, 56]

————. *Manuscript Releases*, vol. 18 [*18MR*] (Silver Spring, MD, E. G. White Estate, 1990), 380 pp. [55]

————. *Manuscript Releases*, vol. 19 [*19MR*] (Silver Spring, MD, E. G. White Estate, 1990), 395 pp. [33]

————. *Manuscript Releases*, vol. 20 [*20MR*] (Silver Spring, MD, E. G. White Estate, 1990), 397 pp. [145]

————. "A Messenger," *Advent Review & Sabbath Herald*, July 26, 1906. [159, 160]

————. *The Ministry of Healing* (Mountain View, CA: Pacific Press Publ. Assn., 1905, 1942), 540 pp. [161]

————. "The New Year," *Advent Review & Sabbath Herald*, Dec. 16, 1884. [38]

————. "Notes of Travel," *Advent Review & Sabbath Herald*, Nov. 25, 1884. [15]

————. "Obedience to the Law Necessary," *Advent Review & Sabbath Herald*, July 15, 1890. [110]

————. "An Opportunity to Give Spiritual Help," *Advent Review & Sabbath Herald*, April 29, 1902. [125]

————. "Our Camp-Meeting in Wisconsin," *The Signs of the Times*, July 22, 1875. [56]

————. "Our Mighty Helper," (Gen. Conf., Nov. 19, 1883), *Advent Review & Sabbath Herald*, July 1, 1884. [103]

————. *Patriarchs and Prophets* [*PP*] (Washington, D.C.: Review and Herald Publ. Assn., 1890, 1958), 805 pp. [34, 49, 50, 59, 157]

————. "The Plan of Salvation," *The Signs of the Times*, Feb. 20, 1893. [54]

————. "The Plan of Salvation the Same in All Ages," *Bible Echo*, July 15, 1893. [56]

————. "The Power of the Truth," *The Signs of the Times*, Aug. 6, 1885. [78]

————. "The Principles of Righteousness Revealed in the Life," *Advent Review & Sabbath Herald*, March 21, 1893. [55]

————. "Prompt and Cheerful Obedience," *The Signs of the Times*, July 22, 1886. [52]

————. "Proper Education," *The Health Reformer*, July 1873. [138]

————. *Prophets and Kings* (Mountain View, CA: Pacific Press Publ. Assn., 1917), 752 pp. [129]

————. "The Purpose and Plan of Grace," *The Signs of the Times*, April 25, 1892. [51]

————. "Questions and Answers," *Advent Review & Sabbath Herald*, Oct. 8, 1867. [124, 139, 141]

————. "Redemption. —No. 1 and No. 2," *Advent Review & Sabbath Herald*, Feb. 24 and March 3, 1874. [18, 130]

————. *Redemption: or the First Advent of Christ, with His Life and Ministry* [*1RL*; leaflets 1–6 of the *Redemption* series also published as *The Life of Christ*, nos. 1–6] (Battle Creek, MI: Steam Press of the Seventh-day Adventist Publ. Assn., 1877), 104 pp. [18, 129, 130, 179, 180, 182]

————. *Redemption: or the Temptation of Christ in the Wilderness* [*2RL*] (Battle Creek, MI: Steam Press of the Seventh-day Adventist Publ. Assn., 1874), 96 pp. [18, 180]

————. *Redemption: or the Miracles of Christ, the Mighty One* [*3RL*] (Battle Creek, MI: Steam Press of the Seventh-day Adventist Publ. Assn., 1877), 126 pp. [18]

————. *Redemption: or the Teachings of Christ, the Anointed One* [*4RL*] (Battle Creek, MI: Steam Press of the Seventh-day Adventist Publ. Assn., 1877), 128 pp. [18]

————. *Redemption: or the Sufferings of Christ; His Trial and Crucifixion* [*5RL*] (Battle Creek, MI: Steam Press of the Seventh-day Adventist Publ. Assn., 1877), 96 pp. [18]

————. *Redemption: or the Resurrection of Christ; and His Ascension* [*6RL*] (Battle Creek, MI: Steam Press of the Seventh-day Adventist Publ. Assn., 1877), 80 pp. [18]

————. *Redemption: or the Ministry of Peter and the Conversion of Saul* [*7RL*] (Battle Creek, MI: Steam Press of the Seventh-day Adventist Publ. Assn., 1878), 78 pp. [138]

————. *Redemption: or the Teachings of Paul, and His Mission to the Gentiles* [*8RL*] (Battle Creek, MI: Steam Press of the Seventh-day Adventist Publ. Assn., 1878), 80 pp. [138]

————. "Sacrifice of Separation," *Advent Review & Sabbath Herald*, Jan. 9, 1883. [52]

————. "Sanctification, The Christian's Privilege," *Advent Review & Sabbath Herald*, May 3, 1881. [120]

————. *The Sanctified Life* (Washington, D.C.: Review and Herald Publ. Assn., 1889, 1937, 1956), 110 pp. [161]

————. "Search the Scriptures," *The Youth's Instructor*, Aug. 31, 1887. [129]

————. "Seek First the Kingdom of God," *Advent Review & Sabbath Herald*, Oct. 27, 1885. [38]

————. *Selected Messages*, book 1 [*1SM*] (Washington, DC, Hagerstown, MD: Review and Herald Publ. Assn., 1958), 448 pp. [24, 144, 154]

————. *Selected Messages*, book 2 [*2SM*] (Washington, DC, Hagerstown, MD: Review and Herald Publ. Assn., 1958), 488 pp. [16, 26, 157]

————. *Selected Messages*, book 3 [*3SM*] (Washington, DC: Review and Herald Publ. Assn., 1980), 510 pp. [12, 13, 18, 20, 22, 29, 32, 34, 35, 58, 112, 119, 128, 129, 137–141, 145, 153, 157, 160, 180]

————. *Sermons and Talks*, vol. 1 [*1SAT*] (Hagerstown, MD: Review and Herald Publ. Assn., 1990), 405 pp. [110]

————. *Sermons and Talks*, vol. 2 [*2SAT*] (Hagerstown, MD: Review and Herald Publ. Assn., 1994), 339 pp. [106, 108]

————. "The Signal of Advance," *Advent Review & Sabbath Herald*, Jan. 20, 1903. [142, 155]

————. *A Sketch of the Christian Experience and Views of Ellen G. White* (Saratoga Springs, NY: James White, 1851), 64 pp. [154]

————. *Sketches from the Life of Paul* [LP] (Battle Creek, MI: Review and Herald Publ. Assn., 1883, 1974 facsimile), 334 pp. [16, 101, 117, 135, 138]

————. *A Solemn Appeal* (Battle Creek, MI: Seventh-day Adventist Publ. Assn., 1870), 272 pp. [161]

————. *The Spirit of Prophecy*, vol. 2 [2SP] (Battle Creek, MI: Steam Press of the SDA Publ. Assn., 1878), 396 pp. [16–19, 25, 40, 50, 59–61, 106, 138, 174]

————. *The Spirit of Prophecy*, vol. 3 [3SP] (Battle Creek, MI: Steam Press of the SDA Publ. Assn., 1879), 442 pp. [16, 18, 25, 63–93, 95–111, 114, 116, 120, 121, 123, 124, 128, 137, 138, 153, 174]

————. *The Spirit of Prophecy*, vol. 4 [4SP; subtitled *The Great Controversy Between Christ and Satan*] (Battle Creek, MI: Steam Press of the SDA Publ. Assn., 1884), 506 pp. [21, 23, 128, 135, 142, 172, 182]

————. *Spiritual Gifts*, vol. 1 [1SG] (Battle Creek, MI: James White Publisher, 1858), 218 pp. [15, 29, 51–53, 55, 65, 68, 73–75, 77–84, 86, 91–95, 98, 99, 101–106, 111, 116, 164, 174]

————. *Spiritual Gifts*, vol. 2 [2SG] (Battle Creek, MI: James White Publisher, 1860), 304 pp. [12, 16, 145, 153]

————. *Spiritual Gifts*, vol. 3 [3SG] (Battle Creek, MI: James White Publisher, 1864), 304 pp. [139]

————. *Spiritual Gifts*, vol. 4a [4aSG] (Battle Creek, MI: James White Publisher, 1864), 156 pp. [16, 52, 61, 62, 130, 139, 140, 174]

————. *Steps to Christ* [SC] (Battle Creek, MI: Review and Herald Publ. Co., 1892), 126 pp. [7, 16, 38, 40, 51, 55, 127, 161, 182]

————. "The Sufferings of Christ" [PH169] (Battle Creek, MI: Review and Herald Publ. Co., 1869), 16 pp. [16, 92, 93, 106–109, 111]

————. "The Sufferings of Christ," *Present Truth*, Feb. 4, 1886. [120]

————. "The Sufferings of Christ," *The Signs of the Times*, Nov./Dec. 1875 and Aug. 7, 21, and 28, 1879. [16, 54, 106]

————. "Take These Things Hence," *Advent Review & Sabbath Herald*, Aug. 27, 1895. [66]

————. "The Temptation of Christ," *Advent Review & Sabbath Herald*, July 28, Aug. 4, 18, Sept. 1, 8, Oct. 13, 1874; March 4, 18, 25, April 1, 15, 1875. [18, 52]

————. *Testimonies for the Church*, vol. 1 [1T; comprised of Testimony 1 (1855), 2 (1856) 3, 4 (1857), 5 (1859), 6 (1861), 7, 8 (1862), 9 (1863) 10 (1864), 11, 12, 13 (1867), 14 (1868)] (Mountain View, CA: Pacific Press Publ. Assn., 1881, 1902, 1948 by the Ellen G. White Publications), 712 pp. [38, 153]

————. *Testimonies for the Church*, vol. 2 [2T; comprised of Testimony 15, 16 (1868), 17 (1869), 18, 19 (1870), 20 (1871)] (Mountain View, CA: Pacific Press Publ. Assn., 1881, 1902, 1948 by the Ellen G. White Publications), 712 pp. [16, 103, 108, 124]

————. *Testimonies for the Church*, vol. 3 [3T; comprised of Testimony 21, 22 (1872), 23 (1873), 24, 25 (1875)] (Mountain View, CA: Pacific Press Publ. Assn., 1881, 1902, 1948 by the Ellen G. White Publications), 575 pp. [38]

————. *Testimonies for the Church*, vol. 4 [4T; comprised of Testimony 26, 27 (1876), 28 (1879), 29 (1880), 30 (1881)]

(Mountain View, CA: Pacific Press Publ. Assn., 1881, 1902, 1948 by the Ellen G. White Publications), 657 pp. [21, 38, 56, 120, 154]

————. *Testimonies for the Church*, vol. 5 [5T; comprised of Testimony 31 (1882), 32 (1885), 33 (1889)] (Mountain View, CA: Pacific Press Publ. Assn., 1902, 1948 by the Ellen G. White Publications), 826 pp. [38, 49, 51, 62, 125, 141, 146, 154, 155, 157, 160, 162]

————. *Testimonies for the Church*, vol. 7 [7T] (Mountain View, CA: Pacific Press Publ. Assn., 1902, 1948 by the Ellen G. White Publications), 298 pp. [126]

————. *Testimonies for the Church*, vol. 8 [8T; comprised of Testimony 36 (1904)] (Mountain View, CA: Pacific Press Publ. Assn., 1904, 1948 by the Ellen G. White Publications), 372 pp. [155]

————. *Testimonies on Sexual Behavior, Adultery, and Divorce* [TSB] (Silver Spring, MD: Ellen G. White Estate, 1989), 270 pp. [126]

————. *Testimonies to Ministers and Gospel Workers* (Boise, ID and Oshawa, Ontario, Canada: Pacific Press Publ. Assn., 1923, 1944, 1962), 566 pp. [24]

————. "The Testing of Character," *The Signs of the Times*, May 25, 1888. [126]

————. *Thoughts from the Mount of Blessing* (Pacific Press Publ. Assn., Mountain View, California, 1956; first published in 1896), 172 pp. [33, 34, 35, 40, 155]

————. "The Treasure of Truth Rejected," *Advent Review & Sabbath Herald*, April 3, 1894. [55]

————. "The True Standard of Righteousness," *Advent Review & Sabbath Herald*, Aug. 25, 1885. [53]

————. "Trust In the Lord," *Advent Review & Sabbath Herald*, Feb. 3, 1885. [38]

————. "Truth to Be Rescued From Error," *Advent Review & Sabbath Herald*, Oct. 23, 1894. [118]

————. "The Value of Bible Study," *Advent Review & Sabbath Herald*, July 17, 1888. [155]

————. "The Vision at Bethel," *The Signs of the Times*, July 31, 1884. [106]

————. "Walk Not in Darkness," *Advent Review & Sabbath Herald*, Sept. 20, 1892. [65]

————. "The Whole Duty of Man," *The Signs of the Times*, May 16, 1895. [132]

————, C. C. Crisler, and D. E. Robinson,. *Life Sketches of Ellen G. White* (Mountain View, CA: Pacific Press Publ. Assn., 1943, 1915), 480 pp. [22]

White, James and Ellen. *Health; or How to Live* (Battle Creek, MI: Steam Press of the Seventh-day Adventist Pub. Assn., 1865), 400 pp. [124, 139, 182]

White, James. *Life Sketches, Ancestry, Early Life, Christian Experience, and Extensive Labors of Elder James White and His Wife, Mrs. Ellen G. White* (Battle Creek, MI: Press of the Seventh-day Adventist Pub. Assn., 1880), 416 pp. [15, 21, 115, 130]

White, William C. "How Ellen White's Books were Written: Addresses to Faculty and Students at the Advanced Bible School, Angwin, California," June 18, 1935, Part I, at <www.whiteestate.org/issues/HowEGWbksWCW.html>. [15]

White, William C., and D. E. Robinson. "Brief Statements Regarding the Writings of Ellen White" (St. Helena, CA: "Elmshaven" Office, 1933), reprinted as an insert in *Adventist Review*, June 4, 1981, 16 pp. [8, 12, 16, 116, 118, 135–137]